JAR OPS in Plain English

JAR OPS 1 & 3, Parts 1 & 2, Translated!

Phil Croucher

About the Author

Phil Croucher holds JAR, UK, UAE, US and Canadian licenses for airplanes and helicopters and around 8000 hours on 35 types, with a considerable operational background, and training experience from the computer industry, in which he is equally well qualified. He has at various times been a Chief Pilot, Ops Manager, Training Captain and Type Rating Examiner. He currently works for Aerogulf Services in Dubai and is responsible for the safety column in *Vertical* magazine and can be contacted at **www.electrocution.com**

Praise for The Helicopter Pilot's Handbook:

"a much needed summary of all the "basics" we live by. It sure is great for an old timer to see how all the things we had to find out the hard way in the 60's and 70's can now be found in a book. A great reference tool."

Robert Eschauzier

"A good insight into the working life of a pilot"

HF

"In short... great book! Thankfully your book illuminates many of the practical aspects of flying rotorcraft that are missing from the intro texts used during training. I'd equate much of the valuable practical information in your book to the to the same valuable information found in "Stick and Rudder.""

Ian Campbell

"The chapters covering your experiences and showing 'the real world' of helicopter ops is a worthwhile addition to any pilots library and knowledge bank."

Paul

".....an excellent book for pilots interested in a career as a helicopter pilot. It answers all the really hard questions like "how does a young pilot get the required experience without having to join the army for 10 years". Great book for anyone interested in fling-wings!"

Reilly Burke, Technical Adviser, Aero Training Products

"Having only completed 20 hours of my CPL(H) in Australia, a lot of the content was very new to me. Your writing style is very clear and flowing, and the content was easy to understand. It's made me more eager than ever to finish my training and get into it. It's also opened my eyes as to how much there is to learn. The section on landing a job was excellent, especially for this industry that seems so hard to break into."

Philip Shelper

"Picked up The Helicopter Pilot's Handbook on Friday and have already read it twice. How you crammed that much very informative info into 178 pages is totally beyond me. WELL DONE. What a wealth of information, even though I only have a CPL-F. OUTSTANDING. I'm starting it again for the third time because I've picked up so much more the second time, that I'll read certainly a dozen more times. I cant wait to apply a lot the ideas and comments that you have supplied.

My wife is totally blown away that I've read it cover to cover twice and going around for a third time. She said it must be an outstanding book as I need real mental stimulus to keep me going.

Have a great nite and thanks for the excellent read."

Will

"Your book is very good and has been read by a few of the guys here with good 'raps'. particularly the Info on slinging etc. is stuff that is never covered in endorsement training. Certainly a worthwhile addition to any pilot library."

Gibbo

"I have only skimmed through the first version. Its already answered and confirmed a few things for me. Just the type of info I am after."

Andrew Harrison

".....provides many insights that wouldn't appear in the standard textbooks.

The next part of the book deals with the specialized tasks that a jobbing pilot may be called upon to do. It covers a very wide range of tasks from Avalanche Control through Aerial Photography and Filming; from Wildlife Capture to Winter Operations; from Pipeline Survey to Dropping Parachutists. This is not an exhaustive list of what he covers. If you need to know then it's probably here. The information given is good, practical and down to earth. It is exactly what you need to know and written from the pilot's point of view.

For anyone with some practical experience of helicopter operations it is worth a read. For someone who is going into civvie street and intends to fly then it is definitely worth a read. For anyone who intends to be a 'jobbing pilot' it could be invaluable as a source of reference."

Colin Morley
Army Air Corps

Praise for The BIOS Companion:

A book that deals with all those secret settings in your computer's BIOS, plus tons of data for troubleshooters.

I already had about HALF of the information, and to get THAT much, I had to get several books and web pages. GOOD JOB!!

I had more time to go thru the book and think that you should change the word "HALF" to "FOURTH".

I commend you on the great job you did. That's a hell of a lot of work for any major company to do, let alone an individual.

Again, Thank you

Craig Stubbs

Thank! I really appreciated this. I read it and was able to adjust my BIOS settings so that my machine runs about twice as fast. Pretty impressive.

Thanks again.

Tony

The computer book of the month is The Bios Companion by Phil Croucher. Long-time readers of this column will recall I have recommended his book before. This tells you everything you ought to know about the BIOS in your system. Post codes, options, upgrades, you name it.

Years ago, I called an earlier edition of this invaluable and I see no reason to change my view. Recommended.

Jerry Pournelle, Byte Magazine

Available from **www.electrocution.com**

Table of Contents

Introduction

This book is a guide - use it to get the gist of the law, but check the real stuff before basing any actions on it - the contents are severely edited!

JAR OPS documents are actually in two parts, although you will only get the first ones from the JAA website. Aeroplane AOC holders come under JAR OPS 1, and helicopters under JAR OPS 3 (JAR OPS 2 and 4, for aerial work and corporate, are on the horizon). To amplify the first part, additional material like *Advisory Circulars Joint* (ACJ), *Advisory Material Joint* (AMJ), *Acceptable Means of Compliance* (AMC) and *Interpretative/Explanatory Material* (IEM, to help illustrate JAR meanings) comes in a second one, which costs an arm and a leg to gain access to, from a company called IHS (cartel, anyone?). If a JAR OPS paragraph does not have a corresponding AMC or IMC, supplementary material is not required. In this book, they have all been combined – for example, JAR OPS 3.255 and AMC 3.255, its partner, are in the same section (they normally use the same numbering system, and cross-reference each other), whereas in the real regulations they would be all over the place.

Thus, JAR OPS tells you *what* is to be done (or gives you permission to do it), whereas the AMC, or whatever, tells you *how* it is to be done, that is, what you need to do to comply (in this respect, the UK authorities tend to give basic guidelines and leave it to operators to produce their own rules, whereas others specify things more tightly). In other words, AMCs illustrate one way, or several alternative ways, but not necessarily the only ways, by which requirements can be met.

A *Temporary Guidance Leaflet* (TGL) is AMC or IEM material being made available in a hurry, while an NPA (*Notice of Proposed Amendment*) is a draft proposal to modify a JAR or propose a new one, similar the *Notice of Proposed Rulemaking* (NPRM) from the FAA.

Where reference is made to JAR codes that have not yet been implemented (such as Flight Duty Times) the equivalent national regulations apply until they are.

Definitions from all documents have been included in Section 1. As much of JAR OPS 3 is a clone of JAR OPS 1, to save space, I have not duplicated it entirely, but referenced back to JAR OPS 1.

For convenience, references to *Acts* include orders or regulations made under them (as amended), licences and endorsements are assumed to be valid and current (and effective until surrendered, suspended or revoked), and aircraft and simulators are suitable and approved, as are airfields and other equipment. In other words, we've left out the painfully obvious, unnecessary repetition, and stuff that is out of date, such as anything to do with Concorde, since it is not flying now.

Some large tables have also been omitted, but most are summaries of the paragraphs they refer to, and are also quite complex– people who actually require them likely have access to the real regulations, and this book is only meant to be a quick reference, to save you either carrying around several large looseleaf volumes, or a CD, which requires a laptop (its other benefit is the comprehensive index).

Most sections start with the phrase: *"An operator must ensure that...."* or *"The operator must provide, and the commander must ensure that......"*. Since this is almost always the case anyway, I have left them out – just be aware that, if you need to check specifically who is responsible for an action, check the real regulations. Procedures are always the responsibility of the operator. The commander, of course, is responsible for everything:

> *"...As a pilot of a machine, you are responsible for that machine all the time, and it is always your fault if you crash it in a forced landing occasioned by any failure, structural or otherwise, of the machine or its engine. It is your fault if, in thick weather, you hit the top of any hill that has its correct height shown on your map.*
>
> *It is entirely your fault if you run out (of petrol) when coming home against a headwind after four or five hours (of flying), or if you fail to come down on the right spot after a couple (of) hours cloud flying.*
>
> *It is your fault if you have nowhere to make a landing when the engine fails just after you have taken off; in the event of a forced landing, your machine is a glider that should take you down safely on any possible landing place.*
>
> *It is your fault – well, it is a golden rule to assume that whatever goes wrong is your fault. You may save yourself a lot of trouble if you act accordingly."*

from *Recollections of an Airman*, by Lt Col L A Strange, 1919. Nothing changes!

The term *commander*, by the way, includes the pilot to whom conduct of the flight is delegated.

I have used the term *Pilot Monitoring* in preference to *Pilot Not Flying*, as it reflects the true function.

Naturally, the Authorities reserve the right to ~~screw it all up~~ change things at any time!

EASA

The *European Aviation Safety Agency* is the European Community's answer to the FAA. Its establishment will cause many changes to the JAA system.

The EASA formally started on 28 September 2003, taking over airworthiness and maintenance issues within the EU Member States. During 2003, airworthiness and maintenance JARs were transposed or converted into EASA regulations, with some, such as JAR 21 and 145 becoming

Implementing Rules (IRs) through a *Commission Regulation*, and others becoming AMCs and *Certification Specifications* (CS) through Agency decisions. As they get converted, they arrive on EASA's website.

Since EASA is likely to affect JAR FCLs, they have been left out of this book, but if the author gets a lot of rainy days in the back of a helicopter, they may well be included at a later date anyway.

JAA will retain its present functions for JAA member states outside EASA.

1 – Terms & Definitions

Abortive Start

An attempt to start, where the (turbine) engine lights up, but fails to accelerate, assuming its handling is under manufacturer's instructions!

Acceleration Datum Conditions

For turbine engines, conditions (such as rotational speed, torque, exhaust gas temperature, etc.) from which, during the type endurance test, the specified accelerations to 95% takeoff power and/or thrust are timed. Unless otherwise agreed, the power and/or thrust is not above 10% and the time to 95% not above 5 seconds.

Accelerate-Stop Distance Available (ASDA)

The length of the TORA plus the stopway.

Acceptance Check List

A document used to help with checking the external appearance of dangerous goods pckages and associated documents to determine that requirements have been met.

Accepted/Acceptable

Not objected to for the purpose intended.

Accident

An occurrence associated with the operation of an aircraft between the time any person boards it with the intention of flight until all persons have disembarked, in which a person is fatally or seriously injured as a result of:

- being in the aircraft

- direct contact with any part of it, including parts which have become detached

- direct exposure to jet blast

except when the injuries are from natural causes, self-inflicted or inflicted by other persons, or happen to stowaways.

Also, when the aircraft sustains damage or structural failure which adversely affects its structural strength, performance or flight characteristics, and would normally require major repair or replacement, except for engine failure or damage (when limited to the engine, its cowlings or accessories), or damage limited to propellers, wing tips, antennas, tyres, brakes, fairings, small dents or punctures in the aircraft skin, plus when the aircraft is missing or is completely inaccessible.

Accountable Manager

The person acceptable to the Authority with corporate authority for ensuring that operations and maintenance can be financed and carried out to the standard required.

Adjustable Pitch Propeller

One whose pitch setting can be changed during field maintenance, but not when it is spinning.

Aerial Work

Where an aircraft is used for specialised services such as agriculture, construction, photography, surveying, observation and patrol, search and rescue, aerial advertising, etc. In other words, not carrying passengers in the normal fare-paying sense, although "essential persons" may be carried.

Aerodynamic Coefficients
Non-dimensional coefficients for aerodynamic forces and moments.

Aeroplane
A heavier-than-air engine-driven fixed-wing aircraft supported in flight by the dynamic reaction of air against its wings.

Airborne
Entirely supported by aerodynamic forces.

Aircraft
A machine that can derive support in the atmosphere from reactions of the air, other than against the earth's surface.

Aircraft Variant
The same basic type, with modifications not causing significant changes in handling or flight characteristics, or crew complement, but still causing significant changes to equipment and/or procedures.

Airframe
The fuselage, booms, nacelles, cowlings, fairings, aerofoil surfaces (including rotors but not propellers and rotating engine aerofoils), and landing gear, and their accessories and controls.

Alternate Airport
Where an aircraft may land if a landing at the intended airport becomes inadvisable.

Appliance
Any instrument, mechanism, equipment, part, apparatus, appurtenance, accessory, including communications equipment, used or intended for operating or controlling an aircraft in flight, installed in or attached to it, and not part of an airframe, engine, or propeller.

Applicant
Someone after approval of aircraft or parts.

Approved
Compliance with the applicable JTSO has been demonstrated, or relevant airworthiness standards where one does not exist.

Approved by the Authority
Documented as suitable for the purpose intended.

Atmosphere, International Standard
As defined in ICAO Document 7488/2, but for JAR purposes, the following is acceptable:

- The air is a perfect dry gas

- The temperature at sea-level is 15°C

- The pressure at sea-level is 1.013250 x 10^5 Pa (29.92 in Hg) (1013.2 mb)

- The temperature gradient from sea level to where the temperature becomes -565°C is 3.25°C/500 m (1.98°C/1000 ft)

- The density at sea level, under the above conditions is 1.2250 kg/m³ (0.002378 slugs/ft³). For density up to 15000 m (50000 ft) see Table 1 (not here)

Authority
The competent body responsible for the safety regulation of Civil Aviation.

Autorotation
Flight with the lifting rotor driven entirely by action of the air when a rotorcraft is in motion.

Auxiliary Power Unit (APU)
Any gas turbine-powered unit delivering rotating shaft power, compressor air, or both, not intended for direct propulsion. Certain definitions apply:

- *Accessory Drives* - any drive shaft or utility mounting pad, used to extract power to drive accessories, components, or controls essential to the operation of the APU or associated systems.

- *Blade* - an energy transforming element of the compressor or turbine rotors, whether integral or attached.

- *Compressor Air* - compressed air from the APU to do work, extracted or bled from the compressor section or a compressor driven by the APU.

- *Containment* - retention within the APU of all high energy rotor fragments resulting from the failure of a high energy rotor.

- *Critical Rotor Stage* - the compressor and turbine stages whose rotors have the smallest margin of safety under the speed and temperature in Appendix 1, para 7.10 of JAR APU.

- *Demonstrate* - to prove by physical test under Appendix 1 of JAR APU.

- *Essential APU* – one which produces bleed air and/or power to drive accessories.

- *High Energy Rotor* - a rotating component or assembly which, when ruptured, will generate high kinetic energy fragments.

- *Major Part* - a part whose failure might adversely affect operational integrity.

- *Maximum Allowable Speed* - the maximum rotor speed which the APU would experience under overload or transient conditions, and limited by safety devices.

- *Maximum Allowable Temperature* - the maximum EGT or TIT the APU would experience during overload or transient conditions, and limited by safety devices.

- *Minor Part* – not a major part.

- *Non-essential APU* – one which may be used for convenience, on the ground or in flight, and may be shut down without jeopardising safe operations.

- *Output Provisions* - any drive pad or compressed air output flange to extract shaft or pneumatic power from the APU.

- *Rated Output* - the approved shaft power or compressed air output, or both, developed statically at standard sea-level atmospheric conditions for unrestricted use.

- *Rated Temperature* - the maximum TIT or EGT at which the engine can operate at rated output and speed.

- *Rotor* – a rotating component or assembly, including blades, except accessory drive shafts and gears.

- *Start* - an acceleration from the initiation of operation or starter torque to a stabilised speed and temperature in the governed ranges without exceeding limits.

- *Substantiate* – to prove by presenting adequate evidence fromdemonstration or analysis, or both.

- *Type* - all of a series of units, developed as an alternative configuration or refinement of the same basic unit.

Auxiliary Rotor

A rotor that principally serves to counteract the effect of main rotor torque on a rotorcraft and/or to manoeuvre it about one or more of its three principal axes.

Beta Control

Where the propeller can be operated at blade angles directly selected, normally used during the approach and ground handling.

Boost Pressure

On piston engines, the manifold pressure measured relative to standard sea-level atmospheric pressure.

Brake Horsepower

Power delivered at the propeller shaft (main drive or main output) of an aircraft engine.

Calibrated Airspeed

Indicated airspeed, corrected for position and instrument error. CAS is equal to TAS in the standard atmosphere at sea level.

Cargo Aircraft

Any aircraft carrying goods or property, but not passengers. In this context, crew members, employees under the Ops Manual, authorised people or people with duties concerning particular shipments on board are not passengers.

Category A

A multi-engined rotorcraft with engine and system isolation features as per JAR 27 or 29, capable of using takeoff and landing data under a critical engine failure concept which assures adequate designated surface area and performance capability for continued safe flight or safe rejected takeoff if an engine fails.

Category B

A single- or multi-engined rotorcraft which does not meet Category A, and with no guaranteed capability for safe flight if an engine fails - an unscheduled landing is assumed.

Charge Cooling

For piston engines, the % degree of charge cooling.

Clearway

Fo turbine-engined aeroplanes certificated after August 29, 1959, an area beyond the runway, at least 152 m (500 ft) wide, centrally about the extended centreline, under control of airport authorities. It is expressed in terms of a clearway plane, from the end of the runway with an upward slope up to 1.25%, above which no object or terrain protrudes, except threshold lights if their height above the end of the runway is up to 0.66 m (26 ins) and if they are on each side of the runway.

Climates, Standard

There are three, *Temperate*, *Tropical* and *Arctic*, whose conditions are unlikely to be exceeded more than one day per year, except that they do not cover the extremes of temperature occasionally reached in tropical deserts or Siberia in winter.

Circling

The visual phase of an approach for a runway not suitably located for a straight-in approach, or a different one than the approach was for.

Civil Aircraft

An aircraft on the civil register of a State, other than in its service, permanently or temporarily.

Class

A group of single-pilot aeroplane types with similar handling and flight characteristics.

Cloud Base

The height of the base of the lowest observed, or forecast, cloud element near an aerodrome or heliport, or within a specified area of operations. The height is normally measured above aerodrome elevation, but, offshore, above mean sea level.

Co-pilot

A pilot serving as other than PIC or commander, but not for the sole purpose of receiving flight instruction for a licence or rating.

Component, Parts, Appliances, Product

The same meaning as in either the *JAA Arrangements or the Council Regulation* (EEC) No. 3922/91, except when defined in another way, either in this JAR, an individual JAR, or unless the contrary is indicated.

Commercial Air Transportation

Transportation by air of passengers, cargo or mail for remuneration or hire.

Committal Point (CP)

The point in the approach where the PF decides that, if a power unit failure is recognised, the safest option is to continue to the deck.

Congested Area

In relation to a city, town or settlement, any area substantially used for residential, commercial or recreational purposes (which may include a golf course - see also definitions of hostile and non-hostile environments).

Contaminated Runway

A runway is contaminated when more than 25% of its surface (in isolated areas or not) is covered by surface water more than 3 mm (0.125 in) deep, or the equivalent in slush, or loose snow, or snow which has been compressed into a solid mass which resists further compression and will hold together or break into lumps if picked up (compacted snow), or ice, including wet ice.

Continuous Maximum Icing

See *Icing, Atmospheric Conditions.*

Crewmember

A person assigned to duty in an aircraft during flight time.

Critical Altitude

The maximum altitude you can maintain, without ram, at max continuous rotational speed, the max continuous power (for engines where this power rating is the same at sea level and rated altitude), or the maximum continuous rated manifold pressure (for engines with the max continuous power governed by a constant manifold pressure).

Critical Engine

The engine whose failure most adversely affects performance or handling qualities.

Critical Part

Where a part must achieve and maintain a particularly high level of integrity if Hazardous Effects are not to occur at a rate over Extremely Remote, it is a Critical Part.

D

The largest dimension of a helicopter with rotors turning.

Damp Runway

A runway is damp when the surface is not dry, but moisture on it does not give it a shiny appearance.

Dangerous Goods Accident

An occurrence associated with and related to the transport of dangerous goods which results in fatal or serious injury or major property damage.

Dangerous Goods Incident

An occurrence, other than a dangerous goods accident, not necessarily on board an aircraft, resulting in injury to a person, property damage, fire, breakage, spillage, leakage of fluid or radiation, or other evidence that integrity of the packaging has not been maintained. Also, any occurrence relating to the transport of dangerous goods which seriously jeopardises the aircraft or its occupants.

Dangerous Goods Transport Document

A document specified by the Technical Instructions, completed by the person who offers dangerous goods for air transport, with information about them. The document bears a signed declaration indicating that the dangerous goods are fully and accurately described by their proper shipping names and UN/ID numbers and that they are correctly classified, packed, marked, labelled and in a proper condition for transport.

Decision Height

The wheel height above runway elevation by which a go-around must be initiated unless adequate visual reference has been established and your position and approach path assessed (visually) as satisfactory to continue in safety.

Defined Point After Takeoff (DPATO)

The point, within the takeoff and initial climb phase, before which a helicopter's ability to continue flight safely, with the critical power unit inoperative, is not assured and a forced landing may be required (only for Performance Class 2).

Defined Point Before Landing (DPBL)

The point in the approach and landing phase, after which a helicopter's ability to continue safely, with the critical power unit inoperative, is not assured and a forced landing may be required (only applies to Performance Class 2).

Detent

A mechanical arrangement which indicates, by feel, a position of an operating control. The detent holds the lever there and an additional-to-normal force is required to move it away (JAR 25 only).

Distance DR

DR is the horizontal distance a helicopter has travelled from the end of the TODA.

Dry Operating Mass

The total mass of an aircraft ready for a specific type of operation, excluding usable fuel and traffic load. This includes crew and baggage, catering and removable passenger service equipment, and potable water and lavatory chemicals.

Dry Runway

One which is neither wet nor contaminated, and includes paved runways which have been specially prepared with grooves or porous pavement and maintained to retain 'effectively dry' braking action even when moisture is present.

Elevated Heliport

One at least 3 m above the surrounding surface.

Engine
One used for propulsion, not including a propeller.

Engine Dry Weight
The weight of an engine as type-certificated, or one clearly derived by specified additions or omissions.

Engine Type
Engines similar in design (see JAR 21).

Equivalent Airspeed
Calibrated airspeed corrected for adiabatic compressible flow at particular altitudes, equal to CAS in standard atmosphere at sea level.

Exhaust Gas Temperature
Average temperature of exhaust gas streams (turbines).

Exposure Time
The period during which the performance of a helicopter with the critical power unit inoperative in still air does not guarantee a safe forced landing or safe continuation of a flight.

External Load
One that is carried, towed or extends outside the aircraft fuselage.

External Load Attaching Means
Structural components that attach an external load to an aircraft, including containers, the backup structure at the attachment points, and quick-release devices to jettison the load.

Extremely Remote
Unlikely to occur when considering the total operational life of a number of aircraft of the type in which an engine is installed, but has to be regarded as being possible.

Fail-Operational Flight Control System
In a failure below alert height, the approach, flare and landing, can be completed automatically, and the automatic landing system reverts to fail-passive.

Fail-Operational Hybrid Landing System
One with a primary fail-passive automatic landing system and a secondary independent guidance system enabling the pilot to complete a landing manually after failure of the primary system.

A typical secondary independent guidance system consists of a monitored HUD providing guidance which normally takes the form of command information, but may alternatively be situation (or deviation) information.

Fail-Passive Flight Control System
A flight control system is fail-passive if, when it fails, there is no significant out-of-trim condition or deviation of flight path or attitude, but the landing is not completed automatically. The pilot assumes control after a failure.

False Start
An attempt to start in which a turbine engine fails to light up, assuming handling is as per manufacturer's instructions.

Feathered Pitch
The setting which, in flight with engine stopped, gives approximately minimum drag, corresponding with a windmilling torque of approximately zero.

Final Approach and Takeoff Area
A defined area over which the final phase of the approach manoeuvre to hover or landing is completed and from which the takeoff manoeuvre is started and, where the FATO is to be used by Performance Class 1 helicopters, includes the rejected takeoff area available.

Final Takeoff Speed
The speed of an aeroplane at the end of the takeoff path in the en-route configuration with OEI.

Fireproof
The ability of materials, components and equipment to withstand heat from a flame, for 15 minutes without any failure that creates a hazard to the aircraft. For materials, this is equivalent to withstanding a fire at least as well as steel or titanium in appropriate dimensions.

Fire Resistant
As for *Fireproof*, but for 5 minutes, and equivalent to aluminium alloy.

First Aid Oxygen

Additional oxygen for passengers who do not satisfactorily recover after subjection to excessive cabin altitudes, when they had been provided with supplemental oxygen.

Fixed Pitch Propeller

One whose pitch cannot be changed, except in the workshop.

Flame Resistant

Not likely to combust if flame is propagated, beyond safe limits, after ignition is removed.

Flammable

Where a fluid or gas is susceptible to igniting readily or exploding.

Flap Extended Speed

The highest speed allowed with wing flaps in a prescribed extended position.

Flash Resistant

Not susceptible to violent burning if ignited.

Flight Control System

A system which includes an automatic landing system and/or a hybrid landing system.

Flight Crewmember

A pilot, flight engineer, or flight navigator assigned to duty in an aircraft during flight.

Freight Container

An article of transport equipment for radioactive materials, designed to facilitate their transport, either packaged or unpackaged, by one or more modes of transport. See *Unit Load Device* for where the dangerous goods are not radioactive.

Ground Emergency Service Personnel

Any (such as policemen, firemen, etc.) involved with HEMS and whose tasks are pertinent to helicopter operations.

Ground Idling Conditions

For turbine engines, conditions of minimum rotational speed associated with zero forward speed and the maximum EGT at this speed.

Gyroplane

A rotorcraft with rotors not engine-driven (except for initial starting), but which rotate from action of the air when moving, and an independent means of propulsion, usually conventional propellers.

Handling Agent

An agency which performs on behalf of an operator some or all of the latter's functions including receiving, loading, unloading, transferring or other processing of passengers or cargo.

Harness

Equipment, consisting of two shoulder straps and a lap belt, that restrains a member of the flight crew against inertia loads in emergency conditions.

Helicopter

A rotorcraft that depends principally on its engine-driven rotors for horizontal motion.

Helicopter Emergency Medical Service Flight

A flight by a helicopter under a HEMS approval, for emergency medical assistance, where immediate and rapid transportation is essential, by carrying medical personnel, supplies, or ill or injured people and others directly involved.

Helicopter Hoist Operations Flight

A flight by a helicopter under an HHO approval, to transfer people and/or cargo by hoist.

Helideck

A heliport on a floating or fixed offshore structure.

Heliport

An area of land or water, or structure used or intended for the landing and takeoff of helicopters.

HEMS Crewmember

A person on a HEMS flight attending to people in need of medical assistance carried in the helicopter and assisting the pilot during the mission.

HEMS Operating Base

A heliport where HEMS crews and helicopters may be on standby for HEMS operations.

Hoist Cycle

One down-and-up cycle of a hoist hook.

Hostile Environment

Where:

- A safe forced landing cannot be made because the surface is inadequate

- The occupants cannot be adequately protected from the elements

- SAR response/capability is not consistent with anticipated exposure

- Unacceptable risk of endangering people or property on the ground

These areas are *always* hostile:

- For overwater operations, the open sea North of 45N and South of 45S, as designated by the Authority of the State

- Congested areas without adequate safe forced landing areas

Icing Atmospheric Conditions

- *Continuous Maximum Icing* – defined by cloud liquid water content, mean effective diameter of cloud droplets, ambient air temperature, and their relationship.

- *Intermittent Maximum Icing* – defined by the cloud liquid water content, mean effective diameter of cloud droplets, ambient air temperature, and their inter-relationship.

ID Number

A temporary identification number for an item of dangerous goods without a UN number.

IFR Conditions

Weather below the minimum for VFR flight.

Incident

An occurrence, not an accident, associated with operation of an aircraft which may affect safety.

Indicated Airspeed

The speed of an aircraft as shown on its ASI, calibrated to reflect standard atmosphere adiabatic compressible flow at sea level, uncorrected for airspeed system errors.

Installed

Complies with applicable airworthiness requirements or the relevant code for Type Certification, and any requirement in JAR OPS.

Instrument

A device with an internal mechanism to show visually or aurally the attitude, altitude or operation of an aircraft or part, including electronic ones for automatically controlling aircraft in flight.

Instrument Flight Time

Time during which a pilot is controlling an aircraft in flight solely by reference to instruments.

Instrument Ground Time

Time when a pilot is receiving instruction in simulated instrument flight in STDs.

Intermittent Maximum Icing

See *Icing Atmospheric Conditions*.

Landing Decision Point (LDP)

The point used to determine landing performance from which, a power unit failure having been recognised, the landing may be safely continued or a baulked landing initiated.

Landing Distance Available (LDA)

The length of the runway declared available by the appropriate Authority and suitable for the ground run of a landing aeroplane.

Landing Distance Required

The horizontal distance required to land and come to a full stop from a point 10.7 m (35 ft) above the landing surface.

Landing Gear Extended Speed

The maximum speed at which an aircraft can be safely flown with the gear extended.

Landing Gear Operating Speed

The maximum speed at which the gear can be safely extended or retracted.

Large Aeroplane

One over 5700 kg (12,500 lbs) MCTOW, not including commuters (see JAR 23.1 and 23.3).

Load Factor

The ratio of a specified load to total weight of an aircraft, in terms of any of: aerodynamic forces, inertia forces, or ground or water reactions.

Low Visibility Procedures (LVP)

Procedures at an aerodrome to ensure safe operations during Cat II and III approaches and Low Visibility Takeoffs.

Low Visibility Takeoff (LVTO)

Where the RVR is less than 400 m.

Mach Number

The ratio of TAS to the speed of sound.

Main Rotor

Rotor or rotors supplying the principal lift of a rotorcraft.

Maintenance

One or a combination of overhaul, air, inspection, replacement, modification or defect rectification of aircraft or components.

Manifold Pressure

Absolute static pressure measured at the appropriate point in an induction system, usually in inches or millimetres of mercury.

Max Approved Pax Seating Configuration

The maximum passenger seating capacity of an aeroplane, excluding pilot, flight deck and cabin crew seats, as approved and in the Ops Manual.

Max Continuous Power and/or Thrust

The power and/or thrust in the performance data for unrestricted duration.

Max Continuous Power and/or Thrust Rating

The minimum test bed acceptance power and/or thrust, as in the engine type certificate data sheet, of series and newly overhauled engines running at the specified conditions within appropriate acceptance limitations.

Maximum Engine Overspeed

- *Piston Engine* - maximum rotational speed, inadvertent occurrence of which for up to 20 seconds does not require rejection or maintenance (other than for correction).

- *Turbine Engine* - maximum rotational speed of each independent main rotating system, inadvertent occurrence of which, for up to 20 seconds, does not require rejection or maintenance (other than to correct the cause). For each main rotating system, this is normally at least the maximum transient RPM in non-fault conditions.

Maximum Engine Overtorque

Maximum torque of a free power-turbine, inadvertent occurrence of which for up to 20 seconds does not require rejection or maintenance (other than to correct the cause).

Maximum Power Turbine Overspeed

The max rotational speed of the free power-turbine (in helicopters), inadvertent occurrence of which, for up to 20 seconds does not require rejection or maintenance (other than to correct the cause).

Microlight

An aeroplane with up to two seats, a V_{SO} up to 35 knots CAS, and maximum takeoff mass up to:

- 300 kg for a landplane, single-seater

- 330 kg, single-seat amphibians, floatplanes

- 450 kg for a landplane, two-seater

- 495 kg for an amphibian or floatplane, two-seater, provided that a microlight that is both a floatplane and a landplane falls below both MTOM limits, as appropriate.

Foot-launched aircraft are excluded.

Maximum Approved Passenger Seating

The maximum passenger seating capacity of an individual aircraft, excluding crew seats, as approved and included in the Ops Manual.

Maximum Contingency Power and/or Thrust

The power and/or thrust for when a power-unit has failed or been shut down during takeoff, baulked landing or before a discontinued approach and limited continuously for up to 2.5 minutes.

Maximum Exhaust Gas Overtemperature

The maximum engine EGT of a turbine, inadvertent use of which for up to 20 seconds does not require rejection or maintenance (other than to correct the cause). Do not confuse with maximum temperatures for starting.

Maximum Permitted Exposure Time

A period, based of the power unit failure rate for the engine type, during which the probability of a power unit failure can be discounted.

Max Power-Turbine Speed for Autorotation

The maximum rotational speed of the power-turbine (in a helicopter) during autorotation for periods of unrestricted duration.

Maximum Propeller Overspeed

Max rotational speed, inadvertent occurrence of which for up to 20 seconds does not need rejection or maintenance (other than to correct the cause).

Maximum Structural Landing Mass

The maximum permissible total aeroplane mass on landing under normal circumstances.

Maximum Structural Take Off Mass

The maximum permissible total aeroplane mass at the start of the takeoff run.

Maximum Takeoff Mass

The maximum permissible total mass at takeoff.

Maximum Zero Fuel Mass

The maximum permissible mass of an aeroplane with no usable fuel or, put another way, where any additional weight comes from fuel. The mass of fuel in particular tanks must be included when explicitly mentioned in Flight Manual limitations.

Medical Passenger

A medical person carried in a helicopter during a HEMS flight, including but not limited to, doctors, nurses and paramedics.

Minimum Drainage Period After a False Start

The minimum period to allow surplus fuel to drain from a turbine engine before trying again, from the time the starter is switched off and/or the engine fuel cock is closed during a false start.

Minimum Governed Rotational Speed

The minimum rotational speed as determined by the setting of the (variable pitch) propeller governor or control mechanism.

Min Takeoff Crankshaft Rotational Speed

Minimum crankshaft rotational speed of a piston engine with max takeoff manifold pressure.

Modified Engine

One previously approved, with unapproved modifications.

Modified Propeller

One previously approved, with unapproved modifications.

Module

A group of engine (or propeller) components defined and replaceable without mechanical or performance difficulties. It is uniquely identified and amenable to the setting of an overhaul life separate from other parts.

Multi-crew Cooperation

The functioning of the flight crew as a team of co-operating members led by the PIC.

New Engine

An engine not operated in-service, essentially identical in design, materials and construction with one which has been type-certificated.

New Propeller

A propeller not operated in-service, essentially identical in design, materials and construction with one which has been type-certificated.

Non-Hostile Environment

An environment where a safe forced landing can be accomplished, occupants can be protected from elements, and SAR is consistent with anticipated exposure. Congested areas with adequate safe forced landing areas are non-hostile.

Normal Operating Differential Pressure

The difference between cabin and outside pressure, including tolerances of normal regulating systems.

Notice of Proposed Amendment
One to a JAR Code.

Obstacle
Includes the surface of the earth, land or sea.

Overhauled Engine or Module
An engine or module which has been repaired or reconditioned to a standard which renders it eligible for the complete overhaul period for the particular type of engine.

Overhauled Propeller
A propeller which has been repaired or re-conditioned to a standard which renders it eligible for the complete overhaul period for the particular type of propeller.

Overpack
An enclosure used by a single shipper to contain one or more packages and form one handling unit for convenience of handling and stowage (not including a unit load device.)

Package
The complete product of a packing operation consisting of the packaging and its contents prepared for transport.

Packaging
Receptacles and other components or materials necessary for the receptacle to perform its containment function and to ensure compliance with packing requirements.

Parts
See *Component, Parts, Appliances, Product.*

Parts and Appliances
See *Component, Parts, Appliances, Product.*

Passenger Classification
Adults, male and female, are 12 years of age and above. *Children* are 2 years old and above, but less than 12. Infants are less than 2 years old.

Performance Class 1
Performance such that, if the critical power unit fails, a helicopter can land within rejected takeoff

distance available or safely go to an appropriate landing area, depending on when the failure occurs.

Performance Class 2
Performance such that, if the critical power unit fails, a helicopter can safely continue, except early in the takeoff or late in the landing, when a forced landing may be required.

Performance Class 3
Performance such that, if a power unit fails, a forced landing *may* be required in a multi-engined helicopter, but *will* be required in a single-engined helicopter.

Pilot Flying (PF)
The pilot in charge of the controls of an aircraft.

Pilot Monitoring (PM)
See *Pilot Not Flying.*

Pilot Not Flying (PNF)
The pilot assisting the Pilot Flying under the multi-crew co-operation concept, when the flight crew is more than one (a better term is *Pilot Monitoring*).

Pilot In Command (PIC)
The pilot responsible for the operation and safety of an aircraft during flight time (not necessarily the handling pilot).

Pitch Setting
The propeller blade setting determined by the blade angle, in the Engine Manual.

Power Definitions
For piston-engined aeroplanes and helicopters:

- *Takeoff Power* - output shaft power for takeoff, discontinued approach and baulked landing, up to 5 continuous minutes.

- *Takeoff Power Rating* - the test bed minimum acceptance output shaft power in the engine type certificate data sheet, of series and newly overhauled engines running at the declared maximum coolant CHTs, within appropriate aceptance limitations.

- *Maximum Continuous Power* - output shaft power in performance data for unrestricted duration (don't assume this is necessarily for normal operations).

- *Maximum Continuous Power Rating* - the minimum test bed acceptance power, as in the type certificate data sheet, of series and newly overhauled engines at declared max coolant CHTs within appropriate acceptance limitations.

- *Maximum Recommended Cruising Power Conditions* - crankshaft rotational speed, manifold pressure and other parameters recommended for cruising.

- *Maximum Best Economy Cruising Power Conditions* - crankshaft rotational speed, manifold pressure and other parameters recommended for economical cruising mixture strength.

Powered Sailplane
An aircraft, with one or more engines, with the characteristics of a sailplane when engines are out.

Product
See *Component, Parts, Appliances, Product.*

Propeller
A complete propeller, including parts attached to and rotating with the hub and blades, and equipment for its control and operation.

Propeller Equipment
Equipment used with, or necessary for the control and operation of, the propeller.

Proper Shipping Name
The name to describe a particular article or substance in shipping documents and notifications and, where appropriate, on packagings.

Protective Breathing Equipment
Breathing equipment for protection against smoke, fumes and other harmful gases.

Prototype Engine
The first engine, of a type and arrangement not previously approved, to be submitted for type-approval test.

Prototype Propeller
The first propeller of a type and arrangement not previously approved, to be submitted for type-approval tests.

Quality Assurance
Planned and systematic actions necessary to provide adequate confidence that operational and maintenance practices satisfy given requirements.

Quality Manager
The manager responsible for the management of the Quality System, monitoring function and requesting remedial actions.

R
Rotor radius.

Reasonably Probable
Unlikely to occur often during operation of the type, but which may occur several times during total operational life.

Reference Landing Speed
The speed of an aeroplane, in a specified landing configuration, descending through the landing screen height in the determination of landing distance for manual landings.

Rejected Takeoff Distance Required
The horizontal distance from the start of takeoff to where a helicopter comes to a full stop after a power unit failure and rejection of takeoff at TDP.

Remote
Unlikely to occur during total operational life but may occur several times in the total operational life of a number of aircraft of the type in which the engine is installed.

Reported Headwind Component
That reported during flight planning which may be used if there is no significant change of unfactored wind before takeoff.

Reverse Pitch
The blade angle used for producing reverse thrust with a propeller.

Rotation Point (RP)

Where a cyclic input is made to initiate a nose-down attitude change during the takeoff. The last point from which, if engine failure is recognised, forced landing on the deck can be achieved.

Rotational Direction of Equipment

The direction of rotation as observed when looking at the drive face ('clockwise' or 'anti-clockwise').

Rotational Speed

- *Engine* - unless otherwise qualified (e.g. propeller rotational speed), the rotational speed in RPM of the engine crankshaft or its equivalent.

- *Propeller* - unless otherwise specified (e.g. prop RPM), the speed in RPM of the engine crankshaft or its equivalent.

Rotorcraft

A heavier-than-air aircraft that depends principally for its support in flight on the lift generated by one or more rotors.

Rotorcraft-Load Combination

The combination of a rotorcraft and an external load, including the load attaching means. They are:

- *Class A* – the load cannot move freely, or be jettisoned, and does not extend below the landing gear.

- *Class B* – the load is jettisonable and is free of land or water.

- *Class C* – the load is jettisonable and remains in contact with land or water.

- *Class D* – the load is other than a Class A, B or C and has been specifically approved. Mostly for human loads.

Safe Forced Landing

Unavoidable landing or ditching with a reasonable expectancy of no injuries to people in the aircraft or on the surface.

Safety Catch

A mechanism which locks a control in position, engaging automatically whenever the control is put there but has to be manually taken out to move it away (JAR 25).

Sailplane

A heavier-than-air aircraft supported in flight by the dynamic reaction of air against its fixed lifting surfaces, the free flight of which does not depend on an engine.

Series Propeller

A propeller essentially identical in design, materials, and construction, with one previously approved.

Serious Incident

An incident involving circumstances indicating that an accident nearly occurred.

Serious Injury

An injury which is sustained by a person in an accident and which:

- Requires hospitalisation for more than 48 hours, starting within seven days from the date the injury was received

- Results in a fracture of any bone (except simple fractures of fingers, toes or nose)

- Involves lacerations causing severe haemorrhage, nerve, muscle or tendon damage

- Involves injury to any internal organ

- Involves second or third degree burns, or any burns affecting more than 5% of the body surface

Standard Atmosphere

See *Atmosphere, International Standard*.

State of Origin

The Authority in whose territory dangerous goods were first loaded on an aircraft.

Stopway

An area beyond the takeoff runway, at least as wide and centred upon the extended centreline, able to support the aeroplane during an abortive takeoff, without causing structural damage, and designated by airport authorities for deceleration.

Supplemental Oxygen

Extra oxygen to protect against adverse effects of excessive cabin altitude and maintain acceptable physiological conditions.

Takeoff Decision Point (TDP)

The point used to determine takeoff performance from which, a power unit failure having been recognised, either a rejected takeoff may be made or a takeoff safely continued.

Takeoff Distance Available (TODA)

The TORA plus clearway.

Takeoff Distance Required

The horizontal distance required from the start of the takeoff to where V_{TOSS}, a height of 10.7 m (35 ft) above the takeoff surface, and a positive climb gradient are achieved, after failure of the critical power unit at TDP, with remaining power units within limits.

Takeoff Mass

The mass, including everything and everyone carried at the start of the takeoff run.

Takeoff Power and/or Thrust

That for takeoff, discontinued approach and baulked landing, up to 5 minutes continuously, or 10 minutes for aeroplanes (if requested) if a power unit fails or is shut down.

Takeoff Power and/or Thrust Rating

The minimum test bed acceptance power and/or thrust as in the type certificate data sheet, of series and newly overhauled engines at the specified conditions and within appropriate acceptance limitations.

Takeoff Run Available (TORA)

The length of runway declared available by the appropriate Authority and suitable for the ground run of an aeroplane taking off.

Takeoff Safety Speed

A referenced airspeed after liftoff where OEI climb performance can be achieved.

Technical Instructions

The latest effective edition of the *Technical Instructions for the Safe Transport of Dangerous Goods by Air* (Doc 9284–AN/905), including Supplement and Addenda, approved and published by ICAO.

Touchdown and Lift-off Area (TLOF)

A load bearing area on which a helicopter may touch down or lift off.

Traffic Load

The total mass of passengers, baggage and cargo, including nonrevenue loads.

True Airspeed

Airspeed relative to undisturbed air.

Type

Aircraft of the same basic design, including modifications, except which result in a change of handling, flight characteristics or crew.

UN Number

The four-digit number assigned by the United Nations Committee of Experts on the Transport of Dangerous Goods to identify a substance or a particular group of substances.

Variable Pitch Propellers

A propeller, the pitch setting of which changes or can be changed, including one directly under control of the flight crew (controllable pitch propeller), and one controlled by a governor or other automatic means, either integral with the propeller or separately mounted equipment and which may or may not be controlled by the flight crew (constant speed propeller), or a combination.

Visual Approach

An approach when either part or all of an instrument approach procedure is not completed and the approach is executed with visual reference.

Wet Runway

A runway is wet when the surface is covered with water, or equivalent, less than specified or when there is enough moisture to cause it to appear reflective, without significant standing water.

JAR OPS 1

1.001 - Applicability

JAR OPS Part 1 is for civil aeroplanes used for commercial air transportation by operators with a principal place of business in a JAA Member State. It does not apply:

- to aeroplanes in military, customs and police service

- parachute dropping and firefighting, and associated positioning and return flights with persons normally carried

- appropriate flights immediately before, during, or immediately after aerial work, carrying up to 6 indispensable people, excluding crew.

Appendix 1

Late compliance dates. The only one left is JAR OPS 1.668 (a)(2) Page 1–K–5–1 Jan 2005

1.005 - General

Aeroplanes used for commercial air transportation must operate under JAR OPS Part 1 (but there are alleviations for Performance B in Appx 1, below), and under their Certificates of Airworthiness and limitations in the Flight Manual.

For Air Taxi and EMS operations, refer to Subpart Q, Appendices A and B, respectively.

Synthetic Training Devices (simulators, etc.) must be qualified under JAR STD and be user-approved.

Appendix 1 - Performance B Aeroplanes

Certain alleviations are allowed:

1.035 - Quality System

For a very small operator, the Quality Manager may a nominated postholder if external auditors are used. This applies where the accountable manager holds one or more nominated posts.

1.037 - Accident Prevention & Flight Safety Program

See ACJ to Appendix 1 to 1.005 (a), below.

1.075 - Methods of Carriage of Persons

Not required for VFR operations of single-engined aeroplanes.

1.100 - Admission to Flight Deck

There must be rules for carrying passengers in pilot seats, which must not cause distraction or interfere with the flight. Passengers must be made familiar with relevant restrictions and safety procedures.

1.105 – Unauthorised Carriage

Not required for VFR operations of single-engined aeroplanes.

JAR OPS 1.135 – Additional Information & Forms

For **A to A VFR** (starting and stopping at the same place) with single-engined aeroplanes by day, these need not be carried:

- Operational Flight Plan (may be simplified, while meeting operational needs)

- Technical Log

- NOTAM/AIS briefing documentation

- Meteorological Information

- Notification of special categories of passengers (except for **A to B VFR** with single-engined aeroplanes by day)

- Notification of special loads including dangerous goods

1.215 - Use of Air Traffic Services
For VFR with single-engined aeroplanes by day, non-mandatory contact with ATS must be maintained to the appropriate extent. SAR service must be ensured as per JAR OPS 1.300.

1.225 - Aerodrome Operating Minima
For VFR, standard VFR minima will normally do. Where necessary, additional requirements, taking into account such factors as radio coverage, terrain, nature of sites for takeoff and landing, flight conditions and ATS capacity, may be specified.

1.235 - Noise Abatement
Not for VFR with single-engined aeroplanes.

1.240 - Routes and Areas of Operation
Subpara (a)(1) does not apply to A to A VFR operations of single-engined aeroplanes by day.

1.250 - Minimum Flight Altitudes
For VFR by day, operations may only be conducted along such routes or within such areas for which safe terrain clearance can be maintained, taking account of such factors as temperature, terrain, shit weather (severe turbulence, etc), corrections for temperature, and pressure variations from standard values.

1.255 - Fuel Policy
For **A to A Flights**, minimum fuel at the end of a flight must be at least 45 minutes' worth.

For **A to B Flights**, the pre-flight calculation of usable fuel for a flight must include:

- *Taxi Fuel* – that used before takeoff, if significant

- *Trip Fuel* (to reach the destination)

- *Reserve Fuel*, consisting of *Contingency Fuel* - at least 5% of planned trip fuel or, in the event of in-flight replanning, 5% of the remainder required, and *Final Reserve Fuel* - for an additional 45 minutes (piston) or 30 minutes (turbine)

- *Alternate Fuel* - to reach the alternate via the destination, if an alternate is required

- *Extra Fuel* –that the commander may require on top.

1.265 - Inadmissible Passengers
For VFR operations of single-engined aeroplanes, and where it is not intended to carry inadmissible passengers, deportees or persons in custody, an operator is not required to establish procedures for their carriage.

1.280 - Passenger Seating
Not for VFR with single-engined aeroplanes.

1.285 - Passenger Briefing
Demonstration and briefing must be given as appropriate to the operation. Single pilots may not be allocated tasks that distract from flying duties.

1.290 - Flight Preparation
An Operational Flight Plan for **A to A** operations is not required, with a simplified one completed for each flight for **A to B** operations under day VFR.

1.295 - Selection of Aerodromes
Not applicable to VFR. The necessary instructions for the use of aerodromes and sites for takeoff and landing must be issued under JAR OPS 1.220.

1.310 - Crew Members at Stations
For VFR, instructions on this are required only for two-pilot operations.

1.375 - In-flight Fuel Management
Appendix 1 is not required to be applied to VFR operations of single-engined aeroplanes by day.

1.405 – Start & Continuation of Approach
Not applicable to VFR.

1.410 - Threshold Crossing Height
Not applicable to VFR.

1.430-1.460, including Appendices
Not applicable to VFR.

1.530 - Takeoff

Subparagraph (a) applies, but the Authority may, case by case, accept other performance data based on demonstration and/or documented experience.

Subparagraphs (b) and (c) apply, but where this paragraph cannot be complied with due to physical limitations relating to extending the runway, and there is a clear public interest and necessity for the operation, the Authority may accept, on a case-by-case basis, other performance data (not conflicting with the Flight Manual) based on demonstration and/or documented experience.

People wishing to conduct such operations must have prior approval of the Authority issuing the AOC, which will specify the type of aeroplane, operation, aerodromes and runways, restrict the takeoff to be under VMC, specify the crew qualificaton, and be limited to aeroplanes where the first type certificate was issued before 1 Jan 2005.

The operation must also be accepted by the state in which the aerodrome is located.

1.535 - Takeoff Obstacle Clearance – Multi-Engined

Subparagraphs (a)(3), (a)(4), (a)(5), (b)(2), (c)(1), (c)(2) and the Appendix do not apply to VFR by day. For IFR or VFR operations by day, sub-paragraphs (b) and (c) apply, but:

- Visual guidance is considered available when visibility is 1500 m or more

- The maximum corridor width is 300 m when flight visibility is 1500 m or more.

1.545 - Landing Destination and Alternates

Where this paragraph cannot be complied with due to physical limitations relating to extending the runway, and there is a clear public interest and necessity for the operation, the Authority may accept, on a case-by-case basis, other performance data (not conflicting with the Flight Manual), relating to special procedures, based on demonstration and/or documented experience.

An operator wishing to conduct such operations must have prior approval of the Authority issuing the AOC, which will specify the type of aeroplane, operation, aerodromes and runways, restrict the takeoff to be under VMC, specify the crew qualificaton, and be limited to aeroplanes where the first type certificate was issued before 1 Jan 2005.

The operation must also be accepted by the state in which the aerodrome is located.

1.550 - Landing - Dry Runways

As above.

1.640 - Operating Lights

The Authority may grant an exemption from some or all of subparagraph (a) until 1 January 2005 for single-engined aeroplanes, under VFR by day, first issued with an individual C of A before 22 May 1995, without an electrical generating system. This is subject to the approval of other states overflown.

1.650 - Day VFR Operations

Single-engined aeroplanes, first issued with an individual C of A before 22 May 1995, may be exempted from subparagraphs (f), (g), (h) and (i) if fulfilment would require retrofitting.

1.905 - Maintenance Management Exposition

The MME may be adapted to the operation.

1.915 – Technical Log

See ACJ to Appendix 1 to JAR OPS 1.1005(a).

The Authority may approve an abbreviated form of Tech Log, relevant to the operation.

1.940 - Composition of Flight Crew

Subparagraphs (a)(2), (a)(4), and (b) do not apply to VFR by day, except that (a)(4) must be applied in full where 2 pilots are required.

1.945 - Conversion Training and Checking

Subparagraph (a)(7) – *Line Flying Under Supervision* (LIFUS) may be performed on any aeroplane within the applicable class. The amount required depends on the complexity of the operation. Subparagraph (a)(8) is not required.

1.955 - Nomination as Commander

For subparagraph (b), the Authority may accept an abbreviated (but relevant) command course.

1.960 - Commanders Holding a CPL

Subparagraph (a)(1)(i) is not applicable to VFR operations by day.

1.965 - Recurrent Training and Checking

For subparagraph (a)(1) (for VFR by day), all training and checking must be relevant to the type of operation and class of aeroplane, with due account taken of specialised equipment.

Subparagraph (a)(3)(ii) applies as follows: Training in the aeroplane may be conducted by a CRE, FE or TRE.

For subparagraph (a)(4)(i), OPCs may be conducted by a TRE, CRE or a suitably qualified commander, trained in CRM concepts and the assessment of CRM skills.

Sub-paragraph (b)(2) applies as follows for VFR by day: Where operations are conducted during seasons up to 8 consecutive months, 1 OPC is enough. This must be undertaken before starting commercial air transport operations.

1.968 - Pilot Qualification for Either Seat
Appendix 1 does not apply to VFR operations of single-engined aeroplanes by day.

1.975 - Route and Aerodrome Competence
For VFR operations by day, subparagraphs (b), (c) and (d) do not apply, except that the operator must ensure that, where a special approval by the state of the aerodrome is required, associated requirements are observed.

For IFR or VFR by night, as an alternative to subparas (b)-(d), route and aerodrome competence may be revalidated as follows:

- Except for the most demanding aerodromes, by at least 10 sectors within the area of operation during the preceding 12 months in addition to any required self briefing.

- Operations to the most demanding aerodromes may be done only if the commander has been qualified at the aerodrome in the preceding 36 months by a visit as flight crew or an observer. The approach must be in VMC from the applicable MSA, and an adequate selfbriefing must have been made before the flight.

1.980 - More than One Type or Variant
Not applicable if operations are limited to single-pilot classes of piston-engined aeroplanes under VFR by day.

For IFR and VFR by night, the requirement in Appendix 1, subparagraph (d)(2)(i) for 500 hours in the relevant crew position before exercising the privileges of 2 licence endorsements, is reduced to

100 hours or sectors if one of the endorsements is related to a class. A check flight must be done before the pilot is let loose as Commander

1.981 - Helicopters and Aeroplanes
Subparagraph (a)(1) does not apply if operations are limited to single-pilot classes of piston-engined aeroplanes.

1.1045 – Ops Manual – Structure and Contents
See AMC OPS 1.1045.

1.1060 - Operational Flight Plan
Not required for A to A VFR by day. For A to B, the flight plan may be in a simplified form relevant to the kind of operations. (cf. JAR OPS 1.135).

1.1070 - Maintenance Management Exposition
The MME may be adapted to the operation (see ACJ to Appendix 1 to JAR OPS 1.005(a))

1.1071 – Technical Log
Applicable as indicated for JAR OPS 1.915.

Subpart R – Dangerous Goods by Air
See ACJ to Appendix 1 below.

1.1235 – Security Requirements
See ACJ to Appendix 1 below.

1.1240 – Training Programs
To be adapted to the operation. A self-study training program may be OK for VFR operations.

1.1250 - Aeroplane Search Procedure Checklist
Not applicable for VFR operations by day.

ACJ to Appendix 1 to 1.005 (a)
1.037 - Accident Prevention and Flight Safety
A simplified program is good enough, which may consist of collecting case-based material (such as relevant accident reports) and submitting or distributing it to the crews concerned, or collection and use of information from flight safety seminars

Appx 2 to 1.175 –Management & Organisation
Supervision may be undertaken by appropriate nominated postholders subject to time available.

1.915 - Technical Log
Two examples of acceptable ways to fulfil the requirement are in attachments 1 and 2 to this ACJ, where a so- called Flight Log is presented.

1.1070 - MME
The MME can be simplified as relevant.

Subpart R - Transport of Dangerous Goods
JAR OPS 1.1155, 1.1160. 1.1165, 1.1215, 1.1220 and 1.1225 apply to all operators, but JAR OPS 1.1165 may be fulfilled by information pamphlets. The remainder of this Subpart applies only when the operator seeks or holds an approval to carry dangerous goods.

Subpart S – Security (1.1235)
Security requirements apply in States where the national security program applies to this Appendix.

1.1240 - Training Programs
These must be adapted to the kind of operation. Self-study may be OK for VFR operations.

1.290(b)(2)
Where there is a CDL for aeroplanes of this size, it is included in the Flight Manual or equivalent.

1.010 - Exemptions

These may be granted if there is a need, subject to compliance with supplementary conditions necessary to ensure an acceptable level of safety in a particular case.

1.015 - Operational Directives

These may be used to direct that an operation be prohibited, limited or subject to certain conditions, in the interests of safety. They are supplementary to JAR OPS Part 1 and will state the reason for issue, applicability, duration, and action required.

1.020 - Laws, Regulations, Procedures

Employees must be made aware that they must comply with pertinent laws, regulations and procedures of States where operations are conducted. Crews must be familiar with pertinent laws, regulations and procedures.

1.025 - Common Language

Crew members must be able to communicate in a common language, and operations personnel must be able to understand the language used in relevant parts of the Ops Manual.

1.030 - Minimum Equipment Lists

These must be established for each aeroplane, based upon, but no less restrictive than, the Master MEL, if one exists.

Aeroplanes must operate under the MEL, unless permitted otherwise, but such permission will, in any case, not be allowed outside the MMEL.

1.035 - Quality System

One must be established, with a Quality Manager (or two, for Ops and Maintenance, if there is one Quality Management Unit) lumbered to monitor compliance with, and the adequacy of, procedures required to ensure safe operational practices and airworthy aeroplanes. This must include a feed-back system to the Accountable Manager to ensure corrective action as necessary (See also JAR OPS 1.175(h)).

There must be a Quality Assurance Program with procedures to verify that operations are conducted under applicable requirements, standards and procedures.

The Quality System and Manager must be acceptable, described in relevant documentation.

AMC OPS 1.035
Note: A general overview is given here, as it's kinda boring – you should read the JARs as well.

Terminology
- *Accountable Manager* - the person acceptable to the Authority *with corporate authority* for ensuring that operations and maintenance can be financed and carried out properly, plus additional requirements defined by the operator. This person is an essential part of management, and the term means CEO/President/General Manager, etc.

- *Quality Assurance*. Planned and systematic actions that provide adequate confidence that operational and maintenance practices satisfy given requirements.

- *Quality Manager*. The manager responsible for the management of the Quality System, monitoring company activities and requesting corrective actions. He should have direct access to the Accountable

Manager, all parts of the organisation, and must not be a nominated postholder. The job may be done by two people over two Quality Assurance Programs.

For small operators (see below), the Accountable and Quality Manager posts may be combined, but audits should then be done by independent people, and the Accountable Manager may not be a nominated postholder.

Quality Policy

Operators should establish a formal written Quality Policy Statement, or a commitment by the Accountable Manager as to what the system should achieve. The Policy should reflect the achievement and continued compliance with JAR OPS 1, with additional standards from the operator.

Purpose of the Quality System

To enable operators to monitor compliance with JAR OPS 1, the Ops Manual, the MME, and other standards specified by operators or the Authority, to ensure safe operations and airworthy aircraft.

Quality System

The Quality System should be structured for the size and complexity of the operation, and should address at least:

- Provisions of JAR OPS

- Additional standards and procedures

- Quality Policy

- Organisational structure

- Responsibility for development, establishment and management of the Quality System

- Documentation, including manuals, reports and records

- Quality Procedures

- Quality Assurance Program

- Financial, material, and human resources

- Training

It should also include a feedback system to the Accountable Manager to ensure that corrective actions are identified and promptly addressed, also

specifying who is required to rectify discrepancies and non-compliance and the procedure if corrective action is not completed within an appropriate timescale.

Relevant Documentation

This includes relevant parts of the Ops Manual and MME, which may be in a separate Quality Manual.

It should also include:

- Quality Policy

- Terminology

- Specified operational standards

- Description of the organisation

- Allocation of duties and responsibilities

- Operational procedures for compliance

- Accident Prevention and Flight Safety Program (see below)

- Quality Assurance Program, reflecting the schedule of the monitoring process, audit and reporting procedures, follow-up and corrective action, and recording systems

- Training syllabus

- Document Control

Quality Assurance Program

This should include planned and systematic actions to provide confidence that operations and maintenance are conducted under applicable requirements, standards and procedures. When establishing one, consideration should at least be given to:

- *Quality Inspection* - to observe a particular event/action/document etc., to verify whether established procedures and requirements are followed and standards are achieved. Typical subject areas include flight operations, Ground De-icing/Anti-icing, Load Control, Maintenance, Technical and Training Standards, etc.

- *Audit* - a systematic, and independent comparison of the way in which an operation is being conducted against the way the procedures say it should be conducted, including interviews or discussions with personnel, a review of documents, witnessing of activities and the preservation of documents and recording of observations. Auditors should not have any day-to-day involvement in the the operation and/or activity to be audited.

- *Monitoring and Corrective Action.* The aim is to investigate and judge effectiveness and ensure that policy, operational, and maintenance standards are continuously complied with. Monitoring activity is based upon quality inspections, audits, corrective action and follow-up.

Recording
Accurate, complete, and readily accessible records documenting the QAP should be maintained. The following should be kept for 5 years:

- Audit Schedules
- Quality inspection and Audit reports
- Responses to findings
- Corrective action reports
- Follow-up and closure reports
- Management Evaluation reports

Subcontractors
These may be used, but the responsibility always lies with the operator.

Training
Effective, well planned and resourced quality related briefings should be established for all personnel. Those responsible for managing the Quality System should get training on:

- The concept of Quality Assurance and the Quality System
- Quality management
- Quality manuals
- Audit techniques
- Reporting and recording

- The way in which the Quality System will function in the company

Courses are available from various National or International Standards Institutions.

Outfits with 20 or less Full Time Employees
The requirement for a Quality System and a Quality Manager applies to all operators, but classifications as to company size according to aircraft carrying capacity or mass do not suit Quality Assurance, due to its complexity.

Operators with 5 or less full time staff are 'very small', while those with 6-20 are 'small' (full-time in this context means at least 35 hours per week, excluding vacations). For such operators, the QAP may use a checklist, with a supporting schedule that requires completion of all items within a specified timescale, with a statement acknowledging completion of a periodic review by top management. An occasional independent overview should be undertaken.

Small operators may decide to use internal or external auditors, or a combination. In these circumstances, it would be acceptable for external specialists and/or qualified organisations to perform quality audits on behalf of the QM.

1.037 - Accident Prevention and Flight Safety Program

This may be integrated with the Quality System, including:

- Programs **for risk awareness**
- An **occurrence reporting scheme** to identify adverse trends or address deficiencies for flight safety. It must protect the identity of the reporter and allow for reports being submitted anonymously
- **Evaluation of relevant information** relating to incidents and accidents and promulgation of related information (but not the attribution of blame)
- **Appointment of a person** to manage the program.

Proposals for corrective action are the responsibility of the person managing the program.

The effectiveness of changes resulting from such proposals must be monitored by the QM.

IEM OPS 1.037
Guidance material for safety programs can be found in:

- ICAO Doc 9422 (*Accident Prevention Manual*)

- ICAO Doc 9376 (*Preparation of an Operational Manual*)

Where available, use may be made of analysis of FDR information (See JAR OPS 1.160(c).)

The *overall* objective of the scheme is to use reported information to improve the level of flight safety and not to attribute blame. The *detailed* objectives are:

- To enable an assessment of the safety implications of each relevant incident and accident, including previous similar occurrences, to initiate necessary action

- To ensure that knowledge of relevant incidents and accidents is disseminated so other persons and organisations may learn from them.

The scheme is an essential part of the overall monitoring function; it is complementary to normal day-to-day procedures and control systems and is not intended to duplicate or supersede any of them. The scheme is a tool to identify those occasions where routine procedures have failed.

Occurrences that have to be reported, and responsibilities for submitting reports, are described in JAR OPS 1.420.

1.040 - Additional Crew Members

Crew members who are not required flight or cabin crew must also be trained in, and be proficient to perform, their assigned duties.

1.050 - Search & Rescue Information

Essential information for intended flights concerning SAR services must be easily accessible on the flight deck.

1.055 - Emergency & Survival Equipment

There must be, for immediate communication to RCCs, lists with information on emergency and survival equipment on board. It must include, as applicable, the number, colour and type of liferafts and pyrotechnics, details of emergency medical supplies, water supplies and the type and frequencies of emergency radio equipment.

1.060 - Ditching

Aeroplanes that can carry more than 30 passengers on overwater flights must be flown no greater than the lesser of 120 minutes at cruising speed, or 400 nm, from land suitable for an emergency landing, unless they comply with the applicable airworthiness code.

1.065 - Weapons & Munitions of War

Approval must be granted by all States concerned. Weapons of war and munitions of war must be:

- Inaccessible to passengers during flight

- Unloaded, unless, before flight, approval has been granted by all States concerned

The commander must be notified before a flight begins of the details and location of such items.

IEM OPS 1.065
There is no internationally agreed definition of weapons and munitions of war, although some States may have defined them for their own purposes or national need. It should be the responsibility of the operator to check.

States that may be concerned with approvals are those of *origin*, *transit*, *overflight* and *destination* of the consignment, and the State of the operator.

Where weapons or munitions of war are also dangerous goods (torpedoes, bombs, etc.), see also Subpart R (and IEM OPS 1.070).

1.070 – Sporting Weapons & Ammunition

Sporting weapons intended to be carried by air must be reported to the operator. Operators accepting their carriage must ensure that they are:

- Inaccessible to passengers during flight, unless compliance is impracticable and other procedures might apply

- For firearms or other weapons that can contain ammunition, unloaded.

Ammunition for sporting weapons may be checked baggage, subject to certain limitations under the (IATA) Technical Instructions (JAR OPS 1.1160(b)(5)) as defined in JAR OPS 1.1150(a)(14).

IMC OPS 1.070

Again, there is no internationally agreed definition of sporting weapons. In general, they may be any weapon which is not a weapon of war or munition of war (See 1.065), but they might include hunting knives, bows and other similar articles. An antique weapon, such as a musket, may now be regarded as a sporting weapon. A *firearm* is a gun, rifle or pistol firing a projectile.

In the absence of a specific definition, for the purpose of JAR OPS, and to provide some guidance, the following firearms are generally regarded as being sporting weapons:

- Those designed for shooting game, birds and other animals

- Those used for target shooting, clay-pigeon shooting and competition shooting, if they are not standard issue for military forces

- Airguns, dart guns, starting pistols, etc.

A firearm, not a weapon or munition of war, should be treated as a sporting weapon for carriage on an aeroplane.

Other procedures may need to be considered if the aeroplane does not have a separate compartment where weapons can be stowed. These should take into account the nature of the flight, its origin and destination, and the possibility of unlawful interference. As far as possible, weapons should be stowed so they are not immediately accessible to passengers (e.g. in locked boxes, or in checked baggage stowed under other baggage or fixed netting). If procedures other than those in JAR OPS 1.070(b)(1) are applied, the commander should be notified accordingly.

1.075 - Method of Carriage of Persons

No person may be in any part of an aeroplane during flight, not designed for their accommodation, unless temporary access has been granted by the commander:

- For taking action necessary for the safety of the aeroplane or of any person, animal or goods in it, or

- Where cargo or stores are carried, if designed to enable a person to have access while the aeroplane is in flight.

1.080 - Dangerous Goods by Air

People offering or accepting dangerous goods for transport by air must be trained, and the goods properly classified, documented, certificated, described, packaged, marked, labelled and fit for transport as per the (IATA) Technical Instructions.

1.085 - Crew Responsibilities

Crew members are responsible for the proper execution of duties related to the safety of the aeroplane and its occupants, and which are specified in the Ops Manual.

Crew members must (unless already reported):

- Report to the commander any fault, failure, malfunction or defect which is believed to affect airworthiness or safe operation, including emergency systems.

- Report to the commander any incident that endangered, or could have endangered, the safety of operation

- Make use of the operator's occurrence reporting schemes under JAR OPS 1.037(a)(2), with a copy communicated to the commander.

A crew member must not perform duties on an aeroplane:

- Under the influence of any drug that may affect faculties contrary to safety

- Until a reasonable time has elapsed after deep water diving

- After blood donation, except when a reasonable time has elapsed

- If in any doubt of being able to accomplish assigned duties

- If knowing or suspecting that he is suffering from fatigue, or feels unfit so that the flight may be endangered

A crew member must not:

- Consume alcohol less than 8 hours before the specified reporting time for flight duty or the start of standby

- Start a flight duty period with a blood alcohol level over 0.2 promille

- Consume alcohol during the flight duty period or while on standby

The commander must:

- Be responsible for the safe operation of the aeroplane and safety of its occupants during flight time

- Have authority to give all commands deemed necessary for securing the safety of the aeroplane and persons or property carried in it

- Have authority to disembark any person, or any part of the cargo, which, in his opinion, may represent a potential hazard to the safety of the aeroplane or its occupants

- Not allow a person to be carried who *appears to be* under the influence of alcohol or drugs to the extent that the safety of the aeroplane or its occupants may be endangered

- Have the right to refuse transportation of inadmissible passengers, deportees or persons in custody if their carriage poses any risk to the safety of the aeroplane or its occupants

- Ensure that all passengers are briefed on the *location* of emergency exits and the *location and use* of relevant safety and emergency equipment

- Ensure that operational procedures and checklists are complied with as per the Ops Manual

- Not permit crew members to perform activities during takeoff, initial climb, final approach and landing, except for safety

- Not permit an FDR to be disabled, switched off or erased during flight, nor permit recorded data to be erased after flight in an accident or an incident subject to mandatory reporting, or permit a CVR to be disabled or switched off during flight, unless he believes that the recorded data, which otherwise would be erased automatically, should be preserved for investigation, nor permit recorded data to be manually erased during or after flight in an accident or incident subject to mandatory reporting

- Decide to accept unserviceabilities allowed by CDLs or MELs

- Ensure that the pre-flight inspection has been carried out

The commander or the pilot to whom flight conduct has been delegated must, in emergencies requiring immediate decision and action, take any action necessary, deviating from rules, procedures and methods in the interest of safety.

1.090 - Authority of the Commander

People carried in the aeroplane must obey all lawful commands given by the commander for securing the safety of the aeroplane and persons or property carried in it.

1.100 - Admission to Flight Deck

Only flight crew members assigned to a flight may be admitted to, or carried on, the flight deck unless that person is:

- An operating crew member

- A representative of the Authority responsible for certification, licensing or inspection on official duty

- Permitted by, and carried under, the Ops Manual

The commander must ensure that, for safety, admission to the flight deck does not cause distraction and/or interfere with the flight's operation, and that all persons on the flight deck are familiar with relevant safety procedures.

Final decisions about admission to the flight deck are the responsibility of the commander.

1.105 - Unauthorised Carriage

Operators must take all reasonable measures to ensure that people do not secrete themselves or cargo on board an aeroplane (i.e. no stowaways).

1.110 - Portable Electronic Devices

Portable electronic devices that can adversely affect systems and equipment may not be used on board.

1.115 - Alcohol and Drugs

Operators must not allow people to enter or be in, and take all reasonable measures to ensure they are not in, an aeroplane when under the influence of alcohol or drugs to the extent that the safety of the aeroplane or its occupants may be endangered.

1.120 - Endangering Safety

People may not recklessly or negligently act or omit to act so as to endanger an aeroplane or person in it, or to cause or permit an aeroplane to endanger any person or property.

1.125 - Documents To Be Carried

These must be carried on each flight:

- Certificate of Registration

- Certificate of Airworthiness

- Noise Certificate (original, if applicable)

- Air Operator Certificate (original or copy)

- Aircraft Radio Licence

- Third Party Liability Insurance Certificate (original or copies)

Flight crew members must also, on each flight, carry valid licences with appropriate rating(s).

Appendix 1

In case of loss or theft, the operation may continue until reaching base or a place where replacements can be provided.

1.130 - Manuals To Be Carried

The current parts of the Ops Manual relevant to crew duties must be carried on each flight, and those required for the conduct of a flight must be easily accessible to the crew. In addition, the current Flight Manual must be carried unless the Ops Manual contains the relevant information.

1.135 - Additional Information and Forms to be Carried

In addition to the documents and manuals above, the following information and forms, relevant to the type and area, must be carried:

- Operational Flight Plan with at least the information in JAR OPS 1.1060

- Technical Log with at least the information in JAR OPS 1.915(a)

- Details of the filed ATS flight plan

- Appropriate NOTAM/AIS briefing documentation

- Appropriate met information

- Mass and balance stuff as per Subpart J

- Notification of special categories of passenger, such as security personnel (if not considered as crew), handicapped persons, inadmissible passengers, deportees and persons in custody

- Notification of special loads, including dangerous goods and written information to the commander as per JAR OPS 1.1215(d)

- Current maps and charts and associated documents as per JAR OPS 1.290(b)(7)

- Any other documentation which may be required by States concerned with the flight, such as cargo and passenger manifests, etc.

• Forms for reporting requirements

The information above may be other than on printed paper (as approved), but an acceptable standard of accessibility, usability and reliability must be assured.

1.140 - Information Kept on Ground

At least for the duration of each flight or series of flights, information relevant to the flight and appropriate for the operation preserved on the ground, and retained until it has been duplicated at the place at which it will be stored (see JAR OPS 1.1065), or, if this is impracticable, carried in a fireproof container in the aeroplane. This includes:

• A copy of the operational flight plan

• Copies of relevant part(s) of the tech log

• Route specific NOTAMs if specifically edited by the operator

• Mass and balance documentation if required (see JAR OPS 1.625)

• Special loads notification

1.145 - Power to Inspect

Authorised people may board and fly in any aeroplane operated under an AOC issued by their Authority, and enter and remain on the flight deck, but the commander may refuse access if, in his opinion, safety would be compromised.

1.150 - Production of Documentation

Authorised people may be given access to any documents and records related to flight operations or maintenance, which must be produced when requested, within a reasonable time.

The commander must, within a reasonable time of a request from an authorised person, produce documentation required to be carried on board.

1.155 - Preservation of Documentation

Original documentation, or copies, to be preserved, must be kept for the required period even if ceasing to be an operator of an aeroplane. When a crew member moves on, his records must be available to the new operator.

1.160 - Preservation, Production and Use of FDR Recordings

Preservation of Recordings

After an accident, the operator of an aeroplane on which a flight recorder is carried must, to the extent possible, preserve the original data, as retained by the recorder for 60 days, unless directed otherwise.

Unless prior permission has been granted, the same applies to an incident subject to mandatory reporting, and when so directed anyway.

When an FDR is required on board, the operator must save the recordings for the time required by JAR OPS 1.715, 1.720 and 1.725 except that, for testing and maintenance, up to one hour of the oldest recorded material (at the time of testing) may be erased, and keep a document which presents the information necessary to retrieve and convert stored data into engineering units.

Production of Recordings

The operator of an aeroplane on which an FDR is carried must, within a reasonable time of a request, produce any recording made by it that is available or has been preserved.

Use of Recordings

CVR recordings may not be used for purposes other than the investigation of an accident or incident subject to mandatory reporting, except with the consent of all crew members.

Neither may FDR recordings, except when used by the operator for airworthiness or maintenance purposes *only*, or de-identified, or disclosed under secure procedures.

1.165 - Leasing

A *Dry Lease* exists when aeroplanes are operated under the AOC of the lessee. A *Wet Lease* exists when the aeroplane is under the AOC of the lessor. A *JAA operator* is one certificated under JAR OPS 1 by a JAA Member State.

Leasing Between JAA Operators
Wet Lease-out
A JAA operator providing an aeroplane and complete crew to another, and retaining the

functions and responsibilities in Subpart C, remains the operator.

All Leases except Wet Lease-out

Except as above, a JAA operator using an aeroplane from, or providing it to, another JAA operator, must obtain prior approval from the respective Authority. Conditions which are part of the approval must be in the agreement.

Elements of lease agreements approved by the Authority, other than agreements with an aeroplane and complete crew, where no transfer of functions and responsibilities is intended, are to be regarded as variations of the AOC under which the flights will be operated.

Between JAA Operators and other Entities

Dry Lease-in

This must be approved, with conditions as part of the approval in the agreement. Differences from Subparts K, L and/or JAR 26 must be notified to, and be acceptable to, the Authority.

Wet Lease-in

This must be approved, and safety standards of the lessor with respect to maintenance and operation must be equivalent to JARs. The lessor must hold an AOC from an ICAO State.

The aeroplane must have a standard C of A under ICAO Annex 8. Standard Certificates issued by a JAA Member State other than the AOC issuer will be accepted without further showing when issued under JAR 21, and any JAR requirement made applicable by the lessee's authority must be complied with.

Dry Lease-out

A JAA operator may dry leaseout an aeroplane for commercial air transport to any ICAO operator, if the JAA operator is exempt from the relevant provisions of JAR OPS 1 and, after the foreign authority has accepted responsibility in writing for surveillance of maintenance and operation, has removed the aeroplane from its AOC, being maintained under an approved program.

Wet Lease-out

A JAA operator providing an aeroplane and complete crew to another entity and retaining the functions and responsibilities in Subpart C, remains the operator.

Leasing At Short Notice

For up to 5 days, where a JAA operator is faced with an immediate, urgent and unforeseen need for a replacement aeroplane, the approval above may be deemed to have been given, if the lessor is an operator holding an ICAO AOC, and the Authority is immediately notified.

1.175 – Air Operator Certification

Appendix 1 specifies the contents and conditions of the AOC. Appendix 2 specifies management and organisation requirements.

Aeroplanes may only operate for commercial air transportation under the terms and conditions of an *Air Operator Certificate* (AOC). In general, you may only hold one AOC from one Authority, with your principal place of business and registered office in the same State (See IEM OPS 1.175(c)(2)) – the aircraft must also be registered there, but you can use aircraft from other States by agreement.

You must satisfy the Authority that you can conduct safe operations, otherwise the AOC will be revoked. For this purpose, the Authorities may inspect your organisation as and when they want to. In addition, you need suitable organisation and management (see Appendix 2), procedures for supervision, an accountable manager, and nominated post holders covering flight and ground operations, the maintenance system and crew training (a person may hold more than one nominated post but, with 21 or more full time staff, you need at least two to cover the four areas. With 20 or less, the accountable manager may fill one).

Flights must be done under the Ops Manual, which the Authorities must get a copy of (see Subpart P). There must be appropriate ground handling, aeroplanes must be equipped and crews qualified for the area and operation.

You must maintain operational support facilities at the main operating base, appropriate for the area and operation.

Appendix 1 – AOC Contents & Conditions

An AOC specifies the:

* Name and location (principal place of business - for proper jurisdiction, this is the State with the administrative headquarters and financial, operational and maintenance management - IEM).

- Date of issue and period of validity

- Description of operations authorised

- Type(s) of aeroplane authorised for use

- Registration markings of authorised aeroplane(s), except that operators may obtain approval for a system to inform the Authority about markings for aeroplanes operated under its AOC

- Authorised areas of operation

- Special limitations

- Special authorisations/approvals, such as CAT II/CAT III (including approved minima), MNPS, ETOPS, RNAV, RVSM and Transportation of Dangerous Goods

Appendix 2 - Management and Organisation

You need a sound and effective management structure to ensure safe conduct of operations. Nominated post holders must have managerial competency, with appropriate technical and operational qualifications in aviation.

Nominated Post Holders

Their functions and responsibilities, including names, must be in the Ops Manual, and the Authority must be notified in writing of any intended or actual changes. There must be continuity during their absence. Post holders may only act for one AOC, and must work enough hours to fulfil their functions.

Crew Members

These must be adequate in number and ability, and trained (see Subpart N and O).

Ground Staff

Numbers depend upon the nature and the scale of operations. Operations and ground handling departments, in particular, must have trained personnel with a thorough understanding of their responsibilities.

Operators contracting out ground services still retain the responsibility for proper standards, under a nominated post holder.

Supervision

The number of supervisors depends on the company structure and number of staff. They need enough experience and personal qualities to ensure the attainment of the standards in the Ops Manual.

Accommodation Facilities

You need enough working space at each base, giving due consideration to the needs of ground staff, those concerned with operational control, storage and display of essential records, and flight planning. Office services must be capable, without delay, of distributing instructions and other information to all concerned.

Documentation

You must make arrangements for production of manuals, amendments and other documentation.

IEM OPS 1.175
See JAR OPS 1.175(g)-(o)

Function and Purpose

Safe conduct of air operations is achieved by an operator and an Authority working in harmony towards a common aim (yeah, right). The functions of the two are different, well defined, but complementary. In essence, the operator complies with standards with a sound and competent management structure. The Authority working within a framework of law, sets and monitors the standards expected from operators.

Responsibilities of Management

The responsibilities of management related to JAR OPS 1 should include at least:

- Determination of the flight safety policy

- Allocation of responsibilities and duties, and issuing instructions, enough for implementation of company policy and maintenance of safety standards

- Monitoring of flight safety standards

- Recording and analysis of deviations from company standards and ensuring corrective action

- Evaluating the safety record of the company to avoid development of undesirable trends

IEM OPS 1.175(c)(2)

Principal Place of Business
See JAR OPS 1.175(c)(2)

Already incorporated.

ACJ OPS 1.175(i)

Nominated Postholders – Competence
See JAR OPS 1.175(i)

Nominated Postholders should normally satisfy the Authority that they possess the appropriate experience and licensing requirements below. In particular cases, and exceptionally, the Authority may accept a nomination which does not meet requirements in full, but the nominee should be able to demonstrate comparable experience.

Nominated postholders should have practical experience and expertise in the application of aviation safety standards and safe operating practices, comprehensive knowledge of JAR OPS and requirements and procedures, and the AOC holder's Operations Specifications, and the need for, and content of, relevant parts of the Ops Manual. Familiarity with Quality Systems, appropriate management experience in a comparable organisation, and five years' relevant work experience of which at least two should be from the aeronautical industry in an appropriate position are also expected.

The **nominated Flight Operations postholder** should hold a Flight Crew Licence as follows:

- For aeroplanes with at least 2 pilots - an ATPL issued or validated by a JAA State

- For aeroplanes with 1 pilot - a CPL, and, if appropriate, an Instrument Rating issued or validated by a JAA State

The nominated **Maintenance System postholder** should possess:

- Relevant engineering degree (from Aeronautical, Mechanical, Electrical, Electronic, Avionic or relevant studies), or be an aircraft maintenance technician with additional acceptable education.

- Thorough familiarity with the Maintenance Management Exposition.

- Knowledge of the types of aircraft

- Knowledge of maintenance methods

The nominated Crew Training postholder should be a current Type Rating Instructor on a type/class operated under the AOC, and have a thorough knowledge of the crew training concept for Flight and Cabin Crew.

The nominated Ground Operations postholder should have a thorough knowledge of the AOC holder's ground operations concept.

ACJ OPS 1.175(j)

Combination of Postholder's Responsibilities
The acceptability of one person holding several posts, possibly in combination with being the accountable manager, depends on the nature and scale of the operation. The two main areas of concern are competence and an individual's capacity to meet the responsibilities (the complexity of the organisation or the operation may prevent, or limit, combinations of posts acceptable in other circumstances).

With regard to competence, there should not be any difference from the requirements for people holding only one post.

In most circumstances, the responsibilities of a nominated postholder will rest with a single individual, but, for ground operations, it may be acceptable for them to be split, if their responsibilities are clearly defined.

The intent of JAR OPS 1.175 is neither to prescribe any specific organisational hierarchy within the operator's organisation on a JAA-wide basis, nor to prevent an Authority from requiring a certain hierarchy before it is satisfied that the management organisation is suitable.

ACJ OPS 1.175(j) & (k)

Employment of Staff
The expression "full-time staff" means employed for at least 35 hours a week, excluding vacations. For establishing the scale of operation, administrative staff, not directly involved in operations or maintenance, should be excluded.

1.180 – AOC Issue, Variation, Validity
You will not be granted an AOC, or a variation, and the AOC will not remain valid, unless:

- Your aeroplanes have a standard C of A under ICAO Annex 8 from a JAA State (those from Member States other than the one responsible for the AOC are accepted directly under JAR 21)

- The maintenance system has been approved by under Subpart M

- You satisfy the Authority that you have the ability to establish and maintain an adequate organisation and quality system, comply with required training programs and maintenance requirements, JAR OPS 1.175, and notify the Authority as soon as practicable of any changes.

If the Authority is not happy, they may require one or more demonstration flights, operated as commercial air transport flights.

1.185 – Administrative Requirements

The following information must be included in the initial application for an AOC and, when applicable, variations or renewals:

- The official and business names, address and mailing address

- A description of the proposed operation and management organisation

- The names of the accountable manager and major post holders, including those responsible for flight operations, the maintenance system, crew training and ground operations, together with their qualifications and experience

- The Ops Manual

For the maintenance system only, the following must also be included:

- The *Maintenance Management Exposition*

- Maintenance program(s)

- Tech Log

- Where appropriate, technical specs of maintenance contract(s)

- The number of aeroplanes

The application must be submitted at least 90 days before the date of intended operation, although the Ops Manual may be submitted later, but at least 60 days before.

Application for variations must be submitted at least 30 days, or as otherwise agreed, before the date of intended operation, and renewals at least 30 days before the end of the validity period.

Other than in exceptional circumstances, the Authority must be given at least 10 days prior notice of a change of a nominated post holder.

IEM OPS 1.185(b)

Maintenance Management Exposition Details
The JAR 145 organisation's MME should reflect details of any subcontract(s). A change of aeroplane type or maintenance organisation may require an amendment.

1.195 - Operational Control

Operators must establish and maintain operational control, and exercise it over any flight operated under the AOC.

ACJ OPS 1.195

Operational control means the exercise, in the interest of safety, of responsibility for the initiation, continuation, termination or diversion of a flight, which does not imply a need for licensed dispatchers or a full flight watch system.

The organisation and methods should be included in the ops manual and cover at least the responsibilities concerning the initiation, continuation, termination or diversion of flights.

1.200 - Ops Manual

Operators must provide an Ops Manual (see Subpart P) for the use and guidance of operations personnel.

1.205 - Competence of Ops Personnel

All personnel assigned to, or directly involved in, ground and flight operations must be properly instructed, demonstrate their abilities, and be aware of their responsibilities and the relationship of their duties to the operation as a whole.

1.210 - Establishment of Procedures

Operators need procedures and instructions for each aeroplane type, containing ground staff and crew members' duties for all types of operations (see AMC OPS 1.210(a)).

Operators must establish a checklist system for crew members for all phases of operation under normal, abnormal and emergency conditions, to ensure that the procedures in the Ops Manual are followed (IEM OPS 1.210 (b)).

Operators may not require crew members to perform activities during critical phases of flight* other than those required for safe operation. *Ttakeoff run and flight path, final approach, landing (including landing roll), and others at the discretion of the commander (IEM OPS 1.210(c)).

AMC OPS 1.210(a)
Operators should specify the contents of safety briefings for all cabin crew members before a flight or series of flights, and specify procedures to be followed by cabin crew with respect to:

- Arming and disarming of slides

- Operation of cabin lights, including emergency lighting

- Prevention and detection of cabin, oven and toilet fires

- Action to be taken in turbulence

- Actions to be taken in emergency and/or evacuation

IEM OPS 1.210(b)
There's a long list of items (not included here) that should be taken into account when compiling cabin crew procedures and checklists.

IEM OPS 1.210(c)
Critical Phases of Flight
Already incorporated above.

1.215 - Use of Air Traffic Services

Air Traffic Services must be used for all flights whenever available.

1.220 - Authorisation of Aerodromes

An operator must only authorise use of aerodromes that are adequate for the type(s) of aeroplane and operation(s) concerned.

IEM OPS 1.220
When defining aerodromes for the type of aeroplane and operation, an *adequate aerodrome* is satisfactory, for performance requirements and runway characteristics. At the expected time of use, the aerodrome should be available and equipped with necessary ancillary services, such as ATS, lighting, communications, weather reporting, navaids and emergency services.

For an ETOPS en-route alternate, also consider the availability of an ATC facility and at least one letdown aid (ground radar would qualify) for an instrument approach.

1.225 - Aerodrome Operating Minima

These must be established under JAR OPS 1.430 for departure, destination or alternate aerodromes authorised under JAR OPS 1.220. Increments from the Authority must be added.

Minima for a specific type of approach and landing are considered applicable if the ground equipment on the chart is operative, with the aeroplane systems required, performance criteria are met and the crew is qualified

1.230 - Instrument Departure and Approach Procedures

Only instrument departure and approach procedures established by the State in which an aerodrome is located may be used, but a commander may accept an ATC clearance to deviate from a published route, if obstacle clearance criteria are observed and full account is taken of the operating conditions. The final approach must be flown visually or under the established procedure.

Different procedures may only be implemented if approved by the State in which the aerodrome is located, and accepted by the Authority.

1.235 - Noise Abatement

Procedures during instrument operations must comply with ICAO PANS OPS Volume 1 (Doc 8168–OPS/611).

Takeoff climb procedures for noise abatement specified by an operator for any one aeroplane type should be the same for all aerodromes.

1.240 - Routes and Areas of Operation

Operations may only be along routes or within areas for which adequate ground facilities and services (including meteorological), are provided. They must be conducted under any restrictions imposed by the Authority.

Performance must be adequate to comply with minimum altitudes, and equipment must meet minimum requirements for the planned operation.

Appropriate maps and charts must also be available (see JAR OPS 1.135(a)(9)).

If two-engined aeroplanes are used, adequate aerodromes must be available within the time/distance limitations of JAR OPS 1.245.

For single-engined aeroplanes, there must be surfaces that permit a safe forced landing.

1.241 Defined Airspace with RVSM

(See JAA Administrative & Guidance Material, Section 1, Part 3, Leaflet 6)

To operate in RVSM airspace, you must be approved (based on Regional Air Navigation Agreements, RVSM has vertical separation minima of 300m (1000 ft) (see also JAR OPS 1.872).

1.243 - Areas with Specific Navigation Performance Requirements

To boldly go where minimum navigation performance specifications are prescribed (e.g. (MNPS/RNP/RNAV), you must be approved (see also JAR OPS 1.865(c)(2) and JAR OPS 1.870).

IEM OPS 1.243

Details of such areas are are in the following documents:

- **MNPS** - ICAO DOC 7030

- **RNP** - ICAO DOC 9613

- **EUROCONTROL** Standards on Area Navigation for RNP/RNAV

- **JAA TGL No 2** - Advisory material for the airworthiness approval of navigation systems in European Airspace designated for Basic RNAV

Objective of RNP

The RNP concept replaces the conventional method of ensuring required navigation performance by specifying worldwide, uniform standards of navigation equipment performance for defined airspace and/or flight procedures.

Navigational Accuracy

RNP is a statement of the navigational accuracy required for operation within defined airspace, based on a combination of signal error, airborne sensor error, display error and flight technical error in the horizontal plane.

The level of accuracy is expressed as a single parameter, defining the distance from an aeroplane's intended position, which must be maintained for at least 95% of total flying time. For example, RNP 4 means that aircraft must remain within 4 nm of their intended positions.

RNP Types

- *RNP 1* requires highly accurate position information and is associated with high-density continental traffic. It should be achieved by a high percentage of aircraft.

- *RNP 4* is normally for continental areas where routes are based on VOR/DME.

- *RNP 12.6* is for the North Atlantic Region.

- *RNP 20* describes the minimum capability for airspace and/or routes with low traffic (other oceanic regions).

- *RNP xxx* (e.g. RNP 2, RNP 5, RNP 10, etc.) describes the minimum capability under procedures based upon Regional Air Navigation Agreements.

1.245 - Max Distance for Two-engined Aeroplanes without ETOPS Approval

Unless specifically approved under JAR OPS 1.246(a) (ETOPS Approval), two-engined aeroplanes may not go further from an adequate aerodrome than, for:

- **Performance A aeroplanes** that can carry **more than 20 passengers** *or* with a maximum takeoff mass of 45 360 kg or more, the distance flown in 60 minutes at the OEI cruise speed determined below

- **Performance A aeroplanes** that can carry **19 or less passengers** *and* with a maximum takeoff mass less than 45 360 kg, the distance flown in 120 minutes or, if approved, 180 minutes for turbojets, at the OEI cruise speed determined below

- For **Performance B or C aeroplanes**, the distance flown in 120 minutes at the OEI cruise speed determined below; or 300 nm, whichever is less.

The speed must not exceed V_{NO}, based on OEI TAS, under ISA in level flight. For turbojets, this will be at FL 170 or the maximum FL to which the aeroplane can climb and maintain OEI, using the gross rate of climb in the Flight Manual, whichever is less (FL 80 for prop-driven aeroplanes).

Max continuous power must be maintained on the remaining engine, and mass must not be less than:

- the maximum at sea-level

- that for all engines climb to the optimum long range cruise altitude

- all engines cruise at long range cruise speed at this altitude, until the approval times above (60, 120 or 180 minutes).

The following type-specific data must be in the Ops Manual:

- The OEI cruise speed above

- The maximum distance from an adequate aerodrome as determined above.

Note: Speeds and altitudes (flight levels) above are only intended for establishing maximum distance from an adequate aerodrome.

AMC OPS 1.245(a)(2) - Non-ETOPS twin turbojets between 120-180 minutes from adequate aerodromes

The 120-minute threshold for twin turbojets may be exceeded by no more than 60 minutes. For between 120-180 minutes, due account should be taken of the aeroplane's design (not type design) and capabilities (see below) and operator experience. Where necessary, information should be included in the Ops Manual and MME.

Aeroplanes should be certificated to JAR-25 as appropriate (or equivalent).

The aeroplane should be capable of safe diversion from the maximum diversion distance with particular emphasis on OEI operations or degraded system capability. To this end, consideration should be given to:

- *Propulsion systems* - power plants should meet JAR 25 and JAR E or equivalents, concerning engine type certification, installation and system operation. In addition to certification performance standards, the engines should comply with all subsequent mandatory safety standards, including those necessary for acceptable reliability. In addition, consideration should be given to the effects of extended duration single-engine operation (e.g. higher power demands, such as bleed and electrical).

- *Airframe systems* - three or more reliable (as defined by JAR 25 or equivalent) and independent electrical power sources should be available, each capable of providing power for all essential services (See Appendix 1). For single-engined operations, the remaining power (electrical, hydraulic, pneumatic) should continue to be available at levels necessary to permit continued safe flight and landing, and to provide services for the overall safety of passengers and crew. As a minimum, following the failure of any two of the three power sources, the remaining one should provide power for all items necessary for the duration of a diversion. To ensure hydraulic power (Hydraulic Motor Generator) reliability, it may be necessary to provide two or more independent energy sources. The ADG/RAT, if fitted, should not require engine dependent power for deployment.

- *APU* - The APU should be an *Essential APU* and meet JAR 25 provisions (Subpart J-APU parts A and B, or equivalent).

- *Fuel Supply* - the fuel supply system should be able to provide enough fuel for the entire diversion taking into account aspects such as fuel boost and fuel transfer.

Powerplant Events and Corrective Action

All powerplant events (shutdowns, flameouts, reduced power, etc.) and operating hours should be reported to the Airframe and Engine manufacturers as well as the State Authority.

Where statistical assessment may not be applicable (small fleet size, etc.), individual events should be reviewed on a case by case basis.

Maintenance

Maintenance requirements should address:

- *Release to Service* - A pre-departure check, on top of the pre-flight inspection required by JAR OPS 1.890(a)(1), should be in the MME. These checks should be done and certified by a JAR 145 organisation or appropriately trained flight crew to ensure that all maintenance actions are complete and fluid levels are at prescribed levels.

- *Engine Oil Consumption Programs* – for engine condition trend monitoring.

- *Engine Condition Trend Monitoring* - a program that monitors performance and degradation trends, so maintenance can be done before significant performance loss or failure.

- *Arrangements* to ensure that all corrective actions required by the type design authority are implemented.

Flight Crew Training

This should include, in addition to JAR OPS 1 Sub part N, particular emphasis on:

- *Fuel Management* - verifying required fuel on board before departure and monitoring it en route, including calculation of fuel remaining. Procedures should provide for independent cross-checks of quantity

indicators (e.g. fuel flow used to calculate fuel burned compared to indicated fuel remaining)

- *Confirmation* - that fuel remaining is enough for critical fuel reserves.

- *Procedures* - for single and multiple failures in flight that may give rise to go/no-go and diversion decisions - policy and guidelines to aid in the diversion decision-making process and the

- *Constant Awareness* - of the closest suitable alternate in terms of time.

- *OEI Performance Data* - drift down procedures and OEI service ceiling data.

Weather Reports and Flight Requirements

METAR and TAF reports and getting in-flight updates on destination and alternate aerodromes. Consideration should also be given to forecast winds (including accuracy compared to actual wind experienced) and conditions along the expected flight path at the OEI cruising altitude and throughout the approach and landing.

Pre-Departure Check

Flight crew should be fully trained and competent. The approved training program should cover relevant maintenance actions with particular emphasis on fluid levels.

MEL

The MEL should take into account all items specified by the manufacturer for this AMC.

Dispatch/Flight Planning

Critical Fuel Scenario

The critical point is the furthest from an alternate, assuming a simultaneous failure of an engine and the pressurisation system (for aeroplanes certificated above FL 450, it is the furthest point from an alternate assuming an engine failure). There should be additional fuel for worst case fuel burn conditions (one engine vs two), if this is greater than the additional fuel calculated under AMC OPS 1.255 1.6 a and b, as follows:

- Fly from the critical point to an alternate at 10 000 ft, or 25 000 ft or the single-engine ceiling, whichever is lower, if all occupants can be supplied with and use supplemental oxygen for the time from the critical point to an alternate, or at the single-engine ceiling, if the aeroplane is certificated above FL 450.

- Descend and hold at 1 500 feet for 15 minutes in ISA conditions

- Descend to the applicable MDA/DH followed by a missed approach (taking into account the complete missed approach procedure), followed by a normal approach and landing.

- Ice Protection - additional fuel used in icing conditions (e.g. for ice protection systems) and take account of ice accumulation on unprotected surfaces if icing is likely to be encountered during a diversion

- APU operation

Communication Facilities
The availability of reliable two-way voice communications between the aeroplane and appropriate ATC units at OEI cruise altitudes.

Technical Log Review
To ensure proper MEL procedures, deferred items, and maintenance checks are completed.

En-route Alternates
Ensuring that en-route alternates are available for the intended route, within 180 minutes at the OEI cruise speed, and confirmation that, based on available information, the weather conditions at en-route alternates are at or above applicable minima for the time during which the aerodrome(s) may be used. (See also JAR OPS 1.297).

Planning Minima

Approach	(RVR & ceiling) for aerodrome with at least:		
	2 separate approaches on 2 separate aids for 2 separate runways (IEM OPS 1.295 (c)(1)(ii))	2 separate approaches based on 2 separate aids serving 1 runway *or*	1 approach based on 1 aid serving 1 runway
Precision Approach Cat II, III (ILS, MLS)	Precision Approach Cat I Minima	Non-Precision Approach Minima	
Precision Approach Cat I (ILS, MLS)	Non-Precision Approach Minima	Circling minima or, if not available, non-precision minima plus 200 ft/1 000 m	
Non-Precision Approach	Lower of non-precision minima plus 200 ft/1 000 m or circling minima	Higher of circling minima or non-precision minima plus 200 ft/1 000 m	
Circling Approach		Circling Minima	

Appendix 1 to AMC OPS 1.245(a)(2) - Power Supply to Essential Services
Any one of the three electrical power sources in sub-paragraph 2.b of AMC OPS 1.245(a)(2) should be able to cope with these essential services:

- Flight crew instruments: at least attitude, heading, airspeed and altitude information

- Pitot heating

- Adequate navigation, radio communication and intercommunication capability

- Adequate flight deck, instrument and emergency lighting

- Adequate flight controls

- Adequate engine controls and restart capability with critical type fuel (from the standpoint of flameout and restart capability) and with the aeroplane initially at the maximum relight altitude

- Adequate engine instrumentation

- Adequate fuel supply system capability including such fuel boost and transfer functions necessary for extended single or dual engine operation

- Warnings, cautions and indications for continued safe flight and landing

- Fire protection (engines and APU)

- Adequate ice protection including windshield de-icing

- Adequate control of the flight deck and cabin environment, including heating and pressurisation

Equipment (including avionics) for extended diversion times should be able to operate after failures in the cooling system or electrical systems.

1.246 - ETOPS

You need approval to go beyond the threshold distances in JAR OPS 1.245, above (see GAI- 20, ACJ 20X6.)

Before conducting an ETOPS flight, a suitable ETOPS en-route alternate must be available, within either the approved diversion time, or one based on the MEL generated serviceability status, whichever is shorter (see also JAR OPS 1.297(d)).

1.250 – Minimum Flight Altitudes

Operators must establish minimum flight altitudes and the (approved) methods of determining them for all route segments to provide required terrain clearance, taking into account Subparts F-I.

Where minimum altitudes established by States overflown are higher, the higher values apply.

The following must be taken into account:

- Accuracy of position determination

- Probable altimeter inaccuracies

- Terrain characteristics (e.g. sudden changes in elevation)

- Probability of unfavourable meteorological conditions (e.g. severe turbulence and descending air currents)

- Possible chart inaccuracies

Due consideration must also be given to corrections for variations in temperature and pressure from standard, ATC requirements, and forseeable contingencies.

IEM OPS 1.250

Here are some examples of methods for calculating minimum flight altitudes:

KSS Formula

Minimum Obstacle Clearance Altitude
MOCA is the sum of:

- The maximum terrain or obstacle elevation, whichever is highest, plus

- 1 000 ft for elevation up to and including 6 000 ft, or

- 2 000 ft for elevations over 6 000 ft, rounded up to the next 100 ft

The lowest MOCA to be indicated is 2 000 ft.

Corridor width is a borderline starting 5 nm either side of a VOR, diverging at 4° until 20 nm wide at 70 nm out, thence paralleling the centreline until 140 nm out, thence again diverging 4° until 40 nm wide at 280 nm out. Then the width remains constant:

Similarly, from an NDB, the borderline starts 5 nm either side of the NDB, diverging 7° until 20 nm wide at 40 nm out, thence paralleling the centreline until 80 nm out, thence again diverging 7° until 60 nm wide at 245 nm out. Then the width remains constant.

MOCA does not cover overlapping of corridors.

Minimum Off-Route Altitude

MORA is calculated for an area bounded by every (or every second) Lat/Long square on the Route Facility Chart (RFC)/Terminal Approach Chart (TAC), based on a terrain clearance as follows:

- Up to 6 000 ft (2 000 m) – 1 000 ft above the highest terrain and obstructions

- Above 6 000 ft (2 000 m) – 2 000 ft above the highest terrain and obstructions

Jeppesen Formula

Two types of MORA are computed by Jeppesen from current ONC or WAC charts:

- **Route MORAs**, e.g. 9800a, are based an area 10 nm either side of route centreline, including a 10 nm radius beyond the radio fix/reporting point or mileage break defining the route segment. They clear all terrain and man-made obstacles by 1 000 ft where the highest terrain elevation or obstacles are up to 5 000 ft. A clearance of 2 000 ft is provided above all terrain or obstacles 5 001 ft and above.

- **Grid MORAs**, e.g. 98, are shown within each grid formed by latitude and longitude lines. Figures are in thousands and hundreds of feet (without the last two digits to avoid chart congestion). Values followed by ± are believed not to exceed the altitudes shown. The same clearance criteria as above apply.

ATLAS Formula

Minimum Safe En-Route Altitude

The MEA is based on the highest point along the segment concerned (from navaid to navaid) within distances either side of track as follows:

- Segment up to 100 nm – 10 nm*

- Segment more than 100 nm – 10% of the segment length, up to 60 nm**

*May be reduced to 5 nm in TMAs which warrant high degrees of navigational accuracy.

**In exceptional cases, where this results in an impracticable value, an additional special MEA may be calculated based on a distance of at least 10 nm either side of track. It will be shown with an indication of the actual width of protected airspace.

The MEA is calculated by adding an increment to the elevation above as appropriate:

Elevation of highest point	Increment
Not above 5 000 ft	1 500 ft
Between 5 000-10 000 ft	2 000 ft
Above 10 000 ft	10% of elevation + 1 000 ft

For the last route segment ending over the IAF, a reduction to 1 000 ft is permissible in TMAs which warrant a high degree of navigational accuracy. The resulting value is adjusted to the nearest 100 ft.

Minimum Safe Grid Altitude

The MGA is based on the highest point within the respective grid area, plus an increment as appropriate (see above table). The resulting value is adjusted to the nearest 100 ft.

1.255 - Fuel Policy

This is required for flight planning and in-flight replanning to ensure that every flight carries enough fuel for the planned operation, and reserves for deviations (no, really? ☺).

Flight planning must at least be based on procedures and data in the Ops Manual, which must be derived from the manufacturer or current aeroplane-specific data from a fuel consumption monitoring system, and operating conditions, which must include:

- Realistic fuel consumption data

- Anticipated masses

- Expected meteorological conditions

- Air Traffic procedures and restrictions

Pre-flight calculation of usable fuel must include:

- *Taxy Fuel*

- *Trip Fuel*

- *Reserve Fuel* consisting of:

- *Contingency Fuel* (see IEM OPS 1.255(c)(3)(i))

- *Alternate Fuel*, if a destination alternate is required (the departure aerodrome can be the destination alternate)

- *Final Reserve Fuel*

- *Additional Fuel*, if required by the operation (e.g. ETOPS)

- *Extra Fuel* as required by the commander

In-flight replanning procedures must include the above, without Taxy Fuel, and the Trip Fuel is for the remainder of the flight.

AMC OPS 1.255

Company fuel policy should be based on the following criteria:

Taxy Fuel
At least the amount, expected to be used before takeoff, taking into account local conditions and APU consumption.

Trip Fuel
This should include:

- Fuel for takeoff and climb from aerodrome elevation to initial cruising level or altitude, for the expected departure routing

- Fuel from top of climb to top of descent, including any steps

- Fuel from top of descent to where the approach is initiated, for the expected arrival procedure

- Fuel for approach and landing at the destination

Contingency Fuel
This should be the higher of:

- The highest of :
  - 5% of planned trip fuel (or remainder)
  - At least 3% of planned trip fuel (or trip remainder) if an en-route alternate is available (see ACJ OPS 1.295)

- Enough fuel for 20 minutes' flying, based on planned trip consumption, if there is a consumption monitoring program for individual aeroplanes using valid data

- Fuel based on approved statistics to cover deviations from planned to actual trip fuel*

- Enough to fly for 5 minutes at holding speed at 1 500 ft (450 m) above the destination aerodrome in standard conditions.

*For example, these values have been agreed:

- 99% coverage plus 3% of trip fuel, if the calculated flight time is less than 2 hours, or more than if no suitable en-route alternate is available

- 99% coverage if the calculated flight time is more than 2 hours and a suitable en-route alternate is available

- 90% coverage if the calculated flight time is more than 2 hours, a suitable en-route alternate is available, and 2 separate runways are available and useable at the destination, one with an ILS/MLS if the weather complies with JAR OPS 1.295(c)(1)(ii) or a Cat II/III ILS/MLS if the weather is at or above 500ft/2 500m.

The data is based on fuel consumption monitoring for each route/aeroplane combination over a rolling two year period.

Alternate Fuel
This should be enough for:

- Missed approach from MDA/DH at the destination to missed approach altitude, through the whole procedure

- Climb from missed approach to cruise

- Cruise from top of climb to top of descent

- From top of descent to where the approach is initiated, through the expected arrival procedure

- Approach and landing at the destination alternate (see JAR OPS 1.295)

If, under JAR OPS 1.295(d), two destination alternates are required, alternate fuel should be enough to go to the one which needs the most fuel.

Final Reserve Fuel

This should be:

- For reciprocating engines, for 45 minutes

- For turbine aeroplanes, fuel to fly for 30 minutes at holding speed at 1 500 ft (450 m) above aerodrome elevation in standard conditions, calculated with the estimated mass at the alternate (or the destination) when no alternate is required.

- Minimum additional fuel, to allow:

  - Holding for 15 minutes at 1 500 ft (450 m) above aerodrome elevation in standard conditions without a destination alternate

  - Following possible failure of a power unit or loss of pressurisation (assuming they occur at the most critical point), the aeroplane to descend as necessary and proceed to an adequate aerodrome, hold there for 15 minutes at 1 500 ft (450 m) above aerodrome elevation in standard conditions, and make an approach and landing, although additional fuel is only required if the minimum amount above is not enough.

Extra Fuel

This is at the discretion of the commander.

Decision Point Procedure

If the fuel policy includes a destination via a decision point, fuel should be the greater of:

- The sum of taxy fuel, trip fuel via the decision point, contingency fuel (at least 5% of the estimated consumption from the decision point to the destination), alternate fuel, final reserve fuel, additional fuel and extra fuel if required by the commander

- The sum of taxy fuel, trip fuel to an alternate via the decision point, contingency fuel (at least 3% of estimated consumption from the departure point to the alternate), final reserve fuel, additional fuel and extra fuel if required by the commander

Isolated Aerodrome Procedure

The amount of fuel at departure should include:

- Taxy fuel

- Trip Fuel

- Contingency Fuel (see above)

- Additional Fuel if required, but at least, for reciprocating engines, fuel to fly for 45 minutes plus 15% of the time to be spent at cruising level, or two hours, whichever is less, or, for turbine engines, fuel to fly for two hours at normal cruise consumption after arriving over the destination, including final reserve fuel

- Extra Fuel if required by the commander.

Pre-Determined Point Procedure

Where the distance between the destination and its alternate means that a flight can only go through a predetermined point, the amount of fuel should be the greater of:

- The sum of taxy fuel, trip fuel via the predetermined point, contingency fuel (see above), additional fuel, but at least, for reciprocating engines, fuel to fly for 45 minutes plus 15% of the time to be spent at cruising level, or two hours, whichever is less, or, for turbine engines, fuel to fly for two hours at normal cruise consumption after arriving over the destination, including final reserve fuel, and extra fuel

- The sum of taxy fuel, trip fuel to an alternate via the predetermined point, contingency fuel (see above), additional fuel, but at least , for reciprocating engines, fuel to fly for 45 minutes or, for turbine engines, 30 minutes at holding speed at 1 500 ft (450 m) above aerodrome elevation in standard conditions, including Final Reserve Fuel, and extra fuel

IEM OPS 1.255(c)(3)(i) - Contingency Fuel

At the planning stage, not all factors can be foreseen, so contingency fuel is carried in case of deviations, such as:

- individual aeroplanes from the expected fuel consumption data

- forecast meteorological conditions

- from planned routings and/or cruising levels/altitudes

1.260 - Persons with Reduced Mobility

PRMs must not be allocated seats where their presence could impede the crew or emergency evacuation, or obstruct access to emergency equipment. The commander must be notified when PRMs are on board.

IEM OPS 1.260

A PRM is one whose mobility is reduced from physical incapacity (sensory or locomotory), intellectual deficiency, age, illness or any other cause. They need special attention, and should not normally be next to emergency exits. Where they form a significant proportion of passengers, they should not exceed the able-bodied persons capable of helping with an emergency evacuation.

1.265 – Inadmissible Passengers, Deportees or Persons in Custody

They must be transported for maximum safety. Commanders must be notified if they are on board.

1.270 - Baggage and Cargo Stowage

Only hand baggage that can be adequately and securely stowed may be taken into the passenger cabin. All baggage and cargo on board which might cause injury or damage, or obstruct aisles and exits if displaced, must be placed in stowages designed to prevent movement.

Appendix 1

Procedures to ensure that hand baggage and cargo are adequately and securely stowed must allow for:

- Items must be stowed only in locations capable of restraining them

- Mass limitations placarded on or adjacent to stowages must not be exceeded

- Underseat stowage must have a restraint bar and the baggage (sizewise) must be adequately restrained by it

- Items must not be stowed in toilets or against bulkheads that are incapable of restraining them forwards, sideways or upwards. Bulkheads must carry a placard stating the greatest mass to be placed there

- Baggage and cargo in lockers must not prevent latched doors from closing securely

- Baggage and cargo must not be placed where it can impede access to emergency equipment

- Checks must be made before takeoff, landing, and when the *fasten seat belts* signs are on, or it is otherwise ordered, to ensure that baggage is stowed where it cannot impede evacuation or cause injury by falling (or other movement) as appropriate

AMC OPS 1.270 - Cargo in Passenger Cabins

The following should be observed:

- Dangerous goods are not permitted (See also JAR OPS 1.1210(a))

- Mixing passengers and live animals is not allowed, except for pets up to 8 kg, and guide dogs

- The weight of cargo must not exceed structural loading limits

- The number and type of restraint devices and attachment points should restrain cargo under JAR 25.789 or equivalent

- The location of cargo should stop it hindering egress or impairing the cabin crew's view in emergency

1.280 - Passenger Seating

Passengers must be seated where, in an emergency evacuation, they may best assist and not hinder.

ACJ OPS 1.280

Passengers allocated seats with direct access to emergency exits must appear to be reasonably fit, strong and able to assist rapid evacuation in emergency after a briefing by the crew. Passengers who might hinder other passengers, or impede the crew, should not be given seats which permit direct access to emergency exits. If this cannot be done at check-in, there must be an alternative procedure.

IEM OPS 1.280

These passengers should not be allocated seats which permit direct access to emergency exits:

- Those suffering from obvious physical or mental handicap, or age and frailty, or obesity, that would have difficulty in moving quickly or getting through a door

- Those who are either substantially blind or deaf, who might not readily assimilate printed or verbal instructions

- Children (accompanied or not) and infants

- Deportees or prisoners in custody

- Passengers with animals.

Direct Access means a seat from which a passenger can proceed directly to the exit without entering an aisle or passing around an obstruction.

1.285 - Passenger Briefing

Passengers must be given a verbal briefing about safety matters. Parts or all of it may be done audio-visually, and it must be supplemented by a safety briefing card on which picture-type instructions show how emergency equipment and exits work.

In an emergency during flight, passengers must be instructed as necessary according to circumstances.

Before Takeoff

Passengers must be briefed on the following items:

- Smoking regulations

- Back of the seat to be in the upright position and tray table stowed

- Location of emergency exits

- Location and use of floor proximity escape path markings

- Stowage of hand baggage

- Restrictions on portable electronic devices

- The location and the contents of the safety briefing card

Passengers must receive a demonstration of:

- Use of safety belts and/or harnesses, including how to fasten and unfasten them

- Location and use of oxygen equipment (see JAR OPS 1.770 and 1.775). Passengers must also be briefed to extinguish all smoking materials when oxygen is used

- Location and use of life jackets (see 1.825).

After Takeoff

Passengers must be reminded of:

- Smoking regulations

- Use of safety belts and/or harnesses

Before Landing

Passengers must be reminded of:

- Smoking regulations

- Use of safety belts and/or harnesses

- Back of the seat to be upright and tray table stowed

- Re-stowage of hand baggage

- Restrictions on portable electronic devices

After Landing

Passengers must be reminded of:

- Smoking regulations

- Use of safety belts and/or harnesses

1.290 - Flight Preparation

An operational flight plan must be completed for each intended flight.

A commander must not commence a flight unless he is satisfied that:

- The aeroplane is airworthy and not operated against the the the CDL

- The instruments and equipment required under Subparts K and L are available and working under the MEL

- Those parts of the ops manual which are required for the flight are available

- The documents, additional information and forms required under JAR OPS 1.125 and 1.135 are on board

- Current maps, charts and documentation or equivalent data are available for the intended operation, including diversions which may reasonably be expected

- Ground facilities and services required are available and adequate

- The provisions in the ops manual for fuel, oil and oxygen, minimum safe altitudes, operating minima and alternate aerodromes, can be complied with

- The load is properly distributed and safely secured

- The mass at the start of takeoff roll, will be such that the flight can be conducted under Subparts F-I

- Operational limitations on top of those above can be complied with

1.295 - Selection of Aerodromes

Operators must establish procedures for selection of destination and/or alternate aerodromes under JAR OPS 1.220 during planning.

Takeoff Alternate

One must be specified in the operational flight plan if it would not be possible to return to the departure aerodrome for meteorological or performance reasons. The takeoff alternate must be located within:

- For two-engined aeroplanes, either one hours' flight time at OEI cruising speed in still air conditions based on actual takeoff mass, or the approved ETOPS diversion time (subject to MEL restriction, up to 2 hours), at the OEI cruising speed as above

- Two hours' flight time at OEI cruising speed in still air standard conditions based on the actual takeoff mass for three- and four-engined aeroplanes

If the Flight Manual does not contain an OEI cruising speed, the speed for calculation must be that achieved with the remaining engines at maximum continuous power.

Destination Alternate

At least one must be selected for IFR flights (and specified in the operational flight plan) unless:

- The duration of the flight from takeoff to landing is not over 6 hours, *and* two separate runways are available (and useable) at the destination, and appropriate weather reports or forecasts for the destination indicate that for one hour either side of ETA, the ceiling will be at least 2 000 ft or circling height + 500 ft, whichever is greater, and the visibility at least 5 km (see IEM OPS 1.295(c)(1)(ii)), or

- The destination is isolated and no adequate alternate exists.

Two Destination Alternates

These must be selected when appropriate weather reports or forecasts indicate that, for 1 hour either side of ETA, the weather (at the destination) will be below planning minima, or no meteorological information is available.

ACJ OPS 1.295 - En Route Alternates

The en-route alternate (see AMC OPS 1.255 1.3 a. ii) should be within a circle of radius equal to 20% of the total flight plan distance, the centre lying on the planned route 25% of the total flight plan distance from the destination, or at least 20% plus 50 nm, whichever is greater, calculated in still air conditions (see example in Appendix 1).

IEM OPS 1.295(c)(1)(ii) - Separate Runways

Runways on the same aerodrome are "separate" when they are separate surfaces which overlay or cross, and one being blocked does not prevent operations on the other one. Each must have a separate approach procedure on a separate aid.

1.297 – IFR Planning Minima

Takeoff Alternates

An aerodrome may not be selected as a takeoff alternate unless the appropriate weather reports or forecasts indicate that, for one hour either side of ETA, the weather will be at or above the landing minima in JAR OPS 1.225. The ceiling must be taken into account when the only approaches are non-precision and/or circling ones. Limitations for OEI operations must be taken into account.

Destination and Alternates

For 1 hour either side of ETA, the weather must be at or above planning minima as follows:

- For destinations, (not isolated aerodromes), RVR/visibility under JAR OPS 1.225, and, for non-precision or circling approaches, ceiling at or above MDH

- For a destination (and enroute) alternates and isolated destinations:

Type of Approach	Planning Minima
Cat II and III	Cat I*
Cat I	Non-precision* **
Non-precision***	Non-precision* ** + 200 ft/1 000 m
Circling	Circling

*RVR **Ceiling must be at or above MDH. *** see ACJ

En-route Alternates

Weather reports or forecasts must indicate that, for 1 hour either side of the ETA, the conditions will be at or above the minima in the table above (see also AMC OPS 1.255, paragraph 1.3.a.ii.).

ETOPS

Weather reports or forecasts must indicate that, for 1 hour either side of the ETA, the conditions will be at or above the minima in the table below, and under the ETOPS approval.

Type of Approach	Planning Minima (RVR/visibility required & ceiling if applicable)	
	Separate runways	1 runway
Precision Approach Cat II, III (ILS,MLS)	Cat I Minima	Non-Precision Approach Minima
Precision Approach Cat I (ILS,MLS)	Non-Precision Approach Minima	Circling minima or, if not available, non-precision approach minima plus 200 ft/1 000m
Non-Precision Approach	Lower of non-precision minima + 200 ft/1 000m or circling minima	Higher of non-precision minima + 200 ft/1 000m or circling minima
Circling Approach	Circling minima	

ACJ OPS 1.297(b)(2) - Alternates

Non-precision minima in the top table above means the next highest available in prevailing wind and serviceability conditions, which includes *Localiser Only* approaches. Choose values that are likely to be appropriate on the majority of occasions (e.g. regardless of wind direction). Unserviceabilities must, however, be fully taken into account.

AMC OPS 1.297 - Aerodrome Forecasts

There's a large table, too big to be included here.

1.300 - ATS Flight Plan

Flight must not start without an ATS flight plan in force, or unless adequate information is deposited to permit alerting services to be activated.

AMC OPS 1.300 - Submission of Plan
Flights without ATS Flight Plan

When unable to submit or close the flight plan due to lack of ATS facilities, there should be procedures, instructions and a list of authorised persons to be responsible for alerting search and rescue services. To ensure that each flight is located at all times, these instructions should:

- Provide the authorised person with at least the information required in a VFR Flight plan, and the location, date and estimated time for re-establishing communications

- If an aeroplane is overdue or missing, provide for notification to the appropriate ATS or SAR, and

- Provide that the information will be retained at a designated place until completion of the flight

1.305 - Re/Defuelling with Passengers

No aeroplane may be re/defuelled with Avgas or wide cut type fuel (e.g. Jet-B), or when a mixture might occur, when passengers are embarking, on board or disembarking. Otherwise, precautions must be taken and the aeroplane properly manned by qualified people ready to initiate and direct an evacuation by the most practical and expeditious means.

Appendix 1
Operational procedures must be established, with the following precautions taken:

- One qualified person must remain at a specified location when fuelling with passengers on board. This person must be able to handle emergency procedures concerning fire protection and fire-fighting, handling communications and initiating and directing an evacuation

- Crew, staff and passengers must be warned that re/defuelling will take place

- *Fasten Seat Belts* signs must be off

- *No Smoking* signs must be on, with interior lighting to enable emergency exits to be identified

- Passengers must be instructed to unfasten their seat belts and refrain from smoking

- Enough qualified people must be on board and prepared for immediate emergency evacuation

- If fuel vapour is detected in the aeroplane, or any other hazard arises, fuelling must be stopped immediately

- Ground areas beneath the exits intended for emergency evacuation and slide deployment must be kept clear

- Provision must be made for a safe and rapid evacuation

IEM OPS 1.305
When re/defuelling with passengers on board, ground servicing activities and work inside the aeroplane, such as catering and cleaning, should not create a hazard, and the aisles and emergency doors must be unobstructed.

1.307 - Wide-cut Fuel
Operators must establish procedures, if required.

IEM OPS 1.307
Wide cut fuel (JET B, JP-4 or AVTAG) is an aviation turbine fuel that falls between gasoline and kerosene in the distillation range and consequently, compared to kerosene (JET A or JET A1), has a higher volatility (vapour pressure), with lower flash and freezing points. Its use should be recorded in the Tech Log. The next two uplifts should be treated as though they also involved wide-cut fuel ("involved" means being supplied or already present in the tanks).

Its use should be avoided, but, if it is the only stuff around, be aware that mixtures of it with kerosene can mean the air/fuel mixture in the tank is in the combustible range at ambient temperatures. The extra precautions below are advisable to avoid arcing from electrostatic discharge. The risk of this can be minimised by a static dissipation additive. When it is present in the proportions in the fuel specification, the normal precautions below are considered adequate. When not present, reduce the fuel flow, which will have the following benefits:

- It allows more time for static build-up to dissipate before the fuel enters the tank

- It reduces charges that build up from splashing

- Until the fuel inlet point is immersed, it reduces misting and extension of the flammable range

Flow rate reduction depends on fuelling equipment and filtration, so it is difficult to quote precise flow rates. Reduction is advisable in any case, whether pressure or over-wing fuelling is used. With over-wing fuelling, avoid splashing by making sure the delivery nozzle extends as far into the tank as practicable, to avoid damaging bag tanks.

1.310 - Crew Members at Stations

Flight Crew
During takeoff and landing, flight crew members on flight deck duty must be at their stations. At all other times, they may be absent for their duties, or physiological needs, if at least one suitably qualified pilot remains at the controls.

Cabin Crew
On all decks occupied by passengers, cabin crew must be seated at assigned stations during takeoff and landing, and whenever deemed necessary by the commander in the interest of safety.

IEM OPS 1.310(b) - Cabin Crew Seating
Cabin crew seating positions should be:

- Close to a floor level exit

- Have a good view of the area(s) of the passenger cabin for which the cabin crew member is responsible

- Evenly distributed throughout the cabin, in the above order of priority.

This does not imply that, with more stations than cabin crew, their numbers should be increased.

1.315 - Assisting Means for Emergency Evacuation

Before taxying, takeoff and landing, and when safe and practicable, an automatic assisting means for emergency evacuation must be armed.

1.320 - Seats, Safety Belts, Harnesses

Crew Members
During takeoff and landing, and whenever deemed necessary by the commander for safety, crew members must be properly secured by all safety belts and harnesses provided. At all other times, those on the flight deck must keep them fastened while at their stations.

Passengers
Before takeoff and landing, and during taxying, and whenever deemed necessary for safety, each passenger must have a seat or berth with safety belt, or harness, where provided, properly secured.

Multiple occupancy may only be allowed on specified seats, and only for one adult and one infant properly secured by a supplementary loop belt or other restraint device.

1.325 - Securing of Passenger Cabin and Galley(s)

Before taxying, takeoff and landing, exits and escape paths must be unobstructed. Whenever deemed necessary for safety, equipment and baggage must be properly secured.

1.330 - Emergency Equipment Accessibility

Relevant emergency equipment must remain easily accessible for immediate use.

1.335 - Smoking On Board

No person on board may smoke:

- Whenever deemed necessary for safety

- While on the ground, unless specifically permitted under the Ops Manual

- Outside designated smoking areas, in the aisles and in toilets

- In cargo compartments and/or other areas where cargo which is not stored in flame resistant containers or covered by flame resistant canvas is carried

- Where oxygen is being supplied

1.340 - Meteorological Conditions

IFR
A commander must not start takeoff, or continue beyond where a revised flight plan applies (in the event of in-flight replanning), unless information indicates that the expected weather at the destination and/or required alternates in JAR OPS 1.295 are at or above the *planning* minima in JAR OPS 1.297.

Neither may the commander fly beyond decision or predetermined points (see AMC OPS 1.255 and the *operating* minima in JAR OPS 1.225), or proceed towards planned destinations or at least one alternate unless, at the ETA, the weather conditions are at or above *operating* minima.

VFR

A commander must not start to takeoff unless current weather reports, or a combination of current reports and forecasts, indicate that conditions along the route, or parts to be flown under VFR will, at appropriate times, allow compliance with these rules.

1.345 - Ice and Other Contaminants

1.345 - Ground Procedures

Procedures for when ground de-icing and anti-icing and related inspections are necessary must be established.

A commander must not start takeoff unless external surfaces are clear of deposits which might adversely affect performance and/or controllability, except as permitted in the Flight Manual.

1.346 - Flight Procedures

Procedures for flights in expected or actual icing conditions must be established (see ACJ OPS 1.346 and JAR OPS 1.675).

Commanders must not start flights, nor intentionally fly into expected or actual icing, unless the aeroplane is certificated and equipped.

ACJ OPS 1.346 - Expected or Actual Icing

Procedures should take account of the design, the equipment or configuration of the aeroplane, and the training. For these reasons, different types operated by the same company may need different procedures. In every case, the relevant limitations are in the Flight Manual and other documents produced by the manufacturer.

For the Ops Manual, the procedural principles for flight in icing conditions are in Appendix 1 to JAR OPS 1.1045, A 8.3.8, and should be cross-referenced, where necessary, to supplementary, type-specific data under B 4.1.1.

Technical Content

Procedures should take account of:

- JAR OPS 1.675

- Equipment and instruments that must be serviceable for icing conditions

- Limitations on flight in icing conditions for each phase. These may be imposed by equipment or performance corrections

- The criteria the flight crew should use to assess the effect of icing on performance and/or controllability

- The means by which the crew detects, by visual cues or the ice detection system, that the flight is entering icing conditions

- The action to be taken in a deteriorating situation (which may develop rapidly) resulting in adverse affects on performance and/or controllability, due to either the failure of the anti-icing or de-icing equipment to control a build-up, and/or ice build-up on unprotected areas.

Training, for Despatch and Flight in Icing

Part D of the Ops Manual should reflect the training (conversion and recurrent), which Flight Crew, Cabin Crew and other relevant operational personnel will require to comply with procedures for despatch and flight in icing conditions.

Flight Crew

Training should include:

- Instruction in how to recognise, from weather reports or forecasts available before flight, or during flight, the risks of encountering icing along the planned route and on how to modify, as necessary, the departure and in-flight routes or profiles

- Instruction in the operational and performance limitations or margins

- The use of in-flight ice detection, anti-icing and de-icing systems in normal and abnormal operation

- Instruction in differing intensities and forms of ice accretion and consequent action

Cabin Crew

Training should include:

- Awareness of conditions likely to produce surface contamination

- The need to inform the Flight Crew of significant ice accretion

1.350 - Fuel and Oil Supply

A commander must not start a flight unless satisfied that the aeroplane carries at least the planned fuel and oil to complete the flight safely, taking into account expected operating conditions.

1.355 - Takeoff Conditions

Before starting takeoff, a commander must satisfy himself that, according to the information available, the weather at the aerodrome and the condition of the runway to be used should not prevent a safe takeoff and departure.

1.360 - Application of Takeoff Minima

Before starting takeoff, a commander must be satisfied that the RVR or visibility in the takeoff direction is equal to or better than the minimum.

1.365 - Minimum Flight Altitudes

See IEM OPS 1.250. The commander must not fly below specified minimum altitudes except when necessary for takeoff or landing.

1.370 - Simulated Abnormal Situations

Situations requiring the application of abnormal or emergency procedures and simulation of IMC by artificial means may not be simulated during commercial air transport flights.

1.375 - In-flight Fuel Management

Procedures must be established to ensure that in-flight fuel checks and management are carried out.

Commanders must ensure that the usable fuel remaining is at least that required to proceed to where a safe landing can be made, with final reserve fuel remaining. Commanders must declare an emergency when actual (usable) fuel on board is less than final reserve fuel.

Appendix 1

In-flight Fuel Checks

Fuel checks must be carried out at regular intervals. Remaining fuel must be recorded and evaluated to compare actual with planned consumption, and check that remaining fuel is enough to complete the flight, as well as determining that expected to remain on arrival. Relevant data must be recorded.

In-flight Fuel Management

If, as a result of an in-flight fuel check, the expected fuel remaining on arrival is less than the required alternate fuel plus final reserve, the commander must take into account the traffic and operational conditions at the destination, along the diversion route to an alternate and at the destination alternate, when deciding whether to proceed to the destination or divert, to land with at least final reserve fuel.

On a flight to an isolated aerodrome, the last possible point of diversion to an en-route alternate must be determined. Before reaching this point, the commander must assess the fuel expected to remain overhead the isolated aerodrome, the weather, traffic and operational conditions prevailing there and at any en-route aerodrome before deciding whether to proceed to the isolated aerodrome or divert to an en-route aerodrome.

AMC to Appendix 1

Isolated Aerodromes

When approaching the last possible point of diversion to an available en-route aerodrome, unless the fuel expected to remain overhead the isolated aerodrome is at least equal to Additional Fuel, or unless two separate runways are available at the isolated aerodrome and the expected weather complies with JAR OPS 1.297(b)(2), the commander should not proceed to the isolated aerodrome, but proceed to the en-route alternate unless, according to information at the time, such a diversion appears inadvisable.

1.385 - Use of Supplemental Oxygen

Flight crew performing duties essential to safe operation in flight must use supplemental oxygen continuously whenever cabin altitude exceeds 10 000 ft for more than 30 minutes, and whenever the cabin altitude exceeds 13 000 ft.

1.390 - Cosmic Radiation

Operators must take account of inflight exposure to cosmic radiation of all crew members on duty (including positioning) and must take the following measures for crews liable to be subject to exposure of more than 1 mSv per year (see ACJ below):

- Assess their exposure

- Take into account the assessed exposure when organising working schedules with a view to reducing doses of highly exposed crew members

- Inform the crews concerned of the health risks their work involves

- Ensure that working schedules for female crews, once they have notified the operator that they are pregnant, keep the equivalent dose to the foetus as low as can reasonably be achieved and, in any case, ensure that the dose does not exceed 1 mSv for the remainder of the pregnancy

- Ensure that individual records are kept for crews liable to high exposure, to be notified to the individual annually, and on leaving

Aeroplanes may not operate above 15 000m (49 000ft) with the equipment in JAR OPS 1.680(a)(1) being serviceable, or the procedure there being complied with. The commander must initiate descent as soon as practicable when the limit values in the Ops Manual are exceeded.

ACJ OPS 1.390(a)(1) – Assessment

To show compliance, operators should assess the likely exposure to determine whether or not action is necessary. Assessment of the exposure level can be made as below (hours exposure for effective dose of 1 mSv), or other acceptable method:

Feet	Km	Hrs at 60°N	Hrs at Equator
27 000	8.23	630	1330
30 000	9.14	440	980
33 000	10.06	320	750
36 000	10.97	250	600
39 000	11.89	200	490
42 000	12.80	160	420
45 000	13.72	140	380
48 000	14.63	120	350

This table is based on the CARI-3 computer program, and may be updated.

The uncertainty on these estimates is about ± 20%. A conservative conversion factor of 0.8 has been used to convert ambient dose equivalent to effective dose.

Doses from cosmic radiation vary greatly with altitude and latitude, and the phase of the solar cycle. The table gives an estimate of the hours at altitudes where 1 mSv would be accumulated for flights at 60° N and the equator. Cosmic radiation dose rates change reasonably slowly with time at altitudes used by conventional jet aircraft (i.e. up to about 15 km/49 000 ft).

The table can be used to identify circumstances where it is unlikely that an annual dosage level of 1 mSv would be exceeded. If flights are limited to less than 8 km (27 000 ft), it is unlikely that annual doses will exceed 1 mSv. No further controls are necessary for crew members whose annual dose can be shown to be less than that.

ACJ OPS 1.390(a)(2) - Schedules and Records

Where in-flight exposure of crews to cosmic radiation is likely to exceed 1 mSv per year, working schedules, where practicable, should be arranged to keep it below 6 mSv. Crews likely to be exposed to more than that considered as highly exposed and individual records of exposure to cosmic radiation should be kept for each one.

ACJ OPS 1.390(a)(3) - Explanatory Stuff

Operators should explain the risks of occupational exposure to cosmic radiation to their crews. Female crew members should know of the need to control doses during pregnancy, and the operator consequently notified so that the necessary dose control measures can be introduced.

1.395 - Ground Proximity Detection

When undue proximity to the ground is detected by flight crews or GPWS, the commander must ensure that corrective action is initiated immediately to establish safe flight conditions.

1.398 - ACAS

ACAS must enable RAs to be produced, unless it would not be appropriate for the conditions. When undue proximity to another aircraft (RA) is detected, corrective action must be initiated *immediately* to establish safe separation, unless the intruder has been visually identified as not a threat.

ACJ OPS 1.398

ACAS operational procedures and training programs should take into account TGL 11 - *Guidance for Operators on Training Programs for the Use of ACAS*. It incorporates advice in:

- ICAO Annex 10 Volume 4
- ICAO Doc 8168 PANS OPS Volume 1
- ICAO Doc 4444 PANS RAC Part X paragraph 3.1.2
- ICAO guidance - *ACAS Performance-Based Training Objectives* (see Attachment E to State letter AN 7/1.3.7.2-97/77)

1.400 - Approach & Landing

Before starting an approach to land, the commander must be satisfied that, according to available information, the weather at the aerodrome and condition of the runway to be used should not prevent a safe approach, landing or missed approach, having regard to performance information in the Ops Manual.

IEM OPS 1.400

The in-flight determination of the landing distance should be based on the latest available report, preferably not more than 30 minutes before the expected landing time.

1.405 – Approach Start & Continuation

The commander may start an instrument approach regardless of reported RVR/Visibility, but it may not be continued beyond the outer marker, or

equivalent position, if the reported RVR/visibility is less than the minima. Where RVR is not available, it may be derived by converting reported visibility under Appendix 1 to JAR OPS 1.430 (h).

If, *after passing* the outer marker or equivalent, the reported RVR/visibility falls below minima, the approach may be continued to DA/H or MDA/H. Where no such position exists, the commander must make the decision to continue or abandon the approach before descending below 1000 ft above the aerodrome on the final approach segment. If the MDA/H is at or higher than that, the operator must establish a height, for each procedure, below which the approach must not be continued if the RVR/visibility is less than the applicable minima.

The approach may be continued below DA/H or MDA/H and the landing may be completed if the required visual reference is established *at the DA/H or MDA/H and is maintained.*

The touch-down zone RVR is always controlling. If reported and relevant*, the mid point and stop end RVR are also controlling. The minimum RVR value for the mid-point is the lesser of 125 m or the RVR required for the touch-down zone, and 75 m for the stop-end. For aeroplanes with a roll-out guidance or control system, the minimum RVR value for the mid-point is 75 m.

Relevant means that bit of runway used in the high speed phase of landing down to approx 60 kts.

IEM OPS 1.405(a) - Equivalent Position

The 'equivalent position' above can be established by DME distance, or a suitably located NDB or VOR, SRE or PAR fix or any other suitable fix that independently establishes position.

1.410 - Threshold Crossing Height

Operators must establish operational procedures to ensure that aeroplanes conducting precision approaches cross the threshold by a safe margin, in the landing configuration and attitude.

1.415 - Journey Log

Commanders must ensure that Journey logs are completed.

1.420 - Occurrence Reporting

Incident Reporting

Commanders or operators must submit reports of incidents that endanger or could endanger the safety of operation (see JAR OPS 1.085(b)), within 72 hours of when the incident was identified, unless prevented by exceptional circumstances.

All known or suspected technical defects and exceedances of technical limitations occurring while a commander was responsible for the flight must be recorded in the tech log. If they endanger, or could endanger, the safety of operation, the commander must also initiate submission of a report as above.

For incidents arising from, or relating to, failures, malfunctions or defects, equipment or any item of ground support equipment, or which cause or might cause adverse effects on continuing airworthiness, the operator must also inform the organisation responsible for the design, or the supplier or, if applicable, whoever is responsible for continued airworthiness.

Accident and Serious Incident Reporting

A commander must notify the operator of any accident or serious incident occurring while he was responsible for the flight, or any other member of the crew if he cannot, according to the succession of command.

The State Authority, the nearest appropriate Authority (if not), and any other organisation required to be informed, must be notified by the quickest means available and – for accidents only - at least before the aeroplane is moved, unless prevented by exceptional circumstances.

The commander or operator must submit a report to the State Authority within 72 hours of when the accident or serious incident occurred.

Specific Reports

Occurrences for which specific notification and reporting methods are used are described below:

Air Traffic Incidents

A commander must without delay notify the ATS unit concerned and inform them of his intention to submit an air traffic incident report after the flight whenever an aircraft in flight is endangered by:

- A near collision with any other flying device

- Faulty air traffic procedures or lack of compliance with procedures by ATS or the flight crew

- Failure of ATS facilities

The commander must notify the Authority as well.

Airborne Collision Avoidance System RA

A commander must notify the ATS unit concerned and submit an ACAS report whenever an aircraft has manoeuvred in response to an ACAS RA.

Bird Hazards and Strikes

The local ATS unit must be informed whenever a potential bird hazard is observed.

If he is aware that a bird strike has occurred, a commander must submit a written report after landing if significant damage has occurred, or there is a loss or malfunction of any essential service. If the strike is discovered when the commander is not available, the operator is responsible.

In-flight Emergencies with Dangerous Goods

If the situation permits, a commander must inform the appropriate ATS unit of any dangerous goods on board. After landing, the commander must, if the occurrence was associated with dangerous goods, comply also with JAR OPS 1.1225 (see AMC OPS 1.420(d)(4))

Unlawful Interference

After an act of unlawful interference on board, the commander or, in his absence, the operator, must submit a report as soon as practicable to the local Authority and the operator's State Authority (see also JAR OPS 1.1245).

Encountering Potentially Hazardous Conditions

A commander must notify the appropriate ATS unit as soon as practicable whenever a potentially hazardous condition, such as an irregularity in a ground or navigational facility, a meteorological phenomenon or volcanic ash cloud is encountered.

AMC OPS 1.420(d)(4) - Dangerous Goods

To assist ground services in preparing for the landing of an aeroplane in an emergency, adequate and accurate information about any dangerous goods on board must be given to the appropriate

ATS unit. Wherever possible, this should include the proper shipping name and/or the UN/ID number, the class/division and, for Class 1, the compatibility group, any subsidiary risk(s), the quantity and the location on board the aeroplane. When it is not possible to include it all, those parts thought most relevant, such as UN/ID numbers or classes/divisions and quantity, should be given.

1.430 - Aerodrome Operating Minima

For each aerodrome planned to be used, operating minima must be established that are not lower than the values in Appendix 1, or any from the State where the aerodrome is, except when approved by that State (this does not prohibit in-flight calculation of minima for a nonplanned alternate).

Full account must be taken of:

- Type, performance and handling

- Composition of flight crew, competence and experience

- Dimensions and characteristics of runways

- Adequacy and performance of ground aids (see AMC OPS 1.430(b)(4))

- Equipment for navigation and/or control of the flight path during takeoff, approach, flare, landing, roll-out and missed approach

- Obstacles

- Obstacle clearance altitude/heights

- Means of determining and reporting weather conditions

Aeroplane categories must be under Appx 2.

Appendix 1

Takeoff Minima

These must be expressed as visibility or RVR limits, taking into account relevant factors for aerodromes and aeroplanes used. Where there is a need to see and avoid obstacles (e.g. low performance aircraft), additional conditions (e.g. ceiling) must be specified.

You may not start to take off unless the weather is equal to or better than landing minima, unless a suitable takeoff alternate is available.

When reported met vis is below that required for takeoff, and RVR is not reported, a takeoff may only be started if you can determine that RVR/visibility along the takeoff runway is equal to or better than required minima. The same applies when no reported vis or RVR is available.

Visual Reference

Takeoff minima must give enough guidance to control the aeroplane for discontinued and continued takeoffs after failure of critical power units.

Required RVR/Visibility

If your **multi-engined aeroplane** can either stop or continue to 1500' above the aerodrome, clearing obstacles by the margins, **takeoff** minima may not be less than:

Facilities	RVR (m)	Vis (m) Cat D
Nil (Day Only)	500	
Rwy Edge Ltg and/or Centreline Marking	250	300
Rwy Edge, Centre Lts	200	250
Rwy Edge, Centre Lights and Multi RVR	150	200

The higher values apply to Category D aeroplanes. At night, at least runway edge and end lights are required. The RVR value must be achieved for all relevant RVR reporting points, except that the initial part may be replaced by your own assessment.

If you need to re-land immediately, and therefore see and avoid obstacles in the takeoff area, refer to the table below. The height at which your engine fails may not be lower than that from which the *one-engine-inoperative net takeoff flight path* can be constructed*. When RVR/met vis is not available you cannot takeoff unless the actual conditions satisfy applicable takeoff minima.

Engine Fail Height	RVR/Vis
<50	200
51-100	300
101-150	400
151-200	500
201-300	1000
>300	1500

Use the higher table for the circumstances.

*1500 m is also applicable if no positive takeoff flight path can be constructed.

Exceptions

Subject to approval, and provided the requirements below are met, an operator may reduce takeoff minima to 125 m RVR (Cat A, B and C) or 150 m RVR (Cat D) when:

- Low Visibility Procedures are in force

- High intensity runway centreline lights 15 m apart or less and high intensity edge lights 60 m or less apart are in operation

- Flight crew have satisfactorily completed training in a simulator

- A 90 m visual segment is available from the cockpit at the start of the takeoff run

- The required RVR value has been achieved for all of the relevant RVR reporting points

Subject to approval, operators of aeroplanes using lateral guidance systems may reduce takeoff minima to an RVR less than 125 m (Cat A, B and C) or 150 m (Cat D), but not lower than 75 m, if runway protection and facilities equivalent to Cat III are available.

Non-Precision Approach

System minima (MDH) for non-precision approaches based on ILS without glidepath, VOR, NDB, SRA and VDF must not be lower than:

Approach Aid	System Min (ft)
ILS No Glide Path	250
SRA (½ nm)	250
SRA (1 nm)	300
SRA (2 nm)	350
VOR	300
VOR/DME	250
NDB	300
NDB/DME	300
VDF (QDM & QGH)	300

Minimum Descent Height

The MDH for a non-precision approach must be higher than the OCH/OCL for the category of aircraft, the system minimum (see table above, or any State minima.

Visual Reference

MDH(ft)	Aeroplane Cat and RVR(m) - Nil			
	A	B	C	D
250–299	1500	1500	1600	1800
300–449	1500	1500	1800	2000
450–649	1500	1500	2000	2000
650 +	1500	1500	2000	2000

You cannot continue below MDH unless you can see (and identify) at least one of:

- elements of approach or runway (edge) lights

- the threshold or touchdown zone, their markings or lights

- visual glideslope indicator(s)

Required RVR

Lowest minima for non-precision approaches:

MDH(ft)	Aeroplane Cat and RVR(m) - Full			
	A	B	C	D
250–299	800	800	800	1200
300–449	900	1000	1000	1400
450–649	1000	1200	1200	1600
650 +	1200	1400	1400	1800

Full facilities comprise runway markings, 720 m or more of HI/MI approach lights, runway edge lights, threshold lights and runway end lights, which must be on.

MDH(ft)	Aeroplane Cat and RVR(m) - Int			
	A	B	C	D
250–299	1000	1100	1200	1400
300–449	1200	1300	1400	1600
450–649	1400	1500	1600	1800
650 +	1500	1500	1800	2000

Intermediate facilities comprise runway markings, 420–719 m of HI/MI approach lights, runway edge lights, threshold lights and runway end lights, which must be on.

MDH(ft)	Aeroplane Cat and RVR(m) - Basic			
	A	**B**	**C**	**D**
250–299	1200	1300	1400	1600
300–449	1300	1400	1600	1800
450–649	1500	1500	1800	2000
650 +	1500	1500	2000	2000

Basic facilities comprise runway markings, <420 m of HI/MI approach lights, any length of LI approach lights, runway edge lights, threshold and runway end lights, which must be on.

Nil approach light facilities comprise runway markings, runway edge lights, threshold lights, runway end lights or no lights at all.

The tables are only applicable to conventional approaches with a nominal descent slope up to 4°. Greater descent slopes will usually require that visual glide slope guidance (e.g. PAPI) is also visible at MDH.

The above figures are either reported RVR or met vis converted to RVR as below.

MDH refers to its initial calculation. When selecting associated RVR, there is no need to round up to the nearest ten feet, which may be done for operational purposes, e.g. conversion to MDA.

Night Operations
For night operations at least runway edge, threshold and runway end lights must be on.

Precision Approach – Cat I
A Category I operation is a precision instrument approach and landing using ILS, MLS or PAR with a DH of at least 200 ft and RVR at least 550 m.

Decision Height
This is at least the highest of:

- OCH/OCL for the category of aircraft

- minimum DH in the Flight Manual

- minimum height without visual reference

- 200 feet

Visual Reference
You cannot continue a precision approach below a DH determined as above, without at least one of these visual references (for the intended runway) visible and identifiable:

- elements of approach or runway (edge) lights

- the threshold or touchdown zone, their markings or lights

- visual glideslope indicator(s)

Required RVR
The lowest minima for Category I ops are:

DH (7)	Facilities/RVR (5)			
	Full (2 & 6)	Intermediate (2 & 6)	Basic (3 & 6)	Nil (4 & 6)
200	550	700	800	1000
201–250	600	700	800	1000
251–300	650	800	900	1200
301 +	800	900	1000	1200

For Notes, see *Non-Precision Aproach*, above.

The DH refers to *initial* calculation; associated RVR does not have to be rounded up to the nearest 10 feet, like when converting to DA.

Single Pilot
The minimum RVR for all approaches must be calculated under JAR OPS 1.430 and this Appendix. RVR may not be less than 800 m, except when using a suitable autopilot coupled to ILS or MLS, in which case normal minima apply. The DH must be at least 1.25 x the minimum use height for the autopilot.

Night Operations
At least runway edge, threshold and runway end lights must be on.

Precision Approach – Cat II Operations
A Category II operation is a precision instrument approach and landing using ILS or MLS with a DH between 100-200 ft and RVR at least 300 m.

Decision Height

DH for Cat II operations must be at least:

- The minimum in the Flight Manual
- The minimum height to which the aid can be used without visual reference
- The OCH/OCL for the category
- The DH the crew is authorised to
- 100 ft

Visual Reference

You may not continue below the Cat II DH above unless visual reference with a segment of at least 3 consecutive lights (centreline, touchdown zone, centreline or edge lights, or a combination) is attained and can be maintained. The reference must include a lateral element, such as an approach lighting crossbar or landing threshold or a barette of touchdown zone lighting.

Required RVR

The lowest minima to be used by an operator for Category II operations are:

DH (ft)	Auto-coupled to Below DH* (m)	
	RVR/ Cat A, B & C	RVR/Cat D
100–120	300 m	300 m**/350 m
121–140	400 m	400 m
> 141	450 m	450 m

*This means continued use of the AFCS down to not greater than 80% of DH. Thus airworthiness requirements may, through minimum engagement height for the AFCS, affect the DH to be applied.

*300 m may be used for a Cat D aeroplane conducting an autoland.

Precision Approach – Cat III

Category III operations are subdivided as follows:

- *III A* - using ILS or MLS with a DH lower than 100 ft, and RVR at least 200 m.
- *III B* - using ILS or MLS with a DH lower than 50 ft, or no DH, and RVR between 75-200 m

Where the DH and RVR do not fall within the same Category, the RVR controls.

Decision Height

This must be at least:

- The minimum in the Flight Manual
- The minimum height to which the aid can be used without visual reference
- The DH the crew is authorised to

No DH Operations

These may only be conducted if authorised in the Flight Manual, if the aid and aerodrome facilities can support them, and the operator is approved (it is assumed that a CAT III runway can support them unless specifically restricted as in the AIP or by NOTAM).

Visual Reference

For Cat IIIA, and Cat IIIB with fail-passive flight control systems, you may not continue below the DH above unless visual reference with a segment of at least 3 consecutive lights (centreline, touchdown zone, centreline or edge lights, or a combination) is attained and can be maintained. The reference must include a lateral element, such as an approach lighting crossbar or landing threshold or a barette of touchdown zone lighting.

For Cat IIIB operations with fail-operational flight control systems using a DH, you may not continue below the DH above unless a visual reference containing at least 1 centreline light is attained and can be maintained. For Cat III operations with no DH, there is no requirement for visual contact.

Required RVR

The lowest minima for Cat III operations are:

Appr Cat	DH (ft)(***)	Roll-out Control	RVR (m)
IIA	< 100	Not required	200*
IIIB	< 100	Fail-passive	150* **
IIIB	< 50	Fail-passive	125
IIIB	< 50/ No DH	Fail-Operational	75

*For fail-passive ops see IEM to Appendix 1 to JAR OPS 1.430 (e)(5) - *Crew actions in case of autopilot failure at or below DH.*

**For aeroplanes certificated under JAR AWO 321(b)(3) or equivalent.

***Flight control system redundancy is determined under JAR AWO by minimum certificated DH. (See IEM to Appendix 1 to JAR OPS 1.430 (d) & (e))

Circling

The lowest minima are:

	Aeroplane Category			
	A	B	C	D
MDH (f)	400	500	600	700
Min Met Vis (m)	1 500	1 600	2 400	3 600

Circling with prescribed tracks is an acceptable procedure within the meaning of this paragraph. (See IEM to Appendix 1 to JAR OPS 1.430 (f)).

Visual Approach

RVR may not be less than 800 m.

Converting Reported Met Vis to RVR

Do not use for calculating takeoff or Cat II or III minima, or if reported RVR is available (if RVR is reported to be above the maximum from the aerodrome operator, it is not a reported RVR in this context so the Table may be used.

When otherwise converting met vis, use this table:

Lighting	RVR = Reported Met Vis x	
	Day	Night
HI approach and runway lighting	1.5	2.0
Any other lighting	1.0	1.5
No lighting	1.0	N/A

IEM to Appendix 1 - Crew Action - Autopilot Failure
At or below DH in fail-passive Cat III Ops

For actual RVR values less than 300m, a go-around is assumed if an autopilot fails at or below DH. This means that a go-around is the normal action, but the wording recognises other circumstances where the safest action is to continue, including the height where the failure occurs, actual visual references, etc. (typically the late stages of the flare). Thus, it is not forbidden to land when the commander determines that this is safest.

All this should be in operational instructions.

IEM to Appendix - (Circling)
The applicable visibility is the met vis (VIS). The MDA/H and OCA/H minima are related to aerodrome elevation.

Missed Approach
If the decision to carry out a missed approach is taken on the approach axis (i.e. track, based on a navaid) the published procedure must be followed.

If visual reference is lost while circling to land from an instrument approach, the missed approach for that particular approach must be followed (the pilot is expected to make an initial climbing turn toward the landing runway and overhead the aerodrome to establish in a climb on the missed approach track). Inasmuch as the circling manoeuvre may be done in more than one direction, different patterns are required to establish on the prescribed missed approach course, depending on its position when visual reference is lost, unless otherwise prescribed.

If the approach is carried out with an ILS, the MAP associated with an ILS without glide path (GP out procedure) should be taken in account.

Approach Followed by Circling Without Tracks

Before Visual Reference, but Above MDA/H
Follow the procedure.

At Start of Level Flight At or Above MDA/H
From the beginning of the level flight phase, maintain the track determined by navaids until it is estimated that, in all probability, visual contact with the runway or its environment will be maintained, that the aircraft is within the circling area before circling, and the pilot

can determine his position against the runway with the external references. If these conditions are not met by the MAP, do the published missed approach.

After leaving the track of the procedure, the phase outbound from the runway should be limited to the distance to align for finals. Manoeuvres should be conducted within the circling area so that visual contact with the runway or its environment is maintained at all times, at least at circling MDA/H.

Descent below MDA/H should not be initiated until the threshold has been identified and the aeroplane can continue with a *normal rate of descent* and land within the touchdown zone.

Approach Followed by Circling With Track

Before Visual Reference, Above MDA/H
Follow the procedure.

The aeroplane should be in level flight at or above MDA/H and the approach track (determined by navaids) maintained until visual contact can be achieved and maintained. At the divergence point, the aeroplane should leave the track and follow the published routing and heights.

If the divergence point is reached before visual reference is acquired, a missed approach should be initiated not later than MAP and carried out as per the procedure. The approach track should only be left at the prescribed divergence point - only published routing and heights should be followed.

Unless otherwise specified in the procedure, final descent should not be initiated until the threshold has been identified and the aeroplane is in a position to continue with a *normal rate of descent* and land within the touchdown zone.

AMC OPS 1.430(b)(4) - Effect on Landing Minima of Failed Ground Equipment
Aerodrome facilities are expected to be installed and maintained to the standards in ICAO Annexes 10 and 14. Deficiencies are expected to be repaired without unnecessary delay. These instructions are for pre- and in-flight use, although it is not expected that commanders would consult them

after passing the outer marker or equivalent - if failures are announced at such a late stage, the approach could be continued at the commander's discretion. If, however, they are announced before then, their effect should be considered as per the tables below, and the approach may have to be abandoned to allow this to happen.

No DH
For aeroplanes authorised to conduct No DH operations with the lowest RVR limitations, the following applies in addition to the content of the tables in JARs (not included here):

- RVR - At least one RVR value must be available

- Runway lights
  - No edge lights, or centre lights – Day – RVR 200 m. Night – Not allowed
  - No TDZ lights – No restrictions
  - No standby power to lights – Day – RVR 200 m. Night – not allowed

- Conditions for Tables
  - Multiple failures of runway lights other than indicated in Table 1B are not acceptable.
  - Deficiencies of approach and runway lights are treated separately.
  - Category II or III operations. A combination of deficiencies in runway lights and RVR assessment equipment is not allowed.
  - Failures other than ILS affect RVR only and not DH.

IEM to Appendix 1 - Minimum RVR
Operators should pay attention to ECAC Doc 17 3rd Edition, Subpart A, which covers the relationship between DH and RVR.

IEM OPS 1.430 – Documents
These documents are related to AWO:

- ICAO Annex 2/*Rules of the Air*
- ICAO Annex 6/*Operation of Aircraft, Part I*

- ICAO Annex 10/*Telecommunications Vol 1*

- ICAO Annex 14/*Aerodromes Vol 1*

- ICAO Doc 8186/PANS OPS *Aircraft Operations*

- ICAO Doc 9365/*AWO Manual*

- ICAO Doc 9476/*SMGCS Manual (Surface Movement Guidance And Control Systems)*

- ICAO Doc 9157/*Aerodrome Design Manual*

- ICAO Doc 9328/*Manual for RVR Assessment*

- ECAC Doc 17, Issue 3 (partly in JAR OPS)

- JAR-AWO (Airworthiness Certification)

IEM to Appendix 1 to JAR OPS 1.430
The minima in this Appendix are based on the experience of commonly used approach aids, but this does not preclude the use of other systems such as HUD and EVS, but minima for them must be developed as the need arises.

Appendix 2 - All Weather Operations
Classifying aeroplanes by categories is based on the indicated airspeed at threshold (V_{AT}) which is equal to V_{SO} multiplied by 1.3, or V_{SIG} multiplied by 1.23 in the landing configuration at max landing mass. If both V_{SO} and V_{S1G} are available, use the higher resulting V_{AT}. The categories corresponding to V_{AT} values are:

Aeroplane Category	V_{AT} (kts)
A	< 91
B	91-120
C	121-140
D	141-165
E	166-210

Operators may impose a permanent, lower, landing mass for determining V_{AT} as approved.

1.440 - Low Visibility Operations

For Category II or III operations:

- Aeroplanes must be appropriately certificated and equipped under JAR AWO or an equivalent

- A suitable system for recording approach and/or automatic landing success and failure must be established and maintained to monitor overall safety

- Operations must approved

- The flight crew must consist of at least 2 pilots

- DH must be determined by a radio altimeter

Low visibility takeoffs may not be conducted in less than 150 m RVR (Category A, B and C) or 200 m RVR (Category D), unless approved.

Appendix 1
Operational Demonstration
At least 30 approaches and landings must be accomplished using the systems in each type if the requested DH is 50 ft or higher. If the DH is less than 50 ft, try at least 100 approaches and landings.

Operators with different variants of the same type using the same basic flight control and display systems, or different ones on the same type, must show satisfactory performance, but a full operational demonstration need not be done for each variant.

A reduced number of approaches and landings may be accepted, based on credit for experience gained by another operator with a JAR OPS 1 AOC using the same type or variant and procedures.

If the unsuccessful approaches exceed 5% of the total (e.g. uns atisfactory landings, system disconnects, etc.) the evaluation program must be extended in steps of at least 10 approaches and landings until the failure rate gets below 5%.

The rest of this is a pile of stuff about sending in reports and data collection. To save space, if you're really interested (yeah, right), check the JARs.

IEM to Appendix 1 - Criteria
An **approach** is successful if:

- *From 500 feet to Start of Flare*, speed is kept up as per ACJ-AWO 231, para 2 *Speed Control*, with no relevant system failure.

- *From 300 feet to DH*, no excess deviation occurs, and no centralised warning gives a go-around command (if installed).

An **automatic landing** is successful if:

- No relevant system failure occurs
- No flare failure occurs
- No de-crab failure occurs (if installed)
- Longitudinal touchdown is beyond a point on the runway 60 metres after the threshold and before the end of the touchdown zone lighting (900 metres from the threshold)
- Lateral touchdown with outboard landing gear is not outside the touchdown zone lighting edge
- Sink rate is not excessive
- Bank angle does not exceed a limit
- No roll-out failure or deviation occurs

More details can be found in JAR AWO 131, JAR AWO 231 and ACJ AWO 231.

ACJ to Appendix 1
Demonstrations may be done in line operations, or any other flight where Operator procedures are being used. The rest of this ACJ just deals with conditions to be observed, data collection, faulty navaids, etc.

1.445 – Aerodrome Considerations
They must be approved by the State in which they are located. Operators must verify that Low Visibility Procedures (LVP) have been established, and will be enforced.

1.450 – Training and Qualifications
Before conducting Low Visibility Takeoff, Category II and III operations, flight crews must complete the training and checking in Appendix 1 (including Flight Simulator) to the appropriate limiting values of RVR and DH. They must be qualified under Appendix 1.

There must be a detailed syllabus in the Ops Manual in addition to the training in Subpart N, and the flight crew qualification must be specific to the operation and aeroplane type.

Appendix 1
Crew training programs for Low Visibility Operations must include structured courses of ground, Flight Sim and/or flight training. Content may be abbreviated as below, if acceptable:

- Crews with no Cat II or III experience must complete the full program.
- Crews with Cat II or III experience with another JAA operator may do an abbreviated ground training course.
- Crews with Cat II or III experience with the operator may do an abbreviated ground, Flight Sim and/or flight training course, to include at least the requirements of sub-paragraphs (d)(1), (d)(2)(i) or (d)(2)(ii) as appropriate and (d)(3)(i).

Ground Training
The initial ground training course for Low Visibility Operations must cover at least:

- Characteristics and limitations of the ILS and/or MLS
- Characteristics of visual aids
- Characteristics of fog
- Operational capabilities and limitations of particular airborne systems
- Effects of precipitation, ice accretion, low level wind shear and turbulence
- Effects of specific malfunctions
- Use and limitations of RVR assessment systems
- Principles of obstacle clearance
- Recognition of and action to be taken if ground equipment fails
- Procedures and precautions with regard to surface movement when RVR is 400 m or less, and any additional procedures for takeoff below 150 m (200 m for Category D aeroplanes)

- Significance of decision heights based upon radio altimeters and the effect of terrain profile in the approach area on radio altimeter readings and automatic approach/landing systems

- The importance and significance of Alert Height and action on failures above and below the Alert Height

- Qualifications for pilots to obtain and retain approval for Low Visibility Takeoffs and Cat II or III operations

- The importance of correct seating and eye position

Flight Simulator and/or Flight Training

The program must include:

- Checks of satisfactory equipment function, on the ground and in flight

- Effect on minima from changes in status of ground installations

- Monitoring of AFCS and autoland status annunciators, with emphasis on actions if they fail

- Actions in the event of failures such as engines, electrical, hydraulics or flight control systems

- The effect of known unserviceabilities and use of MELs

- Operating limitations from airworthiness certification

- Guidance on visual cues required at DH, with information on maximum deviations from glidepath or localiser

- The importance and significance of Alert Height and the action in the event of failures above and below it

Flight crews must be trained for their duties and instructed on the coordination required with other crew members. Maximum use should be made of Flight Simulators.

Training must be in phases covering normal operation with no failures, but including possible weather and detailed scenarios of

aeroplane and equipment failure which could affect Cat II or III operations. If the system involves hybrid or other special systems (e.g. HUDs or Enhanced Vision Equipment), crews must practise in normal and abnormal modes during the Flight Simulator phase.

Appropriate incapacitation procedures must be practised.

For aeroplanes with no representative Flight Simulator, the flight training phase specific to the visual scenarios of Cat II operations must be done in a specifically approved simulator, to include at least 4 approaches.

Type-specific training and procedures must be practised in the aeroplane.

Initial Cat II and III training must include at least the following exercises:

- Approach using appropriate flight guidance, autopilots and control systems to the appropriate DH, to include transition to visual flight and landing, and (with all engines operating) down to DH followed by missed approach, all without external visual reference

- Where appropriate, approaches using automatic flight systems to provide automatic flare, landing and roll-out

- Normal operation of applicable systems, with and without acquisition of visual cues at DH

Subsequent training must include at least:

- Approaches with engine failure at various stages on the approach

- Approaches with critical equipment failures (e.g. electrics, autoflight, ground and/or airborne ILS/MLS systems and status monitors)

- Approaches where failures of autoflight equipment at low level require either reversion to manual flight to control flare, landing and roll out or missed approach, or reversion to manual flight or a downgraded automatic mode to control missed approaches from, at or below DH, including those which may result in a touchdown on the runway

- Failures of systems which will result in excessive localiser and/or glideslope deviation, above and below DH, in minimum visual conditions. As well, a continuation to a manual landing must be practised if a HUD forms a downgraded mode of the automatic system or forms the only flare mode

- Failures and procedures specific to aeroplane type or variant

Programs must provide practice in handling faults requiring reversion to higher minima, and must include handling when, during a fail-passive Cat III approach, the fault causes the autopilot to disconnect at or below DH when the last reported RVR is 300 m or less. With takeoffs in RVRs of 400 m and below, training must cover systems and engine failure resulting in continued and rejected takeoffs.

Conversion Training
The experience requirements for an abbreviated course are above.

Ground Training
The requirements above, allowing for the crew's Cat II and III training and experience.

Flight Simulator and/or Flight Training
At least 8 approaches and/or landings in a Flight Simulator. Where no representative simulator is available, at least 3 approaches, with at least 1 go-around are required on the aeroplane. Appropriate additional training for special equipment (e.g. HUDs) is also needed.

Flight Crew Qualification
These are specific to the operator and type of aeroplane. Flight crews must complete a check before conducting Category II or III operations, but successful completion of the Flight Simulator and/or flight training above will do instead.

Line Flying under Supervision
- *For Cat II,* when a manual landing is required, at least 3 landings from autopilot disconnect

- *For Cat III*, at least 3 autolands, but only 1 is needed when the training above has been done in a simulator usable for zero flight time conversion

Type and Command Experience
Before starting Cat II/III ops, new commanders must have 50 hours or 20 sectors on type, including line flying under supervision. 100 m must be added to RVR minima unless previously qualified for Cat II or III operations with a JAA operator, until 100 hours or 40 sectors, including the line flying, has been achieved (on type).

A reduction may be authorised for flight crews with Cat II or III command experience.

Low Vis Takeoff with RVR under 150/200 m
Before authorisation to conduct takeoffs in RVRs below 150 m (200 m for Category D), the following training must be done:

- Normal takeoff in minimum RVR

- Takeoff in minimum RVR with an engine failure between V1 and V2, or as soon as safety permits

- Takeoff in minimum RVR with an engine failure before V1 for a rejected takeoff

This training musr be done in a flight sim, to include special procedures and equipment. Where no representative simulator is available, it may be authorised in an aeroplane without the requirement for minimum RVR conditions (see Appendix 1 to JAR OPS 1.965).

A flight crew member must complete a check before conducting low visibility takeoffs in RVR below 150 m (200 m for Cat D aeroplanes) if applicable. It may only be replaced by successful completion of the Flight Simulator and/or flight training above on conversion to a type.

Recurrent Training and Checking
In conjunction with normal recurrent training and OPCs, a pilot's knowledge and ability to perform the tasks associated with the category of operation.

The required number of approaches within the OPC validity period (see JAR OPS 1.965(b)) is to be at least three, one of which may be substituted by an approach and landing in the aeroplane using

Cat II or III procedures. One missed approach must be flown during the OPC. If the operator is authorised for RVR less than 150/200 m, at least one LVTO to the lowest minima must be flown during the OPC (See IEM OPS 1.450(b)(i)).

For Cat III, a Flight Simulator must be used.

Operators must ensure that, for Cat III operations with fail passive flight control systems, a missed approach is completed at least once over three consecutive OPCs as the result of an autopilot failure at or below DH when the last reported RVR was 300 m or less.

Recurrent training and checking for Cat II and LVTO in a type where no representative simulator is available may be authorised.

Recency for LVTO and Category II/III based upon automatic approaches and/or auto-lands is maintained by the recurrent training and checking described here.

IEM OPS 1.450(g)(1)

The number of approaches includes one approach and landing in the aeroplane using approved Cat II/III procedures, which may be done in normal line operation or as a training flight. It is assumed they will be conducted by pilots qualified under JAR OPS 1.940 and qualified for the category.

1.455 – Operating Procedures

These must be in the Ops Manual, with crew duties during taxying, takeoff, approach, flare, landing, roll-out and missed approach, as appropriate.

Before starting a Low Visibility Takeoff or a Category II or III approach, the commander must satisfy himself that:

- The status of visual and nonvisual facilities is good enough

- Appropriate LVPs are in force according to information from ATS

- Flight crews are properly qualified (before a Low Visibility Takeoff in an RVR less than 150 m (Cat A, B and C aeroplanes) or 200 m (Cat D))

Appendix 1

Low Visibility Operations include:

- Manual takeoff (with or without electronic guidance systems)

- Auto-coupled approach to below DH, with manual flare, landing and roll-out

- Auto-coupled approach followed by auto-flare, autolanding and manual roll-out

- Auto-coupled approach followed by auto-flare, autolanding and auto-roll-out, when the applicable RVR is less than 400 m.

A hybrid system may be used with any of these modes of operations. Other guidance systems or displays may be certificated and approved.

Procedures and Operating Instructions

The precise nature and scope of procedures and instructions depend upon the airborne equipment and flight deck procedures. Operators must clearly define flight crew duties during takeoff, approach, flare, roll-out and missed approach in the Ops Manual, with particular emphasis on responsibilities during transition from non-visual to visual conditions, and on procedures in deteriorating visibility or when failures occur.

Special attention must be paid to the distribution of flight deck duties to ensure that the workload of the pilot making the decision to land or execute a missed approach enables him to devote himself to supervision and the decision-making process.

The detailed operating procedures and instructions must be in the Ops Manual, and be compatible with the limitations and mandatory procedures in the Flight Manual, covering the following in particular:

- Checks for satisfactory functioning of aeroplane equipment, before departure and in flight

- Effect on minima from changes in the status of the ground installations and airborne equipment

- Procedures for takeoff, approach, flare, landing, roll-out and missed approach

- Procedures in the event of failures, warnings and non-normal situations

- The minimum visual reference

- The importance of correct seating and eye position

- Action which may be necessary from a deterioration of visual reference

- Allocation of crew duties in carrying out the procedures above, to allow the Commander to devote himself mainly to supervision and decision-making

- The requirement for height calls below 200 ft to be based on the radio altimeter and for one pilot to continue monitoring the instruments until the landing is completed

- The requirement for the Localiser Sensitive Area to be protected

- The use of information relating to wind velocity, windshear, turbulence, runway contamination and use of multiple RVR assessments

- Procedures for practice approaches and landing on runways at which the full Category II or Category III aerodrome procedures are not in force

- Operating limitations resulting from airworthiness certification

- Information on the maximum deviation allowed from the ILS glide path and/or localiser.

1.460 - Minimum Equipment

The minimum equipment that has to be serviceable when starting a Low Visibility Takeoff or Category II or III approach under the Flight Manual or other approved document must be in the Ops Manual.

The commander must satisfy himself that the status of the aeroplane and relevant airborne systems is appropriate for the specific operation.

1.465 - VFR Operating Minima

VFR flights must be done under the Visual Flight Rules and the Table in Appendix 1 (below).

Special VFR flights must not be *started* when visibility is less than 3 km and *not otherwise conducted* when it is less than 1.5 km.

Appendix 1 - Minimum Visibilities

Airspace	B	CDE	FG	
			Highest of above 900 m (3 000') AMSL or above 300 m (1 000') above terrain	Highest of at and below 900 m (3 000') AMSL or 300 m (1 000') above terrain
Distance from cloud	Clear	1 500 m horizontally 300 m (1 000 ft) vertically		Clear of cloud in sight of surface
Vis	8 km at and above 3 050 m (10 000 ft) AMSL* 5 km below 3 050 m (10 000 ft) AMSL			5 km**

*When the height of the transition altitude is lower than 3 050 m (10 000 ft) AMSL, FL 100 should be used instead of 10 000ft.

**Cat A and B aeroplanes may operate in flight visibilities down to 3 000 m, if the appropriate ATS permits a flight visibility less than 5 km, and the circumstances are such that the probability of encounters with other traffic is low, and the IAS is 140 kt or less.

1.470 – Performance (General)

Multi-engined torboprops that can carry more than 9 passsengers, or with a maximum takeoff mass over 5 700 kg, and all multi-engined turbojets, must operate under Subpart G (Performance Class A).

Propeller-driven aeroplanes that can carry 9 or less passengers, and with a maximum takeoff mass of 5700 kg or less come under Subpart H (Class B).

Aeroplanes with reciprocating engines that can carry more than 9 passengers or with a maximum takeoff mass over 5700 kg are under Subpart I (Class C).

Where full compliance with the appropriate Subpart cannot be shown due to specific design characteristics (e.g. supersonic aeroplanes or seaplanes), approved standards that ensure an equivalent level of safety must be used.

1.475 - General

The mass at the start of takeoff, or from where a revised operational flight plan applies, must not be greater than that at which the appropriate Subpart can be complied with, allowing for expected reductions in mass as the flight proceeds, and fuel jettisoning as is provided for.

Performance data in the Flight Manual must be used to determine compliance, supplemented with other data in the relevant Subpart. When applying those factors, account may be taken of operational factors already in Flight Manual data to avoid double application.

When showing compliance, due account must be taken of aeroplane configuration, environmental conditions and systems with an adverse effect on performance. For performance purposes, a damp runway, other than a grass one, is considered to be dry.

AMC OPS 1.475(b) - Reverse Thrust Credit

Landing distance data in the Flight Manual (or POH, etc.) with credit for reverse thrust can only be considered as approved for compliance if it contains a specific statement from the appropriate airworthiness authority that it complies with a recognised airworthiness code (e.g. FAR 23/25, JAR 23/25, BCAR Section 'D'/'K').

IEM OPS 1.475(b) - Factoring of Automatic Landing Distance Data (Performance A Only)

Where the landing requires an automatic landing system, and the distance in the Flight Manual includes safety margins equivalent to those in JAR OPS 1.515(a)(1) and 1.520, the landing mass should be the lesser of that determined under them, or that for the automatic landing distance for the surface condition (as in the Flight Manual). Increments due to features such as beam location or elevations, or procedures like overspeed, should also be included.

1.480 - Terminology

See *Definitions.*

1.485 – Performance A

Performance data in the Flight Manual must be supplemented with other data, if the stuff in the Flight Manual is not good enough for reasonably expected adverse operating conditions, such as takeoff and landing on contaminated runways, and consideration of engine failure in all flight phases.

For wet and contaminated runways, performance data under JAR 25.1591 or equivalent must be used (see IEM OPS 1.485(b)).

IEM OPS 1.485(b) - Data

If performance data has been based on measured runway friction coefficient, the operator should use a procedure correlating it and the effective braking coefficient of friction of the type over the required speed range for the conditions.

1.490 - Takeoff

The mass must not exceed the maximum for the pressure altitude and ambient temperature. The following requirements must be met:

- The accelerate-stop distance must not exceed accelerate-stop distance available

- The takeoff distance must not exceed takeoff distance available, with a clearway up to half of the takeoff run available

- The takeoff run must not exceed the takeoff run available

- Compliance with this paragraph must be shown with a single value of V_1 for the rejected and continued takeoff

- On a wet or contaminated runway, the takeoff mass must not exceed that permitted for a takeoff on a dry runway under the same conditions

When showing compliance with the above, operators must take account of:

- Pressure altitude and ambient temperature at the aerodrome

- Runway surface and condition

- Runway slope in the direction of takeoff

- Up to 50% of the reported head-wind or at least 150% of the tailwind

• The loss of runway length due to alignment before takeoff

IEM OPS 1.490(c)(3) - Runway Surface (T/O)

Operation on runways contaminated with water, slush, snow or ice implies uncertainties with regard to runway friction and contaminant drag, and therefore to the achievable performance and control during takeoff, since the actual conditions may not completely match the assumptions on which performance information is based. For a contaminated runway, the first option is to wait until the runway is cleared, but, if this is impracticable, a commander may consider a takeoff, if he has applied the performance adjustments, and any further safety measures justified under the prevailing conditions.

An adequate overall level of safety will only be maintained if operations under JAR 25 AMJ 25.1591 are limited to rare occasions. Where the frequency is higher, operators should provide additional measures for an equivalent level of safety, which could include special crew training, additional distance factoring, and more restrictive wind limitations.

IEM OPS 1.490(c)(6) - Loss of Runway Length Due to Alignment

The length of the runway declared for calculation of TODA, ASDA and TORA does not account for lining up in the direction of takeoff, usually a 90° taxiway entry to the runway and 180° turnaround on it. There are two distances to be considered:

• The minimum distance of the mainwheels from the start of the runway for determining TODA and TORA (L below)

• The minimum distance of the most forward wheel(s) from the start of the runway for determining ASDA (N below)

Where the manufacturer does not provide the appropriate data, the calculation in paragraph 2 (not included here) may be used.

1.495 - Takeoff Obstacle Clearance

The net takeoff flight path must clear all obstacles vertically by at least 35 ft, or at least 90 m plus 0.125 x D horizontally, where D is the horizontal distance the aeroplane has travelled from the end of the TODA or the end of the takeoff distance if a turn is scheduled before the end of TODA. For aeroplanes with a wingspan of less than 60 m, a horizontal obstacle clearance of half the wingspan plus 60 m, plus 0.125 x D may be used.

Account must be taken of:

• The mass at the start of the takeoff run

• The aerodrome pressure altitude and ambient temperature

• Up to 50% of the reported headwind or at least 150% of the tailwind

Track changes are not allowed up to where the net takeoff flight path is half the wingspan (but at least 50 ft above the elevation of the end of the TORA). Thereafter, up to 400 ft, it is assumed that the angle of bank is only up to 15°. Above 400 ft, you can use between 15-25°.

Where the bank is over 15°, obstacles within the horizontal distances below must be cleared vertically by at least 50 ft, and special procedures must be applied when applying bank angles up to 20° between 200-400 ft, or up to 30° above 400 ft (see Appendix 1).

Adequate allowance must be made for the effect of bank angle on operating speeds and flight paths, including the distance increments from increased operating speeds (see AMC OPS 1.495(c)(4)).

Where the flight path does not require track changes over 15°, obstacles over 300 m away need not be considered, if the pilot can maintain the required navigational accuracy through the obstacle accountability area (see AMC OPS 1.495(d)(1) & (e)(1), below, or 600 m, for all other conditions. For track changes over 15°, use 600 m and 900 m, respectively.

Contingency procedures for JAR OPS 1.495 must be established, to provide a safe route, avoiding obstacles, and enable the aeroplane to either comply with JAR OPS 1.500, or land at either the aerodrome of departure or at a takeoff alternate (see IEM OPS 1.495(f)).

IEM OPS 1.495(a)

The net takeoff flight path begins 35 ft above the runway or clearway at the end of the takeoff distance, which is the longest of 115% of the distance from the start of the takeoff to 35 ft above the runway or clearway, or just that distance, if the critical engine fails at V_1 for a dry runway (if it is wet or contaminated, from the start of the takeoff to where the aeroplane is 15 ft above the runway or clearway).

JAR OPS 1.495(a) specifies that the net takeoff flight path must clear all relevant obstacles vertically by 35 ft. On a wet or contaminated runway, an engine failure at V_1 implies that the aeroplane can initially be as much as 20 ft below it, and therefore may clear close-in obstacles by only 15 ft. Take care!

AMC OPS 1.495(c)(4)

The Flight Manual generally provides a climb gradient decrement for a 15° bank turn. For less than 15°, proportionate amounts should be applied, unless the manufacturer or Flight Manual says otherwise.

Acceptable adjustments to assure adequate stall margins and gradient corrections are:

Bank	Speed	Gradient Correction
15°	V_2	1 x Flight Manual 15° Gradient Loss
20°	V_2 + 5 kt	2 x Flight Manual 15° Gradient Loss
25°	V_2 + 10 kt	3 x Flight Manual 15° Gradient Loss

AMC OPS 1.495(d)(1) & (e)(1) - Navigational Accuracy

Flight Deck Systems

The obstacle accountability semi-widths of 300 m and 600 m may be used if the navigation system under OEI provides a two standard deviation (2 s) accuracy of 150 and 300 m, respectively.

Visual Course Guidance

The obstacle accountability semi-widths of 300 m and 600 m may be used where navigational accuracy is ensured at all relevant points on the flight path by use of external references. These references may be considered visible from the flight deck if they are situated more than 45° either side of the intended track and not greater than 20° depresswed from the horizontal.

For visual navigation, the weather at the time, including ceiling and visibility, must ensure that obstacle and/or ground reference points can be seen and identified. The Ops Manual should specify the minimum conditions that will enable the flight crew to continuously determine and maintain the correct flight path with respect to ground reference points, to provide safe clearance with respect to obstructions and terrain as follows:

- The procedure should be well defined with respect to ground reference points so the track can be analysed for obstacle clearance

- The procedure should be within the capabilities of the aeroplane for speed, bank angle and wind effects

- A written and/or pictorial description of the procedure should be there for the crew

- The limiting environmental conditions (such as wind, lowest cloud base, ceiling, visibility, day/night, ambient lighting, obstruction lighting) should be specified

IEM OPS 1.495(f) - Engine Failure Procedures

If compliance is based on an engine failure route that differs from the all-engine departure route or normal SID, a Deviation Point can be identified. Adequate obstacle clearance along the normal departure with failure of the critical engine at that point will normally be available, but, in certain situations, the obstacle clearance along the normal route may be marginal and should be checked to ensure that, if an engine fails after the point, a flight can safely proceed along the normal departure.

Appendix 1 - Increased Bank Angles

The following criteria must be met:

- The Flight Manual must contain approved data for the speed increase and must allow the construction of the new flight path

- Visual guidance must be available for navigation accuracy

- Weather minima and wind limitations must be specified for each runway and approved

- Training under JAR OPS 1.975

1.500 - En-route – OEI

The OEI en-route net flight path data (for the expected weather conditions) must comply with the paragraphs below at all points. There must be a positive gradient at 1 500 ft above the aerodrome where the landing is assumed to be made after engine failure, allowing for the effect of ice protection systems.

The gradient must be positive, at least 1 000 ft above all terrain and obstructions within 9.3 km (5 nm) either side of the intended track.

The aeroplane must continue flight from cruising altitude to where a landing can be made (see JAR OPS 1.515 or 1.520), clearing vertically, by at least 2 000 ft, all terrain and obstructions within 9.3 km (5 nm) either side of track as follows:

- The engine is assumed to fail at the most critical point along the route

- Account is taken of wind effect on the flight path

- Fuel jettisoning is allowed consistent with reaching the aerodrome with fuel reserves, if a safe procedure is used

- The aerodrome where the aeroplane is assumed to land after engine failure must meet certain performance criteria for the expected landing mass, weather reports or forecasts and field condition reports indicate that a safe landing can be accomplished at the ETA.

The width margins above must be increased to 18.5 km (10 nm) if navigational accuracy does not meet the 95% containment level.

AMC OPS 1.500

The high terrain or obstacle analysis for showing compliance with JAR OPS 1.500 may be carried out in two ways, as explained below.

A detailed analysis of the route should be made with contour maps, plotting the highest points within the prescribed corridor's width along the route. The next step is to determine whether it is

possible to maintain level flight OEI 1000 ft above the highest point of the crossing. If this is not possible, or if the associated weight penalties are unacceptable, a driftdown procedure should be worked out, based on engine failure at the most critical point, and clearing critical obstacles by at least 2000 ft. The minimum cruise altitude is determined by the intersection of the two driftdown paths, taking into account allowances for decision-making (see Figure 1). However, this is time consuming and requires detailed terrain maps.

Alternatively, the published minimum altitudes (MEA or MORA) may be used to determine whether OEI level flight is feasible at the minimum altitude or if it is necessary to use the published minimum altitudes as the basis for driftdown construction (see Figure 1). This avoids a detailed contour analysis, but may be more penalising.

To comply with JAR OPS 1.500(c), one means of compliance is the use of MORA and, with JAR OPS 1.500(d), MEA, if the aeroplane meets the navigational equipment standard assumed in the definition of MEA.

MEA or MORA normally provide the required 2000 ft obstacle clearance for driftdown, but, at and below 6000 ft, they cannot be used directly, as only 1000 ft. clearance is assured.

1.505 - En-route – Aeroplanes With 3 Or More Engines, 2 Engines Inoperative

At no point will an aeroplane with three or more engines be more than 90 minutes, at the all-engines long range cruising speed at standard temperature in still air, away from a suitable aerodrome, unless:

- The two engines inoperative en-route net flight path allows the flight to continue, in expected weather, from where two engines are assumed to fail simultaneously, to a suitable aerodrome (that is, where you can land and come to a complete stop using the prescribed procedures). The NFP must clear vertically, by at least 2 000 ft, all terrain and obstructions within 9.3 km (5 nm) either side of the track, allowing for ice protection. If navigational accuracy does not meet the 95% containment level, width must be increased to 18.5 km (10 nm).

- The two engines are assumed to fail at the most critical point where the route is more than 90 minutes, at the all engines long range cruising speed, etc. etc.), away from a suitable aerodrome.

- The gradient must be positive at 1500 ft above the suitable aerodrome after the failure of two engines.

- Fuel jettisoning is allowed, consistent with reaching the aerodrome with required fuel reserves, if a safe procedure is used

- The expected mass where the two engines are assumed to fail must allow for enough fuel to proceed to a suitable aerodrome, and to arrive there at least 1 500 ft directly over the landing area and thereafter to fly level for 15 minutes.

1.510 - Landing – Destinations And Alternates

The landing mass (see JAR OPS 1.475(a)) must not exceed the maximum for altitude and temperature at the ETA.

For instrument approaches with a missed approach gradient greater than 2.5%, the expected landing mass must allow a missed approach with a climb gradient equal to or greater than that in the OEI missed approach configuration and speed (see JAR 25.121(d)). Alternative methods must be approved.

With a DH below 200 ft, the expected landing mass must allow a missed approach gradient of climb, with the critical engine failed and the speed and configuration for go-around of at least 2.5%, or the published gradient, whichever is the greater (see JAR AWO 243). Alternative methods must be approved.

IEM OPS 1.510(b) and (c)

The required missed approach gradient may not be achieved by all aeroplanes at or near maximum landing mass in engine-out conditions. Mass, altitude, temperature limitations and wind for the missed approach must all be considered. As an alternative, an increase in the DA/H or MDA/H and/or a contingency procedure (see JAR OPS 1.495(f)) providing a safe route and avoiding obstacles, can be approved.

AMC OPS 1.510 & 1.515 – Landing – Dry Runways

Pressure or geometric altitude may be used, but reflected in the Operations Manual.

1.515 - Landing – Dry Runways

The landing mass for the ETA must allow a full stop landing from 50 ft above the threshold within 60% of the landing distance available (turbojets), or 70% for turboprops. For steep approaches, factored data may be approved for a screen height between 35-50 ft. (see (see Appendix 1).

Short landings may be exceptionally approved if a need is demonstrated (Appendices 1 & 2), but the following must be taken into account:

- Altitude at the aerodrome

- Up to 50% of the headwind or at least 150% of the tailwind

- The slope in the direction of landing if greater than +/-2%

However, it must be assumed that the aeroplane will land on the most favourable runway, in still air, and the one most likely to be assigned given the probable wind speed and direction and ground handling characteristics of the aeroplane, and other conditions, such as landing aids and terrain (see IEM OPS 1.515(c)).

If an operator cannot comply with the above for a destination with a single runway where a landing depends upon a specified wind component, an aeroplane may be despatched if 2 alternates are designated which permit full compliance. Before starting an approach to land at the destination, the commander must satisfy himself that a landing can be made under JAR OPS 1.510 and the above.

If an operator cannot comply with the above for the destination, the aeroplane may be despatched if there is an alternate which permits full compliance.

IEM OPS 1.515(c)

There are two considerations when determining the max permissible landing mass. Firstly, the aeroplane must be landed within 60 or 70% of the landing distance available on the most favourable (normally the longest) runway in still air. *Regardless of the wind, the maximum landing mass for an aerodrome or aeroplane configuration at a particular aerodrome, cannot be exceeded.*

Secondly, consideration should be given to anticipated conditions and circumstances. The expected wind*, or ATC and noise abatement procedures, may indicate the use of a different runway. These may result in a lower landing mass than that above, in which case, to show compliance despatch should be based on this lesser mass.

*The expected wind is that expected to exist at the time of arrival.

Appendix 1

Steep Approaches
Steep Approaches with glideslope angles of 4.5° or more may be approved, with screen heights between 35-50 ft, if:

- The Flight Manual states the maximum approved glideslope angle, other limitations, normal, abnormal or emergency procedures as well as amendments to the field length data when using steep approach criteria

- A suitable glidepath reference system comprising at least a visual glidepath indicating system is available at each aerodrome where steep approaches are to be conducted

- Weather minima are specified and approved for each runway.

Consideration must be given to:

- obstacles

- the glidepath reference and runway guidance, such as visual aids, MLS, 3D–NAV, ILS, LLZ, VOR, NDB

- the minimum visual reference at DH and MDA

- Available airborne equipment

- Pilot qualification and special aerodrome familiarisation

- Flight Manual limitations and procedures

- Missed approach criteria

Short Landings
The distance used to calculate the permitted landing mass may consist of the usable length of the declared safe area, plus the declared landing distance available. Operations may be approved if there is a clear public interest and operational necessity for the operation, due to the remoteness of the airport or physical limitations relating to extending the runway.

Short landing operation will only be approved where the vertical distance between the path of the pilot's eye and the lowest part of the wheels, with the aeroplane on the normal glide path, does not exceed 3 m. When establishing operating minima, the visibility/RVR must be at least 1.5 km. In addition, wind limitations must be in the Ops Manual, as must minimum pilot experience, training requirements and special aerodrome familiarisation.

It is assumed that the crossing height over the beginning of the usable length of the declared safe area is 50 ft.

Additional conditions may be imposed as deemed necessary for a safe operation.

Appendix 2 – Short Landing Airfield Criteria
The use of the safe area must be approved by the airport authority. Its useable length must not exceed 90 metres, with a width of at least twice the runway width or twice the wing span, whichever is the greater, on the extended runway centre line.

The declared safe area must be clear of obstructions or depressions which would endanger an aeroplane undershooting, and no mobile object is allowed on it area while the runway is used for short landing operations.

The slope of the declared safe area must not exceed 5% upward nor 2% downward in the direction of landing.

For the purpose of this operation, bearing strength requirements (of JAR OPS 1.480(a)(5)) need not apply to the declared safe area.

1.520 - Landing – Wet and Contaminated Runways
If the runway at the ETA is likely to be **wet**, the landing distance available must be at least 115% of the required landing distance. A distance shorter than that, but at least that required by JAR OPS 1.515(a), may be used if the Flight Manual includes specific additional information.

If the runway is likely to be **contaminated**, the landing distance available must be the greater of at least the distance above, or 115% of the landing distance determined under approved contaminated landing distance data or equivalent. A distance shorter than that, but at least that required by JAR OPS 1.515(a), may be used if the Flight Manual includes specific additional information (JAR OPS 1.515(a)(1) and (2) do not apply).

1.525 – Performance Class B

Single-engined aeroplanes may not operate at night or in IMC, except under Special VFR.

Limitations on the operation of single-engined aeroplanes are covered by JAR OPS 1.240(a)(6).

Twin-engined aeroplanes which do not meet the climb requirements of Appendix 1* are treated as single-engined aeroplanes.

Appendix 1* - Takeoff and Landing, Climb

This Appendix is based on JAR 23.63(c)(1) and 23.63(c)(2).

Takeoff Climb

All Engines Operating

The steady gradient of climb must be at least 4% with takeoff power on each engine, gear extended (if it can be retracted in 7 seconds, it may be assumed to be retracted), flaps at takeoff, and a climb speed of at least the greater of 1.1 V_{MC} and 1.2 V_{S1}.

OEI

The steady gradient of climb at 400 ft above the takeoff surface must be measurably positive with the critical engine out and its propeller in the minimum drag position, and with the remaining engine at takeoff power, with gear retracted and flaps at takeoff, a climb speed equal to that achieved at 50 ft.

The steady gradient of climb must be at least 0.75% at 1500 ft above the takeoff surface with the critical engine out and its propeller in the minimum drag position, with the remaining engine at up to maximum continuous power, gear and flaps retracted, and a climb speed of at least 1.2 V_{S1}.

Landing Climb

All Engines Operating

The steady gradient of climb must be at least 2.5% with not more than the power or thrust available 8 seconds after initiation of movement of the power controls from the minimum flight idle position, gear extended, flaps at landing position and a climb speed equal to V_{REF}.

OEI

The steady gradient of climb must be at least 0.75% at 1500 ft above the takeoff surface with the critical engine out and its propeller in the minimum drag position, with the remaining engine at up to maximum continuous power, gear and flaps retracted, and a climb speed of at least 1.2 V_{S1}.

1.530 - Takeoff

Takeoff mass must not exceed the maximum in the Flight Manual for the pressure altitude and ambient temperature.

The unfactored takeoff distance must not exceed the takeoff run available (when multiplied by a factor of 1.25) or, when stopway and/or clearway is available, the takeoff run available:

- When multiplied by a factor of 1.15, the takeoff distance available

- When multiplied by a factor of 1.3, the accelerate-stop distance available

The following must be taken into account:

- Mass at the start of the takeoff run

- Pressure altitude and ambient temperature

- Runway surface condition, type and slope

- Up to 50% of the reported headwind or at least 150% of the tailwind.

AMC OPS 1.530(c)(4) - Correction Factors

Unless otherwise specified in the Flight Manual or equivalent, the variables affecting takeoff performance and associated factors are shown in the table below. They should be applied in addition to the factors in JAR OPS 1.530(b).

Surface	Condition	Factor
Grass (on firm soil) up to 20 cm long	Dry	1.20
	Wet	1.30
Paved	Wet	1.00

Soil is *firm* when there are wheel impressions but no rutting. When taking off on grass with a single-engined aeroplane, care should be taken to assess the rate of acceleration and consequent distance increase. When making a rejected takeoff on very short grass which is wet, and with a firm subsoil, the surface may be slippery, in which case the distances may increase significantly.

IEM OPS 1.530(c)(4)
Operations from contaminated runways should be avoided whenever possible, and you should delay takeoff until the runway is cleared, but, when this is impracticable, you should also consider the excess runway length available, including the criticality of the overrun area.

AMC OPS 1.530(c)(5) - Slope
Unless otherwise specified in the Flight Manual, takeoff distance should be increased by 5% for each 1% of upslope, except that correction factors for runways with slopes over 2% require approval.

1.535 - Obstacle Clearance – Multi-Engine
The takeoff flight path must clear all obstacles vertically by at least 50 ft, or horizontally by at least 90 m, plus 0.125 x D, where D is the horizontal distance travelled from the end of the TODA or the end of the takeoff distance if a turn is scheduled before the end of the TODA, except as provided below. For aeroplanes with a wingspan of less than 60 m, use half the wingspan plus 60 m, plus 0.125 x D instead. Assume that:

- The takeoff flight path begins at 50 ft above the surface at the end of the TODR (see JAR OPS 1.530(b)) and ends at 1500 ft above the surface

- There is no bank before 50 ft, and angle of bank is not over 15° afterwards

- Failure of the critical engine occurs where visual reference is expected to be lost

- The gradient from 50 ft to the assumed engine failure height is equal to the average all-engine gradient during climb and transition to the enroute configuration, multiplied by a factor of 0.77

- The gradient from the height above to the end of the takeoff flight path is equal to the OEI en-route gradient in the Flight Manual

Where the intended flight path does not require track changes over 15°, obstacles more than 300 m away need not be considered, if visual guidance is used, or if navaids enable you to maintain the flight path with the same accuracy (otherwise, ignore any over 600 m away. Where the intended flight path requires track changes of more than 15°, the figures change to 600 m and 900 m, respectively).

The following must be taken into account:

- Mass at the start of the takeoff run

- Pressure altitude and ambient temperature

- Runway surface condition, type and slope

- Up to 50% of the reported headwind or at least 150% of the tailwind.

Appendix 1– Visual Guidance Navigation
The weather at the time of operation, including ceiling and visibility, must allow obstacle and/or ground reference points to be seen and identified. The Ops Manual must specify minimum weather that enables flight crews to continuously determine and maintain the correct flight path to provide safe clearance with respect to obstructions and terrain.

The procedure must be well defined with respect to ground reference points, so that the track can be analysed for obstacle clearance requirements

The procedure must be within the capabilities of the aeroplane with respect to forward speed, bank angle and wind effects

A written and/or pictorial description must be provided for crew use, and the limiting environmental conditions must be specified (e.g. wind, cloud, visibility, day/night, ambient lighting, obstruction lighting).

IEM OPS 1.535 - Limited Visibility
The idea behind the complementary requirements JAR OPS 1.535 and Appendix 1 to JAR OPS 1.430 (a)(3)(ii) is to enhance safety with Performance B aeroplanes in limited visibility, which do not necessarily provide for engine failure in all phases

of flight. It is accepted that accountability for engine failure need not be considered until 300 ft.

The weather minima in Appendix 1 to JAR OPS 1.430 (a)(3)(ii) up to and including 300 ft imply that, if a takeoff is undertaken with minima below 300 ft, a one engine inoperative flight path must be plotted starting on the all-engine takeoff flight path at the assumed engine failure height. This path must meet the vertical and lateral obstacle clearance in JAR OPS 1.535. Should engine failure occur below this height, the associated visibility is taken as being the minimum which would enable the pilot to make, if necessary, a forced landing broadly in the direction of the takeoff, as, below 300 ft, a circle and land procedure is extremely inadvisable. Appendix 1 to JAR OPS 1.430 (a)(3)(ii) specifies that, if the assumed engine failure height is more than 300 ft, the visibility must be at least 1500 m and, to allow for manoeuvring, the same should apply whenever the obstacle clearance criteria for a continued takeoff cannot be met.

AMC OPS 1.535(a) - Flight Path Construction
For demonstrating that an aeroplane clears all obstacles vertically, a flight path should be constructed with an all-engine segment to the assumed engine failure height, followed by an engine-out segment. Where the Flight Manual does not contain appropriate data, the formulae in this section (not included here) may be used for the all-engine segment for an assumed engine failure height of 200 ft, 300 ft, or higher.

IEM OPS 1.535(a)
This IEM provides examples to illustrate the method of takeoff flight path construction given above – there are formulae and pictures which are not given here.

1.540 - En-Route – Multi-engined Aeroplanes
The aeroplane, in the expected meteorological conditions, and if an engine fails, with the others within maximum continuous power, must be capable of continuing at or above the relevant minimum safe altitudes in the Ops Manual to 1000 ft above an aerodrome at which the performance requirements can be met.

The aeroplane must not be assumed to be at a higher altitude than that at which the rate of climb equals 300 ft per minute* with all engines operating at maximum continuous power. The assumed en-

route gradient with OEI must be the gross gradient of descent or climb, respectively increased or decreased by a gradient of 0.5%.

IEM OPS 1.540*
This is not a restriction on the maximum cruising altitude, but merely the maximum altitude from which driftdown can be planned to start.

Aeroplanes may be planned to clear en-route obstacles assuming a driftdown procedure, having first increased the scheduled en-route OEI descent data by 0.5% gradient.

1.542 - En-Route – Single-engined Aeroplanes
The aeroplane, in the expected weather conditions, and if an engine fails, must be able to reach a place where a safe forced landing can be made. For landplanes, this means on land, unless otherwise approved (see AMC OPS 1.542(a)).

The aeroplane must not be assumed to be flying, with the engine within maximum continuous power conditions specified, higher than that at which the rate of climb equals 300 ft per minute, and the assumed en-route gradient must be the gross gradient of descent increased by 0.5%.

IEM OPS 1.542 – Cloud Below MSA
If an engine fails, single-engined aeroplanes have to rely on gliding to a suitable safe forced landing point, which is clearly incompatible with flight above a cloud layer which extends below MSA. In such cases, the scheduled engine-inoperative gliding performance data should be increased by 0.5% gradient.

The altitude where the rate of climb equals 300 ft per minute is not a restriction on the maximum cruising altitude, but the maximum altitude from which engine-out procedures can be planned.

AMC OPS 1.542(a)
If an engine fails, the aeroplane should be able to reach a point from where a successful forced landing can be made which, unless otherwise specified, should be 1000ft above the intended landing area.

1.545 - Landing – Destination & Alternates
The landing mass must not exceed the maximum for the altitude and temperature expected for the estimated time of landing.

AMC OPS 1.545 & 1.550 - Dry Runway
Use pressure or geometric altitude; reflect this in the Operations Manual.

1.550 - Landing – Dry Runway
The landing mass for the estimated time of landing must allow a full stop landing from 50 ft above the threshold within 70% of the LDA, although a screen height between 35-50 ft may be approved (if you say please). Short Landing Operations may also be approved (pretty please). See Appendix 2.

The following must be taken into account:

- Altitude

- Runway surface condition, type and slope

- Up to 50% of the reported headwind or at least 150% of the tailwind.

Assume that the aeroplane will land on the most favourable runway, in still air, and the one most likely to be assigned, considering probable wind speed and direction, ground handling characteristics, and other conditions, such as landing aids and terrain. If this cannot be complied with for the destination, the aeroplane may still be despatched if an alternate permits full compliance.

Appendix 1 - Steep Approaches
Steep Approaches with glideslope angles of 4.5° or more may be approved, with screen heights between 35-50 ft, if:

- The Flight Manual states the maximum approved glideslope angle, other limitations, normal, abnormal or emergency procedures as well as amendments to the field length data when using steep approach criteria

- A suitable glidepath reference system comprising at least a visual glidepath indicating system is available at each aerodrome where steep approaches are to be conducted

- Weather minima are specified and approved for each runway.

Consideration must be given to:

- obstacles

- the glidepath reference and runway guidance, such as visual aids, MLS, 3D–NAV, ILS, LLZ, VOR, NDB

- the minimum visual reference at DH and MDA

- Available airborne equipment

- Pilot qualification and special aerodrome familiarisation

- Flight Manual limitations and procedures

- Missed approach criteria

Appendix 2 - Short Landings
The distance used to calculate landing mass may consist of the usable length of the declared safe area, plus the landing distance available. Operations may be approved if the use of the safe area is approved by the aerodrome authority, and is clear of obstructions or depressions which would endanger an undershooting aeroplane, with no mobile object permitted on it while the runway is used for short landing operations.

The slope must not exceed 5% upward nor 2% downward in the direction of landing, and its useable length must not exceed 90 metres, with width is be at least twice the runway width, centred on the extended runway centreline.

It is assumed that the crossing height over the start of the usable length is at least 50 ft.

For the purpose of this operation, the bearing strength requirement of JAR OPS 1.480(a)(5) need not apply to the declared safe area.

Weather minima must be specified and approved for each runway, being at least the greater of VFR or non-precision approach minima.

Pilot requirements must be specified (see 1.975(a))

AMC OPS 1.550(b)(3) - Landing Distance Correction Factors
Unless otherwise specified in the Flight Manual, the variables affecting landing performance and associated factors are shown in the table below. They should be applied in addition to the factors in JAR OPS 1.530(a).

Surface	Factor
Grass (on firm soil) up to 20 cm long	1.15

Soil is firm when there are wheel impressions but no rutting.

AMC OPS 1.550(b)(4) - Runway Slope
Landing distances required should be increased by 5% for each 1% of downslope, except that corrections for slopes over 2% need approval.

IEM OPS 1.550(c) - Landing – Dry Runway
On arrival, the mass must allow landing within 70% of the LDA on the most favourable (normally the longest) runway in still air. Regardless of the wind, the maximum cannot be exceeded.

Consideration should also be given to anticipated conditions and circumstances. The expected wind*, or ATC and noise abatement procedures, may indicate the use of a different runway that may result in a lower landing mass than before.

*That expected to exist at the time of arrival.

1.555 - Landing – Wet & Contaminated Runways
When appropriate weather reports or forecasts indicate that the runway at the ETA may be **wet**, the LDA must be equal to or exceed the required landing distance multiplied by a factor of 1.15 (although it may be shorter, giving due consideration to JAR OPS 1.550(a), if the Flight Manual includes specific additional information. When it is **contaminated**, the landing distance must not exceed the LDA.

IEM OPS 1.555(a) - Wet Grass Runways
On very short wet grass, with a firm subsoil, the slippery surface may increase distances by as much as 60% (1.60 factor). As it may not be possible to determine the degree of wetness when airborne, in case of doubt, use the wet factor (1.15).

1.560 – Performance Class C
Performance data in the Flight Manual must be supplemented, as necessary, with other acceptable data if it isn't good enough.

1.565 - Takeoff
The takeoff mass must not exceed the maximum in the Flight Manual for the pressure altitude and ambient temperature.

For aeroplanes with Flight Manuals that do not cover engine failure, the distance from the start of the takeoff roll to reach 50 ft above the surface with all engines operating within maximum takeoff power conditions, when multiplied by a factor of either 1.33 (for aeroplanes with two engines), 1.25 (three), or 1.18 (four), must not exceed the TORA.

Otherwise:

- The accelerate-stop distance must not exceed ASDA

- Takeoff distance must not exceed TODA, with a clearway up to half TORA

- The takeoff run must not exceed the TORA

- Compliance must be shown with a single value of V1 for the rejected and continued takeoff, and, on wet or contaminated runways, mass must not exceed that for a dry runway under the same conditions.

The following must be taken into account:

- Mass at the start of the takeoff run

- Pressure altitude and ambient temperature

- Runway surface condition, type and slope

- Up to 50% of the reported headwind or at least 150% of the tailwind.

- Loss of runway length due to alignment before takeoff.

IEM OPS 1.565(d)(3)
Operation on runways contaminated with water, slush, snow or ice implies uncertainties with regard to runway friction and contaminant drag, and therefore to achievable performance and control during takeoff, since the actual conditions may not completely match the assumptions on which performance information is based. An adequate overall level of safety can, therefore, only be maintained if such operations are limited to rare occasions. The first option is to wait until the runway is cleared. If this is impracticable, you may consider a takeoff, if you have applied applicable performance adjustments, and any further safety measures considered justified under the conditions.

AMC OPS 1.565(d)(4) - Runway Slope

Takeoff distance should be increased by 5% for each 1% of upslope, except that correction factors for runways with slopes over 2% need approval.

IEM OPS 1.565(d)(6) - Loss of Runway Length Due to Alignment

Same as IEM OPS 1.490(c)(6).

1.570 - Takeoff Obstacle Clearance

The flight path with OEI must clear all obstacles vertically by at least 50 ft plus 0.01 x D, or horizontally by at least 90 m plus 0.125 x D, where D is the horizontal distance from the end of the TODA. For aeroplanes with a wingspan of less than 60 m, you can use a horizontal obstacle clearance of half the wingspan plus 60 m, plus 0.125 x D instead.

The flight path must begin at 50 ft above the surface at the end of the TODR by JAR OPS 1.565(b) or as applicable, and end at 1 500 ft above the surface.

The following must be taken into account:

- Mass at the start of the takeoff run
- Pressure altitude and ambient temperature
- Up to 50% of the reported headwind or at least 150% of the tailwind.

Track changes are not allowed up to 50 ft. Up to 400 ft, it is assumed that the aeroplane is banked by no more than 15°. Above 400 ft, bank angles between 15-25° may be scheduled.

Where track changes more than 15° are not required, obstacles further away than 300 m need not be considered if you can maintain the required navigational accuracy. Otherwise, try 600 m.

Where track changes more than 15° are required, the figures change to 600 and 900 m, respectively.

AMC OPS 1.570(d) - Takeoff Flight Path

Same as AMC OPS 1.495(c)(4).

AMC OPS 1.570(e)(1) & (f)(1) - Required Navigational Accuracy

Looks the same as AMC OPS 1.495(d)(1) & (e)(1).

1.575 - En-Route – All Engines Operating

The aeroplane must, in the expected weather, be able to climb at least 300 ft per minute with all engines operating at maximum continuous power at the minimum safe altitudes, and the minimum altitudes for compliance with the conditions in JAR OPS 1.580 and 1.585, as appropriate.

1.580 - En-Route – One Engine Inoperative

The aeroplane must, in the expected weather, if an engine fails, and with the others within maximum continuous power conditions, be able to continue from cruising altitude to where a landing can be made under JAR OPS 1.595 or 1.600, clearing obstacles within 9.3 km (5 nm) either side of track vertically by at least 1000 ft when the rate of climb is zero or greater, or 2000 ft when the rate of climb is less than zero (18.5 km (10 nm) if the navigational accuracy does not meet the 95% containment level).

The flight path must have a positive slope at 450 m (1 500 ft) above the aerodrome where the landing is assumed to be made after one engine fails. The available rate of climb is taken to be 150 ft per minute less than the gross rate specified.

Fuel jettisoning is allowed, consistent with reaching the aerodrome with the required fuel reserves, if a safe procedure is used.

AMC OPS 1.580

The high terrain or obstacle analysis can be done with a detailed analysis using contour maps, and plotting the highest points within the prescribed corridor width. The next step is to determine whether it is possible to maintain level flight with one engine out 1000 ft above the highest point of the crossing. If this is not possible, or if the associated weight penalties are unacceptable, a drift-down procedure must be evaluated, based on engine failure at the most critical point, and must show obstacle clearance during the drift-down by at least 2000 ft. The minimum cruise altitude is determined from the drift-down path, taking into account allowances for decision making, and the reduction in the scheduled rate of climb.

1.585 - En-Route – Aeroplanes With Three Or More Engines, Two Engines Inoperative

At no point will an aeroplane with three or more engines be more than 90 minutes, at the all-engines long range cruising speed at standard temperature in still air, away from a suitable aerodrome, unless:

- The two engines inoperative en-route net flight path allows the flight to continue, in expected weather, to a suitable aerodrome, clearing vertically, by at least 2 000 ft, all terrain and obstructions within 9.3 km (5 nm) either side of the track. If navigational accuracy does not meet 95% containment, increase the width to 18.5 km (10 nm).

- The two engines are assumed to fail at the most critical point where the route is more than 90 minutes (at the all engines long range cruising speed, etc. etc.), away from a suitable aerodrome.

- Fuel jettisoning is allowed, consistent with reaching the aerodrome with required fuel reserves, if a safe procedure is used

- The expected mass where the two engines are assumed to fail must allow for enough fuel to proceed to a suitable aerodrome, and to arrive there at least 1 500 ft directly over the landing area and thereafter to fly level for 15 minutes.

The available rate of climb is taken to be 150 ft per minute less than that specified.

1.590 - Landing – Destinations and Alternates
The landing mass must not exceed that in the Flight Manual for the altitude and temperature at the ETA.

AMC OPS 1.590 & 1.595
Use either pressure or geometric altitude, as should be reflected in the Operations Manual.

1.595 - Landing – Dry Runways
The landing mass for the ETA must allow a full stop landing from 50 ft above the threshold within 70% of the LDA.

The following must be taken into account:

- Altitude at the aerodrome

- Up to 50% of the headwind component or at least 150% of the tailwind

- The slope and type of runway

However, it must be assumed that the aeroplane will land on the most favourable runway, in still air, and the one most likely to be assigned given the probable wind speed and direction and ground handling characteristics of the aeroplane, and other conditions, such as landing aids and terrain (see IEM OPS 1.515(c)).

If an operator cannot comply with the above for a destination with a single runway where a landing depends upon a specified wind component, an aeroplane may be despatched if 2 alternates are designated which permit full compliance. Before starting an approach to land at the destination, the commander must satisfy himself that a landing can be made under JAR OPS 1.510 and the above.

If an operator cannot comply with the above for the destination, the aeroplane may be despatched if there is an alternate which permits full compliance.

AMC OPS 1.595(b)(3) - Landing Distance Correction Factors
Same as AMC OPS 1.550(b)(3).

AMC OPS 1.595(b)(4) - Runway Slope
Same as AMC OPS 1.550(b)(4).

IEM OPS 1.595(c) - Landing Runway
Same as AMC OPS 1.550(c).

1.600 - Landing – Wet and Contaminated Runways
When appropriate weather reports or forecasts indicate that the runway at the ETA may be **wet**, the LDA must be equal to or exceed the required landing distance multiplied by 1.15 (although it may be shorter, giving due consideration to JAR OPS 1.550(a)), if the Flight Manual includes specific additional information. When it is **contaminated**, the landing distance must not exceed the LDA.

1.605 – Mass and Balance
The loading, mass and centre of gravity must comply with the more restrictive limitations of the Flight Manual or the Ops Manual.

Mass and C of G must be established by actual weighing before initial entry into service, and thereafter every 4 years, if individual masses are used, and 9 years for fleet masses. The accumulated effects of modifications and repairs must be accounted for and properly documented - aeroplanes must be reweighed if the effects are not accurately known.

The mass of all operating items and crew members in the dry operating mass must be determined by weighing or using standard masses, as must the influence of their position on the C of G.

The mass of the traffic load, including ballast, must be determined by actual weighing or under standard passenger and baggage masses (see JAR OPS 1.620).

The mass of the fuel load must be found with the actual density* or, if not known, an alternative method in the Ops Manual.

IEM OPS 1.605(e) - *Fuel Density

If the actual density is not known, you can use the standard density values in the Ops Manual, which should be based on current measurements for the airports or areas concerned. Typical values are:

- AVGAS – 0.71
- JP 1 – 0.79
- JP 4 – 0.76
- Oil – 0.88

ACJ OPS 1.605 - Mass Values

Weight is a force rather than a mass, but the words can be used interchangeably.

Appendix 1

Determination of DOM

Weighing of Aeroplanes

New aeroplanes are normally weighed at the factory and may be operated without reweighing if the mass and balance records have been adjusted for alterations or modifications. Aeroplanes transferred from one JAA operator with an approved mass control program to another need not be weighed unless more than 4 years have elapsed since the last weighing.

Individual mass and C of G positions are re-established periodically (by weighing or calculation*), as in JAR OPS 1.605(b).

*Whenever the cumulative changes exceed ± 0.5% of the maximum landing mass, or the cumulative change in C of G position exceeds 0.5% of the MAC.

Fleet Mass and C of G Position

For a fleet or group of aeroplanes of the same model and configuration, an average DOM and C of G position may be used, if individual ones meet tolerances below. Sub-paragraphs (iii), (iv) and (a)(3) are also applicable.

Tolerances

If the DOM of any aeroplane weighed, or the calculated DOM of any aeroplane of a fleet, varies by more than ±0.5% of the maximum structural landing mass from the fleet mass, or the C of G position varies by more than ±0.5 % of the MAC from the fleet C of G, that aeroplane must be dishonourably discharged from the fleet (joke). Separate fleets may be established, each with differing mean masses.

Where the mass is within the tolerance but the C of G position isn't, the aeroplane may still be operated, but with an individual C of G position.

Individual aeroplanes with differences that cause exceedance of fleet tolerances may be kept in the fleet, if appropriate corrections are applied to mass and/or C of G position.

Aeroplanes with no published MAC must operate with their individual mass and C of G, or be subject to special study and approval.

Use of Fleet Values

After weighing, or if any change occurs in equipment or configuration, the aeroplane must fall within the tolerances above.

Aeroplanes which have not been weighed since the last fleet evaluation can still be kept in the fleet, if the individual values are revised by computation and stay in the tolerances. If they don't, the operator must either determine new fleet values or operate the aeroplanes with their individual values.

To add an aeroplane to a fleet, the operator must verify by weighing or computation that actual values fall within the tolerances.

Fleet values must be updated at least at the end of each fleet evaluation.

Number of Aeroplanes to be Weighed
There is a formula for calculating this, which is not included here. Those that have not been weighed for the longest time must be selected.

The interval between 2 fleet mass evaluations must not be over 48 months.

Weighing Procedure
This must be done either by the manufacturer or an AMO. Normal precautions must be taken, consistent with good practices such as checking for completeness of the aeroplane and equipment, determining that fluids are properly accounted for, ensuring that the aeroplane is clean and that it is done in an enclosed building.

Equipment must be properly calibrated, zeroed, and used under the manufacturer's instructions. Each scale must be calibrated either by the manufacturer, a civil department of weights and measures or an appropriately authorised organisation within 2 years, or a time period defined by the manufacturer, whichever is less.

Special Standard Masses
In addition to standard masses for passengers and checked baggage, an operator can submit them for other items.

Aeroplane Loading
Loading must be supervised by qualified people, consistent with the data used for calculation of aeroplane mass and balance.

Additional structural limits must be observed, such as floor strength, maximum per running metre, maximum per cargo compartment, and/or the maximum seating limits.

Centre of Gravity Limits
Unless seat allocation is applied and the effects of the number of passengers per seat row, of cargo in individual compartments and fuel in individual tanks is accounted for accurately, operational margins must be applied to the certificated C of G envelope.

Possible deviations from the assumed load distribution must be considered.

If free seating is applied, there must be a way of ensuring corrective action if extreme longitudinal seat selection occurs. The C of G margins and operational procedures, including assumptions with regard to passenger seating, must be acceptable (see IEM to Appendix 1 to JAR OPS 1.605 subpara (d))

In-flight Centre of Gravity
Further to the above, procedures must fully account for the extreme variation in C of G travel caused by passenger/crew movement and fuel consumption/transfer.

AMC to Appendix 1 - Accuracy of Equipment
The mass of the aeroplane must be established accurately, but single criteria for weighing equipment cannot be given. However, accuracy is considered satisfactory if the following are met by individual scales or cells:

- Scale/cell loads below 2 000 kg: $\pm$ 1%

- Scale/cells loads 2000-20000 kg: $\pm$ 20 kg

- Scale/cell loads above 20 000 kg: $\pm$ 0.1%

IEM to Appendix 1 – C of G Limits
In the Limitations section of the Flight Manual, forward and aft C of G limits are specified, which ensure that certification stability and control criteria are met throughout the flight and allow the proper trim setting for takeoff. These limits must be observed by defining operational procedures or a C of G envelope which compensates for deviations and errors as listed below:

- Deviations of actual C of G, empty or operating, from published values due to weighing errors, modifications, etc

- Deviations in fuel distribution

- Deviations in baggage and cargo distribution from the assumed distribution, plus errors in mass calculation

- Deviations in actual seating from that assumed when preparing documentation*

- Deviations of actual C of G of cargo and passenger load within individual compartments or cabin sections from the normally assumed mid position

- Deviations of the C of G caused by gear and flap positions and application of fuel usage procedures (unless already covered by the certified limits)

- Deviations caused by in-flight movement of crew, pantry equipment and passengers

*Large C of G errors may occur when free seating is allowed (that is, for passengers to select any seat). Although reasonably even longitudinal passenger seating can mostly be expected, there is a risk of an extreme forward or aft selection causing very large and unacceptable C of G errors (assuming the balance calculation is done on an assumed even distribution). The largest errors may occur at a load factor of around 50% if all passengers are in either the forward or aft half of the cabin. Statistics show that the risk is greatest on small aeroplanes.

1.607 – Terminology

See *Terms & Definitions.*

1.610 - Loading, Mass and Balance

The Ops Manual must contain the principles and methods involved in loading and mass and balance systems under JAR OPS 1.605. The system must cover all types of intended operation.

1.615 - Mass Values For Crew

Use actual masses, including crew baggage, or standard masses, including hand baggage, of 85 kg for flight crew and 75 kg for cabin crew, or anything else otherwise approved. The DOM and C of G must be corrected for additional baggage.

1.620 - Mass Values for Pax and Baggage

Use actual values or the standard ones in the tables below, except where there are less than 10 seats available, in which case you can use a verbal statement by or on behalf of each passenger with a predetermined constant for hand baggage and clothing (see AMC below). When to select either must be in the Ops Manual.

If determining actual mass by weighing, include personal belongings and hand baggage, and do it immediately before boarding, and nearby.

If using standard values, use Tables 1 and 2 below. They include hand baggage and infants below 2 carried by an adult on one passenger seat. Infants occupying separate seats are children.

20 Passenger Seats or More

With 30 or more seats, *All Adult* values apply.

Pax Seats	20 +	30 and more	
	Male	*Female*	*All Adult*
Non-charters	88 kg	70 kg	84 kg
Holiday charters	83 kg	69 kg	76 kg
Children (2-12)	35 kg	35 kg	35 kg

Holiday charter means part of holiday packages. Mass values apply with up to 5% of seats used for certain non-revenue passengers (see IEM).

Checked Baggage

Type of Flight	Standard Mass
Domestic	11 kg
Within Europe	13 kg
Intercontinental	15 kg
All Other	13 kg

With 19 passenger seats or less, use actual mass. *Domestic flight* means one with origin and destination(s) within one state, *within Europe* means flights, other than Domestic, with origin and destination in the EEC (see Appendix 1), and *Intercontinental flight*, other than in Europe, means with origin and destination in different continents.

19 Passenger Seats or Less

Pax Seats	1–5	6–9	10–19
Male	104 kg	96 kg	92 kg
Female	86 kg	78 kg	74 kg
Children 2-12	35 kg	35 kg	35 kg

Use actual baggage values. With no hand baggage, or if separate, deduct 6 kg from male and female (except overcoats, umbrellas, handbags, etc). With more than usual large passengers, use actual values or add an increment. The same goes for baggage. The commander must be advised when a non-standard method has been used. It must be stated in mass and balance documentation.

Appendix 1 (f) - Flights Within Europe
For JAR OPS 1.620(f), flights within the European region (other than domestic ones), are conducted within the area bounded by rhumb lines between:

N7200 E04500   N4000 E04500

N3500 E03700   N3000 E03700

N3000 W00600   N2700 W00900

N2700 W03000   N6700 W03000

N7200 W01000   N7200 E04500

There is also a map, not included here.

Appendix 1 (g) - Revised Standard Values
Average mass with hand baggage must be determined by weighing random samples, based on normal statistical analysis (sample sizes, according to aeroplane size, etc. are not given here).

Baggage follows essentially the same idea. At least 2000 pieces of checked baggage must be weighed.

On aeroplanes with 20 or more passenger seats, these averages apply as revised standard male and female mass values. On smaller aeroplanes, the following increments must be added to average passenger mass to obtain the revised values:

Pax Seats	Increment
1 – 5	16 kg
6 – 9	8 kg
10 – 19	4 kg

Alternatively, adult revised values may be applied on aeroplanes with 30 or more passenger seats. Revised baggage values apply to aeroplanes with 20 or more passenger seats. Deviations must be approved and reviewed at least every 5 years.

Adult revised values are based on a male/female ratio of 80/20, except for holiday charters, which are 50/50. Different suggestions must show that the alternative ratio is conservative and covers at least 84% of the actual ratios on a sample of at least 100 representative flights.

The average values are rounded to the nearest whole number in kg. Checked baggage values are rounded to the nearest 0.5 kg, as appropriate.

AMC OPS 1.620(a) – Verbal Statements
Specific constants should be added to account for hand baggage and clothing. They should be determined on the basis of studies relevant to particular routes, etc. and should be at least 4 kg for clothing and 6 kg for hand baggage.

Stated masses should be checked to see if they are reasonable (assessors must be trained)

IEM OPS 1.620(d)(2) - Holiday Charter
A *charter flight solely intended as an element of a holiday travel package* is one where the entire capacity is hired by one or more Charterer(s) for passengers travelling, all or in part by air, on a round- or circle-trip. Company personnel, tour staff, the press, JAA/Authority officials etc. can be included within the 5% alleviation without negating mass values.

IEM OPS 1.620(g) - Statistical Evaluation
You're not *really* interested in this are you? ☺

IEM OPS 1.620(h) & (i) - Adjustment
When standard mass values are used, JAR OPS 1.620 (h) and 1.620(i) require the operator to identify and adjust passenger and baggage masses where significant numbers may exceed standard values. This implies that the Ops Manual should ensure that check-in, operations and cabin staff and loading personnel report or take appropriate action when such a flight is identified. On small aeroplanes, where risks of overload and/or C of G errors are the greatest, commanders should pay special attention to the load and its distribution.

AMC to Appendix 1 – Survey Guidance
Weighing surveys may be pooled by operators on similar routes or networks, under conditions specified here.

IEM to Appendix 1 - Survey Guidance
This IEM summarises several elements of passenger weighing surveys and provides explanatory and interpretative information.

The weighing survey report should be prepared in a standard format not included here.

1.625 - Mass and Balance Documentation
This must be established before each flight, and specify the load and its distribution. The documentation must enable the commander to determine that mass and balance limits are not exceeded. The person preparing the documentation must be named on it. The person supervising the loading must confirm by signature that the load and its distribution are under it. This must be

acceptable to the commander, his acceptance being indicated by countersignature or equivalent (see also JAR OPS 1.1055(a)(12)).

There must be Last Minute Change procedures. Subject to approval, alternatives may be used.

Appendix 1

Mass and balance documentation must contain the following information:

- Registration and type
- Flight identification and date
- Identity of Commander
- Who prepared the document
- DOM dry operating mass and C of G
- Mass of fuel at takeoff and trip fuel
- Mass of consumables other than fuel
- Components of the load including passengers, baggage, freight and ballast
- Takeoff, Landing and Zero Fuel Mass
- Load distribution
- C of G positions
- Limiting mass and C of G values

Subject to approval, some of this may be left out.

Last Minute Changes

If any occur after the documentation is done, this must be brought to the attention of the commander, and the change entered. The maximum allowed changes must be in the Ops Manual. If this is exceeded, new documentation must be prepared.

Computerised Systems

The integrity of the system's output must be verified. Amendments must be incorporated properly and the system operating correctly on a continuous basis by verifying the output up to every 6 months.

Onboard Systems

Approval must be obtained to use one as a primary source for despatch.

Datalink

A copy of final documentation as accepted by the commander must be on the ground.

IEM to Appendix 1

For Performance Class B, the C of G position need not be mentioned on mass and balance documentation if, for example, the distribution is under a precalculated balance table, or if it can be shown that a correct balance can be ensured, whatever the real load is.

1.630 – Instruments & Equipment

Flights may not start unless required instruments and equipment are approved (but see below), and installed under the relevant requirements, including minimum performance standards and operational and airworthiness requirements, and working.

Minimum performance standards are in *Joint Technical Standard Orders* (JTSO) as in JAR TSO, unless different standards are prescribed in operational or airworthiness codes.

The following items are not required to have an equipment approval:

- Fuses referred in JAR OPS 1.635
- Electric torches in JAR OPS 1.640(a)(4)
- Accurate time piece in JAR OPS 1.650(b) & 1.652(b)
- Chart holder in JAR OPS 1.652(n)
- First aid kits in JAR OPS 1.745
- Emergency medical kit in JAR OPS 1.755
- Megaphones in JAR OPS 1.810
- Survival and pyrotechnic equipment in JAR OPS 1.835(a) and (c)
- Sea anchors and equipment for mooring, anchoring or manoeuvring seaplanes and amphibians in JAR OPS 1.840

Equipment and Instruments must be readily operable or viewable from where they are used.

IEM OPS 1.630 - Approval and Installation

Instruments and Equipment approved otherwise than in JTSOs, before the applicability dates in JAR OPS 1.001(b), are acceptable for commercial air transportation, if relevant JAR OPS requirements are complied with.

When a new version of a JTSO (or other specification) is issued, Instruments and Equipment approved under earlier requirements may be used or installed if they are operational, unless removal or withdrawal is required by amendments to JAR OPS 1 or JAR 26.

1.635 - Circuit Protection Devices
You need at least 10% of spare fuses relative to the number of each rating, or three of each rating, whichever is the greater.

1.640 - Operating Lights
By **day**, aeroplanes must have:

- Anti-collision lights

- Lighting from the electrical system for instruments and equipment essential to safe operation, and for passenger compartments

- An electric torch for each crew member, readily accessible at their stations

By **night**, this as well:

- Navigation/position lights

- Two landing lights or a single light with two separately energised filaments

- Lights to conform with International regulations for preventing collisions at sea (if a Seaplane or Amphibian)

1.645 - Windshield Wipers
Aeroplanes over 5 700 kg must have a windshield wiper or equivalent at each pilot station.

1.650 - Day VFR
This equipment is required:

- Magnetic compass

- Accurate timepiece showing hours, minutes, and seconds

- Sensitive pressure altimeter in feet with a sub-scale setting in hectopascals/millibars, adjustable for any likely pressure

- ASI calibrated in knots

- VSI

- Turn and slip indicator, or turn coordinator incorporating a slip indicator

- Attitude indicator

- Stabilised direction indicator

- OAT indicator in °C for the crew compartment (see below)

Where two pilots are required, the second pilot's station must have:

- Sensitive pressure altimeter in feet with a sub-scale setting in hectopascals/millibars, adjustable for any likely pressure

- ASI calibrated in knots

- VSI

- Turn and slip indicator, or turn coordinator incorporating a slip indicator

- Attitude indicator

For flights under 1 hour, taking off and landing at the same aerodrome, and remaining within 50 nm, the turn and slip, attitude and stabilised direction indicators may be replaced by either a turn and slip indicator, a turn coordinator with a slip indicator, or an attitude and a slip indicator.

Airspeed indicating systems for aeroplanes over 5700 kg or with more than 9 passenger seats, or those with a JAA C of A issued on or after 1 April 1999, must have a heated pitot tube or equivalent.

Whenever duplicates are required, the requirement embraces separate displays for each pilot and separate selectors, etc. appropriate.

Aeroplanes must have a means for indicating when power is not adequately supplied to instruments, and those with compressibility limitations not otherwise indicated by the ASI need a Mach number indicator at each pilot's station.

Each flight crew member must also have a headset with boom microphone.

AMC OPS 1.650/1.652
Individual requirements may be met by combinations of instruments or integrated flight systems, or a combination of parameters on

electronic displays, if the information available is at least that normally provided.

Equipment may be substituted by alternative means with equivalent safety.

IEM OPS 1.650/1.652

This is just a big chart summarising the above, but, for **IFR or at night**, a Turn and Slip indicator, or a slip indicator and a third (standby) attitude indicator certified under JAR 25.1303(b)(4) or equivalent, as required. Three Pointer and Drum Pointer altimeters do not satisfy the requirements.

AMC OPS 1.650(i) & 1.652(i)

An OAT indicator may be a temperature indicator providing indications convertible to OAT.

IEM OPS 1.650(p)/1.652(s) - Headset, Boom Mike and Associated Equipment

A headset, as required by JAR OPS 1.650(p) and 1.652(s), has an earphone (or earphones) to receive, and a microphone to transmit, audio signals to the aeroplane's communication system. They should naturally match the system's characteristics and the flight deck environment. Headsets should be adequately adjustable. Boom microphones should be noise-cancelling.

1.652 - IFR or Night – Flight and Navigational Instruments and Associated Equipment

Aeroplanes must have flight and navigational instruments and associated equipment as follows:

- Magnetic compass
- Accurate timepiece showing hours, minutes and seconds
- Two sensitive pressure altimeters calibrated in feet with sub-scales in hectopascals or millibars, adjustable for likely barometric pressures.
- ASI with heated pitot tube or equivalent, with a warning indication of heater failure (except with 9 or less passenger seats or below 5700 kg, and C of A before 1 April 1998)
- VSI
- Turn and slip indicator

- Attitude indicator
- Stabilised Direction Indicator
- A means of indicating in the flight crew compartment the OAT in °C
- Two independent static systems, except that propeller driven aeroplanes of 5 700 kg or less can have one
- A chart holder in an easily readable position which can be lit at night

When two pilots are required, the second pilot's station must have separate instruments as follows:

- Two sensitive pressure altimeters calibrated in feet with sub-scale settings in hectopascals/millibars, adjustable for likely barometric pressures (it may be one of the 2 altimeters above)
- An ASI with heated pitot tube or equivalent, with a warning indication of heater failure (except with 9 or less passenger seats or below 5700 kg, and C of A before 1 April 1998
- VSI
- Turn and slip indicator
- Attitude indicator
- Stabilised Direction Indicator

Aeroplanes over 5 700 kg or with more than 9 passenger seats must have an additional, separate, standby, attitude indicator (artificial horizon), capable of use from either pilot's station, normally powered continuously, but automatically for at least 30 minutes, taking other loads into account, from an independent source after the normal generating system fails. It must be appropriately illuminated during all phases of operation, except for aeroplanes of 5 700 kg or less, already registered in a JAA State on 1 April 1995, with one on the left-hand instrument panel. It must be clear when it is on emergency power, or when it own system is in use, if it has one

If the standby attitude system is certified under JAR 25.1303(b)(4) or equivalent, the turn and slip indicators may be replaced by slip indicators.

Whenever duplicate instruments are required, the requirement includes separate displays for each pilot and separate selectors or other equipment.

There must be a way of indicating when power is not there for flight instruments, and those with compressibility limitations not shown by ASIs need a Mach number indicator at each pilot station.

There must also be a headset with a boom microphone or equivalent for each crew member, with a transmit button on the control wheel.

AMC OPS 1.652(d) & (k)(2)
A combined pitot heater warning indicator is OK, if you can identify the failed heater in systems with two or more sensors.

1.655 - Additional Equipment - Single Pilot IFR
Aeroplanes must have an autopilot with at least altitude hold and heading mode.

1.660 - Altitude Alerting System
Turboprops over 5 700 kg or with more than 9 passenger seats, or turbojets, must have altitude alerting systems that can warn the flight crew on approaching, or deviating from, a preselected altitude (by at least an aural signal), except for aeroplanes below 5 700 kg or less with more than 9 passenger seats and first certificated before 1 April 1972 and already registered in a JAA Member State on 1 April 1995.

1.665 – GPWS & TAWS
Turbojets over 5 700 kg or with more than 9 passenger seats need a GPWS, except those between 5 700-15 000 kg or with between 9-30 passenger seats on or after 1 January 2003 for aeroplanes first certificated on or after 1 January 2003, or 1 October 2001 for aeroplanes without a GPWS, unless they have one with a forward looking terrain avoidance function (TAWS).

The GPWS must automatically provide, with aural and maybe visual signals, timely and distinctive warning of sink rate, ground proximity, altitude loss after takeoff or go-around, incorrect landing configuration and downward glideslope deviation.

Turbojets over 15 000 kg or with more than 30 passenger seats on or after 1 October 2001 for aeroplanes first certificated on or after this date, or 1 January 2005 for aeroplanes first certificated before 1 October 2001, unless they have a GPWS

that includes a forward looking terrain avoidance function (TAWS).

TAWS must automatically provide crews, visually and aurally (using a Terrain Awareness Display), with enough time to prevent CFIT, plus a forward looking capability and terrain clearance floor.

1.668 - Airborne Collision Avoidance System
Turbojets over 15 000 kg or with more than 30 passenger seats after 1 January 2000, or those between 5 700-15 000 kg, or with between 19-30 passenger seats, after 1 January 2005, need an airborne collision avoidance system with a minimum performance of at least ACAS II.

IEM OPS 1.668
The minimum performance level for ACAS II is in ICAO Annex 10, Volume IV, Chapter 4.

1.670 - Airborne Weather Radar
Pressurised aeroplanes, or unpressurised ones over 5 700 kg or with more than 9 passenger seats need AWR at night or in IMC where thunderstorms or other potentially hazardous weather conditions, which may detectable with it, might be expected along the route.

Prop-driven pressurised aeroplanes up to 5 700 kg and with up to 9 passenger seats may use thunderstorm detection equipment instead.

1.675 – Icing Equipment
Aeroplanes may not be operated in expected or actual icing conditions unless they are certificated and equipped for it. At night, a means to illuminate or detect the formation of ice is needed as well, as long as it doesn't cause glare or reflection.

1.680 - Cosmic Radiation Detection
Aeroplanes operating above 15 000 m (49 000 ft) must have an instrument to indicate continuously the dose rate of total cosmic radiation (i.e. the total of ionizing and neutron radiation of galactic and solar origin) and the cumulative dose on each flight, or use an approved system of on-board quarterly radiation sampling.

ACJ OPS 1.680(a)(2) - Quarterly Sampling
Sampling should be carried out with a Radiological Agency or similar acceptable organisation. 16 route sectors, which include flight above 49 000 ft,

should be sampled every quarter (three months). For less than that, sample all sectors.

Neutron and non-neutron components of the radiation field should be included.

The results of the sampling, including a cumulative summary quarter on quarter, should be reported under acceptable arrangements.

1.685 - Flight Crew Interphone
With a flight crew of more than one, you need a flight crew interphone system, including headsets and microphones (not handheld).

1.690 - Crew Interphone
Aeroplanes over 15 000 kg, or with more than 19 passenger seats need a crew member interphone system, except those first certificated before 1 April 1965 and registered in a JAA State on 1 April 1995.

The system must be independent of the public address system, except for handsets, headsets, microphones, selector switches and signalling devices, and provide a means of two-way communication between crew and passenger compartments, galleys not on passenger deck levels, and remote crew compartments not on the passenger deck and not easily accessible from a passenger compartment.

The system must also be readily accessible from each flight crew station and cabin crew stations close to each separate or pair of floor level emergency exits, and have an alerting system with aural or visual signals for the flight crew to alert the cabin crew and *vice versa*, and allow the recipient of a call to determine whether it is a normal or an emergency call, together with a means of two-way communication between ground personnel and at least two flight crew members.

AMC OPS 1.690(b)(6)
The means of determining whether or not a call is a normal or emergency one may be one or a combination of different lights, or codes defined by the operator (e.g. different number of rings), or any other acceptable signal.

IEM OPS 1.690(b)(7)
At least one interphone system station for use by ground personnel should be located so that people using the system may avoid detection from inside.

1.695 - Public Address System
Aeroplanes with more than 19 passenger seats need a public address system independent of the interphone, except for handsets, headsets, microphones, selector switches and signalling devices. It must be readily accessible for immediate use from each flight crew station.

For floor level passenger emergency exits with a cabin crew seat nearby, you need a microphone which is readily accessible to the seated cabin crew member, except that one microphone may serve more than one exit, if the exits are near enough to allow unassisted verbal communication between seated cabin crew members.

The system must be capable of operation within 10 seconds by a cabin crew member at each station in the compartment from which its use is accessible, and be audible and intelligible at all passenger seats, toilets and cabin crew seats and work stations.

1.700 - Cockpit Voice Recorders
Multi-engined turbine aeroplanes over 5700 kg or with more than 9 passenger seats first certificated on or after 1 April 1998 need a CVR which, against a time scale, records:

- Radio communications
- The aural environment of the flight deck, including, without interruption, audio signals from boom and mask microphones
- Voice communications of flight crew over the interphone or public address system
- Voice or audio signals identifying aids introduced into a headset or speaker

The CVR must be able to retain information from at least the last 2 hours, except for aeroplanes 5 700 kg or below, which may use 30 minutes (see 1.705). It must start automatically before the aeroplane moves under its own power and continue until it can no longer do so (depending on power, the CVR must start as early as possible during the cockpit checks before engine start until the cockpit checks immediately following engine shutdown).

CVRs need an underwater location device.

ACJ OPS 1.700
The operational performance requirements for CVRs should be those in EUROCAE Document

ED56A (*Minimum Operational Performance Requirements For Cockpit Voice Recorder Systems*) December 1993 (it's on the New York Times bestseller list. Lots of information, but no plot).

1.705 Cockpit Voice Recorders–2

Multi-engined turbine aeroplanes first certificated between 1 January 1990 and 31 March 1998 (inclusive, 5 700 kg or less with over 9 passenger seats, need a CVR that records the same stuff under the same conditions in 1.700 for 30 minutes.

ACJ OPS 1.705/1.710

See ACJ OPS 1.700.

1.710 Cockpit Voice Recorders–3

Any aeroplane over 5 700 kg first certificated before 1 April 1998 needs a CVR which records the same stuff under the same conditions in 1.700 for 30 minutes, leaving out the audio signals from boom and mask microphones and checklists.

1.715 - Flight Data Recorders

Multi-engined turbine aeroplanes first certificated on or after 1 April 1998 with more than 9 passenger seats or over 5 700 kg require a digital FDR with a method of readily retrieving its data.

The FDR must be able to retain data recorded during at least the last 25 hours, or 10 for aeroplanes below 5700 kg. Data must be obtained from sources which enable accurate correlation with information displayed to the flight crew.

Refer to Appendix 1 for what needs to be recorded against a timescale. There must be special arrangements for novel or unique designs.

The FDR must start automatically before the aeroplane is capable of moving under its own power and must stop automatically after it is incapable of doing so. It must have an underwater locating device.

Aeroplanes first certificated between 1 April 1998 and 1 April 2001, may not need to comply with JAR OPS 1.715(c), if it cannot be done without extensive modifications (See ACJ-OPS 1.715(g)) to aeroplane systems and equipment, and the aeroplane complies with JAROPS 1.720(c), except that parameter 15b in Table A of Appendix 1 need not to be recorded.

ACJ OPS 1.715

Operational performance requirements for FDRs should be those in EUROCAE Document ED55 (*Minimum Operational Performance Specification For Flight Data Recorder Systems*) dated May 1990.

For aeroplanes with novel or unique design or operational characteristics, the additional parameters should be those in JAR 25.1459(e) during type certification or validation.

If recording capacity is available, as many of the additional parameters in table A1.5 of Document ED 55 as possible should be recorded.

ACJ OPS 1.715(g) - Extensive Modifications

The alleviation policy in JAR OPS 1.715(g) affects a small number of aeroplanes first issued with a C of A on or after 1st April 1998 that were either made before then or to a specification in force just before. They may not comply fully with JAR OPS 1.715, but can comply with 1.720. In granting such an alleviation, the Authority should confirm that the above conditions have been met and that compliance with JAR OPS 1.715 would imply significant modifications to the aeroplane with a severe re-certification effort.

Appendix 1 - Parameters to be Recorded

There is a large summary table, not included here (it's the usual stuff).

1.720 - Flight Data Recorders–2

Aeroplanes over 5 700 kg first certificated on or after 1 June 1990, up to and including 31 March 1998 must have a digital FDR and a method of readily retrieving data. It must be able to retain data for at least the last 25 hours.

The FDR must record the parameters in Table A of Appendix 1 to JAR OPS 1.720 against a timescale and, for aeroplanes over 27 000 kg the extras in Table B (for aeroplanes of 27 000 kg or below, parameters 14 and 15b of Table A need not be recorded when the sensor is not readily available, there is not enough capacity, or a change is required in equipment that generates the data. The same applies for aeroplanes over 27 000 kg, for 15 b of Table A and 23, 24, 25, 26, 27, 28, 29, 30 and 31 of Table B if nav signals are not available in digital form either).

Individual parameters that can be derived by calculation from other recorded parameters need not to be recorded, by approval.

Data must be obtained from aeroplane sources which enable accurate correlation with information displayed to the flight crew.

The FDR must start to record before the aeroplane is capable of moving under its own power, and stop after the aeroplane it is incapable of doing so.

The flight data recorder must have an underwater location device.

ACJ OPS 1.720/1.725

The parameters to be recorded should meet the performance specifications (designated ranges, recording intervals and accuracy limits) in Table 1 of Appendix 1 to ACJ OPS 1.720/1.725. Remarks in Table 1 are acceptable means of compliance.

FDRs, for which recorded parameters do not comply with Table 1 (i.e. range, sampling intervals, accuracy limits and recommended resolution readout) may be acceptable.

For all aeroplanes, as far as practicable, when further capacity is available, recording these extra parameters should be considered:

- Remaining parameters in Table B of Appendix 1 to JAR OPS 1.720 or 1.725

- Dedicated parameters relating to novel or unique design or operational characteristics

- Operational information from electronic display systems, with this order of priority:

  - parameters selected by the flight crew relating to the desired flight path, e.g. barometric pressure setting, selected altitude, selected airspeed, decision height, and autoflight system engagement and mode indications if not recorded from another source

  - display system selection/status, e.g. SECTOR, PLAN, ROSE, NAV, WXR, COMPOSITE, COPY, etc

  - warning and alerts

  - the identity of displayed pages from emergency procedures and checklists

- retardation information including brake application for use in the investigation of landing overruns or rejected take offs

- additional engine parameters (EPR, N1, EGT, fuel flow, etc.)

For the purpose of JAR OPS 1.720(d), 1.720(e) and 1.725(c)(2), the alleviation should be acceptable only when adding the missing parameters to the existing system would require a major upgrade of the system itself. Account should be taken of:

- The extent of the modification required

- The down-time period

- Equipment software development

For the purpose of JAR OPS 1.720(d), 1.720(e), 1.725(c)(2) and 1.725(c)(3), *capacity available* refers to space not allocated for recording parameters, or parameters recorded for JAR OPS 1.037 (Accident prevention and flight safety program) as acceptable.

For the purpose of JAR OPS 1.720(d)(1), 1.720(e)(1), 1.725(c)(2)(i) and 1.725(c)(3), a sensor is *readily available* when it is already available or can be easily incorporated.

Appendix 1
Table of parameters, not included here.

1.725 - Flight Data Recorders–3
Turbine-engined aeroplanes over 5 700 kg first certificated before 1 June 1990 must have a digital FDR and a method of readily retrieving data from it. The FDR must be able to retain data from at least the last 25 hours and, against a timescale, record the parameters in Table A of Appendix 1 to JAR OPS 1.725, plus the extras from 6-15b of Table B for aeroplanes over 27 000 kg first certificated after 30 September 1969.

However, the following need not be recorded, as acceptable: 13, 14 and 15b in Table B if the sensor is not readily available, there is not enough capacity, or a change is required in equipment that generates the data. Otherwise, for aeroplanes between 5 700-27 000 kg first certificated on or after 1 January 1989, 6-15b of Table B, and those over 27 000 kg first certificated on or after 1 January 1987, the remaining parameters of Table B.

Individual parameters that can be derived by calculation from the other recorded parameters need not be recorded as acceptable.

Data must be obtained from aeroplane sources which enable accurate correlation with information displayed to the flight crew.

The FDR must start to record before the aeroplane is capable of moving under its own power, and stop after the aeroplane it is incapable of doing so.

The flight data recorder must have an underwater location device.

Appendix 1 - Parameters to be Recorded
A large and boring table, not included here.

ACJ OPS 1.715, 1.720 and 1.725
Summary table, not included here.

1.727 - Combination Recorder
You can use a combination recorder if the aeroplane needs a CVR and FDR only, or if the aeroplane of 5 700 kg or less needs a CVR or FDR. You can also use two combination recorders if the aeroplane over 5 700 kg needs a CVR or FDR.

ACJ OPS 1.727
With two combination recorders, one should be near the cockpit, to minimise risk of a data loss due to wiring failure. The other should be at the rear to minimise data loss from damage in a crash.

1.730 - Seats, Safety Belts, Harnesses and Child Restraint
Aeroplanes must have:

- a seat or berth for each person aged two years or more

- a safety belt, with or without a diagonal shoulder strap, or a safety harness for each passenger seat for each passenger aged 2 years or more

- A supplementary loop belt or other restraint device for each infant

- a safety belt with shoulder harness for each flight crew seat and any next to a pilot's seat, with a device that automatically restrains the torso in a rapid deceleration (all safety belts with shoulder harness must have a single point release)

- a safety belt with shoulder harness for each cabin crew and observer seat (this does not preclude use of passenger seats by extra cabin crew. All safety belts with shoulder harness must have a single point release)

- seats for cabin crew near floor level emergency exits except that, if the emergency evacuation of passengers would be enhanced by seating them elsewhere, other locations are acceptable. Seats must be forward or rearward facing within 15° of the longitudinal axis.

A safety belt with a diagonal shoulder strap for aeroplanes up to 5 700 kg, or a safety belt for aeroplanes up to 2 730 kg, may be used instead of a safety belt with shoulder harness if it is not reasonably practicable to fit one.

1.731 - Signs
Aeroplanes in which all passenger seats are not visible from the flight deck must have a means of indicating to all passengers and cabin crew when seat belts must be fastened and when smoking is not allowed.

1.735 - Internal Doors and Curtains
The following equipment must be installed:

- With more than 19 passenger seats, a door between the passenger compartment and flight deck saying *Crew Only, Push Off* (only joking!) and a means of locking it to stop passengers opening it without permission

- A means for opening each door that separates a passenger compartment from another with emergency exits (the means must be readily accessible)

- If you have to pass through a doorway or curtain separating the passenger cabin from other areas to reach an emergency exit from a passenger seat, the door or curtain must have a means to keep it open.

- A placard on each internal door or any next to a curtain that is the means of access to an emergency exit, to indicate that it must be secured open on take off and landing

- A means for any member of the crew to unlock any door that can normally be locked by passengers

1.745 – First Aid Kits

Aeroplanes require first aid kits, readily accessible for use, to the following scale:

Passenger Seats	First Aid Kits
0 to 99	1
100 to 199	2
200 to 299	3
300 +	4

Kits must be inspected periodically and replenished as necessary.

AMC OPS 1.745

First Aid kits should have this stuff in them:

- Bandages (unspecified)

- Burns dressings (unspecified)

- Wound dressings, large and small

- Adhesive tape, safety pins and scissors

- Small adhesive dressings

- Antiseptic wound cleaner

- Adhesive wound closures

- Adhesive tape

- Disposable resuscitation aid

- Simple analgesic e.g. paracetamol

- Antiemetic e.g. cinnarizine

- Nasal decongestant

- First-Aid handbook

- Splints, suitable for upper and lower limbs

- Gastrointestinal Antacid*

- Anti-diarrhoeal medication*

- Ground/Air visual code for survivors

- Disposable Gloves

- A list of contents in at least 2 languages (one being English), to include the effects and side effects of drugs carried

An eye irrigator, whilst not required, should, where possible, be available on the ground.

*For aeroplanes with more than 9 passenger seats.

1.755 - Emergency Medical Kit

Aeroplanes with more than 30 passenger seats must have an emergency medical kit if you plan to be more than 60 minutes flying time (at normal cruising speed) from where qualified medical assistance could be expected.

Drugs may not be administered except by qualified doctors, nurses or similarly qualified personnel.

Conditions for Carriage

The kit must be dust- and moisture-proof and be carried under security, where practicable, on the flight deck, inspected periodically and replenished as necessary.

AMC OPS 1.755

This stuff should be in the emergency medical kit:

- Sphygmomanometer – non mercury

- Stethoscope

- Syringes and needles

- Oropharyngeal airways (2 sizes)

- Tourniquet

- Coronary vasodilator e.g. nitro-glycerine

- Anti-smasmodic e.g. hyascene

- Epinephrine 1:1 000

- Adrenocortical steroid e.g. hydrocortisone

- Major analgesic e.g. nalbuphine

- Diuretic e.g. fursemide

- Antihistamine e.g. diphenhydramine hydrochloride

- Sedative/anticonvulsant e.g. diazepam

- Medication for Hypoglycaemia e.g. hypertonic glucose

- Antiemetic e.g. metoclopramide
- Atropine
- Digoxin
- Uterine contractant e.g. Ergometrine/Oxytocin
- Disposable Gloves
- Bronchial Dilator – including an injectable form
- Needle Disposal Box
- Anti-spasmodic drugs
- Catheter
- A list of contents in at least 2 languages (one being English), to include the effects and side effects of drugs carried.

1.760 – First Aid Oxygen

Pressurised aeroplanes above 25 000 ft, when cabin crew are required, must have a supply of undiluted oxygen for passengers who might need oxygen after a depressurisation.

The amount is based on an average flow of at least 3 litres STPD/minute/person and must be enough for the rest of the flight when cabin altitude is between 8 000-15 000 ft, for at least 2% of the passengers, but at least one. There must be enough dispensing units (can be portable), but at least two, with a means for cabin crew to use the supply.

The amount for a particular operation is based on cabin pressure altitudes and flight duration, consistent with procedures.

The equipment must be able to generate a mass flow to each user of at least four litres per minute, STPD. This may be decreased to at least two litres per minute, STPD, at any altitude.

IEM OPS 1.760

First aid oxygen is for passengers who still need undiluted oxygen when supplemental oxygen has run out (see Appendix 1 to 1.770), although, after a depressurisation, the supplemental stuff should be enough to cope with hypoxic problems for all passengers when the cabin altitude is above 15 000 ft, and a proportion between 10 000-15 000 ft. For these reasons, first-aid oxygen should be calculated

for the time after depressurisation when cabin altitude is between 8 000-15 000 ft, when supplemental oxygen may no longer be available.

Moreover, after depressurisation, an emergency descent should be carried out to the lowest altitude compatible with safety, and the aeroplane should land at the first available aerodrome asap.

The conditions above should reduce the time during which first-aid oxygen may be required, and the amount to be carried on board.

1.770 - Supplemental Oxygen – Pressurised Aeroplanes

Pressurised aeroplanes at pressure altitudes above 10 000 ft need supplemental oxygen equipment, capable of storing and dispensing the oxygen required by this paragraph, which is determined on the basis of cabin pressure altitude, flight duration and the assumption that a pressurisation failure will occur at the most critical pressure altitude or point of flight (from the standpoint of oxygen need), and that, after the failure, the aeroplane will descend under emergency procedures in the Flight Manual to a safe altitude that will allow continued safe flight and landing.

Afetr a cabin pressurisation failure, the cabin pressure altitude is considered to be the same as the aeroplane pressure altitude, unless it is demonstrated otherwise. In this case, the demonstrated maximum cabin pressure altitude may be used as a basis for determination of supply.

Equipment and Supply Requirements

Flight Crew

Members on flight deck duty require oxygen under Appendix 1. If they use the same source, they are "flight crew". Otherwise, flight deck seat occupants, not supplied by the flight crew source, are "passengers".

Oxygen masks must be within the immediate reach of flight crew at their assigned stations. Those for crews in pressurised aeroplanes at pressure altitudes above 25 000 ft must be the quick donning type.

Cabin Crew, Additional Crew and Passengers

Cabin crew and passengers must have supplemental oxygen as per Appendix 1, except*. Extra cabin crew, and additional crew, are passengers for this purpose.

Aeroplanes that operate at pressure altitudes above 25 000 ft must have enough spare outlets and masks and/or portable oxygen units with masks for use by all cabin crew. They must be distributed evenly to ensure immediate availability of oxygen to each cabin crew member, regardless of location at pressurisation failure. They must also have an oxygen dispensing unit connected to supply terminals immediately available to each occupant, wherever seated. The total number must exceed seats by at least 10%, and be evenly distributed throughout the cabin.

If such aeroplanes, when at or below 25 000 ft, cannot descend safely within 4 minutes to 13 000 ft (and which were first certificated on or after 9 November 1998), they must have automatically deployable oxygen equipment immediately available to each occupant. The total number of dispensing units and outlets must exceed seats by at least 10% and be evenly distributed throughout the cabin.

*The oxygen supply for aeroplanes not certificated above 25 000 ft may be reduced to the entire time between 10 000-13 000 ft cabin PAs for all required cabin crew and at least 10% of passengers if the aeroplane can descend safely within 4 minutes to a cabin pressure altitude of 13 000 ft.

Appendix 1– Minimum Requirements

Supply for	Duration & Cabin PA
Occupants of flight deck seats on flight deck duty	Entire flight time when cabin PA exceeds 13 000 ft and between 10 000-13 000 ft after the first 30 minutes, but in no case less than 30 minutes for aeroplanes that fly up to 25 000 ft (2), and 2 hours for aeroplanes certificated above that (3).
All cabin crew	Entire flight time when cabin PA exceeds 13 000 ft, but at least 30 minutes, and between 10 000-13 000 ft after first 30 mins
100% Passengers (5)	Entire flight time when cabin PA is over 15 000 ft, but at least 10 minutes (4)
30% passengers (5)	Entire flight time between 14 000-15 000 ft.

Supply for	Duration & Cabin PA
10% of passengers (5)	Entire flight time when cabin PA is between 10 000-14 000 ft after the first 30 minutes.

Note 1: The supply must take account of the cabin PA and descent profile for the routes.

Note 2: That necessary for a constant rate of descent from maximum certificated altitude to 10 000 ft in 10 minutes, and followed by 20 minutes at 10 000 ft.

Note 3: That necessary for a constant rate of descent from maximum certificated altitude to 10 000 ft in 10 minutes and followed by 110 minutes at 10 000 ft. The oxygen in JAR OPS 1.780(a)(1) may be included.

Note 4: That necessary for a constant rate of descent from maximum certificated altitude to 15 000 ft in 10 minutes.

Note 5: "Passengers" means those actually carried and includes infants.

IEM OPS 1.770

A *quick donning mask* can be placed on the face from its ready position, properly secured, sealed, and supplying oxygen on demand, with one hand and within 5 seconds, and will thereafter remain in position, freeing both hands. It will not disturb eye glasses or delay crew members from proceeding with emergency duties, or prevent immediate communication over the intercom or radio.

In determining supplemental oxygen, it is assumed that the aeroplane will descend under emergency procedures in the Ops Manual, without exceeding operating limitations, to an altitude that allows the flight to be completed safely (i.e. terrain clearance, navigational accuracy, weather avoidance etc.)

ACJ OPS 1.770(b)(2)(v)

The maximum altitude up to which an aeroplane can operate without passenger oxygen and be capable of providing oxygen to each cabin occupant should be established using an emergency descent profile which takes into account:

- 17 seconds delay for pilot recognition and reaction, including mask donning, for troubleshooting and configuring for the emergency descent

- maximum operational speed (VMO) or the airspeed in the Flight Manual for emergency descent, whichever is the less

- all engines working

- the estimated mass at the top of climb

Emergency descent data (charts) from the manufacturer and in the Flight Manual should be used to ensure uniform application.

Where oxygen is needed for 10% of the passengers between 10 000-13 000ft, it may be provided either by a plug-in or drop-out system with enough outlets and dispensing units uniformly distributed throughout the cabin, or by portable bottles when fully trained cabin crews are carried.

1.775 - Supplemental Oxygen – Non-Pressurised Aeroplanes

Supplemental equipment is needed above 10 000 ft. What you need is based on altitude and flight time, consistent with the flight manual, routes, etc (see Appendix 1).

People using the flight crew source are flight crew for this purpose. Extra crew are passengers.

Appendix 1

Supply for	Duration & Cabin PA
Occupants of flight deck seats on flight deck duty	Entire time at PAs over 10 000 ft
All cabin crew	Entire flight time when cabin PA exceeds 13 000 ft, and between 10 000-13 000 ft after the first 30 minutes
100% Passengers*	Entire time PAs over 13 000 ft
10% of passengers*	Entire flight time at PAs between 10 000-13 000 ft after the first 30 minutes.

*Passengers means those actually carried and includes infants under 2.

1.780 - Crew Protective Breathing Equipment

Pressurised aeroplanes or unpressurised ones over 5 700 kg or with more than 19 passenger seats must have equipment to protect the eyes, nose and mouth of each flight crew member on flight deck duty and to provide oxygen for at least 15 minutes (this may be supplemental oxygen).

In addition, when the flight crew is more than one and there is no cabin crew, portable PBE must be provided for one member, to last for at least 15 minutes. The same for cabin crew, if carried.

PBE for the flight crew must be conveniently located on the flight deck and be easily accessible for immediate use at assigned duty stations. PBE for cabin crew must be next to each duty station.

An additional, easily accessible portable PBE must next to the hand fire extinguishers in JAR OPS 1.790(c) and (d) except that PBE must be outside but next to the entrance of cargo compartments.

PBE in use must not prevent communication.

1.790 - Hand Fire Extinguishers

These must be provided for crew, passenger and cargo compartments and galleys as follows:

- The extinguishing agent must be suitable and minimise the hazard of toxic gas concentration.

- At least one hand fire extinguisher, containing Halon 1211 (BCF) must be conveniently located on the flight deck. At least one must be in, or readily accessible for use in, each galley not on the main passenger deck.

- At least one readily accessible hand extinguisher must be available in each Class A or B cargo or baggage compartment and in each Class E cargo compartment accessible to the crew in flight, and a least the following number must be conveniently located in the passenger compartment(s):

Seats	Extinguishers
7-30	1
31-60	2
61-200	3
201-300	4
301-400	5
401-500	6
501-600	7
601 or more	8

- When two or more extinguishers are needed, they must be evenly distributed.

- At least one extinguisher in the passenger compartment of an aeroplane with at least 31, and not more than 60, passenger seats, and at least two in the passenger compartment of an aeroplane with 61 or more passenger seats must contain Halon 1211 (BCF), or equivalent.

AMC OPS 1.790

The number and location of hand extinguishers should provide adequate availability for use, according to the number and size of passenger compartments, the need to minimise the hazard of toxic gas concentrations and the location of toilets, galleys etc. These considerations may result in the number being greater than the minima.

There should be at least one extinguisher for flammable fluid and electrical equipment fires on the flight deck. Extras may be required for other compartments accessible to the crew in flight. Dry chemical extinguishers should not be used on the flight deck, or in any compartment not separated by a partition from it, because of the adverse effect on vision and, if non-conductive, interference with electrical contacts by chemical residues.

Where only one hand extinguisher is required in the passenger compartments, it should be near the cabin crew member's station, where provided.

Where two or more hand extinguishers are needed in the passenger compartments and their location is not otherwise dictated as above, one extinguisher should be near each end of the cabin with the remainder distributed evenly throughout.

Unless an extinguisher is clearly visible, its location should be indicated by a placard or sign, supplemented by appropriate symbols.

1.795 - Crash Axes and Crowbars

Aeroplanes over 5 700 kg or with more than 9 passenger seats must have at least one crash axe or crowbar on the flight deck. Another is needed if there are more than 200 passenger seats, in or near the most rearward galley area.

Crash axes and crowbars in passenger compartments must not be visible to passengers.

1.800 - Marking of Break-in Points

External break-in areas must be marked as shown in the regulations (diagram not included here).

They must be red or yellow, and outlined in white to contrast with the background. If the corner markings are more than 2 m apart, intermediate lines 9 x 3 cm must be inserted so there is no more than 2 m between adjacent marks.

1.805 - Means for Emergency Evacuation

Passenger emergency exit sill heights must not be more than 1.83 m (6 feet) above the ground (with the aeroplane on the ground and the gear extended) or if the gear collapses or fails to extend (if the type certificate was first applied for on or after 1 April 2000), unless there is equipment at each exit to enable passengers and crew to reach the ground safely in an emergency.

Such equipment need not be provided at overwing exits if the escape route terminates less than 1.83 m (6 feet) from the ground with the aeroplane on the ground, the gear extended, and flaps in the take off or landing position, whichever is higher.

In aeroplanes that need a separate emergency exit for the flight crew and with the lowest point of the emergency exit more than 1.83 m (6 feet) above the ground with the gear extended, or (if a Type Certificate was first applied for on or after 1 April 2000) would be if the gear collapses or fails to extend, there must be a device to assist the flight crew to reach the ground safely in an emergency.

1.810 - Megaphones

Aeroplanes with more than 60 passenger seats, and carrying at least one, must have portable battery-powered megaphones readily accessible by crew members during an emergency evacuation, to the following scales:

- For each passenger deck:

Seats	Megaphones
61-99	1
100 or more	2

- For aeroplanes with more than one passenger deck, when total passenger seating configuration is more than 60, at least 1 megaphone is required.

AMC OPS 1.810

A single megaphone should be readily accessible from a cabin crew seat. Where two or more are required, they should be suitably distributed in the passenger cabin(s) and readily accessible to crew members directing emergency evacuations (this does not necessarily mean they have to be reached by a crew member strapped in a cabin crew seat).

1.815 - Emergency Lighting

Passenger carrying aeroplanes with more than 9 passenger seats must have emergency lighting systems with independent power supplies to facilitate evacuation. The system must include:

- For aeroplanes with **more than 19** passenger seats:

    - Sources of general cabin illumination

    - Internal lighting in floor level emergency exit areas

    - Illuminated emergency exit marking and locating signs

    - For aeroplanes with an application for type certificate before 1 May 1972, at night, exterior emergency lighting at overwing exits, and where descent assist means are required. Otherwise (after that date), exterior emergency lighting at passenger emergency exits

    - For aeroplanes certificated on or after 1 January 1958, floor proximity emergency escape path markings in the passenger compartment(s)

- For JAR 23/25 aeroplanes with **19 or less** passenger seats:

    - Sources of general cabin illumination

    - Internal lighting in emergency exit areas

    - Illuminated emergency exit marking and locating signs

- For **non-JAR 23/25 aeroplanes with 19 or less** passenger seats, sources of general cabin illumination.

- **At night**, passenger carrying aeroplanes with **9 or less** passenger seats must have a source of general cabin illumination for evacuation (dome lights or other sources of illumination already fitted are OK), which

can stay on after the battery has been switched off.

1.820 - ELT

Aeroplanes first certificated on or after 1 January 2002 must have an ELT that can transmit on 121.5 and 406 MHz.

Aeroplanes first certificated before 1 January 2002 must have any type of ELT that can transmit on 121.5 and 406 MHz, except that those already with an automatic ELT before 1 April 2000 that can only transmit on 121.5 MHz may continue in service until 31 December 2004.

All ELTs capable of transmitting on 406 MHz must be coded under ICAO Annex 10 and registered with the national agency for SAR or similar.

IEM OPS 1.820

ELTs are defined as follows:

- *Automatic Fixed.* Permanently attached to the aeroplane before and after a crash, and designed to aid SAR in locating a crash site

- *Automatic Portable.* Rigidly attached to the aeroplane before a crash, but readily removable afterwards, functioning as an ELT during the crash sequence. If it does not have an integral antenna, the aircraft-mounted one may be disconnected and an auxiliary (on the ELT case) attached. The ELT can be tethered to a survivor or a life-raft. This type is intended to aid SAR teams in locating the crash site or survivor(s)

- *Automatic Deployable.* Rigidly attached to the aeroplane before the crash and automatically ejected and deployed after the crash sensor has determined that one has occurred. This type should float in water and is intended to aid SAR teams in locating the crash site.

To minimise the possibility of damage in crash impact, Automatic ELTs should be rigidly fixed as far aft as practicable with antenna and connections arranged to maximise the probability of the signal being radiated after a crash.

1.825 - Lifejackets

Land Aeroplanes

Land aeroplanes over water more than 50 nm from the shore or when taking off or landing at an aerodrome where the takeoff or approach path produces a likelihood of a ditching must have lifejackets with survivor locator lights for each person on board. Each must be easily accessible from the seat or berth. Lifejackets for infants may be substituted by other approved devices with survivor locator lights.

Seaplanes and Amphibians

Seaplanes or amphibians on water must have lifejackets with survivor locator lights for each person on board. Each must be easily accessible from the seat or berth. Life jackets for infants may be substituted by other approved devices with survivor locator lights.

IEM OPS 1.825

Seat cushions are not flotation devices.

1.830 - Liferafts and Survival ELTs for Extended Overwater Flights

Over water, aeroplanes must not be further away from land suitable for emergency landings than the lesser of 120 minutes at cruising speed or 400 nm, for aeroplanes that can continue to an aerodrome with the critical power unit(s) inoperative. Otherwise, 30 minutes or 100 nm, unless this equipment is carried:

- Enough liferafts to carry everyone on board. Unless extras with enough capacity are provided, buoyancy and seating capacities beyond rated ones must accommodate all occupants if one of the largest ones are lost. Liferafts must have a survivor locator light and life saving equipment including appropriate means of sustaining life.

- At least two survival ELTs that can transmit on the distress frequencies in ICAO Annex 10, Volume V, Chapter 2. (See AMC OPS 1.830(c).)

AMC OPS 1.830(b)(2)

The following should be readily available with each liferaft:

- Means for maintaining buoyancy

- Sea anchor

- Lifelines, and means of attaching one liferaft to another

- Paddles for liferafts with capacities of 6 or less

- Means of protecting occupants from the elements

- Water resistant torch

- Equipment to make the pyrotechnic distress signals in ICAO Annex 2

- 100 g of glucose tablet for each 4, or fraction of 4, persons the liferaft is designed to carry

- At least 2 litres of drinkable water in durable containers, or means of making sea water drinkable, or a combination

- First-aid equipment

The items above should be in a pack.

AMC OPS 1.830(c)

A survival ELT is intended to be removed and activated by survivors. Thus, it should be stowed for ready removal and use in an emergency. It may be activated manually or automatically (e.g. by water activation), and designed to be tethered to a liferaft or a survivor.

An automatic portable ELT, as in JAR OPS 1.820, may replace one ELT(S) if it meets ELT(S) requirements (not a water activated ELT(S)).

1.835 - Survival Equipment

Aeroplane over areas in which search and rescue would be especially difficult must have:

- Signalling equipment for the pyrotechnical distress signals in ICAO Annex 2

- At least one ELT(S) that can transmit on the distress frequencies in ICAO Annex 10, Volume V, Chapter 2 (AMC OPS 1.830(c))

- Additional survival equipment for the route and persons on board (See AMC OPS 1.835(c)), except that the equipment in sub-para (c) need not be carried when the aeroplane either remains within 120 minutes at the OEI cruising speed (for aeroplanes capable of continuing to an aerodrome with critical power unit(s) inoperative), or 30 minutes at cruising speed for all others, from where SAR is not especially difficult. For JAR 25 aeroplanes or equivalent, no greater distance than 90 minutes at cruising speed from a suitable area for emergency landings

IEM OPS 1.835
"Areas in which search and rescue would be especially difficult" means those so designated by the State responsible for SAR or areas that are largely uninhabited and where the State responsible has not published any information to confirm that SAR would not be especially difficult, and the State does not designate areas as being especially difficult for search and rescue.

AMC OPS 1.835(c)
At least the following equipment should be carried:

- 2 litres of drinkable water for each 50, or fraction of 50, persons on board, in durable containers
- One knife
- One set of Air/Ground codes

In addition, when polar conditions are expected:

- A means for melting snow
- Sleeping bags for use by one third of all persons on board and space blankets for the remainder, or space blankets for all passengers on board
- Arctic/Polar suit for each crew member

If any item in the above list is already on board for another requirement, it need not be duplicated.

1.840 - Seaplanes and Amphibians – Miscellaneous Equipment
Seaplanes or amphibians on water must have a sea anchor and other equipment necessary to facilitate mooring, anchoring or manoeuvring on water, appropriate to its size, weight and handling characteristics, and equipment for making the sound signals in the International Regulations for preventing collisions at sea, where applicable.

1.845 – Communication & Nav Eqpt

This must be approved and installed as required, under minimum performance standards* and operational and airworthiness requirements, and be working, except under an MEL. The failure of any single unit must not result in the failure of another.

Equipment must be readily operable from any station at which it is required to be used.

*Those in the applicable JTSO, unless otherwise prescribed in operational or airworthiness codes.

IEM OPS 1.845 - Approval and Installation
Approved means that compliance with the applicable JTSO design requirements and performance specifications, or equivalent, in force at the time of the approval application, has been demonstrated. Where a JTSO does not exist, the applicable airworthiness standards or equivalent apply unless otherwise in JAR OPS 1 or JAR 26.

Installed means that the installation has been demonstrated to comply with the applicable airworthiness requirements of JAR 23/25, or the relevant code for Type Certification, and any requirement in JAR OPS 1.

1.850 - Radio Equipment
Radio equipment is required for the operation.

Where two independent (separate and complete) radio systems are required, each must have an independent antenna except that, where rigidly supported non-wire antennae or equivalent are used, only one is required.

Radio communication must provide 121.5 MHz.

1.855 - Audio Selector Panel
Aeroplanes under IFR must have audio selector panels accessible to each flight crew member.

1.860 - VFR
Under VFR over routes that can be navigated by reference to visual landmarks, radio equipment must communicate with appropriate ground stations and ATC from any point in controlled airspace within which flights are intended, and receive weather information.

1.865 - IFR or VFR Without Reference to Visual Landmarks

Radio communication and navigation equipment for ATS requirements in the area(s) of operation is required.

Radio Equipment

At least two independent radio communication systems under normal operating conditions to communicate with an appropriate ground station from any point on the route including diversions.

Navigation equipment must comprise of at least:

- One VOR, one ADF, one DME

- One ILS or MLS, as required

- One Marker Beacon as required

- An Area Navigation System, as required

- An additional DME, VOR or ADF where navigation is based only on those signals

- An additional VOR where navigation is based only on VOR signals

- An additional ADF where navigation is based only on NDB signals

It must comply with the RNP Type for the airspace concerned.

Alternative equipment may be authorised, if it allows safe navigation for the intended route.

VHF communication equipment, ILS Localisers and VORs for IFR must be of a type that complies with FM immunity performance standards.

AMC OPS 1.865 - Combinations

Individual requirements of JAR OPS 1.865 may be met by combinations of instruments or integrated flight systems, or a combination of parameters on electronic displays, if the information available is at least that provided by whatever is specified.

ACJ OPS 1.865(e) - FM Immunity

Refer to ICAO Annex 10, Volume I - *Radio Navigation Aids, Fifth Edition* dated July 1996, Chapter 3, Paragraphs 3.1.4, 3.3.8 and Volume III, Part II - *Voice Communications Systems*, Para 2.3.3.

Acceptable equipment standards, consistent with ICAO Annex 10, are in EUROCAE Minimum Operational Performance Specifications,

documents ED-22B for VORs, ED-23B for VHF communications and ED-46B for LOC receivers and the corresponding RTCA documents DO-186, DO-195 and DO-196.

1.866 - Transponder Equipment

Aeroplanes must have a pressure altitude reporting SSR transponder and any other for the route.

1.870 - Additional Equipment for MNPS

Navigation equipment is required that complies with MNPS, as in ICAO Doc 7030, in the form of Regional Supplementary Procedures. It must be visible and usable by either pilot at his duty station.

For unrestricted operation in MNPS airspace, an aeroplane must have two independent Long Range Navigation Systems (LRNS). Along notified special routes, one LRNS is required.

IEM OPS 1.870

An LRNS may be an INS or Omega, or one system using inputs from one or more Inertial Reference Systems (IRS), or Omega Sensor Systems (OSS) or other MNPS sensor system.

An integrated system which offers equivalent functional availability, integrity and redundancy may, for this requirement, be considered as two independent Long Range Navigation Systems.

1.872 - Equipment for RVSM

Aeroplanes operated in RVSM airspace must have:

- Two independent altitude measurement systems

- An altitude alerting system

- An automatic altitude control system

- SSR transponder with altitude reporting that can be connected to the altitude measurement system.

1.875 – Maintenance

Aeroplanes must be maintained and released to service by appropriately approved and accepted JAR 145 organisations, although preflight inspections are exempt.

This Subpart prescribes aeroplane maintenance needed for certification requirements under JAR OPS 1.180.

IEM OPS 1.875

Reference to *aeroplanes* includes *components*.

De-icing and anti-icing activities do not require JAR 145 approval.

1.880 - Terminology

The following definitions apply:

- *Preflight Inspection.* The inspection done before flight to ensure that the aeroplane is fit. It does not include defect rectification.

- *Approved Standard.* An approved manufacturing/ design/maintenance/quality standard.

- *Approved by the Authority.* What it says.

1.885 - Application and Approval

For approval of the maintenance system, applicants for initial issue, variation and renewal of an AOC must submit the documents specified in JAR OPS 1.185(b) (see IEM OPS 1.885(a).)

Detailed requirements are in JAR OPS 1.180(a)(3) and 1.180(b), and JAR OPS 1.185.

IEM OPS 1.885(b)

Approval of a maintenance system is indicated by a statement containing the following information:

- AOC number

- Name of Operator

- Type(s) of aeroplane

- Reference identification of the maintenance program(s) related to types and MME

- Any limitations imposed

Approval may be limited to specified aeroplanes or locations, or operational limitations if considered necessary for safety.

IEM OPS 1.885(a) - Application and Approval

The documents in JAR OPS 1.185(b) are not expected to be completed with the initial application, since each will require approval in its own right and may be subject to amendments. Draft documents should be submitted at the earliest opportunity so that the process can begin,

but the Authority must have the completed documents for it to finish.

Applicants should inform the Authority where base and scheduled line maintenance takes place and give details of contracted maintenance as well.

At the time of application, the Operator should have arrangements for all base and scheduled line maintenance in place for an appropriate time, as acceptable. Further arrangements should be establishd before the maintenance is due.

Base maintenance contracts for high-life time checks may be based on one-time contracts, when the Authority considers that this is compatible with the fleet size.

1.890 - Maintenance Responsibility

Airworthiness and serviceability must be accomplished by:

- Preflight inspections

- Rectification of defects and damage, as per the MEL and CDL

- Maintenance under the approved program in JAR OPS 1.910, and analysis of its effectiveness

- Operational directives, ADs and other requirements made mandatory

- Until adoption of JAR 39, compliance with current national aviation regulations

- Modifications. For non-mandatory ones, an embodiment policy

The C of A must remain valid in respect of the requirements above and any expiry date or maintenance condition in the Certificate.

AMC OPS 1.890(a)

The requirement means that the operator is responsible for determining what maintenance is required, when it has to be done, by whom and to what standard, to ensure continued airworthiness. Operators should have adequate knowledge of the design status (type specification, customer options, ADs, modifications, operational equipment) and required and performed maintenance.

Status of design and maintenance should be adequately documented to support the quality system (See JAR OPS 1.900).

There should be adequate co-ordination between flight operations and maintenance to ensure that both receive necessary information on the condition of aircraft to perform their tasks.

Operators themselves need not perform maintenance (which is to be done by a JAR 145 AMO (See JAR OPS 1.895) but they do carry the responsibility for airworthiness. They should thus be satisfied before the flight that all required maintenance has been properly carried out.

Operators not approved under JAR 145 should provide a clear work order to the maintenance contractor. The fact that operators contract a JAR 145 AMO should not prevent them from checking the work.

AMC OPS 1.890(a)(1)
The term *preflight inspection* is intended to mean all actions necessary to ensure that the aeroplane is fit for the intended flight. These should typically include, but are not necessarily limited to:

- A walk-around type inspection for condition including obvious signs of wear, damage or leakage. In addition, the presence of required emergency equipment should be established.

- Inspection of the Tech Log to ensure that the intended flight is not adversely affected by deferred defects and that no required maintenance action is overdue or will become due during the flight.

- Consumable fluids, gases etc. uplifted before flight are correct, free from contamination, and correctly recorded.

- All doors are securely fastened.

- Control surface and landing gear locks, pitot/static covers, restraint devices and engine/aperture blanks have been removed

- All external surfaces and engines are free from ice, snow, sand, dust etc.

Tasks such as oil and hydraulic fluid uplift and tyre inflation may be part of the preflight inspection, if acceptable. The related instructions should address

procedures to determine whether the uplift or inflation results from an abnormal consumption and may need action by the JAR 145 AMO.

Operators should publish guidance to maintenance and flight personnel (and any others doing preflight inspection tasks, as appropriate), defining responsibilities for these actions and, where tasks are contracted to other organisations, how they are subject to the quality system of JAR OPS 1.900. It should be demonstrated that preflight inspection personnel have appropriate training for the relevant tasks. The training standard should be in the MME.

IEM OPS 1 890(a)(1)
The fact that preflight inspections are an operator's maintenance responsibility does not necessarily mean that people doing them should report to the Nominated Postholder for Maintenance, but that that person is responsible for determining the content of the preflight inspection and setting qualification standards. In addition, compliance with the qualification standard should be monitored by the Quality System.

AMC OPS 1.890(a)(2)
There should be a system to ensure that defects affecting safe operation are rectified within the limits in the MEL or CDL, and postponements are not allowed without the Operator's agreement and under approved procedures.

AMC OPS 1.890(a)(3)
There should be a system to ensure that maintenance checks are done within the limits of the maintenance program and that, whenever a check cannot be done within the time limit, its postponement is allowed with the Operator's agreement and under approved procedures.

AMC OPS 1.890(a)(4)
An operator should have a system to analyse the effectiveness of the maintenance program, with regard to spares, established defects, malfunctions and damage, and to amend the maintenance program (this will involve approval unless the operator has been approved to amend things without direct involvement of the Authority).

IEM OPS 1.890(a)(5)
"Any other continued airworthiness requirement made mandatory by the Authority" includes Type Certification related requirements, such as

Certification Maintenance Requirements (CMRs), Life Limited Parts, Airworthiness Limitations, etc.

AMC OPS 1.890(a)(6)
Operators should establish a policy to assess non-mandatory information related to airworthiness, such as Service Bulletins, Service Letters and other information on the aircraft and its components from the design organisation, the manufacturer or the related airworthiness authorities.

1.895 - Maintenance Management
Operators must be JAR 145 approved to work under JAR OPS 1.890(a)(2), (3), (5) and (6), except when contracting out to a JAR 145 organisation is approved.

An acceptable person must be employed to ensure that maintenance is done on time to approved standards, for JAR OPS 1.890. This, or the senior person, is the *nominated postholder* in 1.175(i)(2), who is also responsible for corrective action from the quality monitoring of JAR OPS 1.900(a). The Nominated Postholder should not be employed by a JAR 145 organisation under contract, unless specifically approved.

Except as otherwise specified below, the arrangement must be a written maintenance contract (commercial elements of which are not required) detailing the functions in JAR OPS 1.890(a)(2), (3), (5) and (6), and defining the support of the quality functions of 1.900.

A contract may exist with a non-JAR 145 organisation, if it is a JAR Operator of the same type, with all maintenance ultimately performed by JAR 145 organisations, the contract details the functions in JAR OPS 1.890(a)(2), (3), (5) and (6) and the support of the quality functions of 1.900, and the contract, with amendments, but ignoring commercial elements, is acceptable.

For occasional line or component maintenance (including engine maintenance), the "contract" may be individual work orders.

Suitable office accommodation must be provided.

AMC OPS 1.895(a)
The requirement is intended to provide for the possibility of three alternatives:

* An operator approved under JAR 145 to carry out *all* maintenance

* An operator approved under JAR 145 to carry out *some* maintenance, which, at least, could be limited line maintenance, or more, but still short of the above

* An operator not approved under JAR 145 to carry out *any* maintenance

The Authority determines which may be accepted, applying the primary criteria of relevant experience on comparable aeroplanes. For example, for the all maintenance option, assuming experience is satisfactory, it is reasonable to add a different wide-bodied aircraft to an existing wide bodied fleet. If the experience is not satisfactory or too limited, the Authority may require more experienced management and/or release to service staff, or may refuse to accept the new aircraft if experienced staff cannot be found.

For the *some maintenance* option, or where the Authority has been unable to accept an application for *all maintenance*, satisfactory experience is again the key, but related to the reduced maintenance. If the experience is not satisfactory or too limited, the Authority may require more experienced staff or refuse to accept the application if such staff cannot be found, leaving the final option, which accepts that the operator either does not have experience or has only limited experience of some maintenance.

An operator must enter into a contract with a JAR 145 organisation, except that, in some cases where the Authority believes that enough experienced staff can be found for the minimal maintenance option, in which case that option would apply.

Experience means staff with proven evidence that they were directly involved with at least line maintenance of similar types for at least 12 months, as demonstrated. Operators must have enough people for JAR OPS 1.895(b) to manage the maintenance responsibility, whichever is used.

AMC OPS 1.895(b)
People employed should represent the maintenance management structure (for maintenance) and be responsible for all maintenance functions. Depending on the size and setup, functions may be divided under individual managers or combined in any number of ways. This includes combining the functions of 'accountable manager' (see JAR OPS 1.175(h)), the 'nominated postholder' (see JAR OPS 1.175(i)) and the quality monitoring function

(see JAR OPS 1.900) so long as it remains independent of whatever is monitored. In the smallest organisation this may lead to the quality function being done by the accountable manager, if suitably qualified. Consequently, the smallest organisation consists of at least two persons, except that the Authority may agree to the quality monitoring function being contracted out.

The actual number of people to be employed and their qualifications depends on the tasks, so is dependent on the size and complexity of the operation (route network, line or charter, ETOPS, number of aircraft and the aircraft types, complexity and age), number and locations of maintenance facilities and the amount and complexity of maintenance contracting. Thus, the number of people needed, and their qualifications, may differ greatly and a simple formula covering the whole range of possibilities is not feasible.

To enable the Authority to accept the number of persons and their qualifications, operators should make an analysis of the tasks to be performed, the way in which they may be divided and/or combined, how responsibilities will be assigned and establish the number of man/hours and the qualifications needed to perform the tasks, and updated as necessary.

The authority does not necessarily expect the credentials of the Maintenance Management Group to be individually submitted, but the Manager of the Group, and any reporting directly to him should be individually acceptable.

AMC OPS 1.895(c)
The Authority should only accept that the proposed person be employed by the JAR 145 Organisation when it is manifest that he/she is the only available competent person within a practical working distance from the Operator's offices.

IEM OPS 1.895(c)
This only applies to contracted maintenance, so does not affect situations where the JAR 145 Organisation and Operator are the same.

AMC OPS 1.895(d)
Where an operator is JAR 145 approved, or an operator's maintenance organisation is independent, a contract should be agreed between the operator and the JAR 145 AMO that specifies, in detail, the work to be performed.

Both the specification of work and assignment of responsibilities should be clear, unambiguous and detailed so that misunderstandings do not arise between the parties (operator, MO and the Authority) that could result in a situation where work that has a bearing on airworthiness or serviceability or will not be properly done.

Special attention should be paid to procedures and responsibilities to ensure that all maintenance work is performed, service bulletins are analysed and decisions taken on accomplishment, airworthiness directives are completed on time and that all work, including non-mandatory modifications is carried out to approved data and to the latest standards.

For the layout of the contract, the IATA *Standard Ground Handling Agreement* may be used, but this does not preclude the Authority from ensuring that the content is acceptable, and especially that the contract allows the Operator to properly exercise its maintenance responsibility. Parts of a contract that have no bearing on the technical or operational aspects of airworthiness are outside the scope of this paragraph.

AMC OPS 1.895(e)
For a contract with a non-JAR 145 organisation, the MME should include procedures to ensure that all this contracted maintenance is ultimately performed on time by JAR 145 organisations under data acceptable to the Authority. In particular, Quality procedures should place great emphasis on monitoring compliance. The list of JAR 145 contractors, or a reference to this list, should be in the MME.

Such maintenance arrangements do not absolve Operators from overall Maintenance responsibility. Specifically, to accept the arrangement, the Authority should be satisfied that it allows the Operator to ensure full compliance with JAR OPS 1.890 - *Maintenance Responsibility*.

IEM OPS 1.895(e)
The purpose of JAR OPS 1.895(e) is to authorise a primary maintenance arrangement with a non-JAR 145 Maintenance Organisation, when it proves that such an arrangement is in the interest of the Operator by simplifying maintenance management, and the Operator keeps appropriate control. Such an arrangement should not preclude the Operator from ensuring that all maintenance is performed by a JAR 145 organisation and complying with the

JAR OPS 1.890. Typical examples of such arrangements follow:

Component Maintenance

The Operator may find it more appropriate to have a primary contractor to despatch components to appropriate organisations, rather than sending them to various JAR 145 organisations. The benefit is that management is simplified by having a single contact point. The Operator retains responsibility.

Aeroplanes, Engines and Components

The operator may have a maintenance contract with another non-JAR 145 operator of the same type. A typical case is that of a dry-leased aeroplane between operators, where the parties find it appropriate to keep the aeroplane under current maintenance arrangements. Where this involves various JAR 145 contractors, it might be more manageable for the lessee to have a single contract with the lessor, although this is not as a transfer of responsibility - the lessee, being the JAR OPS approved Operator, remains responsible for maintenance.

In essence, JAR OPS 1.895(e) does not alter the intent of JAR OPS 1.895(a), (b) and (d), in that it also requires that the Operator has to establish a written maintenance contract acceptable to the Authority and, whatever type of arrangement is made, the Operator must exercise the same level of control on contracted maintenance, particularly through the Maintenance Management Group and Quality System.

IEM - OPS 1.895 (f & g)

The intent of this paragraph is that maintenance contracts are not necessary when the maintenance system, as approved, specifies that the relevant activity may be ordered through one-time work orders. This includes, for obvious reasons, occasional line maintenance and may also include component maintenance up to engines, as long as the Authority considers that the maintenance is manageable this way, in terms of volume and complexity. This paragraph implies that, even where base maintenance is ordered on a case-by-case basis, there must be a written contract.

AMC OPS 1.895(h)

Office accommodation means such that incumbents can carry out their tasks in a way that contributes to good maintenance standards. For smaller operators, the Authority may agree to these tasks being conducted from one office, subject to space and undue disturbance. Office accommodation should also include an adequate technical library and room for document consultation.

1.900 - Quality System

For maintenance purposes, the quality system (see JAR OPS 1.035), must include at least:

- Checking that the activities of JAR OPS 1.890 are done under accepted procedures

- Checking that contracted maintenance is carried out under the contract

- Checking compliance with this Subpart

The quality system may be combined with the one required by JAR–145, if the operator is approved.

AMC OPS 1.900

An operator should establish a plan to show when and how often the activities as required by JAR OPS 1.890 will be monitored. In addition, reports should be produced at the completion of each investigation and include details of discrepancies.

The feedback part of the system should address who is required to rectify discrepancies and non-compliance and the procedure if rectification is not done within appropriate timescales. The procedure should lead to the Accountable Manager in JAR OPS 1.175(h).

To ensure effective compliance with JAR OPS 1.900, the following have been shown to work well:

- *Product sampling* – the part inspection of a representative sample of the aeroplane fleet

- *Defect sampling* – the monitoring of defect rectification performance

- *Concession sampling* – monitoring concessions to *not* carry out maintenance on time

- *On time maintenance sampling* – monitoring of when (flying hours/calendar time/flight cycles etc) aeroplanes and components are brought in for maintenance

• *Sampling reports* of unairworthy conditions and maintenance errors

Note that JAR OPS 1.900 includes other self-explanatory monitoring elements.

IEM OPS 1.900

The primary purpose of the Quality System is to monitor compliance with an MME to ensure compliance with Subpart M and thereby ensure the maintenance aspects of operational safety. In particular, this part of the Quality System provides a monitor of the effectiveness of maintenance (see JAR OPS 1.890), and should include a feedback system to ensure that corrective actions are identified and carried out in a timely manner.

1.905 – MME

Operators must provide a MME, which must be approved, with details of the organisation structure (See AMC OPS 1.905(a)), including:

• The nominated postholder responsible for the maintenance system (see JAR OPS 1.175(i)(2)) and the person, or group, referred to in JAR OPS 1.895(b)

• The procedures to satisfy the maintenance responsibility of JAR OPS 1.890 and the quality functions of 1.900, except that where the operator is JAR 145 approved, such details may be included in the JAR–145 exposition

AMC OPS 1.905(a)

The purpose of the MME is to set forth the procedures, means and methods of the operator. Compliance with its contents will assure compliance with JAR OPS 1 Subpart M, which, in conjunction with an appropriate JAR 145 AMO Exposition, is a prerequisite for acceptance of the operator's maintenance system.

Where an operator is appropriately approved as a JAR 145 AMO, the Exposition of the maintenance organisation may form the basis of the Operator's MME in a combined document as follows:

JAR 145 Exposition

• Part 1 - Management

• Part 2 - Maintenance Procedures

• Part L2 - Additional Line Maintenance

• Part 3 - Quality System Procedures*

• Part 4 - Contracted JAA Operators

• Part 5 - Appendices (samples)

*Must also cover Quality functions (1.900).

Additional parts should cover:

• Part 0 - General Organisation

• Part 6 - Maintenance Procedures

Where an operator is not approved under JAR 145 but has a maintenance contract with a JAR 145 AMO, the MME should comprise:

• Part 0 - General Organisation

• Part 1 - Maintenance Procedures

• Part 2 - Quality System

• Part 3 - Contracted Maintenance

Personnel are expected to be familiar with relevant parts of the Exposition.

The operator must specify who should amend the document, particularly when there are several parts.

The person responsible for management of the Quality System should be responsible for monitoring and amending the Exposition, unless otherwise agreed, including associated procedures manuals, and submission of proposed amendments. The Authority may agree a procedure, which will be stated in the amendment control section, defining the class of amendments which can be incorporated without the prior consent.

The MME may be published electronically, and be made available to the Authority in an acceptable form. Attention should be paid to compatibility.

Part 0 (General Organisation) should include a corporate commitment, signed by the Accountable Manager, confirming that the MME and associated manuals define compliance with JAR OPS 1 Subpart M and will be complied with at all times. The statement should embrace the intent of the following paragraph (thouh it may be used without amendment). Modifications should not alter the intent:

This exposition defines the organisation and procedures upon which the Authority* Approval under JAR OPS 1 Subpart M is based.

These procedures are approved by the undersigned and must be complied with, as applicable, in order to ensure that all maintenance of .....(quote Operator's name)...... fleet of aircraft is carried out on time to an approved standard.

It is accepted that these procedures do not override the necessity of complying with any new or amended regulation published by the Authority* from time to time where these new or amended regulations are in conflict with these procedures .

It is understood that the Authority* will approve this organisation whilst the Authority* is satisfied that the procedures are being followed and the work standard maintained. It is understood that the Authority* reserves the right to suspend, vary or revoke the JAR OPS Subpart M maintenance system approval of the organisation, as applicable, if the Authority* has evidence that the procedures are not followed and the standards not upheld.

It is further understood that suspension or revocation of the approval of the maintenance system would invalidate the AOC.

Signed ....

Dated ....

Accountable Manager and ...(quote position).......

For and on behalf of .....(organisation's name)...... "

*For *Authority* insert the actual name of the JAA-NAA, for example, RLD, RAI, LBA, DGAC, CAA, etc. etc.

When the accountable manager is changed, the new one must sign the statement at the earliest opportunity as part of the acceptance by the JAA-NAA. Failure to carry out this action invalidates the JAR OPS M approval.

Appendices 1 and 2 contain examples of Exposition layouts for JAR 145 and non-JAR 145 operators (not included here).

1.910 – Maintenance Program

Aeroplanes must be maintained under the operator's maintenance program, which must be approved and contain details, including frequency, of the maintenance to be carried out. It must include a reliability program when one is necessary (see AMC OPS 1.910(a).)

AMC OPS 1.910(a)

The maintenance program should be managed and presented by the operator to the Authority.

Where implementation of the content of a program is accomplished by a JAR 145 AMO, the AMO should have access to the relevant parts of the program when the organisation is not the author. *Implementation* means preparation and planning of maintenance tasks under the program.

The aeroplane should only be maintained to one program at any time. Where an operator wishes to change to another, a transfer Check/Inspection may need to be done.

The program should contain a preface which will define the program contents, inspection standards to be applied, permitted variations to task frequencies and, where applicable, any procedure to escalate established check/inspection intervals.

Appendix 1 to AMC OPS 1.910 (a) &(b) provides detailed guidance on the content of an approved maintenance program (see below).

Where an operator wishes to use an aeroplane with the initial program based upon the MRBR process, associated programs for continuous surveillance of reliability or health monitoring should be considered as part of the maintenance program. Where an type has been subjected to MRBR, an operator should normally develop the initial maintenance program on the MRBR.

The documentation supporting the development of maintenance programs for types subjected to MRBR should contain cross-references to MRBR tasks, such that it is always possible to relate them to the current program. This does not prevent the program from being developed in the light of service experience to beyond MRBR recommendations, but will show their relationship.

Some operator's programs, not developed from the MRB Process, utilise reliability programs, which should be considered as a part of the program.

Reliability programs should be developed for programs based upon MSG logic, or those that include condition monitored components, or that do not contain overhaul time periods for all significant system components. However, they need not be developed for programs of aeroplanes of 5700 kg and below, or that do contain overhaul time periods for all significant system components.

The purpose of a reliability program is to ensure that maintenance program tasks are effective and their periodicity is adequate. It follows that actions resulting from the reliability program may be not only to escalate or delete maintenance tasks, but also to de-escalate or add them, as necessary.

A reliability program provides an appropriate means of monitoring the effectiveness of the maintenance program.

AMC OPS 1.910(b)

The documentation that approves the maintenance program may include details of who may issue certificates of release to service, and define which tasks are considered as base maintenance activity. Development of the program depends on satisfactory in-service experience which has been properly processed. In general, the task being considered for escalation beyond MRB limits should have been satisfactorily repeated at the existing frequency several times before being proposed for escalation. Appendix 1 to AMC OPS 1.910 (a) & (b) gives further guidance (below).

The Authority may approve a part of or an incomplete program at the start of operating a new type or with a new operator, but the program is only valid for a period not exceeding required maintenance not yet approved. The following examples illustrate two possibilities:

- A new type may not have completed the acceptance process for structural inspection or corrosion control. The operator's program cannot be approved as complete but it is reasonable to approve for a limited period, say, 3000 hrs or 1 year

- A new operator may not have established suitable arrangements for high-life time checks. The Authority may be unable to approve the complete program, preferring to opt for a limited period.

If the Authority is no longer satisfied that a safe operation can be maintained, approval may be suspended or revoked. Events giving rise to such action include:

- Suspending the operation of that type for at least one year (by the operator)

- Periodic review of the program showing that the operator has failed to ensure that it reflects maintenance needs, such that safe operation can be assured.

Appendix 1 to AMC OPS 1.910(a) & (b)

The maintenance program should contain.

- Type/model and registration number of the aeroplane, engines, auxiliary power units and propellers

- Name and address of the operator

- Reference identification of the program document; date of issue and issue number

- A statement signed by the operator to the effect that the specified aeroplanes will be maintained to the program and that the program will be reviewed and updated as required by paragraph 5

- Contents/list of effective pages

- Check periods which reflect anticipated utilisation of the aeroplane. Such utilisation should be stated and include a tolerance of up to 25%. Where utilisation cannot be anticipated, calendar time limits should also be included

- Procedures for escalation of check periods, where applicable and acceptable

- Provision to record date and reference to approved amendments

- Details of preflight maintenance tasks done by maintenance staff and not flight crew

- The tasks and when each part of the aeroplane, engines, APUs, propellers, components, accessories, equipment, instruments, electrical and radio apparatus, and associated systems and installations should be inspected, with the type and degree of inspection

- When items should be checked, cleaned, lubricated, replenished, adjusted and tested

- Details of specific structural inspections or sampling programs

- Details of the corrosion control program

- Periods and procedures for the collection of engine health monitoring data

- When overhauls and/or replacements by new or overhauled parts should be made

- A cross-reference to other documents which contain the details of maintenance tasks related to mandatory life limitations, CMRs and ADs

> **Note**: To prevent inadvertent variations to such tasks or intervals these items should not be included in the main portion of the maintenance program document, or any planning control system, without specific identification of their mandatory status.

- Details of, or cross-reference to, any required Reliability Program or statistical methods of continuous Surveillance

- A statement that practices and procedures to satisfy the Program should be to the standards in the Type Certificate Holder's Maintenance Instructions. When practices and procedures are included in a customised Operator's Maintenance Manual approved by the Authority, the statement should refer to it.

- Each maintenance task should be defined in a definition section

Program Basis
Programs should normally be based upon the Maintenance Review Board Report, where available, and the Type Certificate holder's Maintenance Planning Document or Chapter 5 of the Maintenance Manual, (i.e. the Manufacturer's recommended Maintenance Program). The structure and format of these maintenance recommendations may be rewritten to better suit operations and control of the program.

For a newly type-certificated aeroplane, where no previously approved Maintenance Program exists, the operator must comprehensively appraise the manufacturer's recommendations (and the MRB Report), together with other airworthiness information, to produce a realistic Program for approval.

For existing types, it is permissible to make comparisons with programs previously approved, alhough it should not be assumed that approval is automatic. Evaluation is to be made of aircraft/fleet utilisation, landing rate, equipment fit and, in particular, experience of the maintenance organisation. Where the Authority is not satisfied that the proposed program can be used as-is, the Authority should request the Operator to introduce appropriate changes, such as additional maintenance tasks or de-escalation of check frequencies, or to develop the initial maintenance program based upon Manufacturer's recommendations.

Amendments
Amendments (revisions) should be raised by the operator, to reflect changes in the type certificate holder's recommendations, modifications, service experience, or as required by the Authority. Reliability programs form one important method of updating approved programs.

Permitted Variations to Maintenance Periods
The Operator may only vary the periods prescribed by the Program with approval.

Periodic Review of Contents
Programs should be subject to periodic review to ensure they reflect current Type Certificate holder's recommendations, revisions to the MRBR, mandatory requirements and maintenance needs. Detailed requirements should be reviewed at least annually for continued validity in the light of experience.

1.915 - Technical Log
Operators must use an approved tech log system with the following information for each aeroplane:

- Information about each flight to ensure continued flight safety

- The current certificate of release to service

- The current maintenance statement giving the status of what scheduled and out-of-phase maintenance is next due, except that the maintenance statement may be kept elsewhere with approval

- Outstanding deferred defects

- Necessary guidance on support

AMC OPS 1.915

The technical log is a system for recording defects and malfunctions discovered during operation and for recording details of maintenance between scheduled visits to base maintenance. In addition, it is used for recording operating information relevant to flight safety and should contain data that the operating crew needs to know. Where a separate means of recording defects or malfunctions in the cabin or galleys that affect safe operation or the safety of occupants is used, this forms part of the tech log.

The system may range from a simple single-section document to a complex system with many sections, but in all cases it should include the information specified for the example used here which happens to use a 5 section document/computer system:

Section 1
Contains the registered name and address of the operator, aeroplane type and complete international registration marks.

Section 2
When the next scheduled maintenance is due, including out-of-phase component changes. In addition, the current Certificate of Release to Service, for the complete aeroplane, issued normally after the last maintenance check.

Note: The flight crew does not need such details if the next scheduled maintenance is controlled by other acceptable means.

Section 3
Information considered necessary for continued flight safety, including:

- Aeroplane type and registration mark

- Date and place of takeoff and landing

- Times of takeoff and landing

- Running total of flying hours, to check time to the next maintenance (the flight crew does not need such details if the next scheduled maintenance is controlled by other acceptable means)

- Details of failures, defects or malfunctions affecting airworthiness or safe operation, including emergency systems, and any in the cabin or galleys known to the commander. Provision should be made for the commander to date and sign such entries, including, where appropriate, the nil defect state for continuity. Provision should be made for a Certificate of Release to Service or the alternate abbreviated Certificate of Release to Service after rectification of a defect or any deferred defect or maintenance check. Such a certificate appearing on each page of this section should readily identify the defect(s) to which it relates or the particular check. The alternate abbreviated C of RS consists of the following statement "JAR 145.50 release to service" in place of the full certification statement in AMC 145.50(b) para 1 (when used, the introductory section of the tech log should have an example of the full statement from AMC 145.50(b) para 1, with a note stating; "The alternate abbreviated certificate of release to service used in this technical log satisfies the intent of JAR 145.50(a) only. All other aspects of JAR 145.50(b) must be complied with")

- Fuel and oil uplifted and the fuel in the tanks at the beginning and end of each flight; provision to show, in the same units, the amount of fuel planned to be uplifted and the amount actually uplifted; provision for when ground de-icing and/or anti-icing was started and the type of fluid applied, including mixture ratio fluid/water

- The pre-flight inspection signature

In addition, it may be necessary to record the following supplementary information:

- The time spent in particular engine power ranges where power used affects the life of the engine or module. Maximum or Inter Contingency Power are two examples.

- The number of landings where they affect the life of an aeroplane or component.

- Flight cycles or flight pressure cycles where they affect the life of an aeroplane or component.

Note 1: Where Section 3 is of the multisector 'part removable' type then such 'part removable' sections should contain all of the foregoing information where appropriate.

Note 2: Section 3 should be designed such that one copy of each page may remain on the aeroplane and another on the ground until completion of the flight. See also JAR OPS 1.140 *Information Retained on the Ground* (Subpart B).

Note 3: Section 3 lay-out should be divided to show clearly what is required after flight and for the next flight.

Section 4

Details of all deferred defects that affect or may affect safe operation and which should be known to the commander. Each page should be pre-printed with the operator's name and page serial number and record:

- A cross reference for each deferred defect, so that the original can be identified in the particular Section 3 Sector Record Page

- The original date of occurrence of the defect deferred

- Brief details of the defect

- Details of the eventual rectification carried out and its Certificate of Release to Service or a clear cross-reference back to the document that contains the details

Section 5

Any necessary information the commander needs to know, such as how to contact maintenance if problems arise en route, etc.

The Tech Log System can be either a paper or computer system, or any combination.

1.920 - Maintenance Records

The tech log must be retained for 24 months after the date of last entry. A system must be established to keep the following records:

All detailed maintenance records for the aeroplane and components	24 months after the aeroplane or component was released to service
Total time and flight cycles of the aeroplane and life-limited components	12 months after the aeroplane is permanently withdrawn from service
Time and flight cycles since last overhaul	Until an overhaul has been superseded by another of equivalent scope and detail
The current aeroplane inspection status, so compliance with the maintenance program can be established	Until the inspection has been superseded by another of equivalent scope and detail
The current status of ADs	12 months after the aeroplane is permanently withdrawn from service
Details of current modifications and repairs to the aeroplane, engine(s), propeller(s) and other components vital to flight safety	12 months after the aeroplane is permanently withdrawn from service

When an aeroplane is permanently transferred from one operator to another, the first two records must also be transferred, and the time periods will continue to apply to the new operator.

AMC OPS 1.920

Operators should ensure that a complete JAR 145 Certificate of Release to Service is received such that the required records can be retained. The system to keep the records should be described in the MME or the relevant JAR 145 exposition.

When operators arrange for the maintenance organisation to retain copies of records on their behalf, they will still be responsible for them. If they cease to be operators, they are also responsible for transferring the records to the next operator.

Keeping maintenance records in a form acceptable to the Authority normally means in paper form, or on a computer database, or a combination. Microfilm or optical discs are also acceptable (which may be carried out at any time. Records should be as legible as the original record, and remain so for the required retention period). Paper systems should use robust material that withstands normal handling and filing. The record should remain legible throughout the required retention period.

Computer systems should have at least one backup system, updated at least within 24 hours of any maintenance. Terminals must contain safeguards against unauthorised personnel altering things.

Information on times, dates, cycles etc. (see JAR OPS 1.920) or *summary maintenance records* are those that give an overall picture on the state of maintenance. The current status of life-limited components should indicate the component life limitation, total number of hours, accumulated cycles or calendar time and the number of hours/cycles/time remaining before the retirement time of the component is reached.

The current status of ADs should identify the applicable ones, including revision or amendment numbers. Where an AD is generally applicable to the aeroplane or component type but not to the particular aeroplane or component, this should be identified. The AD status includes when the AD was accomplished, and, where the AD is controlled by flight hours or cycles, it should include the total flight hours or cycles, as appropriate. For repetitive ADs, only the last application should be recorded in the AD status. The status should also specify which part of a multi-part directive has been accomplished and the method, where a choice is available in the AD.

Details of current modification and repairs means the substantiating data* supporting compliance with airworthiness. This can be in the form of an STC, Service Bulletin, Structural Repair Manual or similar. If the airworthiness data for modification and repair is produced by the JAR 145 organisation under existing national regulations, all documentation necessary to define the change and its approval should be retained.

*The *substantiating data* may include:

- Compliance program

- Master drawing or drawing list, production drawings, installation instructions

- Engineering reports (static strength, fatigue, damage tolerance, fault analysis, etc.)

- Ground and flight test program and results

- Mass and balance change data

- Maintenance and repair manual supplements

- Maintenance program changes and instructions for continuing airworthiness

- Aeroplane flight manual supplement

Records should be stored in a safe way with regard to fire, flood, theft and alteration. Computer backup discs, tapes etc., should be stored in a different, safe, location.

IEM OPS 1.920(b)(6)
A "component vital to flight safety" means one that includes Life Limited Parts, or is subject to Airworthiness Limitations, or a major component such as undercarriage and flight controls.

AMC OPS 1.920(c)
Where an operator terminates operations, all retained maintenance records should be passed on to the new operator or, if there is none, stored as required. A "permanent transfer" does not generally include the dry lease-out of less than 6 months, but all records necessary for the duration of the lease agreement must be transferred to the lessee or made accessible to them.

1.930 - Continued Validity of AOC
Comply with JAR OPS 1.175 and 1.180 in respect of the maintenance system.

IEM OPS 1.930
This paragraph covers scheduled changes to the maintenance system. Whilst the requirements relating to AOCs, including their issue, variation and continued validity, are in Subpart C, this paragraph is in Subpart M to ensure that operators are aware there is a requirement elsewhere.

1.935 - Equivalent Safety Case

Alternative procedures must not be introduced unless needed, and an equivalent safety case has first been approved and supported by JAA.

IEM OPS 1.935

This paragraph is intended to provide necessary flexibility to the Authority so it can accept alternate means of compliance with Subpart M, particularly for advancement of technology. Once agreed by JAA, the alternative means of compliance will be proposed for inclusion in JAROPS 1 Subpart M, after NPA consultation, but, in the meantime, may be published as a Maintenance TGL.

1.940 - Composition of Flight Crew

Operators must ensure that:

- The composition of the flight crew and their numbers at designated crew stations are in compliance with, and at least the minimum specified in, the Flight Manual

- The flight crew includes additional members when required by the operation, and is not reduced below the numbers in the Ops Manual

- All flight crew members hold applicable and valid licences and are suitably qualified and competent

- Procedures are established to prevent the crewing together of inexperienced flight crews (See AMC OPS 1.940(a)(4))*

- One pilot, qualified as PIC under JAR FCL, is designated as commander, who may delegate conduct of the flight to another suitably qualified pilot

- When a dedicated System Panel Operator is required by the Flight Manual, the flight crew includes one member with a Flight Engineer's licence or is otherwise suitably qualified and acceptable

- When using freelancers or part-timers, Subpart N is complied with

In this respect, particular attention must be paid to the total number of types or variants flown for commercial air transport, which must not exceed the requirements in JAR OPS 1.980 and 1.981,

including when services are engaged by another operator. For crew members as commanders, initial operator's CRM training must be done before starting unsupervised line flying unless the crew member has previously done an initial operator's CRM course (but see also 1.943).

Minimum Crew for IFR or at Night

For turboprops with more than 9 passenger seats and for all turbojets, the minimum flight crew is 2 pilots. Others may be single-pilot if the requirements of Appendix 2 (below) are satisfied. If they are not, minimum flight crew is 2 pilots.

AMC OPS 1.940(a)(4) - *Inexperience

A flight crew member is inexperienced, after a Type Rating or command course, and associated line flying under supervision, until achieving on type either:

- 100 hours and 10 sectors in a consolidation period of 120 consecutive days, or

- 150 hours and 20 sectors (no time limit).

Fewer hours or sectors may be acceptable when:

- A new operator is starting up

- A new type is introduced

- Flight crew have previously done a type conversion course with the same operator

- Maximum Takeoff Mass is below 10 tonnes or there are less than 20 passenger seats

Appendix 1 - In-Flight Relief

A flight crew member may be relieved in flight at the controls by another suitably qualified flight crew member.

Relief of Commander

The commander may delegate conduct of the flight to another qualified commander, or, for operations only above FL 200, a pilot qualified as below.

Minimum Requirements for Relief Pilots
- Valid ATPL

- Conversion training and checking (including Type Rating training) as per JAR OPS 1.945

- All recurrent training and checking as per JAR OPS 1.965 and 1.968

- Route competence as per 1.975

Relief of Co-pilot
The co-pilot may be relieved by a suitably qualified pilot or cruise relief co-pilot qualified as below.

Minimum Requirements for Relief Co-Pilot
- CPL/IR

- Conversion training and checking, including Type Rating training, as per JAR OPS 1.945, except the takeoff and landing training

- All recurrent training and checking as per JAR OPS 1.965, except the takeoff and landing training

- To operate as co-pilot in the cruise only, not below FL 200

- Recent experience as in JAR OPS 1.970 is not required. The pilot must, however, carry out Flight Simulator recency and refresher flying skill training within every 90 days, which may be combined with the training in JAR OPS 1.965

Relief of System Panel Operator
A system panel operator may be relieved in flight by a crew member with a Flight Engineer's licence or flight crew member with a suitable qualification.

Appendix 2 - Single Pilot IFR or Night
Aeroplanes in JAR OPS 1.940(b)(2) may be operated by a single pilot under IFR or at night when the following requirements are satisfied:

- The Ops Manual must include a pilot's conversion and recurrent training program which includes the additional requirements for a single pilot operation

- In particular, cockpit procedures must include engine management and emergency handling, use of normal, abnormal and emergency checklists, ATC communication, departure and approach procedures, autopilot management and use of simplified in-flight documentation

- The recurrent checks required by JAR OPS 1.965 must be performed in the single pilot role on the type or class of aeroplane in a representative environment

- The pilot must have at least 50 hours' flight time on the specific type or class of aeroplane under IFR, of which 10 hours is as commander

- The minimum required recency must be 5 IFR flights, including 3 instrument approaches, during the preceding 90 days on the type or class of aeroplane in the single-pilot role. This may be replaced by an IFR instrument approach check on the type or class of aeroplane

1.943 - Initial CRM Training
When a flight crew member has not previously done initial CRM training (new employees or existing staff), an initial CRM course must be done (new employees must do it within their first year).

If the flight crew member has not previously been trained in Human Factors, a theoretical course, based on the human performance and limitations program for the ATPL (see FCL) must be done before initial CRM training, or combined with it.

Initial CRM training must be conducted by at least one acceptable CRM trainer who may be assisted by experts for specific areas (see AMC OPS 1.943/1.945(a)(9)/1.955(b)(6)/1.965(e)).

Initial CRM training must be done under a detailed syllabus in the Ops Manual.

AMC
See after 1.945

1.945 - Conversion Training and Checking
Flight crews must do a Type Rating course which satisfies the requirements (see JAR FCL) when changing from one type to another, or class for which a new type or class rating is required.

Flight crews must do an operator's conversion course before starting unsupervised line flying when changing to an aeroplane for which a new type or class rating is required, or when changing operators.

Conversion training must be done by suitably qualified people under a detailed syllabus in the

Ops Manual. Personnel integrating CRM into conversion training must be suitably qualified.

The training required by the conversion course must be determined after due note has been taken of the crew member's previous training in the training records in JAR OPS 1.985.

Minimum standards of qualification and experience required of flight crews before conversion training must be specified in the Ops Manual.

Flight crews must undergo the checks required by JAR OPS 1.965(b) and the training and checks required by JAR OPS 1.965(d) before starting line flying under supervision.

On completion of line flying under supervision, the check required by JAR OPS 1.965(c) must be done.

Once a conversion course has been started, a flight crew member must not undertake flying duties on another type or class until the course is completed or terminated.

Elements of CRM must be integrated into the conversion course (see AMC OPS 1.943/1.945(a)(9)/1.955(b)(6)/1.965(e) & IEM OPS 1.943/1.945(a)(9)/1.955(b)(6)/1.965(e) and AMC OPS 1.945(a)(9) and IEM OPS 1.945(a)(9)).

For changing aeroplane type or class, the check required by 1.965(b) may be combined with the type or class rating skill test under FCL.

The operator's conversion course and the Type or Class Rating course required for Flight Crew Licences may be combined.

Appendix 1 - Conversion Course

Conversion courses must include (in this order):

- Ground training and checking, including aeroplane systems, normal, abnormal and emergency procedures

- Emergency and safety equipment training and checking which must be completed before aeroplane training commences

- Aeroplane/STD training and checking

- Line flying under supervision and line check

Elements of CRM must be integrated, and conducted by suitably qualified personnel.

When a flight crew member has not previously completed an operator's conversion course, the operator must ensure that the flight crew member also undergoes general first aid training and, if applicable, ditching procedures training using the equipment in water.

AMC OPS 1.945 - Conversion Syllabuses

Type Rating Training

Type rating training may be conducted separately or as part of conversion training. When it is part of conversion training, the program should include all the requirements of JAR FCL.

Ground Training

There should be a properly organised program of ground instruction by training staff with adequate facilities, including audio, mechanical and visual aids. However, if the aeroplane is relatively simple, private study may be adequate if suitable manuals and/or study notes are provided.

The course should incorporate formal tests on systems, performance and flight planning, etc.

Emergency and Safety Equipment

On the initial conversion course and on subsequent courses, the following should be addressed:

- Instruction on first aid in general (Initial course only), as relevant to type and crew complement including where no cabin crew are required (Initial and subsequent)

- Aeromedical topics including Hypoxia, Hyperventilation, Contamination of the skin/eyes by aviation fuel or hydraulic or other fluids, Hygiene and food poisoning and Malaria

- The effect of smoke in an enclosed area and actual use of relevant equipment in a simulated smoke-filled environment

- Operational procedures of security, rescue and emergency services

- Survival information for the area

- The use of survival equipment carried

- A comprehensive drill to cover ditching procedures should be practised where flotation equipment is carried. This should include the actual donning and inflation of a lifejacket, with a demonstration or film of the inflation of life-rafts and/or slide-rafts and associated equipment. This should, on an initial course, be done with the equipment in water, although previous certificated training with another operator or the use of similar equipment will be accepted in lieu of further wet-drill training.

- The location of emergency and safety equipment, correct use of appropriate drills, and procedures in different emergency situations. Evacuation of the aeroplane (or a representive training device) by use of a slide should be included when the Ops Manual requires early evacuation of flight crew to assist on the ground.

Aeroplane STD Training

Flying training should be structured and comprehensive enough to familiarise the flight crew member thoroughly with all aspects of limitations and normal/abnormal and emergency procedures, and should be carried out by suitably qualified TRIs and/or TREs. For specialised operations such as steep approaches, ETOPS or AWO, additional training should be carried out.

In planning aeroplane/STD training on aeroplanes with a flight crew of two or more, particular emphasis should be placed on LOFT with emphasis on CRM.

Normally, the same training and practice should be given to copilots as well as commanders. The 'flight handling' sections of the syllabus should include all the requirements of the OPC.

Unless the type rating training program has been carried out in a ZFT flight simulator, the training should include at least 3 takeoffs and landings in the aeroplane.

Line Flying Under Supervision

After training and checking on the conversion course, flight crew should do a minimum number of sectors and/or flying hours under the supervision of a suitable flight crew member. Minimum sectors/hours should be specified in the Operations Manual and be determined by previous experience, complexity of the aeroplane, and the type and area of operation.

A line check under JAR OPS 1.945(a)(8) should be completed afterwards.

System Panel Operator

Conversion training should approximate that of pilots. If the flight crew includes a pilot with duties of an SPO, he should, after training and initial checks, operate a minimum number of sectors under the supervision of a nominated additional flight crew member. The minimum figures should be in the Ops Manual and be selected after note has been taken of the complexity of the aeroplane and experience of the flight crew member.

IEM OPS 1.945 - Line Flying under Supervision

This allows a flight crew member to carry into practice the procedures and techniques learned on a conversion course, accomplished under a flight crew member specifically nominated and trained for the task. After line flying under supervision, the respective crew member should be able to perform a safe and efficient flight at his station.

The following minimum figures are guidelines for use when establishing individual requirements.

Turbojets

- *Co-pilot on first conversion*: total 100 hours or at least 40 sectors.

- *Co-pilot upgrading to commander*: At least 20 sectors for new types, or 10 if already qualified.

AMC 1.943/1.945(a)(9)/1.955(b)(6)/1.965(e) - (CRM)

Crew Resource Management (CRM) is the effective utilisation of all available resources (e.g. crew members, aeroplane systems, supporting facilities and people) to achieve safe and efficient operation.

The idea is to enhance the communication and management skills of flight crews, with emphasis on the non-technical aspects of their performance.

Initial CRM Training

These are designed to provide knowledge of, and familiarity with, human factors relevant to flight operations. The course should be at least one day for single-pilot operations and two for others. It should cover all elements in Table 1, column (a) to the level required by column (b) (not given here).

A CRM trainer should possess group facilitation skills and should at least:

- Have current commercial air transport experience as flight crew, and have either successfully passed the HPL examination with a recent ATPL (see FCL), or, if holding a Licence acceptable under JAR OPS 1.940(a)(3) before the introduction of HPL into the ATPL syllabus, followed a theoretical HPL course covering the syllabus of the HPL exam.

- Have completed initial CRM training

- Be supervised by suitably qualified CRM training personnel when conducting their first initial CRM training session

- Have received additional education in group management, group dynamics and personal awareness

However, when acceptable, a flight crew member holding a recent qualification as a CRM trainer may continue to be one even after the cessation of active flying duties, and an experienced non-flight crew CRM trainer with a knowledge of HPL may also continue to be a CRM trainer. A former flight crew member with knowledge of HPL may become a CRM trainer if he maintains adequate knowledge of the operation and aeroplane type and meets the provisions above.

Initial CRM training must address the nature of operations, as well as the associated procedures and culture of the company. This will include areas of operations with particular difficulties or adverse climatic conditions and any unusual hazards.

Other courses may be used as approved, but content must meet operational requirements.

CRM skills should not be assessed during initial CRM training.

Conversion Course CRM

If the flight crew member undergoes a conversion course with a change of type, all elements in Table 1, column (a) should be integrated into all appropriate phases of the conversion course and covered to the level required by column (c), unless the two operators use the same CRM provider.

If the flight crew member undergoes a conversion course with a change of operator, all elements in Table 1, column (a) should be integrated into all appropriate phases of the conversion course and covered to the level required by column (d).

Flight crews should not be assessed when completing elements of CRM training which are part of an operator's conversion course.

Command Course CRM

All elements in Table 1, column (a) must be integrated into the command course and covered to the level required by column (e).

Flight crews should not be assessed on elements of CRM training which are part of the command course, although feedback should be given.

Recurrent CRM Training

Elements of CRM must be integrated into recurrent training every year, with all elements in Table 1, column (a) covered to the level in column (f). Modular CRM training must cover the same areas over periods of 3 years.

Relevant modular CRM training must be conducted by CRM trainers qualified under paragraph 2.2.

Flight crews should not be assessed on elements of CRM training which are part of recurrent training.

Flight and Cabin Crew Training

Operators should provide combined training for flight and cabin crew, including briefing and debriefing, with an effective liaison between training departments. Provision should be made for instructors to observe and comment on each others' training.

Assessment of CRM Skills

Assessment of CRM skills should provide feedback to the individual and serve to identify retraining areas, and be used to improve the training system.

Before the introduction of CRM skills assessment, a detailed description of the CRM methodology including terminology, should be published in the Operations Manual.

Operators should establish procedures to be applied if people do not achieve or maintain the required standards (Appendix 1 to 1.1045, Section D, paragraph 3.2 refers).

If the OPC is combined with the Type Rating revalidation/renewal check, the assessment of CRM skills will satisfy the Multi Crew Co-operation requirements of the Type Rating revalidation/renewal. This will not affect the validity of the Type Rating.

IEM 1.943/1.945(a)(9)/1.955(b)(6)/1.965(e) – CRM

CRM training should reflect the culture of the operator, with classroom training and practical exercises, including group discussions and accident and incident reviews to analyse communication problems and examples of a lack of information or crew management.

Consideration should be given to using synthetic training devices which reproduce a realistic operational environment and permit interaction. This includes, but is not limited to, those with appropriate LOFT scenarios.

Initial CRM training should be conducted in a group session outside the company premises so the opportunity is provided for flight crews to interact and communicate away from their usual working environment.

Assessment of CRM Skills

Assessment is the process of observing, recording, interpreting and evaluating pilot performance and knowledge. It includes the concept of self-critique, and feedback which can be given continuously during training or in summary after a check.

CRM skills assessment should be included in an overall assessment of the crew member's performance and be under approved standards. Suitable methods of assessment should be established, with the selection criteria and training requirements of the assessors and their relevant qualifications, knowledge and skills.

Individual assessments are not appropriate until the crew member has completed the initial CRM course and the first OPC. For first CRM skills assessment, the following methodology is satisfactory:

- Operators should include an agreed terminology, which should be evaluated with regard to methods, length of training, depth of subjects and effectiveness

- A training and standardisation program for training personnel should then be established

- For a transition period, the evaluation system should be crew rather than individually based

Levels of Training.

Overview training will normally be instructional in style. Such training should refresh knowledge gained in earlier training.

In Depth Training will normally be interactive and should include, as appropriate, case studies, group discussions, role play and consolidation of knowledge and skills. Core elements should be tailored to the specific needs of the training phase.

AMC OPS 1.945(a)(9) - Automation

The conversion course should include training in the use and knowledge of automation and the recognition of systems and human limitations associated with its use.

The objective should be to provide appropriate knowledge, skills and behavioural patterns for managing and operating automated systems.

Special attention should be given to how automation increases the need for crews to have a common understanding of the way in which the system performs, and any features of automation which make this understanding difficult.

1.950 - Differences & Familiarisation Training

Flight crew members must complete:

- *Differences Training*, which requires additional knowledge and training on an appropriate training device or the aeroplane when operating another variant of the same type or another type of the same class, or when changing equipment and/or procedures on types or variants currently operated

- *Familiarisation Training,* which requires acquisition of additional knowledge when operating another aeroplane of the same type, or when changing equipment and/or procedures on current types or variants

The Operations Manual should specify when such training is required.

1.955 - Nomination as Commander

For upgrade to commander from co-pilot, and for those joining as commanders, a minimum level of experience must be specified in the Ops Manual and, for multi-crew, the pilot must complete an appropriate command course, which must be specified in the Ops Manual and include at least:

- Training in an STD (including LOFT) and/or flying training

- An OPC as commander

- Commander's responsibilities

- Line training in command under supervision (at least 10 sectors are required for pilots already qualified on type)

- Completion of a commander's line check as per JAR OPS 1.965(c) and route and aerodrome competence qualification as per JAR OPS 1.975

- Elements of CRM

1.960 - Commanders with a CPL

A CPL holder must not operate as a commander of an aeroplane certificated for single-pilot unless:

- When carrying passengers under VFR more than 50 nm from an aerodrome of departure, they have at least 500 hours total aeroplane time, or an IR (in addition, for multi-crew, and before operating as commander, the command course in JAR OPS 1.955(a)(2) must be done), or

- On a multi-engined type under IFR, they have at least 700 hours total aeroplane time, which includes 400 PIC (under JAR FCL), of which 100 hours have been under IFR including 40 multi-engined. The 400 hours PIC may be substituted by co-pilot hours on the basis of two to one, if gained within an established multi- crew system as per the Ops Manual. When single pilot under IFR, Appendix 2 to JAR OPS 1.940 must also be satisfied

1.965 - Recurrent Training & Checking

Flight crews must do recurrent training and checking, relevant to the type or variant operated. A program must be in the Ops Manual and approved by the Authority.

Recurrent Training

This must be done by:

- *Ground and Refresher Training* – suitably qualified personnel

- *Aeroplane/STD Training* - by a TRI, CRI, or for STD content, an SFI, if they satisfy the experience and knowledge requirements enough to instruct on the items in paras (a)(1)(i)(A) and (B) of Appendix 1 to JAR OPS 1.965

- *Emergency and Safety Equipment Training* – suitably qualified personnel

- *CRM* - by the personnel conducting recurrent training, when integrating CRM elements into other phases (assuming they are qualified). Modular CRM training must be done by at least one acceptable CRM trainer, who may be assisted by experts to address specific areas

Recurrent Checking

This must be done by:

- *Operator Proficiency Check* – by a TRE, CRE or, if the check is done in a STD, a TRE, CRE or SFE, trained in CRM concepts and the assessment of CRM skills

- *Line Checks* – by suitably qualified commanders nominated by the operator and acceptable to the Authority

- *Emergency and safety equipment checking* – by suitably qualified personnel

Operator Proficiency Check

Flight crew members must do these to demonstrate competence in their normal, abnormal and emergency procedures. They must be done without external visual reference when required to operate under IFR.

OPCs must be done as part of a normal flight crew complement.

The validity period is 6 calendar months, plus the remainder of the month of issue. If issued within the final 3 months of validity of a previous check, the validity extends from the date of issue until 6 months from the original expiry date.

Line Check

These are for demonstrating competence in normal line operations as described in the Ops Manual. The validity period is 12 calendar months, plus the remainder of the month of issue. If issued within the final 3 months of validity of a previous check, the validity extends from the date of issue until 12 months from the original expiry date.

Emergency and Safety Equipment

The location and use of emergency and safety equipment carried. The validity period is 12 calendar months, plus the remainder of the month of issue. If issued within the final 3 months of validity of a previous check, the validity extends from the date of issue until 12 calendar months from the original expiry date.

CRM

Elements of CRM must be integrated into all appropriate phases of recurrent training, and flight crew members must do specific modular CRM training. All major topics must be covered over a period up to 3 years.

Ground and Refresher Training

Flight crews must do ground and refresher training at least every 12 calendar months. If done within the 3 months before the expiry of the 12-month period, the next must be done within 12 months of the original expiry date.

STD Training

Must be done at least every 12 calendar months. If done within the 3 calendar months before the expiry of the 12-month period, the next must be done within 12 calendar months of the original expiry date.

Appendix 1 – Pilots

Recurrent Training

Ground and refresher training must include:

- Aeroplane systems

- Operational procedures and requirements including ground de-/anti-icing (See AMC OPS 1.345(a)) and pilot incapacitation (see AMC to Appendix 1 to JAROPS 1.965)

- Accident/Incident and occurrence review

Knowledge is verified by a questionnaire or similar.

STD Training

All major failures of systems and associated procedures must have been covered in the preceding 3 year period. Engine failures must be simulated.

Aeroplane/STD training may be combined with the OPC.

Emergency and Safety Equipment

Training may be combined with checking.

Every year, the training must include:

- Actual donning of a lifejacket and protective breathing equipment

- Actual handling of fire extinguishers

- The location and use of emergency and safety equipment, and exits

- Security procedures

Every 3 years, the training must include:

- Actual operation of all types of exits

- Demonstration of how to use slides

- Actual fire-fighting with representative equipment, except that an alternative to Halon may be used

- Effects of smoke in enclosed areas and actual use of equipment in simulated smoke-filled environments

- Actual handling of pyrotechnics, real or simulated

- Demonstration in use of liferaft(s)

Crew Resource Management (CRM)

Elements of CRM must be integrated into all appropriate phases of recurrent training. A specific modular CRM program must ensure that all major topics training are covered over a period up to 3 years, as follows:

- Human error and reliability, error chain, error prevention and detection

- Company safety culture, SOPs, organisational factors

- Stress, stress management, fatigue and vigilance

- Information acquisition and processing, situational awareness, workload management

- Decision making

- Communication and coordination inside and outside the cockpit

- Leadership and team behaviour, synergy

- Automation and philosophy of the use of Automation (if relevant to the type)

- Specific type-related differences

- Case based studies

Additional areas warranting extra attention, as identified by the accident prevention and flight safety program (see JAR OPS 1.037).

Recurrent Checking

Where applicable, **OPCs** must include:

- Rejected takeoff when a flight sim is available for that specific aeroplane, otherwise touch drills only

- Takeoff with engine failure between V_1 and V_2 or as soon as safety permits

- Precision instrument approach to minima with, for multi-engined aeroplanes, one engine out

- Non-precision approach to minima

- Missed approach on instruments from minima with, for multi-engined aeroplanes, one engine out

- Landing with one engine out. For single-engined aeroplanes, a practice forced landing is required.

Engine failures must be simulated. In addition to the above, the requirements for the revalidation or renewal of aircraft Type or Class Ratings must be done every 12 months and may be combined with the OPC.

For VFR only, the last four checks above may be omitted, except for an approach and go-around in a multi-engined aeroplane with one engine out.

OPCs must be done by a TRE.

For **Emergency and Safety Equipment** checks, the items to be checked must be those for which training has been carried out above.

Line checks must establish the ability to do a complete line operation, including pre- and postflight procedures and use of equipment, as specified in the Ops Manual.

The flight crew must be assessed on their CRM skills with a methodology in the Ops Manual. The purpose is to provide feedback to the crew collectively and individually and serve to identify retraining, and be used to improve the CRM training system.

Pilots assigned as PF and PM must be checked in both functions.

Line checks must be done in aeroplanes, by commanders nominated by the operator (see

1.965(a)(4)(ii)), who must be trained in CRM concepts and the assessment of CRM skills. They normally occupy an observer's seat, but for longhaul with additional crew, the person may be a cruise relief pilot not occupying either pilot's seat during takeoff, departure, initial cruise, descent, approach and landing. His CRM assessments must be based solely on observations during the initial briefing, cabin briefing, cockpit briefing and phases where he occupies the observer's seat.

AMC to Appendix 1 - Incapacitation Training
Procedures should be established to train flight crew to recognise and handle pilot incapacitation. This training should be done every year and can form part of other recurrent training. It should take the form of classroom instruction, discussion or video or other similar means. If a suitable Flight Simulator is available, practical training should be done every 3 years.

Appendix 2 – System Panel Operators
Recurrent training and checking is as for pilots, plus additional specific duties, omitting items that do not apply. It must, whenever possible, take place concurrently with pilots.

A line check must be conducted by a commander nominated by the operator, or a System Panel Operator Type Rating Instructor or Examiner.

AMC OPS 1.965 (c) - Line Checks
Pilots required to operate as Pilot Flying and Pilot Monitoring should be checked on alternate sectors as one or the other, but where procedures require integrated flight preparation and cockpit initialisation, and pilots perform both duties on the same sector, the line check may be done on a single sector.

AMC OPS 1.965(d) - Emergency & Safety Equipment Training
The successful resolution of emergencies requires interaction between flight and cabin crew, and emphasis should be placed on the importance of effective co-ordination and communication between crew members in various emergencies.

Emergency and Safety Equipment training should include joint practice in evacuations so that all involved are aware of other peoples' duties. If this is not possible, combined flight and cabin crew training should include joint discussion of emergency scenarios.

Emergency and safety equipment training should, as far as practicable, take place in conjunction with cabin crew on similar training with emphasis on co-ordinated procedures and two-way communication between the flight deck and the cabin.

IEM OPS 1.965 - Recurrent Training and Checking
Line checks, route and aerodrome competency, and recency requirements are intended to ensure the ability to operate efficiently under normal conditions, whereas other checks and emergency and safety equipment training are to prepare crew members for abnormal/emergency procedures.

The line check is done in the aeroplane. All other training and checking should be done in the aeroplane (of the same type) or an STD or flight simulator or, for emergency and safety equipment training, a representative training device. The type of equipment should be representative of the instrumentation, equipment and layout of the type.

Line Checks
The line check is considered to be an important factor in the development, maintenance and refinement of high standards, and can provide a valuable indication of the usefulness of training policy and methods (it is not intended to determine competence on any particular route). Line checks are a test of the ability to perform a complete line operation, including pre- and postflight procedures and use of required equipment as per the Ops Manual. The route should give adequate representation of the scope of normal operations. When weather conditions preclude a manual landing, an automatic one is acceptable. The commander, or any pilot who may be required to relieve the commander, should also demonstrate the ability to 'manage' the operation and take appropriate command decisions.

Proficiency Training and Checking
When an STD is used, the opportunity should be taken, where possible, to use LOFT.

Proficiency training and checking for System Panel Operators should, where practicable, take place at the same time as for the pilot.

1.968 - Pilots in Either Pilot's Seat

Pilots who may be assigned to operate in either pilot's seat must complete appropriate training and checking, and the (acceptable) program must be specified in the Ops Manual.

Appendix 1

Additional training and checking must be done as per the Ops Manual, concurrent with the OPCs in JAR OPS 1.965(b), to include at least:

- An engine failure during takeoff
- A OEI approach and go-around
- A OEI landing

Engine failures must be simulated.

Checks required for the left-hand seat must be valid and current.

Pilots relieving commanders must demonstrate, concurrent with the OPC, practice of drills and procedures which would not normally be their responsibility.

Where the differences between left and right seats are not significant (say, because of the autopilot) practice may be conducted in either seat.

A pilot other than the commander in the left-hand seat must demonstrate practice of drills and procedures, concurrent with the OPC, which would otherwise have been the commander's responsibility acting as Pilot Monitoring.

1.970 - Recent Experience

Commander

Commanders must have carried out at least three takeoffs and landings as PF in an aeroplane of the same type/class or in a Flight Simulator, of the type to be used, in the preceding 90 days*.

Co-pilot

Co-pilots must have operated the controls as a pilot for three takeoffs and landings in an aeroplane of the same type/class or in a relevant Flight Simulator, in the preceding 90 days*.

*This may be extended up to 120 days by line flying under a TRI or TRE. For periods beyond 120 days, the recency requirement is satisfied by a training flight, or use of a relevant flight sim.

AMC OPS 1.970

When using a Flight Simulator for meeting the landing requirements in JAR-OPS 1.970(a)(1) and (a)(2), complete visual traffic patterns or complete IFR procedures starting from the Initial Approach Fix should be flown.

IEM OPS 1.970(a)(2) - Co-pilot Proficiency

A co-pilot at the controls is either PF or PM. The only required takeoff and landing proficiency is for type-rating proficiency checks.

1.975 - Route and Aerodrome Competence

Before being assigned as commander or pilot to whom conduct of a flight may be delegated, pilots must have adequate knowledge of the route and aerodromes (including alternates), facilities and procedures to be used.

The validity period of route and aerodrome competence is 12 calendar months, plus the remainder of the month of qualification or latest operation on the route or to the aerodrome.

Revalidation is done by operating on the route or to the aerodrome within the validity period.

If revalidated within the final 3 months of previous qualifications, validity extends from the date of revalidation until 12 months from the original expiry date.

AMC OPS 1.975

Route Competence

Training should include knowledge of:

- Terrain and minimum safe altitudes
- Seasonal meteorological conditions
- Meteorological, communication and air traffic facilities, services and procedures
- Search and rescue procedures
- Navigational facilities associated with routes along which flight takes place

Depending on the complexity of the route, as assessed by the operator, the following methods of familiarisation should be used:

- For less complex routes, familiarisation by self-briefing with route documentation, or by means of programd instruction

- For more complex routes, in addition to the above, inflight familiarisation as a commander, co-pilot or observers under supervision, or familiarisation in an STD using a database appropriate to the route

Aerodrome Competence

Aerodromes are classified in Categories A, B and C, in ascending order of complexity. The Ops Manual should specify parameters which qualify an aerodrome to be in Category A, then provide a list of those which are B or C.

- *Category A* aerodromes have an approved instrument approach procedure, at least one runway with no performance limitations for takeoff and/or landing, published circling minima up to 1 000 feet above aerodrome level, and night capability.

- *Category B* aerodromes do not satisfy Category A, or require extra considerations, such as non-standard approach aids and/or approach patterns, unusual local weather or characteristics or performance limitations, or any other relevant considerations including obstructions, physical layout, lighting etc. Before operating to a Category B aerodrome, the commander should be briefed, or self-briefed by programmed instruction, and should certify that he has carried out these instructions.

- *Category C* aerodromes require even more consideration. Before operating to one, the commander should be briefed and visit the aerodrome as an observer and/or practice in a Flight Simulator. This instruction should be certified by the operator.

1.978 - Advanced Qualification Program

Validity periods of JAR OPS 1.965 and 1.970 may be extended where the Authority has approved an AQP established by the operator. The Program must contain training and checking which

establishes and maintains a proficiency at least that of JAR OPS 1.945, 1.965 and 1.970.

1.980 - Operation on More Than One Type

To operate on more than one type or variant, flight crews must be competent. Differences must justify such operations, allowing for the level of technology, operational procedures and handling characteristics (see AMC OPS 1.980(b) and IEM OPS 1.980(b))

Flight crew members operating more than one type or variant must comply with Subpart N for each one, unless the Authority has approved credit(s) related to training, checking and recency.

Appropriate procedures and/or operational restrictions must be in the Ops Manual, covering:

- Minimum experience levels

- How crews qualified on one type or variant will be trained and qualified on another

- Recency requirements

Appendix 1

When flight crew members operate more than one class, type or variant in AMC FCL 1.215A (class - single pilot) and/or AMC FCL 1.220 (type - single pilot), but not within a single licence endorsement, they may not operate more than three piston-engined or turboprop type or variant, or one turboprop and one piston engined, or one turboprop type or variant and any aeroplane within a particular class.

For more than one type or variant within one or more licence endorsements (see AMC FCL 1.220B (type - multi-pilot)), the minimum crew in the Ops Manual must be the same for each type or variant.. Crew members may not operate more than two types or variants for which a separate endorsement is required, and only aeroplanes within one licence endorsement may be flown in any duty period, unless procedures ensure adequate preparation.

Note: Where more than one licence endorsement is involved, see below.

When a flight crew member operates more than one type or variant in AMC FCL 1.220 A and B, but not within a single licence endorsement, an operator must comply with the above, and, for 1.220 B (type - multi pilot), but not within a single licence endorsement, before exercising the privileges of 2 licence endorsements:

- Flight crew members must have done two consecutive OPCs with 500 hours in the relevant crew position in commercial operations with the same operator

- For a pilot with experience with an operator and exercising privileges of 2 licence endorsements, and then being promoted to command with the same operator on one of those types, the minimum experience as commander is 6 months and 300 hours, and the pilot must have done 2 consecutive OPCs before again being eligible to exercise 2 licence endorsements

Before starting training for and operating another type or variant, crew members must have done 3 months and 150 hours on the base aeroplane, to include at least one proficiency check. After the initial line check on the new type, 50 hours or 20 sectors must be achieved solely on the new type.

The period within which line experience is required on each type must be in the Ops Manual.

Where credits are sought to reduce training, checking and recency between types, the operator must demonstrate which items need not be repeated because of similarities (See AMC OPS 1.980(c) and IEM OPS 1.980(c)).

JAR OPS 1.965(b) requires two OPCs every year. When credit is given for OPCs and line checks to alternate between the two types, each revalidates the other. If the period between OPCs does not exceed that in JAR FCL for each type, the JAR FCL requirements will be satisfied. In addition, relevant and approved recurrent training must be in the Ops Manual.

Emergency and safety equipment stuff must cover all requirements for each type.

When a flight crew member operates combinations of types or variants as defined by AMC FCL 1.215 (class - single pilot) and Appendix 2 of AMC FCL 1.220 (type - multi pilot) operators must show that specific procedures and/or operational restrictions are approved under JAR OPS 1.980(d).

AMC OPS 1.980 - Difference Levels

Level A
Level A training can be adequately addressed through self-instruction with page revisions, bulletins or differences handouts. Level A introduces a different version of a system or component already understood. The differences result in no, or only minor, changes in procedures.

A check related to differences is not required when training, but the crew member is responsible for acquiring the knowledge and may be checked during proficiency checking.

Level B
Level B training can be adequately addressed through aided instruction, such as slide/tape presentation, computer based instruction which may be interactive, video or classroom instruction. Such training is typically used for part-task systems requiring knowledge and training with, possibly, partial application of procedures (eg. fuel or hydraulic systems etc.).

A written or oral check is required for initial and recurrent differences training.

Level C
Level C training should be accomplished wih "hands on" STDs qualified as per JAR STD 2A, Level 1 or higher. The differences affect skills, abilities as well as knowledge but do not require the use of "real time" devices. Such training covers normal and non-normal procedures (for example, flight management systems).

An STD for level C or higher is used for a check of conversion and recurrent training. The check should utilise a "real time" flight environment such as the demonstration of the use of a flight management system. Manoeuvres not related to the specific task do not need to be tested.

Level D
Level D training addresses differences that affect knowledge, skills and abilities for which training will be given in a simulated flight environment involving, "real time" flight manoeuvres for which the use of an STD under JAR STD 2A, Level 1 would not

suffice, but for which motion and visual clues are not required. Such training would typically involve an STD as per JAR STD 2A, Level 2.

A proficiency check for each type or variant should be done after initial and recurrent training, but credit may be given for common manoeuvres and need not be repeated. Items trained to level D differences may be checked in STDs under JAR STD 2A, Level 2. Level D checks will therefore comprise at least a full proficiency check on one type or variant and a partial check at this level on the other.

Level E
Level E provides a realistic and operationally oriented flight environment achieved only with Level C or D Flight Simulators or the aeroplane itself. Level E training should be conducted for types and variants which are significantly different from the base aeroplane and/or for which there are significant differences in handling qualities.

A proficiency check on each type or variant should be done in a level C or D Flight Simulator or the aeroplane itself. Training or checking on each Level E type or variant should be done every 6 months. If training and checking are alternated, a check on one type or variant should be followed by training on the other so a crew member receives at least one check every 6 months and at least one on each type or variant every 12 months.

AMC OPS 1.980(b) - ODR Tables
Some tables here about using base aeroplanes and differences in designs and systems.

IEM OPS 1.980(b) - Philosophy and Criteria
The concept of operating more than one type or variant depends upon the experience, knowledge and ability of the operator and flight crew.

The first consideration is whether or not the two types or variants are similar enough to allow the safe operation of both. The second is whether or not they are similar enough for the training, checking and recency items done on one type or variant to replace those required on the other. If these aeroplanes are similar in these respects, it is possible to have credit for training, checking and recent experience. Otherwise, all training, checking and recent experience requirements in Subpart N

should be completed for each type or variant within the relevant period.

Differences between Types or Variants
The first stage in any submission for crew multi-type or variant operations is to consider the differences, mainly in the level of technology (flight deck layout, instrumentation, FMS, flight controls, pitch trim systems, engines, etc.

Consideration of operational differences involves mainly the pilot-machine interface, and compatibility of paper or automated checklists, manual vs automatic selection of navaids, navigation equipment, weight and performance. Consideration of handling characteristics includes control response, crew perspective and handling techniques in all stages of operation, encompassing flight and ground characteristics as well as performance influences (eg. number of engines). The capabilities of the autopilot and autothrust systems may affect handling characteristics as well as operational procedures. Alternating training and proficiency checking may be allowed if it is shown that there are enough similarities in technology, operational procedures and handling characteristics.

There are examples of completed ODR tables for proposals, which are not included here.

1.981 – Helicopters and Aeroplanes
Operations are limited to one type of each, with appropriate procedures and/or operational restrictions in the Ops Manual.

1.985 - Training Records
Operators must maintain records of all training, checking and qualification and make them available, on request, to the crew member.

IEM OPS 1.985
A summary of training should be maintained to show a flight crew member's completion of each stage of training and checking.

1.988 – Cabin Crew

All crew members, other than flight crew members, assigned to duties in the passenger compartment must comply with this Subpart, except for extra ones solely assigned to specialist duties.

IEM OPS 1.988 – Extra Crew - Specialist Duty

Additional crew members solely on specialist duties who are exempt Subpart O include:

- Child minders/escorts
- Entertainers
- Ground engineers
- Interpreters
- Medical personnel
- Secretaries
- Security staff

1.990 - Number and Composition

Aeroplanes that can carry more than 19 passengers, when carrying one or more, must have at least one cabin crew member for duties (specified in the Ops Manual), for assenger safety. The minimum number of cabin crew is the greater of:

- one for every 50, or fraction of 50, passenger seats on the same deck
- the number who actively participated in the cabin during the emergency evacuation demonstration, or were assumed to have taken part in the relevant analysis, except that, if the maximum seating configuration is less than the number evacuated by at least 50 seats, the cabin crew may be reduced by 1 for every 50 seats

The Authority may, under exceptional circumstances, require additional cabin crew. However, in unforeseen circumstances, the minimum numbers may be reduced if the number of passengers has been reduced under procedures in the Ops Manual, and a report is submitted after the flight.

For freelancers, Subpart O must be complied with. Particular attention must be paid to the total number of types or variants cabin crew members may fly in commercially, which must not exceed the requirements in JAR OPS 1.1030, including when their services are engaged by other operators.

IEM OPS 1.990

The demonstration or analysis in JAR OPS 1.990(b)(2) should be the most applicable to the type, or variant, and the seating configuration used by the operator.

With reference to JAR OPS 1.990(b), the Authority may require extra cabin crew on certain types of aeroplane or operation. Factors to take into account include:

- The number and type of exits, and associated slides
- The location of exits in relation to cabin crew seats and the cabin layout
- The location of cabin crew seats allowing for duties in an emergency evacuation
- Actions to be performed by cabin crew in ditchings, including deployment of slide-rafts and launching of life-rafts

When the cabin crew is reduced below the minimum required (e.g. by sickness), the procedures in the Ops Manual consider at least:

- Reduction of passenger numbers
- Re-seating of passengers with regard to exits and other limitations
- Relocation of cabin crew and change of procedures

When scheduling cabin crew for a flight, account should be taken of experience - some should have at least 3 months experience as cabin crew.

1.995 - Minimum Requirements

Cabin crew members must be at least 18, pass a medical (see AMC OPS 1.995(a)(2)), and remain medically fit and competent.

AMC OPS 1.995(a)(2)

Initial medical examinations and re-assessments should be conducted by, or be under the supervision of, a suitable medical practitioner.

A medical record should be kept for each cabin crew member.

The following medical requirements apply:

- Good health

- Free from physical or mental illness which might lead to incapacitation or inability to perform duties

- Normal cardiorespiratory function

- Normal central nervous system

- Adequate visual acuity 6/9 with or without glasses

- Adequate hearing

- Normal function of ear, nose and throat

1.1000 - Senior Cabin Crew

Senior cabin crew members must be nominated when more than one cabin crew member is assigned. They are responsible to the commander for the conduct and co-ordination of normal and emergency procedure(s) in the Ops Manual.

Senior cabin crew members must have at least one year's experience and complete an appropriate course (see IEM OPS 1.1000 (c).)

There must be procedures to select the next most suitably qualified cabin crew if the nominated one becomes unable to operate, taking account of operational experience.

IEM OPS 1.1000(c) - Training
Training for senior cabin crew should include:

- Preflight Briefing

  - Operating as a crew

  - Allocation of cabin crew stations and responsibilities

  - Consideration of the particular flight including aeroplane type, equipment, area and type of operation including ETOPS, and categories of passenger, including disabled, infants and stretcher cases

- Cooperation Within the Crew

  - Discipline, responsibilities and chain of command

  - Importance of co-ordination and communication

- Pilot incapacitation

- Review of Operator & Legal Requirements

  - Passengers safety briefing, safety cards

  - Securing of galleys

  - Stowage of cabin baggage

  - Electronic equipment

  - Procedures when fuelling with passengers on board

  - Turbulence

  - Documentation

- Human Factors and CRM (this should ideally include participation in flight simulator LOFT exercises)

- Accident and incident reporting

- Flight and duty time limitations and rest requirements

1.1005 - Initial Training

Cabin crew members must successfully completes initial training. The program must be approved by the Authority, under Appendix 1 to JAR OPS 1.1005, and the checking prescribed in JAR OPS 1.1025 done before conversion training.

Appendix 1
Initial training must be done by suitably qualified people.

Fire and Smoke Training
Must include:

- Emphasis on the responsibility of cabin crew for dealing promptly with emergencies involving fire and smoke and, in particular, the importance of identifying the actual source of fire

- The importance of informing the flight crew immediately, as well as the specific actions for co-ordination and assistance, when fire or smoke is discovered

- The necessity for frequent checking of potential fire-risk areas, including toilets, and associated smoke detectors

- Classification of fires and the appropriate type of extinguishers, the application of extinguishing agents, the consequences of misapplication, and use in a confined space

- General procedures of ground-based emergency services at aerodromes

Water Survival Training

Must include the actual donning and use of personal flotation equipment in water.

Before first operating on an aeroplane with life-rafts or similar, training must be given on its use, as well as actual practice in water.

Survival Training

Must be appropriate to the area, (e.g. polar, desert, jungle or sea).

Medical Aspects and First Aid

Must include:

- Instruction on first aid and use of first aid kits

- First aid associated with survival training and appropriate hygiene

- The physiological effects of flying, with particular emphasis on hypoxia

Passenger Handling

Must include:

- Advice on recognition and management of passengers who are, or become, intoxicated or are under the influence of drugs, or aggressive

- How to motivate passengers and crowd control to expedite evacuation

- Regulations covering the safe stowage of cabin baggage (including cabin service items) and the risk of it becoming a hazard to occupants or otherwise obstructing or damaging safety equipment or exits

- Correct seat allocation with reference to mass and balance. Particular emphasis must also be given on the seating of disabled passengers, and the necessity of seating able-bodied passengers next to unsupervised exits

- Duties in the event of turbulence, including securing the cabin

- Precautions when live animals are carried in the cabin

- Dangerous Goods training as per Subpart R

- Security, including Subpart S

Communication

During training, emphasis must be placed on the importance of communication between cabin and flight crew, including technique, common language and terminology.

Discipline and Responsibilities

Must include:

- The importance of performing duties as per the Ops Manual

- Continuing competence and fitness, with special regard to flight and duty time limitations and rest requirements

- An awareness of the regulations relating to cabin crew and the role of the Authority

- General knowledge of relevant aviation terminology, theory of flight, passenger distribution, meteorology and areas of operation

- Pre-flight briefing and provision of safety information as per their duties

- Ensuring that relevant documents and manuals are kept up-to-date

- Identifying when cabin crew members have the authority and responsibility to initiate evacuation and other emergency procedures

- The importance of safety duties and responsibilities and the need to respond promptly and effectively to emergencies

Crew Resource Management

Appropriate JAR OPS requirements must be included in the training.

IEM OPS 1.1005/1.1010/1.1015/1.1020 - Representative Training Devices

A representative training device may be used instead of the aeroplane or required equipment. However, only items relevant to the training and testing to be given should accurately represent the aeroplane in the following particulars:

- Layout of the cabin in relation to exits, galley areas and safety equipment stowage

- Type and location of passenger and cabin crew seats

- Where practicable, exits in all modes of operation (particularly in relation to method of operation, their mass and balance and operating forces)

- Safety equipment as provided in the aeroplane (may be 'training use only' items and, for oxygen and protective breathing equipment, units charged with or without oxygen may be used)

AMC to Appendix 1 (and Appendix 1 to JAR-OPS 1.1015) - CRM Training

Initial and recurrent CRM training should be provided for cabin crew members, who should not be assessed. It should utilise all available resources (e.g. crews, aeroplane systems and supporting facilities) for safe and efficient operations.

Emphasis should be placed on the importance of co-ordination and two-way communication between flight and cabin crew in various abnormal and emergency situations, and on normal coordination and communication within the crew including the use of correct terminology, common language, and communications equipment.

Initial and recurrent CRM training should ideally include combined flight and cabin crew in practice evacuations.

Combined flight and cabin crew training should, include joint discussion of emergency scenarios.

Cabin crew should be trained to identify unusual situations that might occur inside the passenger compartment, as well as activity outside that could affect the safety of the aeroplane or passengers.

There should be an effective liaison between flight and cabin crew training departments, with provision for instructors to observe and comment on each others' training.

Recurrent CRM training can be part of, and included in, other recurrent training.

IEM to Appendix 1 (and 1.1015) - CRM Training

CRM training should include:

- The nature of operations as well as associated crew operating procedures and areas of operations which produce particular difficulties, such as adverse weather and unusual hazards

- Awareness of flight crew management of various emergency situations and consequential effects on the operation of the aeroplanes

- Where practicable, the participation of the senior cabin crew member in flight sim LOFT exercises.

IEM to Appendix 1 to JAR-OPS 1.1005/1.1015/1.1020 - First Aid Training

This should include the physiology of flight, including oxygen requirements, and hypoxia, and medical emergencies in aviation including:

- Choking

- Stress reactions and allergic reactions

- Hyperventilation

- Gastro-intestinal disturbance

- Air sickness

- Epilepsy

- Heart attacks

- Stroke

- Shock

- Diabetes

- Emergency childbirth

- Asthma

Basic first aid and survival training should also be covered, including care of the unconscious, burns, wounds and fractures and soft tissue injuries.

Also, practical cardio-pulmonary resuscitation by each cabin crew member, wth regard to the aeroplane environment, with a specifically designed dummy, and the use of appropriate equipment including first-aid kits and first-aid oxygen.

IEM to Appendix 1 to JAR-OPS 1.1005/1.1010/1.1015/1.1020 - Crowd Control

This training should include:

- Communications between flight crew and cabin crew and use of all communications equipment, including the difficulties of co-ordination in a smoke-filled environment

- Verbal commands

- Physical contact to encourage people out of an exit and onto a slide (just push!)

- Redirection of passengers away from unusable exits

- Marshalling of passengers away from the aeroplane

- Evacuation of disabled passengers

- Authority and leadership

IEM to Appendix 1 to JAR-OPS 1.1005/1.1010/1.1015/1.1020 - Training Methods

Training may include the use of mock-up facilities, video presentations, computer based training and other types of training. A reasonable balance between the different methods should be achieved.

IEM to Appendix 1 to JAR-OPS 1.1010/1.1015 - Conversion and Recurrent Training

A review should be carried out of previous initial training under JAR OPS 1.1005 to confirm that nothing has been left out. This is especially important for cabin crew first transferring to aeroplanes with liferafts or similar equipment.

Fire and Smoke Training

Training requirement/interval	Required activity
First conversion to type (e.g. new entrant)	Actual fire fighting and handling equipment (Note 1)
Every year during recurrent training	Handling equipment
Every 3 years during recurrent training	Actual fire fighting and handling equipment (Note 1) (Notes 2 & 3)
Subsequent a/c conversion	(Note 1) (Note 1)
New fire fighting equipment	Handling equipment

1. Actual fire fighting during training must include use of at least one extinguisher and extinguishing agent as used on the aeroplane. An alternative may be used in place of Halon.

2. Fire fighting equipment must be handled if it is different to that previously used.

3. Where the equipment between aeroplane types is the same, training is not required if within the validity of the 3 year check.

1.1010 - Conversion & Differences Training

Cabin crew must complete appropriate training, as in the Ops Manual, before duties as follows:

Conversion Training

A conversion course must be done before being first assigned as a cabin crew member, or to operate another type.

Differences Training

Must be done before operating on a variant of a type currently operated, or with different safety equipment, safety equipment location, or normal and emergency procedures on currently operated types or variants.

The content of the training must take account of any previous training as in the training records required by JAR OPS 1.1035.

Training must be done in a structured and realistic manner (see Appendix 1), and must include the use of all safety equipment and all normal and emergency procedures for the type or variant. It must involve training and practice on either a representative training device or the aeroplane.

Appendix 1

Conversion and differences training must be conducted by suitably qualified people, including the location, removal and use of all safety and survival equipment carried, as well as all related normal and emergency procedures.

Fire and Smoke Training

Cabin crews must be given realistic and practical training in the use of all fire fighting equipment, including protective clothing representative of that carried, to include extinguishing a fire characteristic of an interior fire (except that an alternative to Halon may be used), and the donning and use of PBE in an enclosed, simulated smoke-filled environment.

Operation of Doors and Exits

Cabin crew must operate and actually open all normal and emergency exits for passenger evacuation in an aeroplane or representative training device, and be shown the operation of all other exits, such as flight deck windows.

Evacuation Slide Training

Crew members must descend an evacuation slide fitted to an aeroplane or a representative training device from a height representative of the aeroplane main deck sill height

Evacuation and Other Emergencies

Emergency evacuation training must include the recognition of planned or unplanned evacuations on land or water, and recognition of when exits are unusable or evacuation equipment is unserviceable.

Crew members must be trained to deal with:

- In-flight fires, with particular emphasis on identifying the source
- Severe air turbulence
- Sudden decompression, including donning portable oxygen equipment
- Other in-flight emergencies

Crowd Control

Training must be given on practical aspects of crowd control in various emergencies, as applicable to the type.

Pilot Incapacitation

Unless the minimum flight crew is more than two, cabin crew must be trained to assist if a pilot becomes incapacitated, to include a demonstration of:

- The pilot's seat mechanism
- Fastening and unfastening the pilot's seat harness
- Use of pilot's oxygen equipment
- Use of pilots' checklists

Safety Equipment

Cabin crews must be given realistic training on, and demonstration of, the location and use of safety equipment, including:

- Slides, and, for self-supporting slides, the use of associated ropes
- Life-rafts and slide-rafts, including equipment attached, and/or carried
- Lifejackets, infant lifejackets and flotation cots
- Dropout oxygen system
- First-aid oxygen
- Fire extinguishers
- Fire axe or crow-bar
- Emergency lights including torches
- Communications equipment, including megaphones
- Survival packs, including contents
- Pyrotechnics (actual or representative devices)
- First-aid kits, their contents and emergency medical equipment
- Other cabin safety equipment or systems where applicable

Passenger Briefing/Safety Demonstrations
Training must be given in the preparation of passengers for normal and emergency situations under JAR OPS 1.285.

1.1012 - Familiarisation
After conversion training, cabin crews must undergo familiarisation before operating as part of the minimum crew required by JAR OPS 1.990.

AMC OPS 1.1012
New entrant cabin crews with no previous comparable experience should visit the aeroplane and participate in familiarisation flights as described below. Those on a subsequent type with the same operator can do either.

Familiarisation flights should form part of the training record for each cabin crew member. During the flights, cabin crews should be additional to the minimum number (see JAR OPS 1.990). Familiarisation flights should be conducted under the senior cabin crew member, and should be structured to involve cabin crew members in the participation of safety related pre-flight, in-flight and post-flight duties. Uniform should be worn.

The purpose of aeroplane visits is to familiarise cabin crews with the aeroplane environment and its equipment. Thus, they should be conducted by suitably qualified people under a syllabus in the Ops Manual, Part D. The visit should provide an overview of the aeroplane's exterior, interior and systems including:

- Interphone and public address systems
- Evacuation alarm systems
- Emergency lighting
- Smoke detection systems
- Safety/emergency equipment
- Flight deck
- Cabin crew stations
- Toilet compartments
- Galleys, galley security and water shut-off
- Cargo areas if accessible from the passenger compartment during flight
- Circuit breaker panels located in the passenger compartment
- Crew rest areas
- Exit location and its environment

An aeroplane visit may be combined with the conversion training under JAR OPS 1.1010(c)(3).

1.1015 - Recurrent Training
Cabin crews must undergo recurrent training, covering the actions in normal and emergency procedures and drills relevant to the type(s) and/or variant(s) on which they operate (see Appendix 1).

The recurrent training and checking program, as approved, must include theoretical and practical instruction, together with individual practice.

The validity period is 12 calendar months, plus the remainder of the month of issue. If issued within the final 3 months of a previous check, the validity extends from the date of issue until 12 calendar months from the original expiry date.

Appendix 1
Recurrent training must be conducted by suitably qualified people. Every 12 months, the practical training program must include:

- Emergency procedures, including pilot incapacitation
- Evacuation procedures, including crowd control
- Touch-drills for opening normal and emergency exits for passenger evacuation
- Location and handling of emergency equipment, including oxygen systems, and donning of lifejackets and PBE
- First aid and contents of first aid kit(s)
- Stowage of articles in the cabin
- Security procedures
- Incident and accident review
- CRM

Every 3 years, recurrent training must also include:

- Operation and actual opening of normal and emergency exits for evacuation, in an aeroplane or representative training device

- Demonstration of the operation of other exits, including flight deck windows

- Realistic and practical training in the use of firefighting equipment, including protective clothing, representative of that carried, to include extinguishing a typical interior fire (using something else instead of Halon), and donning and using PBE in an enclosed, simulated smoke-filled environment.

- Use of pyrotechnics (actual or representative devices)

- Demonstration of the use of the liferaft, or slide-raft, where fitted

All appropriate JAR OPS requirements must be included in the training of cabin crew members.

IEM OPS 1.1015
A formalised course of recurrent training must be provided for cabin crew to ensure continued proficiency with all equipment relevant to the aeroplane types that they operate.

1.1020 - Refresher Training
Cabin crew who have been absent from flying for more than 6 months, but who are still current must do refresher training as per the Ops Manual, prescribed in Appendix 1, below. When they have been flying, but have not, in the previous 6 months, been a cabin crew member, they must either do refresher training on type or two re-familiarisation sectors (see AMC OPS 1.1012 (3)).

Appendix 1
Refresher training must be conducted by suitably qualified people and must include at least:

- Emergency procedures, including pilot incapacitation

- Evacuation procedures, including crowd control

- Operation and actual opening of normal and emergency exits for evacuation, in an aeroplane or representative training device

- Demonstration of the operation of other exits, including flight deck windows

- Location and handling of emergency equipment, including oxygen systems, and the donning of lifejackets, portable oxygen and PBE

AMC OPS 1.1020
In developing the content of refresher training programs, operators should consider (in consultation with Authorities) whether, for aeroplanes with complex equipment or procedures, refresher training may be necessary for absences less than the 6 months in JAR OPS 1.1020(a).

IEM OPS 1.1020(a)
An operator may substitute recurrent training for refresher training if the re-instatement of the cabin crew member's flying duties commences within the period of validity of the last recurrent training and checking. If the validity period of the last recurrent training and checking has expired, conversion training is required.

1.1025 - Checking
During or after the training required by JAR OPS 1.1005, 1.1010 and 1.1015, cabin crew mut undergo a check covering the training received to verify proficiency in normal and emergency safety duties, to be done by acceptable personnel.

- *Initial Training.* The items in Appendix 1 to JAR OPS 1.1005

- *Conversion and Differences Training.* The items in Appendix 1 to JAR OPS 1.1010

- *Recurrent Training.* The items in Appendix 1 to JAR OPS 1.1015, as appropriate

AMC OPS 1.1025
Elements of training requiring individual practical participation should be combined with practical checks, which should be accomplished by the method appropriate to the training, including:

- Practical demonstration and/or

- Computer based assessment and/or

- In-flight checks and/or

- Oral or written tests

1.1030 - More than One Type or Variant

Cabin crew must not operate on more than three types except that, with approval, they may operate on four, if, for at least two types, non-type specific normal and emergency procedures are identical, and safety equipment and type specific normal and emergency procedures are similar (for this putpose, variants of a type are different if they are not similar in emergency exit operation, location and type of portable safety equipment and type-specific emergency procedures.

ACJ OPS 1.1030

When determining the similarity of exit operation, the following should be assessed:

- Exit arming/disarming

- Direction of movement of the operating handl

- Direction of exit opening

- Power assist mechanisms

- Assist means, e.g. evacuation slides

Self-help exits, for example Type III and Type IV, need not be included.

When determining similarity of location and type of portable safety equipment, all portable safety equipment should be stowed in the same, or, exceptionally, in substantially the same location, and require the same method of operation.

Portable safety equipment includes:

- Fire fighting equipment

- Protective Breathing Equipment (PBE)

- Oxygen equipment

- Crew lifejackets

- Torches

- Megaphones

- First aid equipment

- Survival equipment and signalling equipment

- Other safety equipment where applicable

Type-specific emergency procedures include, but are not limited, to:

- Land and water evacuation

- In-flight fire

- Decompression

- Pilot incapacitation

When changing type or variant during a series of flights, the cabin crew safety briefing should include a representative sample of type-specific normal and emergency procedures and applicable safety equipment.

1.1035 - Training

Operators must maintain records of all training and checking required by JAR OPS 1.1005, 1.1010, 1.1015, 1.1020 and 1.1025, and make them available, on request, to the cabin crew member.

IEM OPS 1.1035 - Training Records

An operator should maintain a summary of training to show a trainee's completion of every stage of training and checking.

1.1040 – Operations Manual

The Operations Manual must contain all instructions and information necessary for operations personnel to perform their duties.

The contents, including amendments or revisions, must not contravene the the AOC or regulations (that is, they are supplemental), and must be acceptable to, or approved by, the Authority (see IEM OPS 1.1040(b).)

Unless otherwise approved, or under national law, the Ops Manual must be in English, although it may be translated into another language (see IEM OPS 1.1040(c).) It may be in separate volumes.

Operations personnel must have easy access to a copy of each relevant part, and crew members must have a personal copy of, or sections from, Parts A and B as relevant for personal study.

The Ops Manual must be amended or revised to keep it up to date. Operations personnel must be made aware of relevant changes, and people responsible for copies must insert the amendments.

The Authority must be supplied with intended amendments and revisions in advance of the effective date. Approval as required (see IEM below) must be obtained before then. When immediate amendments or revisions are required in the interest of safety, they may be published and applied immediately, provided that any approval required has been applied for.

All amendments and revisions required by the Authority must be incorporated.

Information from approved documents, and their amendments, must be correctly reflected in the Ops Manual, which should contain no contrary information. However, this does not prevent using more conservative data and procedures.

The Ops Manual must be useable without difficulty, though not necessarily on printed paper, with approval.

Using an abridged Ops Manual does not exempt operators from JAR OPS 1.130.

IEM OPS 1.1040(b) - Elements for Approval

A number of provisions of JAR OPS require prior approval, which means that related sections of the Ops Manual are subject to special attention. In practice, there are two options:

- The Authority approves a specific item (e.g. with a written response to an application) which is then included in the Ops Manual. In such cases, the Authority merely checks that the Ops Manual accurately reflects the content of the approval. In other words, text has to be acceptable to the Authority

- An application for an approval includes the related, proposed, Ops Manual text, in which case, the Authority's written approval encompasses approval of the text.

In either case, it is not intended that a single item is subject to two approvals. The following list indicates only those elements of the Ops Manual which require specific approval by the Authority (a full list of every approval required by JAR OPS is in Appendix 6 of the *Operations Joint Implementation Procedures* (JAA Administration & Guidance Material Section 4, Part 2, but you knew that anyway ☺).

Ops Manual	Subject	Reference
A 2.4	Operational Control	1.195
A 5.2(f)	Flight crew to operate on more than 1 type or variant	1.980
A 5.3(c)	Cabin crew to operate on four types	1.1030(a)
A 8.1.1	Determination of minimum flight attitudes	1.250(b)
A 8.1.4	En-route single engine safe forced landing area for land planes	1.542(a)
A 8.1.8 (i)	Standard mass values other than in Subpart J	1.620(g)
	(ii) Alternative documentation and related procedures	1.625(c)
Mass & balance:	(iii) Omission of data from documentation	App. 1, 1.625, § (a)(1)(ii)
	(iv) Special standard masses for traffic load	App. 1, 1.605, § (b) (ii)
A 8.1.11	Tech Log	1.915(b)
A 8.4	Cat II/III Operations	1.440(a)(3), (b) & App. 1 to JAR-OPS 1.455, Note
A 8.5	ETOPS Approval	1.246
A 8.6	Use of MEL	1.030(a)
A 9	Dangerous Goods	1.1155
A 8.3.2(b)	MNPS	1.243
A 8.3.2(c)	RNAV (RNP)	1.243
A 8.3.2(f)	RVSM	1.241
B 1.1(b)	Max. approved passenger seating configuration	1.480(a)(6)
B 2(g)	Alternate method for verifying approach mass (DH < 200ft) - Performance A	1.510(b)
B 4.1(h)	Steep Approaches and Short Landings - Performance B	1.515(a)(3) & (a)(4) & 1.550(a)
B 6(b)	Use of on-board mass and balance systems	App. 1 to JAR-OPS 1.625, § (c)
B 9	MEL	1.030(a)
D 2.1	Cat II/III Training syllabus flight crew	1.450(a)(2)
	Recurrent training program flight crew	1.965(a)(2)
	Advanced qualification program	1.978(a)
D 2.2	Initial training cabin crew	1.1005

Ops Manual	Subject	Reference
	Recurrent training program cabin crew	1.1015(b)
D 2.3(a)	Dangerous Goods	1.1220(a)

IEM OPS 1.1040(c) - Language

The Ops Manual should normally be prepared in English, but it is recognised that approval for the use of another language may be justifiable. The criteria on which such an approval may be based should include at least:

- Languages commonly used by the operator

- The language of related documentation, such as the Flight Manual

- Size and scope of the operation, i.e. domestic or international route structure

- Type of operation e.g. VFR/IFR

- The period of time requested for the use of another language

1.1045 – Structure & Contents

The main structure is as follows:

Part A - General/Basic

Non type-related operational policies, instructions and procedures for a safe operation.

0 - Aministration and Control of Ops Manual
0.1 Introduction

- A statement that the manual complies with applicable regulations and the terms and conditions of the AOC

- A statement that the manual contains operational instructions to be complied with by relevant personnel

- A list and brief description of the various parts, contents, applicability and use

- Explanations and definitions needed for use of the manual

0.2 - Amendments and Revisions

- Details of people responsible for issuing and inserting amendments

- A record of amendments with insertion and effective dates

- A statement that handwritten amendments and revisions are not permitted, except where immediately needed for safety

- A description of how pages are annotated and effective dates

- A list of effective pages

- Annotation of changes (on text pages and, as far as practicable, on charts and diagrams)

- Temporary revisions

- The distribution system

1 - Organisation & Responsibilities
1.1 - Organisational Structure

A description of the organisational structure including general company and operations department organigrams, which must depict the relationship between the Operations Department and the others. In particular, the subordination and reporting lines of all Divisions, Departments etc, which pertain to the safety of flight operations, must be shown.

1.2 - Nominated Postholders

The name of the people responsible for flight operations, the maintenance system, crew training and ground operations, as prescribed in JAR OPS 1.175(i), including a description of their function and responsibilities.

1.3 - Responsibilities and Duties of Operations Management Personnel

Pertaining to the safety of flight operations and compliance with applicable regulations.

1.4 - Authority, Duties and Responsibilities of the Commander

A statement defining them.

1.5 - Duties and Responsibilities of Crew Members other than the Commander

As above.

2 - Operational Control and Supervision
2.1 - Supervision of the Operation by the Operator

A description of the system (see JAR OPS 1.175(g)). This must show how the safety of flight operations and qualifications are supervised. In particular, the procedures related to licence and qualification validity, competence of operations personnel and control, analysis and storage of records, flight documents, additional information and data must be described

2.2 - System of Promulgation of Additional Operational Instructions and Information

A description of any system for promulgating operational information supplementary to that in the Operations Manual. The applicability of this information and the responsibilities for its promulgation must be included.

2.3 - Accident Prevention and Flight Safety Program

A description of the main aspects.

2.4 - Operational Control

Procedures and responsibilities necessary to exercise operational control for flight safety.

2.5 - Powers of the Authority

The powers of the Authority and guidance to staff on how to facilitate inspections.

3 – Quality System
A description of the quality system adopted including at least, policy, a description of the organisation of the Quality System, and allocation of duties and responsibilities.

4 – Crew Composition
4.1 Crew Composition

Method for determining crew composition, taking account of:

- The type of aeroplane
- The area and type of operation
- The phase of flight
- The minimum crew requirement and flight duty period planned

- Experience (total and on type), recency and qualification of crews
- Designation of commander and, if necessitated by the duration of the flight, the procedures for relief (see Appendix 1 to JAR OPS 1.940.)
- Designation of senior cabin crew member and, if necessitated by duration of flight, procedures for relief

4.2 - Designation of the Commander

The rules.

4.3 - Flight Crew Incapacitation

Instructions on the succession of command in the event of flight crew incapacitation.

4.4 - Operation on More than One Type

A statement indicating which aeroplanes are considered as one type for crew scheduling.

5 – Qualification Requirements
5.1 – General

A description of the required licence, rating(s), qualification/competency (e.g. for routes and aerodromes), experience, training, checking and recency for operations personnel. Consideration must be given to the aeroplane type, operation and composition of the crew.

5.2 - Flight Crew

Commander, pilot relieving the commander, co-pilot, pilot under supervision, system panel operator, operation on more than one type.

5.3 - Cabin Crew.

Senior cabin crew member, cabin crew member (required , additional and during familiarisation flights), operation on more than one type or variant.

5.4 - Training, Checking and Supervision Personnel

For flight and cabin crew.

5.5 - Other Operations Personnel

6 – Crew Health Precautions

The relevant regulations and guidance to crew members concerning health, including:

- Alcohol and other intoxicating liquor
- Narcotics
- Drugs
- Sleeping tablets
- Pharmaceutical preparations
- Immunisation
- Deep diving
- Blood donation
- Meal precautions before and in flight
- Sleep and rest
- Surgical operations

7 – Flight Time Limitations

7.1 - Flight and Duty Time Limitations and Rest Requirements

The scheme (developed by the operator) under Subpart Q (or national requirements until Subpart Q has been adopted).

7.2 - Exceedances of Flight and Duty Time Limitations and/or Reductions of Rest Periods

Conditions under which flight and duty time may be exceeded or rest periods reduced, and procedures for reporting.

8 – Operating Procedures

8.1 - Flight Preparation Instructions

- *8.1.1 - Minimum Flight Altitudes*
- *8.1.2 - Criteria for Usability of Aerodromes*
- *8.1.3 - Aerodrome Operating Minima.* For IFR flights under JAR OPS 1 Subpart E. Reference must be made to determination of visibility and/or RVR and applying actual visibility observed by the pilots, the reported visibility and the reported RVR.
- *8.1.4 - En-route Minima for VFR* and, for single-engined aeroplanes,

instructions for route selection with respect to surfaces which permit a safe forced landing.

- *8.1.5 - Presentation and Application of Operating Minima*
- *8.1.6 - Interpretation of Meteorological Information.* How to decode MET forecasts and reports.
- *8.1.7 - Determination of Quantities of Fuel, Oil and Water Methanol Carried.* How they are determined and monitored in flight, including the measurement and distribution of fluids on board, allowing for all likely circumstances, including in-flight replanning and failure of one or more engines. The system for maintaining fuel and oil records must also be described.
- *8.1.8 - Mass and Centre of Gravity.* Definitions, standard and/or actual masses, verification of documentation, Last Minute Changes, Specific gravities, Seating policy, etc.
- *8.1.9 - ATS Flight Plan*
- *8.1.10 - Operational Flight Plan*
- *8.1.11 - Technical Log*
- *8.1.12 - Documents To Be Carried*

8.2 - Ground Handling Instructions

- *8.2.1 - Fuelling Procedures.* Safety precautions during refuelling and defuelling, including when APUs or engines are running and prop-brakes are on, refuelling and defuelling when passengers are embarking, on board or disembarking, and precautions for avoiding mixing fuels.
- *8.2.2 - Aeroplane, Passengers and Cargo Handling Related to Safety.* Allocating seats, embarking and disembarking passengers and loading and unloading. Further procedures, aimed at achieving safety on the ramp, must also be given. Handling procedures must cover children/infants, sick passengers and Persons with Reduced

Mobility, inadmissible passengers, deportees or persons in custody, size and weight of hand baggage, loading and securing of items in the aeroplane, special loads and classification of load compartments, positioning of ground equipment, operation of doors, safety on the ramp, ramp procedures, servicing of aeroplanes, documents and forms for handling and multiple occupancy of seats.

- *8.2.3 - Refusal of Embarkation.* People who appear to be intoxicated or demonstrate that they are under the influence of drugs (not medical patients under proper care).

- *8.2.4 - Ground De-icing and Anti-icing*

- *8.3 - Flight Procedures*

- *8.3.1 - VFR/IFR Policy*

- *8.3.2 - Navigation Procedures.* MNPS and POLAR navigation, RNAV, In-flight replanning, system degradation, RVSM, etc.

- *8.3.3 - Altimeter Setting Procedures*

- *8.3.4 - Altitude Alerting System*

- *8.3.5 - GPWS*

- *8.3.6 - Use of TCAS/ACAS*

- *8.3.7 - In-flight Fuel Management*

- *8.3.8 - Adverse and Potentially Hazardou Atmospheric Conditions.*.Thunderstorms, icing conditions, turbulence, windshear, jetstream, volcanic ash clouds, heavy precipitation, sand storms, mountain waves and significant temperature inversions.

- *8.3.9 - Wake Turbulence*

- *8.3.10 - Crew Members at their Stations*

- *8.3.11 - Use of Safety Belts*

- *8.3.12 - Admission to Flight Deck*

- *8.3.13 - Vacant Crew Seats*

- *8.3.14 - Incapacitation*

- *8.3.15 - Cabin Safety Requirements.* Procedures covering cabin preparation for flight, ensuring that passengers are seated where they may best assist evacuation, passenger embarkation and disembarkation, and refuelling or defuelling with passengers embarking, on board or disembarking. Also smoking on board.

- *8.3.16 - Passenger Briefing*

- *8.3.17 - Cosmic or Solar Radiation Detection Equipment*

8.4 - All Weather Ops (see Subparts D & E)

8.5 - ETOPS

8.6 - MEL & CDL

8.7 - Non Revenue Flights

8.8 - Oxygen Requirements

9 – Dangerous Goods & Weapons
Information, instructions and general guidance on the transport of dangerous goods including the conditions under which weapons, munitions of war and sporting weapons may be carried.

10 – Security
Security instructions and guidance of a nonconfidential nature. Policies and procedures for handling and reporting crime on board such as unlawful interference, sabotage, bomb threats, and hijacking must also be included, as must a description of preventative security measures and training, parts of which may be kept confidential.

11 – Occurrences
Definition of occurrences and the relevant responsibilities of people involved, forms used with instructions on how they are to be completed, where they should be sent in what time period. Also:

- In the event of an accident, which company departments, Authorities and other organisations have to be notified, how this will be done and in what sequence

- Verbal notification to ATS units of incidents involving ACAS RAs, bird hazards, dangerous goods and hazardous conditions

- Submitting written reports on air traffic incidents, ACAS RAs, bird strikes, dangerous goods incidents or accidents, and unlawful interference;

- Reporting procedures

12 – Rules of the Air
Including:

- Visual and instrument flight rules

- Territorial application - Rules of the Air

- Communication procedures, including COM failure

- Interception procedures

- How listening watch is to be kept

- Signals

- Time system used

- ATC clearances, adherence to flight plan and position reports

- Visual signals

- Procedures for pilots observing accidents or receiving distress transmissions

- Ground/air visual codes for survivors, description and use of signal aids

- Distress and urgency signals

13 – Leasing
The operational arrangements for leasing, associated procedures and management responsibilities.

Part B - Aeroplane Operating Matters (SOPs)
Type-related instructions and procedures for a safe operation, taking account of differences between types, variants or individual aeroplanes used.

0 – General Information and Units of Measurement
Stuff like aeroplane dimensions, including units of measurement and conversion tables.

1 – Limitations
Limitations, including:

- Certification status (eg. JAR 23, JAR 25, ICAO Annex 16 (JAR 36 and JAR 34) etc)

- Passenger seating configuration, including a pictorial presentation

- Types of operation (e.g. VFR/IFR, CAT II/III, RNP Type, icing etc.)

- Crew composition

- Mass and centre of gravity

- Speed limitations

- Flight envelope(s)

- Wind limits including operations on contaminated runways

- Performance limitations for applicable configurations

- Runway slope

- Wet or contaminated runways

- Airframe contamination

- System limitations

2 – Normal Procedures
Procedures and duties assigned to the crew, checklists, and a statement covering the coordination procedures between flight and cabin crew, including:

- Preflight

- Pre-departure

- Altimeter setting and checking

- Taxy, Takeoff and Climb

- Noise abatement

- Cruise and descent

- Approach, Landing preparation and briefing
- VFR Approach
- Instrument approach
- Visual Approach and circling
- Missed Approach
- Normal Landing
- Post Landing
- Wet and contaminated runways

3 – Abnormal & Emergency Procedures

Procedures and duties assigned to the crew, checklists, and a statement covering the coordination procedures between flight and cabin crew, including:

- Crew Incapacitation
- Fire and Smoke Drills
- Unpressurised and partially pressurised flight
- Exceeding structural limits (overweight landing)
- Exceeding cosmic radiation limits
- Lightning Strikes
- Distress Communications and alerting ATC to Emergencies
- Engine failure
- System failures
- Guidance for Diversion in case of Serious Technical Failure
- Ground Proximity Warning
- TCAS Warning
- Windshear
- Emergency Landing/Ditching

4 – Performance

Data must be in a form that can be used without difficulty.

4.1 - Performance Data

Material providing data for compliance with JAR OPS 1 Subparts F, G, H and I must be included, to allow the determination of:

- Takeoff climb limits – Mass, Altitude, Temperature
- Takeoff field length (dry, wet, contaminated)
- Net flight path data for obstacle clearance or takeoff flight path
- The gradient losses for banked climbouts
- En-route, Approach and Landing climb limits
- Landing field length (dry, wet, contaminated) including the effects of an in-flight failure of a system or device, if it affects the landing distance
- Brake energy limits
- Speeds for various flight stages (also considering wet or contaminated runways)
- 4.1.1- *Supplementary Data for Icing Conditions* If data is not in the Flight Manual, other acceptable data must be included, although the Ops Manual may cross-reference to the Flight Manual if the data is not likely to be used often or in an emergency.

4.2 - Additional Performance Data

- All engine climb gradients
- Drift-down data
- Effect of de-icing/anti-icing fluids
- Flight with landing gear down
- For aeroplanes with 3 or more engines, OEI ferry flights
- Flights conducted under the CDL

5 – Flight Planning
Data and instructions for preflight and in-flight planning, including speed schedules and power settings. Where applicable, procedures for engine(s)-out operations, ETOPS (particularly the OEI cruise speed and maximum distance to an adequate aerodrome under JAR OPS 1.245) and flights to isolated aerodromes must be included.

In addition, how to calculate the fuel for the various stages of flight, under JAR OPS 1.255.

6 – Mass and Balance
Instructions and data for calculation, including:

- Calculation system (e.g. Index)
- Completion of documentation, including manual and computer generated types
- Limiting masses and C of G for the types, variants or individual aeroplanes
- DOM and corresponding centre of gravity or index

7 – Loading
Procedures and provisions for loading and securing the load in the aeroplane.

8 – Configuration Deviation List
The CDL, if provided by the manufacturer, taking account of the types and variants operated, including procedures when an aeroplane is despatched under its CDL.

9 – Minimum Equipment List
The MEL must take account of the types and variants operated and the area(s) of operation. It must include navigational equipment and take into account the navigation performance for the route and area.

10 – Emergency & Survival Equipment, including Oxygen
A list of the survival equipment to be carried and procedures for checking its serviceability before takeoff, with instructions regarding location, accessibility and use.

The procedure for determining the amount of oxygen required and the quantity available.

The flight profile, number of occupants and possible decompression must be considered. The information must be in a form which can be used without difficulty.

11 – Emergency Evacuation Procedures
Instructions for preparation for emergency evacuation, including crew co-ordination and emergency station assignment, plus a description of the duties of crew members for rapid evacuation and handling passengers in a forced landing, ditching or other emergency.

12 – Aeroplane Systems
A description of systems, related controls and indications and operating instructions (see IEM to Appendix 1 to JAR OPS 1.1045).

Part C - Route and Aerodrome Guide
Instructions and information relating to communications, navigation and aerodromes, including minimum flight levels and altitudes for each route and operating minima for each aerodrome, including:

- Minimum flight level/altitude
- Operating minima for departure, destination and alternate aerodromes
- Communication facilities and navaids
- Runway data and aerodrome facilities
- Approach, missed approach and departure procedures including noise abatement
- COM failure procedures
- Search and rescue facilities for the area
- Aeronautical charts to be carried in relation to the flight and route, including validity
- Availability of aeronautical information and MET services
- En-route COM/NAV procedures
- Aerodrome categorisation for flight crew competence (See AMC OPS 1.975)

- Special aerodrome limitations (performance limitations and operating procedures etc.)

Part D - Training

Training syllabuses and checking programs for all operations personnel in connection with the preparation and/or conduct of a flight, to include:

- *2.1 - Flight Crew.* All relevant items in Subparts E and N

- *2.2 - Cabin Crew.* All relevant items in Subpart O

- *2.3 - Operations Personnel, including Crew Members.* All relevant items in Subpart R (Transport of Dangerous Goods by Air) and Subpart S (Security).

- *2.4 - Operations Personnel other than Crew Members.* All other relevant items.

3 - Procedures

- 3.1 - Training and checking

- 3.2 – If personnel do not achieve or maintain standards

- 3.3 - To ensure that abnormal or emergency situations requiring abnormal or emergency procedures and artificial simulation of IMC are not simulated during commercial air transportation flights.

- 4 - Description of documentation to be stored and storage periods (see Appendix 1 to JAR OPS 1.1065.)

Appendix 1

Has been included in the above.

IEM to Appendix 1

With reference to Operations Manual Part A, paragraph 8.3.17 (cosmic radiation), limit values should be published in the Ops Manual only after the results of scientific research are available and internationally accepted.

With reference to Operations Manual Part B, paragraph 9 (Minimum Equipment List) and 12 (Aeroplane Systems) operators should give consideration to using ATA numbering for chapters and numbers for aeroplane systems.

AMC OPS 1.1045

When compiling an Operations Manual, operators may use the contents of other relevant documents. Material produced for Part B may be supplemented with, or substituted by, parts of the Flight Manual or an Operating Manual produced by the manufacturer. For Performance B aeroplanes, a POH or equivalent may be used as Part B, if it covers the necessary items. For Part C (Route Guide), material may be supplemented with or substituted by material produced by a specialised professional company (Jep, Aerad).

If operators choose to use material from other sources, they should either copy it and include it directly in the relevant part, or the Ops Manual should contain a statement to the effect that a specific manual (or parts) may be used instead of the specified parts.

This does not absolve operators from the responsibility of verifying the applicability and suitability of other material. Material from an external source should be given its status by a statement in the Ops Manual.

IEM OPS 1.1045(c)

Since a high degree of standardisation of Ops Manuals within JAA should lead to improved overall flight safety, it is strongly recommended that the structure here should be used as far as possible (see above for a List of Contents). Operators are recommended not to deviate from the numbering system. If there are sections which do not apply, insert 'Not applicable' or 'Intentionally blank' where appropriate.

1.1050 - Flight Manual

Operators must keep a current approved Flight Manual or equivalent for each aeroplane operated.

1.1055 – Journey Log

The following information for each flight must be kept in the form of a Journey Log (entries must be made concurrently and be permanent in nature):

- Registration

- Date

- Name(s) and assignment of crew member(s)

- Place of departure and arrival

- Time of departure (off-block time)

- Time of arrival (on-block time)

- Hours of flight

- Nature of flight

- Incidents, observations (if any)

- Commander's signature (or equivalent)

Operators may be allowed not to keep a journey log, or parts, if the relevant information is available in other documentation (see IEM OPS 1.1055(b).)

IEM OPS 1.1055(a)(12) – Equivalent Signature
This IEM discusses how to arrange the electronic equivalent of a handwritten signature – a PIN code which, from a legal and responsibility point of view, is considered to be the same.

Entering the PIN code should generate a print-out of the individual's name and professional capacity on the relevant documents in such a way that it is obvious who has signed them.

The computer system should log when and where each PIN code was entered.

The requirements for record keeping remain unchanged, and all personnel should be made aware of the conditions associated with electronic signatures and should confirm this in writing.

IEM OPS 1.1055(b)
'Other documentation' might include the operational flight plan, tech log, flight report, crew lists, etc.

1.1060 - Operational Flight Plan

The operational flight plan used and the entries made during flight must contain:

- Registration, type and variant

- Date of flight

- Flight identification

- Names and duty assignments of flight crew

- Place and time of departure (actual off-block time, takeoff time)

- Place and time of arrival (planned and actual, actual landing and on-block time)

- Type of operation (ETOPS, VFR, Ferry flight, HEMS, etc.)

- Route and segments with checkpoints, waypoints, distances, time and tracks

- Planned cruising speed and flying times between check-points/waypoints. Estimated and actual times overhead

- Safe altitudes and minimum levels

- Planned altitudes and flight levels

- Fuel calculations (records of in-flight fuel checks)

- Fuel on board when starting engines

- Alternate(s) for destination and, where applicable, takeoff and en-route, including information required above

- Initial ATS Flight Plan clearance and subsequent re-clearance

- In-flight re-planning calculations

- Relevant meteorological information

Items readily available in other documentation or other acceptable sources, or which are irrelevant, may be omitted. The operational flight plan and its use must be described in the Ops Manual. Entries must be made concurrently and be permanent.

1.1065 - Document Storage Periods

All records and relevant operational and technical information for each flight must be stored for the periods in Appendix 1.

Appendix 1
For maintenance records, see Subpart M.

Preparation and Execution of Flights
- Operational flight plan: 3 months

- Technical log: 24 months after last entry

- Route-specific NOTAM/AIS briefing docs if edited by operator: 3 months

- Mass and balance: 3 months

- Notification of special loads, including written information to the commander about dangerous goods: 3 months

Reports

- Journey log: 3 months

- Details of any occurrence (see JAR OPS 1.420), or any event the commander deems necessary to report or record: 3 months

- Exceedances of duty and/or reducing rest periods: 3 months

Flight Crew Records

- Flight, Duty and Rest time: 15 months

- Licence: As long as the flight crew member is exercising the privileges for the operator

- Conversion training and checking: 3 years

- Command course (inc checking): 3 years

- Recurrent training and checking: 3 years

- Operation in either pilot's seat: 3 years

- Recency (JAR OPS 1.970): 15 months

- Route and aerodrome competence (JAR OPS 1.975): 3 years

- Specific operations when required by JAR OPS (e.g. ETOPS CATII/III): 3 years

- Dangerous Goods Training: 3 years

Cabin Crew Records

- Flight, Duty and Rest Time: 15 months

- Initial training, conversion and differences training (inc checking): When employed

- Recurrent training and refresher (including checking): until 12 months s after leaving

- Dangerous Goods Tining: 3 years

Other Operations Personnel

Training/qualification records of other personnel for whom an approved training program is required by JAR OPS: Last 2 training records

Other Records

- Cosmic and solar radiation dosage: Until 12 months after leaving

- Quality System: 5 years

- Dangerous Goods Transport Document: 3 months after completion of the flight

- Dangerous Goods Acceptance Checklist: 3 months after completion of the flight

1.1070 – MME

Operators must keep a current approved MME as per JAR OPS 1.905.

1.1071 - Technical Log

Operators must keep an aeroplane technical log as per in JAR OPS 1.915.

1.1150 – Dangerous Goods

For Terminology, see *Terms & Definitions*.

IEM OPS 1.1150(a)(3) & (a)(4)

As a dangerous goods accident or incident may also constitute an aircraft accident or incident, the criteria for the reporting both should be satisfied.

1.1155 - Approval

To transport dangerous goods, operators must be approved by the Authority.

IEM OPS 1.1155

Permanent approval will be reflected on the AOC. Otherwise, approvals may be issued separately.

Before issuing an approval, operators should satisfy the Authority that adequate training has been given, that all relevant documents (e.g. for ground handling, aeroplane handling, training) contain information and instructions on dangerous goods, and that there are procedures in place to ensure the safe handling of dangerous goods at all stages of air transport.

The exemption or approval under JAR OPS 1.1165(b)(1) or (2) is in addition to that indicated by JAR-OPS 1.1155.

1.1160 - Scope

Operators must comply with the (IATA) Technical Instructions when dangerous goods are carried, irrespective of whether the flight is wholly or partly within or wholly outside the territory of a State.

Articles and substances which would otherwise be dangerous are excluded from this Subpart, to the extent in the Technical Instructions, if:

- They are required to be on board under the relevant JARs or for operating reasons*

- They are catering or cabin service supplies*

- They are for use *in flight* as veterinary aid or as a humane killer for an animal

- They are for use *in flight* for medical aid for a patient, if:

  - Gas cylinders have been manufactured specifically for containing and transporting that particular gas

  - Drugs, medicines and other medical matter are under the control of trained people when they are in use

  - Equipment containing wet cell batteries is kept and, when necessary secured, in an upright position to prevent spillage

  - Proper provision is made to stow and secure the equipment during takeoff and landing and at all other times deemed necessary by the commander in the interests of safety

- They are carried by passengers or crew

*Replacements, however, must be transported as per the Technical Instructions.

IEM OPS 1.1160(b)(1) – Operating Reasons

Dangerous goods required to be on board under JARs or for operating reasons are those for:

- Airworthiness

- Safe operation

- Health of passengers or crew

They include, but are not limited to:

- Batteries

- Fire extinguishers

- First-aid kits

- Insecticides/Air fresheners

- Life saving appliances

- Portable oxygen supplies

IEM OPS 1.1160(b)(3) - Veterinary Aid or Humane Killer for an Animal

These may also be carried on a flight made by the same aeroplane (to collect the animal, maybe), or preceding the flight on which the animal is carried and/or on a flight made by the same aeroplane after the animal has been carried when it is impracticable to load or unload the goods when the animal is carried.

IEM OPS 1.1160(b)(4) - Medical Aid for a Patient

Gas cylinders, drugs, medicines, other medical material (such as sterilising wipes) and wet cell or lithium batteries are dangerous goods which are normally provided as medical aid for a patient – they are not those which are a part of the normal equipment of the aeroplane.

They may also be carried on a flight made by the same aeroplane to collect a patient, or after that patient has been delivered when it is impracticable to load or unload the goods at the time.

IEM OPS 1.1160(b)(5) - Passengers or Crew

The Technical Instructions exclude some dangerous goods when carried by passengers or crew, subject to certain conditions. For the convenience of operators who may not be familiar with the Technical Instructions, these include:

- Alcoholic beverages in receptacles under 5 litres, containing 24-70% by volume, up to 5 litres per person

- Non-radioactive medicinal or toilet articles (including aerosols, hair sprays, perfumes, medicines containing alcohol), and, in checked baggage only, aerosols which are non-flammable, non-toxic and without subsidiary risk, for sporting or home use. Not more than ½ ltr or ½ kg per item, total 2 litres or 2 kg

- Safety matches or lighters, for own use, *carried on one's person* . 'Strike anywhere' matches, lighters with unabsorbed liquid fuel (other than liquefied gas), lighter fuel and refills are *not* permitted

- Hydrocarbon gas powered hair curlers, if the safety cover is securely over the heating element. No gas refills

- Small CO_2 cylinders for mechanical limbs, etc., and spares for long journeys

- Pacemakers or other implants for medical purposes

- Mercurial barometers or thermometers, carried by officials of a weather bureau, in a strong packaging with a sealed inner liner or bag of strong leak-proof and puncture-resistant material impervious to mercury, closed to prevent the escape of mercury irrespective of position. The commander should be informed

- Small personal thermometers containing mercury, cased.

- Dry ice, for perishable items, not above 2 kg, and the package must allow release of the gas. Carriage may be in carry-on (cabin) baggage, but agreement is required for checked baggage

- Up to 2 small non-flammable gas cylinders in self-inflating life-jackets, and 2 spares.

- Heat producing articles, such as underwater torches and soldering irons. Disable.

- Wheelchairs or other battery-powered mobility aids with non-spillable batteries, as checked baggage. When the equipment can always be upright, the battery must be securely attached and disconnected, with the terminals insulated against short circuits. Otherwise, it must be removed and carried upright in strong, rigid, leak-proof packaging (the package itself must have on it *Battery wet, with wheelchair* or *Battery wet, with mobility aid*, bear a *Corrosives* label and be marked for correct orientation). The commander should be informed.

- Not more than 5 kg of cartridges for sporting weapons, if they are in Division 1.4S*, are for that person's own use, are securely boxed and in checked baggage. Cartridges with explosive or incendiary projectiles are not permitted (*Division 1.4S is assigned to an explosive, in this case

cartridges packed or designed so that dangerous effects are confined within the package, unless it has been degraded by fire, and which do not hinder fire fighting). Mercurial barometers in cabin baggage of representatives of government weather bureaux or similar official agencies must be packed in strong packaging with a sealed inner liner, or bag of strong leak-proof and puncture resistant material impervious to mercury, closed to prevent its escape whichever way up it is.

1.1165 - Limitations

Operators must take all reasonable measures to ensure that articles and substances that are specifically identified by name or generic description in the Technical Instructions as being forbidden for transport under any circumstances are not carried on any aeroplane. Also, that articles and substances or other goods identified as being forbidden for transport in normal circumstances are only transported when:

- They are exempted by the States concerned under the Technical Instructions (see below), or

- The Technical Instructions indicate they may be transported under an approval issued by the State of Origin

IEM OPS 1.1165(b)(1) - States Concerned with Exemptions

The Technical Instructions provide that, in certain circumstances, dangerous goods which are normally forbidden on an aeroplane, may be carried. These circumstances include cases of extreme urgency or when other forms of transport are inappropriate or when full compliance with the requirements is contrary to the public interest. In these circumstances all the States concerned may grant exemptions provided that every effort is made to achieve an equivalent level of safety.

The States concerned are those of origin, transit, overflight and destination, and that of the operator.

Where the Technical Instructions indicate that dangerous goods which are normally forbidden may be carried with an approval, the exemption procedure does not apply.

The exemption is in addition to the approval required by JAR OPS 1.1155.

1.1170 - Classification

Articles and substances must be classified as dangerous goods as in the Technical Instructions.

1.1175 - Packing

Dangerous goods must be packed as specified in the Technical Instructions.

1.1180 - Labelling and Marking

Packages, overpacks & freight containers must be labelled and marked as in the Technical Instructions. Where dangerous goods are carried on a flight wholly or partly outside the territory of a State, labelling and marking must be in English in addition to any other requirements.

1.1185 - Transport Document

Except when otherwise specified in the Technical Instructions, dangerous goods must travel with a dangerous goods transport document.

Where dangerous goods are carried on a flight which takes place wholly or partly outside the territory of a State, English must be used in addition to any other language requirements.

1.1195 - Acceptance

Dangerous goods must not be accepted for transport until the package, overpack or freight container has been inspected under the acceptance procedures in the Technical Instructions.

An acceptance check list must be used, which allows for relevant details to be checked, and for recording of the results of the acceptance check by manual, mechanical or computerised means.

1.1200 - Inspection for Damage

Packages, overpacks and freight containers must be inspected for leakage or damage immediately before loading, as specified in the Technical Instructions.

A unit load device must not be loaded unless it has been inspected as per the Technical Instructions and found free from any leakage from, or damage to, the dangerous goods in it.

Leaking or damaged packages, overpacks or freight containers must not be loaded.

Any package of dangerous goods found on an aeroplane which appears to be damaged or leaking must be removed, or arrangements made for its removal. In this case, the remainder of the consignment must be inspected for damage or contamination, together with the aeroplane.

Packages, overpacks and freight containers must be inspected for signs of damage or leakage upon unloading. If there is evidence of damage or leakage, the area where the dangerous goods were stowed must also be inspected.

1.1205 - Removal of Contamination

Any contamination from the leakage or damage of dangerous goods must be removed without delay. An aeroplane which has been contaminated by radioactive materials must immediately be taken out of service and not returned until the radiation level at any accessible surface and the non-fixed contamination are not more than the values in the Technical Instructions.

1.1210 - Loading Restrictions

Passenger Cabin and Flight Deck

Dangerous goods must not be carried in a cabin occupied by passengers or on the flight deck, unless specified in the Technical Instructions.

Cargo Compartments

Dangerous goods must be loaded, segregated, stowed and secured as per Technical Instructions.

Carriage Only on Cargo Aircraft

Dangerous goods bearing the 'Cargo Aircraft Only' label must be carried on a cargo aircraft and loaded as per the Technical Instructions.

1.1215 - Provision of Information

Information to Ground Staff

Information must be provided to enable ground staff to carry out their duties with regard to dangerous goods, including actions in the event of incidents and accidents involving dangerous goods. This information should also be provided to the handling agent.

Information to Passengers and Others

Information must be promulgated as required by the Technical Instructions so that passengers are warned as to the types of goods which they are forbidden from transporting on board. As a minimum, this information should consist of:

- Enough prominently displayed warning notices or placards, at each place where tickets are issued and passengers checked in, in boarding areas and at any other place where passengers are checked in

- A warning with the passenger ticket. This may be printed on it, on a ticket wallet or on a leaflet, and may include reference to dangerous goods which may be carried.

Operators and handling agents must ensure that notices are provided at acceptance points for cargo giving information about dangerous goods.

Information to persons offering cargo for transport by air should be promulgated so that they are warned as to the need to properly identify and declare dangerous goods. This information should at least consist of enough warning notices or placards prominently displayed at any location where cargo is accepted.

Information to Crew Members
Information must be provided in the Ops Manual to enable crew members to carry out their responsibilities in regard to dangerous goods, including actions in emergencies arising involving dangerous goods.

Information to the Commander
The commander must be provided with written information, as per the Technical Instructions (see Table 1 of Appendix 1 to JAR OPS 1.1065 for storage periods).

Information in Incidents or Accidents
Operators of aeroplanes involved in incidents must, on request, provide any information required to minimise hazards created by dangerous goods.

Operators of aeroplanes involved in accidents must, as soon as possible, inform the appropriate authority of the State in which the accident occurred of any dangerous goods carried.

AMC OPS 1.1215(b)
Mostly incorporated above. Otherwise, information should be easily understood and identify that there are various classes of dangerous goods. Pictographs may be used as alternatives to written information, or to supplement it.

AMC OPS 1.1215(e) - Information in the Event of an Incident or Accident
This should include the proper shipping name, UN/ID number, class, subsidiary risk(s) for which labels are required, the compatibility group for Class 1 and the quantity and location on board.

1.1220 - Training Programs
Operators must establish and maintain staff training Programs, as required by the Technical Instructions, as approved by the Authority.

Operators Without Permanent Approval
Staff engaged in general cargo and baggage handling must receive training to carry out their duties in respect of dangerous goods. This training must at least cover the areas in Column 1 of the table below and be to a depth enough to ensure that an awareness is gained of the hazards, how to identify them and what requirements apply to the carriage of such goods by passengers and:

- Crew members

- Passenger handling staff

- Security staff employed by the operator who deal with the screening of passengers and their baggage

AREAS OF TRAINING	1	2
General philosophy	X	X
Limitations on Dangerous Goods in air transport		X
Package marking and labelling	X	X
Dangerous Goods in passengers baggage	X	X
Emergency procedures	X	X

Note: 'X' indicates an area to be covered.

Operators with Permanent Approval
Staff engaged in the **acceptance** of dangerous goods must have received training and be qualified. This training must at least cover the areas in **Column 1** of the table below and be to a depth enough to ensure the staff can take decisions.

Staff engaged in **ground handling, storage and loading** of dangerous goods must have received training, which must at least cover the areas in **Column 2** of the table below and be to a depth enough to ensure that an awareness is gained of the hazards associated with dangerous goods, how to identify them and how to handle and load them.

Staff engaged in **general cargo** and **baggage handling** must have received training, which must at least cover the areas in **Column 3** of the table below and be to a depth enough to ensure that an awareness is gained of the hazards, how to identify dangerous goods, how to handle and load them and what requirements apply to their carriage.

Flight crew members must have received training which, at least, must cover the areas in **Column 4** of the table below. Training must be to a depth enough to ensure that an awareness is gained of the hazards and how dangerous goods should be carried on an aeroplane.

Passenger handling staff, Security staff employed by the operator who deal with screening passengers and baggage, and **crew other than flight crew**, must have received training which must at least cover the areas in **Column 5** of the table below. Training must be to a depth enough to ensure that an awareness is gained of the hazards associated with dangerous goods, and what requirements apply to their carriage by passengers or, more generally, their carriage on an aeroplane.

Staff who receive training must undertake a test to verify understanding of their responsibilities.

Staff who require dangerous goods training must receive recurrent training within every 2 years.

Records of dangerous goods training must be maintained for all staff as per the Technical Instructions.

AREAS OF TRAINING	1	2	3	4	5
General Philosophy	X	X	X	X	X
Limitations on Dangerous Goods in air transport	X	X		X	X
Classification of Dangerous Goods	X				
List of Dangerous Goods	X	X		X	
General packing requirements and Packing instructions	X				
Packaging specifications and markings	X				
Package marking and labelling	X	X	X	X	X
Documentation from the shipper	X				

AREAS OF TRAINING	1	2	3	4	5
Acceptance of Dangerous Goods, including the use of a checklist	X				
Storage and loading procedures	X	X	X	X	
Inspections for damage or leakage and decontamination procedures	X	X			
Provision of information to commander	X	X		X	
Dangerous Goods in passengers' baggage	X	X	X	X	X
Emergency procedures	X	X	X	X	X

AMC OPS 1.1220

Application for Approval
Applications for approval of training programs should indicate how the training will be carried out. Training to give general information and guidance may be by any means including handouts, leaflets, circulars, slide presentations, videos, etc, and may take place on- or off-the-job. Training to give an in-depth and detailed appreciation of the whole subject or particular aspects of it should be by formal courses, which should include a written examination, the successful passing of which will result in the issue of the proof of qualification. Applications for formal training courses should include the course objectives, the training program syllabus/curricula and examples of the written examination to be undertaken.

Instructors
Instructors should have knowledge not only of training techniques but also of the transport of dangerous goods by air, so the subject be covered fully and questions adequately answered.

Areas of Training
The areas of training in Tables 1 and 2 of JAR-OPS 1.1220 apply whether the training is for general information and guidance or an in-depth and detailed appreciation, which affects the extent to which any area should be covered. Additional areas not identified in Tables 1 and 2 may be needed, or some areas omitted, depending on the responsibilities of the individual.

Levels of Training

There are two levels of training:

- An in-depth and detailed appreciation, so the person being trained gains knowledge enough to apply the Technical Instructions

- General information and guidance so the person being trained receives an overall awareness of the subject

In the absence of other guidance, the staff in JAR-OPS 1.1220(c)(1) should receive training to the extent in the first paragraph above; others should follow the second. However, where flight crew or other crew members, such as loadmasters, are responsible for checking dangerous goods, their training should also be as per the first paragraph.

Emergency Procedures

This should include at least:

- For personnel covered by JAR-OPS 1.1220(b) and (c), except for crew members whose emergency procedures training is covered below, dealing with damaged or leaking packages and other actions in the event of ground emergencies arising from dangerous goods

- For flight crew members, actions in emergencies in flight in the passenger cabin or the cargo compartments, and the notification to ATS should an in-flight emergency occur

- For crew members other than flight crew, dealing with incidents arising from dangerous goods carried by passengers, or dealing with damaged or leaking packages in flight

Recurrent Training

This should cover the areas in Table 1 or 2 above, relevant to initial Dangerous Goods training, unless the responsibility of the individual has changed.

Testing

There should be some way of establishing that a person has gained in understanding from the training; this is achieved with a test, whose complexity, manner of being conducting and questions asked should be commensurate with the duties of the person being trained. The test should demonstrate that the training has been adequate. If it is completed satisfactorily a certificate should be issued.

IEM OPS 1.1220

Areas of Training

Pretty much as for AMC OPS 1.1220, except tat, if a crew member is a loadmaster, column 4 may be used instead of column 5.

How to Achieve Training

Pretty much as for AMC OPS 1.1220, except that the formal training may be done by tuition or self-study, or a mixture.

1.1225 – Incident and Accident Reports

Dangerous goods incidents and accidents must be reported. An initial report must be despatched within 72 hours unless exceptional circumstances prevent this. Undeclared or misdeclared dangerous goods discovered in cargo or passengers' baggage must also be reported, in the same timescale.

AMC OPS 1.1225

Any type of dangerous goods incident or accident should be reported, irrespective of where the dangerous goods are found.

Initial reports may be made by any means, but in all cases a written report should be made as soon as possible. The report should be as precise as possible and contain all data known at the time it is made, for example:

- Date of the incident or accident, or the finding of undeclared or misdeclared dangerous goods

- Location, the flight number and flight date, if applicable

- Description of the goods and the reference number of the air waybill, pouch, baggage tag, ticket, etc

- Proper shipping name (including the technical name, if appropriate) and UN/ID number, where known

- Class or division and any subsidiary risk

- Type of packaging, and the packaging specification marking on it

- Quantity involved

- Name and address of the shipper, passenger, etc

- Any other relevant details

- Suspected cause of the incident or accident

- Action taken

- Any other reporting action taken

- Name, title, address and contact number of the person making the report

Copies of the relevant documents and any photographs should be attached to the report.

1.1235 - Security

Operators must ensure that all appropriate personnel are familiar, and comply, with the relevant requirements of the national security Programs of the State of the operator.

1.1240 - Training Programs

Operators must establish, maintain and conduct approved training Programs which enable personnel to take appropriate action to prevent acts of unlawful interference, such as sabotage or unlawful seizure of aeroplanes and to minimise the consequences of such events should they occur.

1.1245 - Reporting Unlawful interference

Following an act of unlawful interference on board an aeroplane the commander or, in his absence the operator, must submit, without delay, a report of such an act to the designated local authority and the Authority in the State of the operator.

1.1250 – Search Procedure Checklist

Aeroplanes must carry a checklist of the procedures to be followed (for that type) in searching for concealed weapons, explosives, or other dangerous devices. It must be supported with guidance on the action to be taken should a bomb or suspicious object be found.

1.1255 – Flight Crew Compartment

If installed, the flight crew door on all aeroplanes operated for the carrying of passengers must be capable of being locked from within the compartment to prevent unauthorised access.

Notes

JAR OPS 3

3.001 - Applicability

JAR OPS 3 concerns AOC holders for civil helicopters on commercial air transportation by operators with principal places of business in JAA Member States. It does not apply:

- To helicopters in military, customs, police and SAR service

- To parachute dropping and firefighting, and associated positioning and return flights, carrying people who would normally be carried on them

- To flights immediately before, during, or immediately after aerial work if they are connected with that activity and, excluding crew members, no more than 6 persons indispensable to the activity are carried.

3.005 - General

Helicopters used for commercial air transportation must do so under JAR OPS 3 (except for the variations below*, which require specific approval) and comply with JAR 26, although current national regulations apply until its formal adoption.

Helicopters must be operated under their C of As as per the Flight Manual (Appendix 1).

*Variations apply to (see appendices):

- HEMS

- Operations over a hostile environment outside a congested area

- Small helicopters, Day VFR (i.e. 3 175 kg or less, with 9 or less passenger seats, by day, over routes navigated visually)

- Local area operations (Day VFR only - where the helicopter is over 3 175 kg and working within a local and defined geographical area, starting and ending at the same location on the same day

- Helicopter Hoist Operations (HHO)

- Operations to or from a public interest site

*Appendix 1 to JAR OPS 3.005(c) - Limitations

For Category A helicopters, momentary flight through the height velocity (HV) envelope is allowed during takeoff and landing to or from a helideck or elevated heliport, when the helicopter is operated under:

- JAR OPS 3.517

- Sub-para (c)(2)(i) of Appendix 1 to JAR OPS 3.005(d)

- Appendix 1 to JAR OPS 3.005(e)

Appendix 1 to JAR OPS 3.005(d) – HEMS

Note: The Authority may decide what is a HEMS operation in the sense of this Appendix.

Terminology
See *Terms & Definitions*.

Ops Manual
The Ops Manual must include a HEMS supplement. Relevant extracts must be made available to the organisation for which HEMS is being provided.

Operating Requirements

The Helicopter
Performance 3 operations (single-engine) must not be conducted over a hostile environment.

Performance Requirements

Takeoff and Landing - 5 700 kg or Less
Helicopters operating to or from **heliports** at **hospitals** in hostile environments must operate under Subpart G (Performance 1), except that helicopters first certificated before 1 January 2000 are exempt from:

- JAR OPS 3.490(a)(3)(i)
- Clearing the elevated heliport in JAR OPS 3.490(a)(3)(ii) and 3.510(a)(3)(i)
- JAR OPS 3.510(a)(3)(ii)

until 31 December 2004, if there is a relevant approval (see Appendix 1 to JAR OPS 3.517(a), (a)(2)(ii) and (v), (b)(2) and (b)(5).)

Helicopters operating to or from a **HEMS site** in a hostile environment must, as far as possible, be operated under Subpart G (Performance 1). The commander must make every reasonable effort to minimise danger to occupants and people on the surface if a power unit fails (see ACJ to Appendix 1 to JAR OPS 3.005(d) (c)(2)(i)(B)). The site must be big enough for adequate clearance from obstructions. At night, it must be illuminated, from the ground or the helicopter (see ACJ to Appendix 1 to 3.005(d), (c)(2)(i)(C).)

Guidance on takeoff and landing procedures at previously unsurveyed sites must be in the Ops Manual.

Takeoff and Landing – Over 5 700 kg
HEMS helicopters must operate under Performance Class 1.

The Crew
Regardless of Subpart N, the following apply for HEMS:

- *Selection.* The Ops Manual must contain specific criteria for selection, taking previous experience into account.

- *Experience.* The minimum for commanders conducting HEMS flights must be at least:

  - Either 1 000 hours PIC of aircraft, of which 500 hours is on helicopters, or 1 000 hours as co-pilot on HEMS, of which 500 hours is as PICUS, and 100 hours PIC of helicopters.

  - 500 hours on helicopters gained in an operational environment similar to the intended operation

  - For night operations, 20 hours VMC at night as PIC

  - Successful completion of training under sub-paragraph (e) of this Appendix

- *Recency.* Pilots on HEMS must have done at least 30 minutes by sole reference to instruments in an STD or helicopter in the last 6 months

- *Crew composition.* The minimum crew by day must be one pilot and one HEMS crew member, which can be reduced to one pilot in exceptional circumstances. By night, there must be two pilots, but one pilot and one HEMS crew member may be employed in specific areas defined in the Ops Manual, taking into account:

  - Adequate ground reference

  - Flight following

  - Reliability of weather reporting

  - HEMS MEL

  - Continuity of a crew concept

- Minimum crew qualification, initial and recurrent training

- Operating procedures, including crew co-ordination

- Weather minima

- Additional considerations due to specific local conditions

HEMS Operating Minima.

Performance Class 1 and 2. Weather minima for despatch and en-route phases of HEMS flights are in the table below. If, during the en-route phase, the weather falls below the cloud base or visibility shown, VMC-only helicopters must abandon the flight or return to base. IFR ones may abandon the flight, return to base or convert to IFR, if the crew are qualified.

2 PILOTS		1 PILOT	
DAY			
Ceiling	Visibility	Ceiling	Visibility
500 ft and above	(See JAR OPS 3.465)	500 ft and above	(See JAR OPS 3.465)
499–400 ft	1 000 m (Note 1)	499–400 ft	2 000 m
399–300 ft	2 000 m	399–300 ft	3 000 m
NIGHT			
Cloud base	Visibility	Cloud base	Visibility
1 200 ft (Note 2)	2 500 m	1 200 ft (Note 2)	3 000 m

Note 1: Visibility may be reduced to 800 m for short periods in sight of land if the helicopter is manoeuvred at a speed that gives the opportunity to observe obstacles in time to avoid a collision. (See ACJ OPS 3.465.)

Note 2: Cloud base may be reduced to 1000 ft for short periods.

Performance Class 3. The minima are a 600 ft cloud ceiling and 1 500 m visibility, which may be reduced to 800 m for short periods in sight of land if the helicopter is manoeuvred at a speed that gives adequate opportunity to observe obstacles and avoid collision.

Additional Requirements

Medical Equipment. Installations must be approved. Procedures must be established for the use of portable equipment.

Communication and Navigation Equipment. There must be communications equipment in addition to that required by Subpart L, for two-way communication with the organisation for which the HEMS is being provided and, where possible, with ground emergency services (airworthiness approval is required).

HEMS Base Facilities. If standby is required with a reaction time of less than 45 minutes, dedicated suitable accommodation must be provided close to each operating base, where pilots must have facilities for obtaining current and forecast weather information and satisfactory communications with the appropriate ATC. Satisfactory planning facilities must be available.

Refuelling with Passengers on Board. When this is necessary, it can be done either rotors stopped or rotors turning, if doors on the refuelling side are closed, and those on the non-refuelling side are open, weather permitting.

Appropriate fire fighting facilities must be positioned with enough people immediately available to move patients clear in a fire.

Training and Checking

For **flight crew members**, Subpart N training and checking with:

- Meteorological training, concentrating on understanding and interpretation of available weather information

- Preparing the helicopter and specialist medical equipment for subsequent HEMS departure

- Practice of HEMS departures

- Assessment from the air of the suitability of HEMS operating sites

- The medical effects air transport may have on the patient

- VMC proficiency day and/or night checks as appropriate, including flying, landing and takeoff profiles likely at HEMS operating sites

- Line checks with special emphasis on:
  - Local area meteorology
  - HEMS flight planning
  - HEMS departures
  - Selection from the air of HEMS operating sites
  - Low level flight in poor weather
  - Familiarity with established HEMS operating sites in operators local area register

For **HEMS crewmembers**, Subpart O with:

- Duties in the HEMS role
- Navigation (map reading, navigation aid principles and use)
- Operation of radio equipment
- Use of onboard medical equipment
- Preparing the helicopter and specialist medical equipment for subsequent HEMS departure
- Instrument reading, warnings, use of normal and emergency check lists
- Basic understanding of the helicopter in terms of location and design of normal and emergency systems and equipment
- Crew coordination
- Practice of response to HEMS call out
- Refuelling (and rotors running)
- HEMS site selection and use
- Techniques for handling patients, medical consequences of air transport and knowledge of casualty reception
- Marmusting signals
- Underslung loads as appropriate

- Winching as appropriate
- The dangers of rotors running including loading of patients
- The use of the helicopter inter-communications system

Medical passengers must be briefed on the following before any HEMS flight:

- Familiarisation with types operated
- Entry and exit under normal and emergency conditions for self and patients
- Use of relevant onboard specialist medical equipment and the need for commander's approval before its use
- Method of supervision of other medical staff
- Use of helicopter intercom systems
- Location and use of fire extinguishers

Ground emergency service personnel must be familiar with:

- Two way radio procedures
- Selection of suitable HEMS sites
- Physical danger areas of helicopters
- Crowd control for helicopters
- Evacuation of occupants after an on-site helicopter accident

ACJ to Appendix 1 - JAA HEMS Philosophy

Starting with a description of acceptable risk and introducing stuff from other industries, this ACJ describes how risk is addressed in the HEMS appendix for safety. It discusses the difference between HEMS, Air Ambulance and SAR in regulatory terms, plus application of Operations to Public Interest Sites in the HEMS context.

Acceptable Risk

The broad aim of any aviation legislation is to balance the widest spectrum of operations with the minimum risk (in fact it may be worth considering who or what is at risk and who or what is being protected). In the view of the JAA Helicopter Sub-Committee (HSC) three groups are being protected:

- Third parties (including property) - highest protection.

- Passengers (including patients)

- Crew (including specialists) - lowest

It is for the Authority to facilitate a method for the assessment of risk - or as it is more commonly known, safety management.

Risk Management

Safety management textbooks describe four approaches to the management of risk. All but the first have been used in the production of the HEMS appendix and, if we consider that the engine failure accountability of Class I performance equates to zero risk, then all four are used (this of course is not strictly true as there are a number of helicopter parts - such as the tail rotor which, due to lack of redundancy, cannot satisfy the criteria). Applying the taxonomy to HEMS gives:

- *Zero Risk* - no risk of accident with a harmful consequence - Class 1 performance (within the qualification above) - the HEMS Operating Base.

- *De Minimis* - minimised to an acceptable safety target - for example the exposure time concept where the target is less than 5×10^{-8} (for elevated landing sites at hospitals in a congested hostile environment, the risk is contained to the deck edge strike case - and in effect minimised to an exposure of seconds).

- *Comparative Risk* - comparison to other exposure - the carriage of a patient with a spinal injury in an ambulance subject to ground effect compared to the risk of a HEMS flight (consequential and comparative risk).

- *As Low as Reasonably Practical* - where additional controls are not economically or reasonably practical - operations at the HEMS operational site (the accident site).

Put simply, there are three areas in HEMS where risk, beyond that in the main body of JAR OPS 3, is defined and accepted:

- en-route, where alleviation is given from height and visibility rules

- on site, with alleviation from performance and size requirements

- at an elevated hospital site in a congested hostile environment, with alleviation from the deck edge strike – if elements of Appendix 1 to JAR OPS 3.517(a) are satisfied

Against these additional and considered risks, experience levels are set, specialist training is required (such as instrument training against the increased risk of inadvertent entry into cloud), and operation with two crew (two pilots, or one pilot and a HEMS crew member) is mandated (HEMS crews - including medical passengers - are also expected to operate under good CRM).

Air Ambulance

Air ambulance is a normal transport task where the risk is *no higher* than for full JAR OPS 3. This is not to contradict or complement medical terminology, but a statement of policy; none of the risk elements of HEMS should be extant, so no additional HEMS requirements need be applied. Applying a road ambulance analogy:

- If called to an emergency, an ambulance would proceed at great speed, making lots of noise and proceeding against traffic lights, matching the risk of operation to that of a potential death (= HEMS)

- For patient transfer (or equipment) where life and death (or consequential injury of ground transport) is not an issue, the journey would be done without sirens and within normal traffic rules, again matching the risk to the task (air ambulance)

The underlying principle is; the aviation risk should be proportional to the task.

The *medical professional* should decide between the two - not the pilot! For that reason, medical staff who task medical sorties should be fully aware of the additional risks that are (potentially) present with HEMS operations (and the prerequisite for operators to hold HEMS approval. For example. in some countries, hospitals have principal and alternative sites, with the patient landed at the safer alternative (usually in the grounds of a hospital) to eliminate risk - against the small inconvenience of a short ambulance transfer from the site to the hospital. Once the decision has been taken by the professional, the commander makes operational judgements over the conduct of the flight.

The above air ambulance operations *could* be done by any AOC operator (although some HEMS operators hold an AOC) - usually when medical supplies (equipment, blood, organs, drugs etc.) are involved and urgency is not an issue.

Search and Rescue (SAR)
SAR operations, because they qualify for substantial alleviations, are strictly controlled; the crews are trained and held at a high state of readiness. Control and tasking is usually exercised by the Police (or the Military or Coastguard in a maritime State) and mandated under State Regulations.

When JAR OPS 3 was introduced, it was not intended that HEMS would be conducted by operators without AOCs, or operating to other than HEMS standards. It was also not expected that the SAR label would be used to circumvent the intent of JAR OPS 3 or permit HEMS operations to a lesser standard.

Operating Under a HEMS Approval
The HEMS appendix originally contained the definitions for Air Ambulance and SAR to clarify any differences but, because of confusion, all references to activities other than HEMS have been put into an ACJ.

There are only two possibilities - transport as passengers or cargo under JAR OPS 3 (with no alleviations from the HEMS appendix) or operations under a HEMS approval.

HEMS Operational Sites
The HEMS philosophy attributes appropriate levels of risk for each site, derived from practical considerations and the probability of use, with which the risk is expected to be inversely proportional. The types of site are:

- **HEMS Operating Base**, from which all operations will start and finish, with a high probability of a large number of takeoffs and landings, which is why there are no alleviations

- **HEMS Operating Site**. Because this is the primary pickup site, its use can never be pre-planned, so it gets alleviations from procedures and performance when appropriate

- The **Hospital Site** is usually at ground level or on a building (when performance was not a consideration). Their use depends on location and facilities; normally, it will be greater than the HEMS site but less than a HEMS base. They attract some alleviations under HEMS rules

Problems with Hospital Sites
During the implementation of JAR OPS 3, it was found that some States had problems with performance rules for HEMS. Although they accept that progress should be towards operations where risks associated with critical power unit failure are eliminated, or limited by the exposure time concept, a number of sites exist which do not (or never can) allow Performance Class 1 or 2 operations (as mentioned above, sites generally found in a congested hostile environment include those in the grounds of hospitals or on hospital buildings). If the rules were strictly applied, many operations would not be able to run, even though the rule for sites in hospital grounds attract alleviation until 2005.

Thus, if adequate safety is maintained, because such operations are in the public interest, the Authorities exercise their discretion to allow continued use of such sites. However, use of public interest sites is controlled, requiring that a State directory of sites be kept and approval given *only* when there is entry in the Route Manual Section of the Ops Manual.

The information required the dimensions, any non-conformance with Annex 14, the main risks, and the contingency plan should an incident occur. Each entry should also contain a diagram (or annotated photograph) showing the main aspects of the site.

Summary
In summary, the following are considered to be germane to JAA philosophy and HEMS regulations:

- Absolute levels of safety are conditioned by society

- Potential risk must only be to a level appropriate to the task

- Protection is afforded at levels appropriate to the occupants

- The HEMS appendix addresses a number of risk areas and mitigation is built in

- Only HEMS operations are dealt with by the appendix

- There are three main categories of HEMS sites and each is addressed appropriately

- State alleviation from requirements at hospital sites is available, but are strictly controlled by registration

- SAR is a State controlled activity and the label should not be used circumvent HEMS regulations

ACJ to Appendix 1 - Contents of the Ops Manual
The Ops Manual should contain instructions for the conduct of flights, adapted to the area, including at least:

- operating minima

- recommended routes for regular flights to surveyed sites (with the minimum altitude)

- guidance for the selection of the HEMS site in case of flight to an unsurveyed site

- the safety altitude for the area overflown

- procedures for inadvertent entry into cloud

ACJ to Appendix 1 – Sites in Hostile Environments
The alleviation from engine failure accountability at a HEMS site extends to HEMS/HHO where a HEMS crew member, a medical passenger, or ill or injured people and others directly involved in the HEMS flight must be hoisted.

IEM to Appendix 1 - HEMS Site
A HEMS site should have a minimum dimension of at least 2D. At night, unsurveyed sites should be at least 4D in length and 2D in width.

ACJ to Appendix 1 - Relevant Experience
This should allow for geographical characteristics (sea, mountain, big cities with heavy traffic, etc.)

ACJ to Appendix 1 - Recency
This may be obtained in a VFR helicopter with vision-limiting devices, such as goggles or screens, or in a STD.

ACJ to Appendix 1 - HEMS Crew Member
When the crew consists of one pilot and a HEMS crew member, the latter should be in the copilot's seat, to accomplish the usual tasks the commander may delegate, such as navigation or radio assistance, reading checklists, collision avoidance, etc. (tasks may also be delegated on the ground). It is a HEMS crew member's primary task to assist the commander, although there will be occasions when this may not be possible, in which case, reduction of operating minima in Appendix 1 to JAR OPS 3.005(d), sub-paragraph (c)(4) should not be used.

Except where a commander may fly off to get more supplies, leaving the HEMS crew member to give assistance to ill or injured people (exceptional), a commander should not land at a HEMS site without the HEMS crew member assisting from the copilot's seat.

With two pilots, there is no requirement for a HEMS crew member if the Pilot Monitoring (PM) does whatever the HEMS crew member does.

AMC to Appendix 1 – HEMS
A flight following system provides contact with the helicopter throughout its operational area.

ACJ to Appendix 1 - Line Checks
Where, due to size, configuration, or performance, the line check cannot be done on an operational flight, a specially arranged one may be used. It may

be immediately next to, but not simultaneous with, a biennial proficiency check.

IEM to Appendix 1 - Ground Emergency Services

The task of training large numbers of emergency service personnel is a pain in the bum, so operators should afford every assistance to those responsible for training them.

Appendix 1 to JAR OPS 3.005(e) - Hostile Environments outside Congested Areas

Prior approval from the AOC Authority and the State of intended operations is required, which will specify the type of helicopter and operation.

This Appendix only applies to turbine helicopters over a hostile environment outside a congested area where helicopter limitations, or other justifiable considerations, preclude the use of appropriate performance criteria.

Performance Class 2 Alleviation

Helicopters with 9 or less passenger seats are exempt from the following requirements of Subpart H:

- JAR OPS 3.520(a)(2)(i)(A)
- JAR OPS 3.535(a)(2)(i)(B)

Performance Class 3 Alleviation

Helicopters with 6 or less passenger seats are exempt from JAR OPS 3.240(a)(5), if the operator complies with Appendix 1 to JAR OPS 3.517(a), sub-paragraphs (a)(2)(ii) & (v).

Operation

Specific procedures if a power unit fails during takeoff and landing must be in the Ops Manual.

Supplemental Oxygen for Non-Pressurised Helicopters

Non-pressurised helicopters may fly at pressure altitudes above 10 000 ft without supplemental oxygen equipment, if the cabin altitude does not exceed 10 000 ft for more than 30 minutes and never exceeds 13 000 ft pressure altitude.

IEM to Appendix 1

The subject Appendix has been produced to allow some existing operations to continue. It is expected that the alleviation will be used only as follows:

- *Mountain Operations,* where present generation multi-engined aircraft cannot meet Performance Class 1 or 2 requirements at altitude

- *Operations in Remote Areas,* where existing operations are conducted safely, and surface transport does not provide the same level of safety as single-engined helicopters, and where, because of low population density, economics do not justify the cost of multi-engined helicopters (remote arctic settlements)

The AOC State and the State in which operations are conducted should give prior approval. If both approvals have been given by a single State, it should not withhold, without justification, approval for aircraft of another State. Such approvals should only be given after both States have considered the technical and economic justifications.

Appendix 1 to JAR OPS 3.005(f) - Small Helicopters (Day VFR)

Prior approval of the AOC Authority is required, who must specify the type of helicopter and operation, and the geographical limitations of local operations (flights within a local and defined geographical area which start and end at the same location on the same day).

Prohibition

The following activities are prohibited:

- 3.065 - Carriage of Weapons of War and Munitions of War
- 3.265 - Carriage of Inadmissible Passengers, Deportees or Persons in Custody
- 3.305 - Refuelling/defuelling with Passengers Embarking, On Board or Disembarking
- 3.335 - Smoking on Board

Alleviation

The following rules are alleviated:

3.100 - Admission to Cockpit

Carriage of passengers in the pilot seat must not cause distraction and/or interference with the flight's operation, and the passenger occupying a pilot seat must be made familiar with restrictions and safety procedures.

3.135 - Additional Stuff To Be Carried

For **local flights**, these need not be carried:

- 3.135(a)(1) - Operational Flight Plan*

- 3.135(a)(2) - Tech Log (except for land-away)

- 3.135(a)(4) - Notam/AIS docs

- 3.135(a)(5) - Met information

- 3.135(a)(7) - Notification of special passengers, etc.

- 3.135(a)(8) - Notification of special loads, etc.

For **non-local operations**:

- 3.135(a)(1) - Operational Flight Plan. This may simplified, relevant to the operations and acceptable*

- 3.135(a)(7) - Notification of special passengers is not required

- 3.140 - Information need not be kept on the ground when other methods of recording are used

- 3.165 – Leasing applies only where a formal agreement exists (the case where the contract to carry passengers is transferred to another operator who the passengers will pay for transport is not considered to be leasing)

- 3.215 - Use of Air Traffic Services. Not applicable unless mandated by air space requirements and providing SAR arrangements are acceptable

- 3.220 - Authorisation of Heliports. Procedures must be established to qualify commanders for selection of heliports or landing sites, suitable for the type of helicopter and operation

- 3.255 - Fuel Policy. Subparas (b) to (d) do not apply when, on completion of the flight, or series of flights, the fuel remaining allows at least 30 minutes flying time at normal cruising speed

(which may be reduced to 20 minutes in areas with continuous and suitable precautionary landing sites). Final reserve fuel must be specified in the Ops Manual to comply with JAR OPS 3.375(c)

- 3.280 - Passenger Seating. Procedures need not be established. The intent of this paragraph is achieved by the pilot using normal judgement. JAR OPS 3.260 is applicable and is considered to address the need for procedures

- 3.285 Passenger Briefing. Paragraph (a)(1). Unless it would be unsafe, passengers are verbally briefed about safety, parts or all of which may be given by an audio-visual presentation. Prior approval must be given to use portable electronic devices

- 3.290 - Flight Preparation. For local operations, under JAR OPS 3.290(a), an operational flight plan is not required. For non-local operations, it may be in a relevant, simplified form.

- 3.375 - In-flight Fuel Management. Appendix 1 to JAR OPS 3.375 need not be applied (see (d)(14) below). Appendix 1 is not applicable

- 3.385 - Use of Supplemental Oxygen. With prior approval, excursions between 10000-16 000ft for a short time may be undertaken without supplemental oxygen under the Ops Manual (passengers must be informed before departure that supplemental oxygen will not be provided). Appendix 1 to JAR OPS 3.775 is not applicable

- Appendix 1 to 3.270 - Stowage of baggage and cargo. As appropriate

- 3.630 - Instruments and Equipment. Alternative equipment that does not meet current JTSO standards but does meet the safety standard of the original equipment may be acceptable. Appendix 1 to JAR OPS 3.775 is not applicable

- 3.775 - Supplemental Oxygen - Non pressurised helicopters. With prior approval, excursions of short duration between 10000-16000ft may be undertaken without supplemental oxygen, under procedures in the Ops Manual. Appendix 1 is not applicable

- 3.955(b) - Upgrading to Commander. The Authority may accept relevant abbreviated command courses

- Appendix 1 to 3.965 - Recurrent Training and Checking. A syllabus for the type of operation may be accepted

- *3.1060 - Operational Flight Plan

- 3.1235 - Security. Applicable only in States where the national security program applies to the operations in this Appendix

- 3.1240 - Training Programs. To be adapted to the operation. A suitable self-study program may be acceptable

- 3.1250 - Helicopter search procedure checklist. No checklist is required

IEM to Appendix 1

Appendix 1 to JAR OPS 3.005(f) contains prohibitions and alleviations for small helicopters under day VFR. Where a JAR OPS 3 rule contains a paragraph that already allows alternative compliance for approval it is not discussed (in this IEM or the Appendix).

Where a rule is partially applicable (some paragraphs IFR, some VFR), the rule is not referenced (in this IEM or the Appendix) and normal interpretation should be applied.

The following rules are considered not to apply for small helicopters operating to Appendix 1:

- 3.075 - Method of Carriage of Persons

- 3.105 - Unauthorised Carriage

- 3.225 - Heliport Operating Minima

- 3.230 - Departure & Approach Procedures

- 3.295 - Selection of Heliports

- 3.395 - Ground Proximity Detection

- 3.405 - Commencement and Continuation of Approach

- Subpart E, except JAR-OPS 3.465 and Appendix 1

- 3.652 – IFR/Night - Instruments & Equipment

- 3.655 - Additional Stuff Single-Pilot IFR

- 3.670 - Airborne Weather Radar

- 3.695 - Public Address System

- 3.700 - Cockpit Voice Recorders 1

- 3.705 - Cockpit Voice Recorders 2

- 3.715 - Flight Data Recorders 1

- 3.720 - Flight Data Recorders 2

- 3.810 - Megaphones

- 3.815 - Emergency Lighting

- 3.855 - Audio Selector Panel

- 3.865 - Communication and Navigation Equipment for IFR, or VFR over routes not navigated visually

Appendix 1 to JAR OPS 3.005(g) - Local Area Operations (Day VFR)

Prior approval from the AOC Authority is required, which will specify the type of helicopter and operation, and the geographical limits.

Prohibition

The following activities are prohibited:

- 3.065. Carriage of Weapons of War and Munitions of War

- 3.265. Carriage of Inadmissible Passengers, Deportees or Persons in Custody

- 3.305. Refuelling/defuelling with Passengers Embarking, On Board or Disembarking

- 3.335. Smoking on Board

Alleviation

The following rules are alleviated:

- 3.135 - Additional Information and Forms To Be Carried

- 3.135(a)(1) - Operational Flight Plan. This may be simplified, relevant to the operation and acceptable

- 3.135(a)(4) - Notam/AIS Documentation. Not required

- 3.135(a)(5) - Meteorological Information. Not required

- 3.135(a)(7) - Notification of Special Passengers, etc. Not required

- 3.135(a)(8) - Notification of Special Loads, etc. Not required.

- 3.140 - Information On The Ground. It need not be so when other recording methods are employed

- 3.165 - Leasing. Applies only where a formal agreement exists (where the contract to carry the passengers is transferred to another operator who is paid by the passengers is not leasing)

- 3.215 - Use of Air Traffic Services. Not applicable unless mandated by air space requirements, and if SAR arrangements are acceptable to the Authority

- 3.220 - Authorisation of Heliports by the operator. Procedures to qualify commanders for selection of suitable heliports or landing sites must be established

- 3.255 - Fuel Policy. Subparas (b) to (d) are not applicable when, after the flight, the fuel remaining allows at least 30 minutes flying at normal cruising speed, which may be reduced to 20 minutes when in an area with continuous and suitable precautionary landing sites. Final reserve fuel must be established in the Ops Manual to comply with JAR OPS 3.375(c)

- 3.290(a). See (C)(1)(i)

- 3.375 - In-flight Fuel Management. Appendix 1 need not be applied*

- 3.385 - Use of Supplemental Oxygen. With prior approval, excursions between 10 000-13 000ft for a short duration may be undertaken without supplemental oxygen under the Ops Manual (passengers must be informed before departure that supplemental oxygen will not be provided)

- *Appendix 1 to JAR OPS 3.375 - In-flight Fuel Management. Not applicable.

- 3.630 - Instruments and Equipment. Alternative equipment that does not meet current JTSO standards, but does meet standards of the original equipment may be acceptable

- 3.775 - Supplemental Oxygen - Non Pressurised Helicopters. With prior approval, excursions of a short duration between 10 000-16 000ft may be undertaken without supplemental oxygen, under the Ops Manual. Appendix 1 is not applicable

- 3.1060 - Operational Flight Plan. See (C)(1)(i)

- 3.1235 - Security. Applicable only in States where the national security program applies to operation in this Appendix

ACJ to Appendix 1

Part of Appendix 1 to 3.005(f) (and the whole of Appendix 1 to 3.005(g)) contain alleviations for "local operations". Approval should constrain the definition of "local" to be within 20-25 nm, but such arbitrary distances have always presented difficulties as there are always special factors. Authorities are therefore not expected to authorise local operations beyond 25 nm without good operational reasons.

In defining "local operations" (as above), the Authority should, except where such operations specifically "include" cross border excursions (such as sight seeing flights in the Mont Blanc or Matterhorn areas), constrain operations to be within the State boundary.

Appendix 1 to JAR OPS 3.005(h) - Helicopter Hoist Operations (HHO)

Note: The Authority may decide what are HHO operations for this Appendix.

Ops Manual

The Ops Manual must include a supplement with material specific to HHO, in particular:

- Performance

- Conditions under which offshore HHO transfer may be conducted, with limitations on vessel movement and wind speed

- Weather limitations

- Criteria for determining minimum size of HHO sites

- Procedures for determining minimum crew

- How crew members record hoist cycles

When required, relevant extracts must be made available to the organisation for which HHO is being provided.

Maintenance of HHO Equipment

Maintenance instructions must be established by the operator, in liaison with the manufacturer, and included in the maintenance program.

Operating Requirements

The Helicopter

The helicopter must be able to sustain a critical power unit failure with the remaining engine(s) at the appropriate power setting, without hazard to suspended people or cargo, third parties, or property (except for HEMS HHO at a HEMS site where the requirement need not be applied.)

The Crew

Regardless of Subpart N, the following apply to HHO operations:

- *Selection* - the Ops Manual must contain criteria for selection of flight crew members, taking previous experience into account

- *Experience*. The minimum experience level for commanders must be at least:

- *Offshore*: 1 000 hours PIC of helicopters or 1 000 as co-pilot in HHO, of which 200 is as PICUS, plus 50 offshore hoist cycles, of which 20 are at night as required

- *Onshore*: 500 hours PIC of helicopters or 500 hours as co-pilot in HHO, of which 100 is as PICUS, plus 200 in helicopters in a similar environment, and 50 hoist cycles, of which 20 are at night as applicable

- Successful completion of training under the Ops Manual and relevant experience in the role and environment under which HHO is conducted

- *Recency*. Pilots and crew conducting HHO must, as well as JAR OPS 3.970(a), have done, in the last 90 days, any combination of 3 day or night hoist cycles, each with a transition to and from the hover (by day), and, by night, 3 night cycles, with a transition to and from the hover.

- *Crew Composition*. The minimum crew for day or night must be as per the Ops Manual supplement, and depends on the type of helicopter, weather, the task, and, for offshore, the HHO site environment, sea state and movement of the vessel but always at least one pilot and one HHO crew member.

Additional Requirements

- *HHO Equipment*. Installation and operation of hoist equipment (including mods) requires appropriate airworthiness approval. Ancillary items must be designed & tested to appropriate standards & be acceptable

- *Communication Equipment*. Radio equipment, on top of that required by Subpart L, requires airworthiness approval. Day and night offshore or night onshore operations require two-way communication with the organisation for which HHO is being provided, and with ground personnel

Training and Checking

Flight crew members must be trained in Subpart N training and checking, plus:

- Fitting and use of the hoist

- Preparing the helicopter and hoist

- Normal and emergency hoisting by day and, when required, by night

- Crew co-ordination specific to HHO

- Practice of HHO procedures

- Dangers of static discharge

- Proficiency checks, appropriate to day operations, which must also be done by night as necessary. The checks should include procedures likely to be used at HHO sites with special emphasis on:

  - Local meteorology

  - HHO flight planning

  - HHO departures

  - A transition to and from the hover at the site

  - Normal and simulated emergency HHO procedures

  - Crew co-ordination

HHO crew members must be trained under Subpart O, plus:

- Duties in the HHO role

- Fitting and use of the hoist

- Operating hoist equipment

- Preparing the helicopter and specialist equipment for HHO

- Normal and emergency procedures

- Crew coordination specific to HHO

- Operation of intercoms and radio equipment

- Knowledge of emergency hoist equipment

- Handling HHO passengers

- Effect of movement of personnel on C of G and mass, and performance

- Guiding pilots over HHO sites

- Awareness of specific dangers in the operating environment

- The dangers of static electricity

HHO Passengers must be briefed and made aware of the dangers of static electricity and other HHO considerations, before flight

ACJ to Appendix 1 – Two-Pilot HHO

Two pilots may be required when:

- Weather is below VFR minima at the offshore vessel or structure

- There is adverse weather at the site (i.e. turbulence, vessel movement, visibility)

- A second pilot is required because of visibility or handling, or lack of AFCS

Appendix 1 to JAR OPS 3.005(i) - Public Interest Sites

Operators wishing to conduct operations under this Appendix must have prior approval of the AOC Authority and the State where operations will take place. Such approvals must specify the site(s), type(s) of helicopter and operation. This Appendix only applies to turbine helicopters operating to or from public interest sites which were established up to six months after the effective date of this amendment. It is therefore out of date and not included here.

3.010 - Exemptions

Exemptions from JAR OPS 3 may be granted if there is a need, subject to compliance with supplementary conditions that ensure an acceptable level of safety.

3.015 - Operational Directives

These are used to direct that an operation must be prohibited, limited or subject to certain conditions, in the interests of safety. Operational Directives state the reason for issue, applicability and duration, and action required by the operator(s). They are supplementary to JAR OPS 3.

3.020 - Laws and Procedures

Employees must be made aware that they must comply with relevant laws, regulations and procedures of relevant States operated in.

3.025 - Common Language

Crews must be able to communicate in a common language or other acceptable means. Ops personnel must be able to understand the language used in relevant parts of the Ops Manual.

3.030 - MEL

Helicopters must have an approved Minimum Equipment List, based on, but at least as restrictive as, the relevant Master MEL, if there is one. Helicopters may not operate outside the MEL.

3.035 - Quality System

As for JAR OPS 1.035.

IEM OPS 3.035 - Organisation Examples

Two diagrams illustrate typical examples of Quality organisations (not included here). Otherwise, as for JAR OPS 1.035.

AMC OPS 3.035

As for JAR OPS 1.035.

Small Organisations
(with 20 or less full-time employees)

The requirement to establish and document a Quality System and employ a Quality Manager applies to all operators. References to large and small operators are governed by aircraft capacity (i.e. more or less than 10 seats) and mass (greater or less than 3 175 kg), but such terminology is not relevant when considering Quality Systems, which actually use the number of full time employees. Operators employing 5 or less full time staff are 'very small' while those with between 6-20 are 'small'. *Full-time* in this context means employed for at lest 35 hours per week, excluding holidays.

Complex quality systems are inappropriate for small or very small operators and the clerical effort required to draw up manuals and procedures may stretch their resources. It is therefore accepted that they should tailor their quality systems to suit the operation and allocate resources accordingly.

For 'very small' operators, it may be appropriate to develop a Quality Assurance Program with a checklist, which should have a supporting schedule that completes all items within a timescale, with a statement acknowledging completion of a periodic review by top management. An occasional independent overview of the checklist content and achievement of the Quality Assurance should be undertaken.

The 'small' operator may decide to use an internal or external system, or a combination. In these circumstances it would be acceptable for external specialists and or qualified organisations to manage the system on behalf of the Quality Manager.

If the independent monitoring function is being conducted by an organisation other than the one carrying out the operations, the audit schedule must be shown in the relevant documentation.

Whatever arrangements are made, the operator retains the ultimate responsibility.

3.037 - Accident Prevention and Flight Safety

A program must be established, and may be integrated with the Quality System, including programs to achieve and maintain risk awareness and evaluation of relevant information relating to accidents and incidents and promulgation of related information.

IEM OPS 3.037

Guidance material for establishing a safety program can be found in:

- ICAO Doc 9422 (*Accident Prevention Manual*)
- ICAO Doc 9376 (*Preparation of an Operational Manual*)

Where available, use may be made of flight data recorder information.

3.040 - Additional Crew Members

Crew members who are not required flight or cabin crew members must also be trained in, and be proficient to perform, their assigned duties.

3.050 - Search & Rescue Information

Essential information pertinent to the intended flight concerning search and rescue services must be easily accessible in the cockpit.

3.055 - Information on Emergency and Survival Equipment Carried

Lists containing information on the emergency and survival equipment carried on board must be available for immediate communication to RCCs, to include the number, colour and type of life-rafts and pyrotechnics, details of emergency medical and water supplies and the type and frequencies of emergency portable radio equipment.

3.065 - Weapons and Munitions of War

See JAR OPS 1.065.

IEM OPS 3.065
See JAR OPS 1.065..

3.070 - Sporting Weapons & Ammunition

See JAR OPS 1.070.

IEM OPS 3.070
See JAR OPS 1.070.

3.075 - Method of Carriage of Persons

People are not allowed in any part of a helicopter in flight not designed for them, unless temporary access is granted by the commander for safety or where cargo or stores are carried, if so designed.

3.080 - Dangerous Goods

People offering or accepting dangerous goods for transport by air must be trained and the goods properly classified, documented, certificated, described, packaged, marked, labelled and fit for transport as per the Technical Instructions.

3.085 - Crew Responsibilities

Crew members are responsible for the proper execution of their duties related to the safety of the helicopter and its occupants in the Ops Manual.

Crew members must report to the commander any incident that has endangered, or may have endangered, safety, or use the operator's incident reporting schemes under JAR OPS 3.420. Copies must be communicated to the commander.

Crew members may not perform duties:

- Under the influence of any drug that may affect their faculties contrary to safety

- Until a reasonable time period has elapsed after deep water diving or blood donation

- If in any doubt of being able to accomplish assigned duties

- If they know or suspect that they are suffering from fatigue, or feel unfit to the extent that the flight may be endangered

Crew members may not:

- Consume alcohol inside 8 hours of the reporting time for flight duty or start of standby

- Start a flight duty period with a blood alcohol level over 0.2 promille

- Consume alcohol during the flight duty period or on standby

The commander must:

- Be responsible for the safe operation of the helicopter and safety of its occupants when the rotors are turning

- Have authority to give all commands deemed necessary for the purpose of securing the safety of the helicopter and people or property carried inside

- Have authority to disembark any person, or part of the cargo, which may represent a potential hazard to the safety of the helicopter or its occupants

- *Not* allow people to be carried who *appear* to be under the influence of alcohol or drugs so that the safety of the helicopter or its occupants may be endangered

- Have the right to refuse transportation of inadmissible passengers, deportees or persons in custody if their carriage poses a risk to the safety of the helicopter or its occupants

- Ensure that all passengers are briefed on the location of emergency exits and the location and use of relevant safety and emergency equipment

- Ensure that operational procedures and check lists are complied with under the Ops Manual

- *Not* permit any crew member to perform any activity during a critical phase of flight except duties required for safe operation of the helicopter

- *Not* permit:
  - A flight data recorder to be disabled, switched off or erased during flight, nor permit recorded data to be erased after flight in the event of an accident or an incident subject to mandatory reporting

  - A cockpit voice recorder to be disabled or switched off during flight unless believing that the recorded data, which otherwise would be erased automatically, should be preserved for incident or accident investigation, nor permit recorded data to be manually erased during or after flight in the event of an accident or an incident subject to mandatory reporting

- Decide whether or not to accept a helicopter with unserviceabilities allowed by the CDL or MEL

- Ensure that the pre-flight inspection has been carried out

The commander must, in an emergency that requires immediate decision and action, take any action considered necessary under the circumstances, deviating from rules, operational procedures and methods in the interest of safety.

3.090 - Authority of the Commander
All people carried in the helicopter must obey all lawful commands given by the commander for the purpose of securing the safety of the helicopter and people or property carried inside.

3.100 - Admission to Cockpit
No person (other than a flight crew member assigned to a flight) may be admitted to, or carried in, the cockpit unless that person is:

- An operating crew member

- A representative of the Authority responsible for certification, licensing or inspection if required for official duties

- Permitted by, and carried under, the Ops Manual

The commander must ensure that, in the interests of safety, admission to the cockpit does not cause distraction and/or interfere with the flight's operation, and all persons carried in the cockpit are made familiar with relevant safety procedures.

The final decision regarding admission to the cockpit is the responsibility of the commander.

3.105 - Unauthorised Carriage
Operators must take all reasonable measures to ensure that no person secretes himself or cargo on board a helicopter (stowaway).

3.110 - Portable Electronic Devices
Operators may not permit any person to use, and must take all reasonable measures to ensure, that no person uses on board a portable electronic device that can adversely affect performance of helicopter systems and equipment.

3.115 - Alcohol and Drugs
People may not enter or be in a helicopter when under the influence of alcohol or drugs to the extent that the safety of the helicopter or its occupants is likely to be endangered.

3.120 - Endangering Safety
People may not recklessly or negligently act or omit to act as to endanger a helicopter or people inside, or cause or permit a helicopter to endanger people or property.

3.125 - Documents to be Carried
The following must be carried on each flight:

- Certificate of Registration
- Certificate of Airworthiness
- Noise Certificate (may be a copy)
- Air Operator Certificate (may be a copy)
- Aircraft Radio Licence

- Third party liability Insurance Certificate(s) (may be a copy)

Flight crew members must, on each flight (when practicable), carry a valid flight crew licence with appropriate rating(s) for the flight. See 3.130/135.

ACJ OPS 3.125
In case of loss or theft, the operation may continue until the flight reaches the base or a place where replacement documents can be provided.

3.130 - Manuals to be Carried
Current parts of the Ops Manual relevant to crew duties must be carried on each flight. Those required for the conduct of a flight and be accessible if required for flight. The current Flight Manual must also be carried unless the Ops Manual contains enough relevant information.

3.135 - Additional Information and Forms
The following information and forms, relevant to type and area, must be on each flight:

- Operational Flight Plan with at least the information in JAR OPS 3.1060*

- Tech Log with at least the information in JAR OPS 3.915(a)

- Details of the filed ATS flight plan

- Appropriate NOTAM/AIS documentation

- Appropriate meteorological information

- Mass and balance documentation as per Subpart J

- Notification of special categories of passenger, such as security personnel (if not considered as crew), handicapped people, inadmissible passengers, deportees and people in custody

- Notification of special loads, including dangerous goods, with written information to the commander as per JAR OPS 3.1215(d)

- Current maps and charts and associated documents as per JAR OPS 3.290(b)(7)

- Any other documentation which may be required by the States concerned, such as cargo or passenger manifest, etc

- Forms for reporting requirements

The above may be other than on printed paper if otherwise easily accessible.

3.140 - Information on the Ground
At least for the duration of flight(s), relevant information must be preserved on the ground, and retained until it has been duplicated at the place it will normally be stored or, if this is impracticable, carried in a fireproof container.

The information above includes:

- A copy of the operational flight plan

- Copies of relevant part(s) of the tech log

- Route-specific NOTAM documentation if specifically edited by the operator

- Mass and balance documentation

- Special loads notification

3.145 - Power to Inspect
Authorised people must be allowed to board and fly in any helicopter operated under an AOC from their Authority and enter and remain in the cockpit, provided that the commander may refuse access if, in his opinion, the safety of the helicopter would be endangered.

3.150 - Production of Documentation
Operators must give any authorised person access to documents and records related to flight operations or maintenance, and produce them when requested to do so by the Authority, within a reasonable time. The commander must, within a reasonable time of being requested to do so by an authorised person, produce the documentation required to be carried.

3.155 - Preservation of Documentation
Original documentation, or copies, that are required to be preserved must be kept for the required periods even if ceasing to be the operator. Where a crew member, for whom a record has been kept, becomes a crew member for another

operator, that record must be made available to the new operator.

3.160 - Flight Recorder Recordings
Preservation of Recordings
After an accident or an incident subject to mandatory reporting, or as directed, the operator of a helicopter with a flight recorder must, as far as possible*, preserve original data pertaining to the accident for 60 days unless otherwise directed by the investigating authority.

When a flight data recorder must be carried, the operator must save the recordings for the time required by JAR OPS 3.715 and 3.720 (except that, for testing and maintenance, up to one hour of the oldest material may be erased), and provide instructions for converting stored data into engineering units.

IEM OPS 3.160(a) - Preservation
*The phrase 'to the extent possible' means either for technical reasons, or the helicopter has been despatched with unserviceable equipment

Production of Recordings
The operator of a helicopter on which a flight recorder is carried must, within a reasonable time after being requested to do so by the Authority, produce any recording made by a flight recorder which is available or has been preserved.

Use of Recordings
CVR recordings may not be used any other purpose than investigation of accidents or incidents subject to mandatory reporting, except with the consent of *all* crew members concerned. The same applies to FDR recordings, except when they are used by the operator for airworthiness or maintenance purposes only, or de-identified, or disclosed under secure procedures.

3.165 - Leasing
Between JAA Operators
Wet Lease-out
A JAA operator providing a helicopter and crew to another, retaining the functions and responsibilities in Subpart C, remains the operator.

All except Wet Lease-out
Except as above, a JAA operator using a helicopter from, or providing it to, another, must obtain prior approval from the respective Authority. Any conditions in the approval must be included in the lease agreement.

Elements of lease agreements which are approved, other than those in which a helicopter and complete crew are involved and no transfer of functions and responsibilities is intended, are all to be regarded, with respect to the leased helicopter, as variations of the AOC under which the flights will be operated.

Between a JAA and Other Operators
Dry Lease-in
Not without approval. Any conditions which are part of the approval must be in the agreement. Differences from Subparts K, L and/or JAR 26 must be notified and acceptable to the Authority.

Wet Lease-in
Not for more than 3 consecutive months in any 12 without approval. The lessor's safety standards for maintenance and operation must be equivalent to JARs, and the lessor must be an ICAO AOC holder. The helicopter must also have a standard C of A under ICAO Annex 8 (standard C of As issued by a JAA Member State other than the AOC State will be accepted when issued under JAR 21). Any JAA requirement made applicable by the lessee's Authority must be complied with.

Dry Lease-out
A JAA operator may dry lease-out a helicopter for commercial air transport to any ICAO operator if the JAA operator has been exempted from JAR OPS 3 and, after the foreign regulatory authority has accepted responsibility in writing for surveillance of maintenance and operation, has removed the helicopter from its AOC. Maintenance must be under an approved program.

Wet Lease-out

A JAA operator providing a helicopter and complete crew to another entity, retaining all the functions and responsibilities in Subpart C, remains the operator.

Short Notice

Where a JAA operator is faced with an immediate, urgent and unforeseen need for a helicopter, the approval required by (c)(2)(i) above may be deemed to have been given for up to fourteen consecutive days if the lessor holds an ICAO AOC and the Authority is immediately notified.

3.175 - General Rules for Air Operator Certification and Supervision

Helicopter used for commercial air transportation must do so under the terms and conditions of an *Air Operator Certificate* (AOC). An applicant for one, or a variation, must allow the Authority to examine all safety aspects of the proposed operation.

An applicant for an AOC must:

- Not hold an AOC from another Authority unless approved by those concerned

- Have his principal place of business and, if any, registered office in the AOC State

- Have registered the helicopters in the AOC State*

- Satisfy the Authority that he can operate safely (an AOC will be varied, suspended or revoked if the Authority is no longer satisfied that safety can be maintained)

*An operator may operate, with the mutual agreement of the AOC Authority and another, helicopters on the national register of the other

Operators must grant the Authority access to their organisation and helicopters, including any associated JAR 145 maintenance organisation.

Operators must satisfy the Authority that their organisation and management are suitable and properly matched to the scale and scope of operations, and procedures for supervision have been defined.

There must be an Accountable Manager with corporate authority to ensure that operations and

maintenance activities can be financed and carried out to the appropriate standards. There must also be nominated post holders who are responsible for the management and supervision of certain areas, such as flight operations, maintenance, crew training and ground operations.

A person may hold more than one nominated post but, for operators with 21 or more full time staff, at least two people are required for the four areas of responsibility. For operators with 20 or less full time staff, one or more of the nominated posts may be filled by the accountable manager.

Every flight must be conducted in accordance with the Operations Manual.

The operator must arrange appropriate ground handling facilities for safe handling, and ensure that helicopters are equipped and crews qualified for the area and type of operation.

The operator must comply with maintenance requirements under subpart M for all helicopters operated under the terms of its AOC.

The operator must provide the Authority with a copy of the Operations Manual, as per Subpart P and all amendments or revisions to it.

The operator must maintain operational support facilities at the main base, appropriate for the area and type of operation.

IEM OPS 3.175 - Management Organisation

Function and Purpose

The safe conduct of air operations is achieved by an operator and an Authority working in harmony. The functions of the two bodies are different, well defined, but complementary. In essence, the operator complies with the standards with a sound and competent management structure. The Authority, working within the law, sets and monitors the standards expected from operators.

Responsibilities of Management

For JAR OPS 3, these should include at least:

- Determination of the flight safety policy

- Allocation of responsibilities and duties and issuing instructions to individuals, sufficient for implementation of company policy and the maintenance of safety standards

- Monitoring of flight safety standards

- Recording and analysis of deviations from standards and ensuring corrective action

- Evaluating the safety record of the company to avoid undesirable trends

IEM OPS 3.175(c)(2) - Principal Place of Business

JAR OPS 3.175(c)(2) requires operators to have their principal place of business in the AOC State, which means where the administrative headquarters and operational and maintenance management are based.

3.180 – Air Operator Certificates

To be issued with an AOC, or be granted a variation to one, or to keep one valid:

- Helicopters must have a standard C of A under ICAO Annex 8 from a JAA Member State. Standard certificates issued by a JAA Member State other than the AOC issuer will be accepted without further showing under JAR 21

- The maintenance system must be approved under Subpart M, and have the ability to:

  - Establish and maintain an adequate organisation and quality system (see JAR OPS 3.035)

  - Comply with required training programs

  - Comply with maintenance requirements, consistent with the nature and extent of the operations, including the relevant items in JAR OPS 3.175(g) to (o)

  - Comply with JAR OPS 3.175

Notwithstanding JAR OPS 3.185(f), the operator must notify the Authority as soon as practicable of changes to the information above.

If the Authority is not satisfied that the above requirements have been met, it may require one or more demonstration flights, operated as if they were commercial air transport flights.

3.185 - Administrative Requirements

The following information must be included in the initial application, or variation or renewal:

- Official name and business name, address and mailing address

- Description of the proposed operation and management organisation

- Name of accountable manager

- Names of major post holders, including those responsible for flight operations, the maintenance system, crew training and ground operations, together with qualifications and experience

- The Ops Manual (the *application* for an initial issue of an AOC must be submitted at least 90 days before the date of intended operation, but the Ops Manual may follow, in the next 30 days)

For the maintenance system only, this information must also be included in the initial application, any variation or renewal, and for each type:

- MME

- Maintenance program(s)

- Tech log

- Technical specification(s) of the maintenance contract(s)

- The number of helicopters

Applications for variations must be submitted at least 30 days, or as otherwise agreed, before the date of intended operation (before the end of the existing period of validity for renewals).

Other than in exceptional circumstances, the Authority must be given at least 10 days' notice of proposed changes of nominated post holders.

Certificate

An AOC specifies the:

- Name and location (main place of business)

- Date of issue and period of validity

- Description of the operations authorised

- Type(s) of helicopter(s) authorised

- Registration markings of authorised helicopter(s) except that operators may obtain approval for a system to inform the Authority about them

- Authorised areas of operation

- Special limitations (e.g. VFR only)

- Special authorisations/approvals

  - CAT II/CAT III (including minima)

  - Offshore Operations

  - HEMS

  - Transportation of Dangerous Goods

  - Operations over hostile environments outside congested areas

  - Small helicopters (Day VFR)

  - Local Area Operations (Day VFR)

  - Helicopter Hoist Operations

  - Operations to Public Interest Sites

  - Operations with exposure to a power unit failure during takeoff or landing

Management and Organisation

General
Operators must have a sound and effective management structure to ensure safe conduct of operations. Nominated post holders must have proven competency in civil aviation, which means that an individual must have a technical qualification and managerial experience acceptable to the Authority.

Nominated Post Holders
A description of their functions and responsibilities, including names, must be in the Ops Manual and the Authority given notice in writing of any change. There must be arrangements to ensure continuity of supervision in their absence.

Post holders may only act for one AOC, unless approved. Nominated post holders must be contracted to work enough hours to fulfil their management functions. One person may hold several posts if approved.

Note: See JAR OPS 3.895 for post holders responsible for maintenance.

Adequacy and Supervision of Staff
- *Crew Members.* Enough flight and cabin crew must be employed for the planned operation, trained and checked under Subparts N and O.

- *Ground Staff.* Their numbers are dependent on the nature and the scale of operations. Operations and ground handling departments, in particular, must be staffed by trained people with a thorough understanding of their responsibilities. Operators contracting other organisations for certain services retain responsibility for the proper standards. In such circumstances, a nominated post holder must ensure that contractors meet the required standards.

- *Supervision.* The number of supervisors depends on the structure of the operator and the number of staff. Their duties and responsibilities must be defined, and any flying commitments arranged so that they can discharge their supervisory responsibilities. The supervision of crew members must be exercised by individuals with enough experience and personal qualities to ensure the attainment of the standards in the Ops Manual.

Accommodation Facilities
Working space at each base must be enough for the safety of operations. Consideration must be given to the needs of ground staff, those concerned with operational control, the storage and display of essential records, and flight planning by crews.

Office services must be capable, without delay, of distributing operational instructions and other information to all concerned.

Documentation
Operators must make arrangements for the production of manuals, amendments and other documentation.

IEM OPS 3.185(b) – MME Details
The MME should reflect the details of any sub-contract(s). A change of type or the maintenance organisation may require an amendment.

3.195 – Operational Control

Operators must exercise operational control and establish and maintain a method of supervision of flight operations.

3.200 - Ops Manual
An Ops Manual under JAR OPS 3, Subpart P for the use and guidance of operations personnel must be provided.

3.205 - Competence of Ops Personnel
People assigned to, or directly involved in, ground and flight operations must be properly instructed, have demonstrated their abilities and be aware of their responsibilities and the relationship of such duties to the operation as a whole.

3.210 - Establishment of Procedures
Procedures and instructions for each helicopter type, containing ground staff and crew members' duties for all types of operation on the ground and in flight, must be established.

A checklist system for use by crew members for all phases of operation of the helicopter under normal, abnormal and emergency conditions must also be set up, to ensure that the procedures in the Ops Manual are followed.

Crew members may not be allowed to perform any activities during critical phases of the flight other than those required for safe operation.

Rotors may not be turned under power without a qualified *pilot* at the controls.

AMC OPS 3.210(a)
Operators should specify the contents of safety briefings for all cabin crew before starting flights.

IEM OPS 3.210(b)
When an operator establishes procedures and a checklist system for *cabin crew* with respect to the

helicopter cabin, at least the items in a huge table (not included here) should be taken into account

3.215 - Use of Air Traffic Services
Air Traffic Services must be used for all flights whenever available.

3.220 - Authorisation of Heliports
Only heliports adequate for the type(s) of helicopter and operation(s) may be authorised.

AMC No 1
An adequate site is one that takes account of performance and site characteristics (see ICAO Annex 14 Volume 2 and the ICAO Heliport Manual (Doc 9261-AN/903)).

The operator should have a procedure for site survey by competent people, which allows for possible changes which may have taken place since the last survey.

Sites which are pre-surveyed should be specifically authorised in the Ops Manual, which should contain diagrams and/or ground and aerial photographs, and (pictorial) depiction and description of:

- Overall dimensions*
- Location and height of relevant obstacles*
- Approach and takeoff flight paths*
- Surface condition (blowing dust, snow or sand)*
- Helicopter types authorised with reference to performance*
- Provision of control of third parties on the ground*
- Procedure for activating site with land owner or controlling authority
- Other useful information, e.g. appropriate ATS agency and frequency
- Lighting (if applicable)

*For sites which are not pre-surveyed, there should be a procedure which enables the pilot to make, from the air, a judgment on suitability. These items should be considered.

Operations to non pre-surveyed sites by night (except under Appendix 1 to 3.005(d) - (c)(2)(i)(C)) should not be permitted.

AMC No 2 - Helidecks

Part C of the Operations Manual should contain the listing of helideck limitations in a Helideck Limitations List (HLL) and a pictorial representation (template) showing all necessary information of a permanent nature. The HLL will show the most recent status concerning non-compliance with ICAO Annex 14 Volume 2, limitations, warnings, cautions or other comments of operational importance. An example of a typical template is shown in JAR OPS (not included here).

Relevant information and details and pictorial representations should be obtained from the owner/operator of the helideck.

If there is more than one name for the helideck, the most common should be used, although others should also be included. After renaming, the old name should be in the HLL for the next 6 months.

All limitations should be included in the HLL. Helidecks without limitations should also be listed. With complex installations and combinations of installations (e.g. co-locations), a separate listing in the HLL, with diagrams, may be required.

Helidecks should be assessed (based on limitations, warnings, cautions or comments) to determine acceptability with respect to the following which, as a minimum, should cover these factors:

- Physical characteristics
- The preservation of obstacle-protected surfaces is the most basic safeguard for all flights, which are:
  - The minimum 210° obstacle free surface (OFS)
  - The 150° limited obstacle surface (LOS)
  - The minimum 180° falling "5:1" - gradient for significant obstacles. If this is infringed or if an adjacent installation or vessel infringes the obstacle clearance surfaces or criteria related to a helideck, an assessment should be made to determine any possible negative effect

- Marking and lighting:
  - Adequate perimeter lighting and floodlighting
  - Status lights (for night and day operations e.g. Aldis Lamp)
  - Dominant obstacle paint schemes and lighting
  - Helideck markings
  - General installation lighting levels. Any limited authorisation in this respect should be annotated "daylight only operations" on the HLL

- Deck surface:
  - Surface friction
  - Helideck net
  - Drainage system
  - Deck edge netting
  - Tie down system
  - Cleaning of all contaminant

- Environment:
  - Foreign Object Damage
  - Physical turbulence generators
  - Bird control
  - Air quality degradation from exhaust emissions, hot or cold gas vents (adjacent helidecks may need to be included in air quality assessment)

- Rescue and fire fighting:
  - Primary and complementary media types, quantities, capacity and systems personal protective equipment and clothing, breathing apparatus
  - Crash box

- Communications & Navigation:
  - Aeronautical Radio(s)

- R/T callsign to match helideck name and side identification which should be simple and unique

- NDB or equivalent (as appropriate)

- Radio log

- Light signal (e.g. Aldis Lamp)

- Fuelling facilities:

  - In accordance with the relevant national guidance and regulations

- Additional operational & handling equipment:

  - Windsock

  - Wind recording

  - Deck motion recording and reporting

  - Passenger briefing system

  - Chocks

  - Tie downs

  - Weighing scales

- Personnel:

  - Trained helideck staff (e.g. Helicopter Landing Officer/Helicopter Deck Assistant and fire fighters etc.)

For helidecks with incomplete information, a 'limited' authorisation based on information available may be issued before the first visit. During subsequent operations and before full authorisation is given, information should be gathered and the following should apply for the pictorial (static) representation:

- Template (see figure 1) blanks should be available, to be filled out during flight preparation on the basis of the information given by the helideck owner/operator and flight crew observations

- Where possible, suitably annotated photographs may be used until the HLL and template has been completed

- Until the HLL and Template has been completed, operational restrictions (e.g. performance, routing etc.) may be applied

- Any previous inspection reports should be obtained by the operator

- An inspection of the helideck should be carried out to verify the content of the completed HLL and template, following which the helideck may be fully authorised for operations

With reference to the above, the HLL should contain at least:

- HLL revision date and number

- Generic list of helideck motion limitations

- Name of Helideck

- 'D'-value of the helideck

- Limitations, warnings, cautions and comments

The template should contain at least:

- Installation/Vessel name

- R/T Callsign

- Helideck Identification Marking

- Side Panel Identification Marking

- Helideck elevation

- Maximum installation/vessel height

- 'D' Value

- Type of installation/vessel (Fixed manned, Fixed unmanned, Ship type (e.g. diving support vessel), Semi-submersible, Jack-up)

- Name of owner/operator

- Geographical position

- Com/Nav Frequencies and Ident

- General drawing preferably looking into the helideck with annotations showing location of derrick, masts, cranes, flare stack, turbine and gas exhausts, side identification panels, windsock etc.

- Plan view drawing, chart orientation from the general drawing, to show the above. The plan view will also show the 210 degree bisector orientation in degrees true

- Type of fuelling (Pressure and Gravity, Pressure only, Gravity only, None)

- Type and nature of fire fighting equipment

- Availability of GPU

- Deck heading

- Maximum allowable mass

- Status light (Yes/No)

- Revision date

3.225 - Heliport Operating Minima
These must be established under JAR OPS 3.430 for each departure, destination or alternate heliport under JAR OPS 3.220, and must take into account any increment imposed by the Authority.

The minima for a specific type of approach and landing are considered applicable if ground equipment on the respective chart and helicopter systems for the type of approach are operative, performance criteria are met and crews are qualified accordingly.

3.230 - Departure and Approach Procedures
Departure and approach procedures, if specified by the State where the heliport is, must be used, although a commander may accept an ATC clearance to deviate if obstacle clearance is observed and full account is taken of the operating conditions. The final approach must be flown visually or under the established procedure.

Different procedures may only be implemented if they have been approved by the State in which the heliport is located and the AOC Authority.

3.235 - Noise Abatement
Takeoff and landing procedures must take into account the need to minimise effects of noise.

3.240 - Routes and Areas of Operation
Operations may only be conducted along such routes or within such areas, for which:

- Ground facilities and services, including weather, are provided which are adequate

- Performance is enough to comply with minimum flight altitude requirements

- The helicopter equipment meets minimum requirements

- Appropriate maps and charts are available

- For Performance 3 helicopters, surfaces allow a safe forced landing, except under approval to operate under Appendix 1 to JAR OPS 3.005(e). In addition, on Coastal Transit operations, Part C of the Ops Manual must contain procedures to ensure that the width of the Coastal Corridor, and equipment carried, are consistent with the conditions at the time

Operations must be conducted under any restriction on the routes or the areas of operation imposed by the Authority.

IEM OPS 3.240(a)(6) - Coastal Transit
A Performance 3 helicopter operating overwater needs certain equipment fitted, which varies with the distance from land. The aim of this IEM is to discuss that distance, bring into focus what fit is required and to clarify the operator's responsibility.

When North of 45N or South of 45S, the coastal corridor facility *may* or *may not* be available, as it is related to the State definition of open sea area as per the definition of *hostile environment* and IEM 3.480(a)(12).

Coastal Transit means overwater operations within the coastal corridor where there is reasonable expectation that the flight can be conducted safely in the conditions, and, after an engine failure, a safe forced landing and successful evacuation can be made with survival of the crew and passengers assured until rescue is effected.

Coastal Corridor is a variable distance from the coastline to a distance corresponding to 3 minutes flying at normal cruising speed.

Coastal Corridor Width
The distance from land is the boundary of a corridor that extends from the land up to 3 minutes at normal cruising speed (around 5-6 nm). *Land* in this context includes sustainable

ice (see below). If the coastal region includes islands, surrounding waters may be included and aggregated with the coast and each other. Coastal transit need not be applied to inland waterways, estuary crossing or river transit.

Unless it is considered that operating to, or over, suitable ice fields is unacceptable, the definition of the "land" extends to these areas (the interpretation of the following rules may be conditional on this):

- JAR-OPS 3.240(a)(6)
- JAR-OPS 3.825
- JAR-OPS 3.827
- JAR-OPS 3.830
- JAR-OPS 3.843

However, because of the possibility of whiteout and other hazards, the following rules are excluded:

- JAR-OPS 3.650(i)
- JAR-OPS 3.660

The width of the corridor varies from *not safe under the conditions* to the maximum of *3 minutes wide*. A number of factors will, on the day, indicate if it can be used, and how wide it can be. These will include but not be restricted to:

- The prevailing weather
- Instrument fit
- Certification of the aircraft - particularly with regard to floats
- The sea state
- Temperature of the water
- Time to rescue
- Survival equipment carried

Requirement for Safe Flying
It is generally recognised that when out of sight of land in certain conditions, such as in high pressure patterns (goldfish bowl - no horizon, light winds and low visibility), the absence of a basic panel (and training) can lead to disorientation. In addition, lack of

depth perception demands a radio altimeter with an audio voice warning as an added safety benefit - particularly when autorotation to the surface may be required.

In these conditions, a helicopter, without the required instruments and radio altimeter, should be confined to a corridor in which a pilot can maintain visual land reference.

Safe Forced Landing and Evacuation
Weather and sea state both affect the outcome of an autorotation. It is recognised that the measurement of sea state is problematical and good judgement has to be exercised by the operator and the commander.

Where floats have been certificated only for emergency use (as opposed to *ditching*, which requires compliance many requirements relating to water entry, flotation and trim, occupant egress and occupant survival), operations must be limited to sea states which meet those requirements – with safe evacuation possible.

Requirements for Survival
Survival of crew and passengers after a successful autorotation and evacuation depends on the clothing and equipment carried and worn, and the temperature and state of the sea state. SAR response/capability consistent with anticipated exposure should be available before the conditions in the corridor can be considered non-hostile.

Coastal Transit can be conducted (including North of 45N and South of 45S, when the definition of open sea areas allows) if the requirements above are met, and conditions for a non-hostile coastal corridor are satisfied.

3.243 - Navigation Performance Requirements
Helicopter must not be operated where minimum navigation performance specifications are prescribed, unless approved.

IEM OPS 3.243
The requirements and procedures for areas where minimum navigation performance specifications are prescribed (based on Regional Air Navigation Agreements) are covered in the following:

- RNP - ICAO DOC 9613

- EUROCONTROL - Standards on Area Navigation to comply with RNP/RNAV

- JAA TGL n° 2 - Advisory material for the airworthiness approval of navigation systems for use in European Airspace designated for Basic RNAV Operations.

The following explanatory material has been developed to explain RNP more fully:

- *Objective of RNP* - The concept will replace the conventional method of ensuring required navigation performance by requiring specific navigation equipment by worldwide, uniform standards for defined airspace and/or flight procedures. It is therefore up to an operator to decide which system(s) he will utilise to meet the requirements. However, the the system(s) must be certificated for the airspace.

- *Navigational Accuracy* - RNP is defined as a statement of the navigational accuracy for operation within defined airspace, which is based on a combination of navigation and airborne sensor error, display error and flight technical error in the horizontal plane. The level of accuracy is expressed as a single parameter which defines the distance from intended position within which the aircraft must be maintained for at least 95% of the total flying time (RNP 4 means that aircraft remain within 4 nm of intended positions for at least 95% of the total flying time).

- *RNP Types for En-Route Operations* - RNP types have been defined for worldwide, uniform application as follows:

  - RNP 1 requires highly accurate position information and will be associated with high-density continental traffic. Full exploitation of the benefits (in connection with RNAV) will require high percentage of aircraft achieving this level

  - RNP 4 will normally be applied in continental reas where the route structure is based on VOR/DME

3.250 - Minimum Flight Altitudes

These must be established, with the methods to determine them, for all route segments, providing required terrain clearance, taking into account Subparts F to I. When higher, minimum flight altitudes established by States overflown apply.

The following must be taken into account:

- Accuracy of position
- Probable inaccuracies of altimeters
- Characteristics of terrain
- Probability of encountering shit weather
- Possible inaccuracies in charts

In fulfilling the above requirements, due consideration must be given to:

- Corrections for temperature and pressure variations from standard values
- ATC requirements
- Contingencies along the planned route

IEM OPS 3.250
Same as IEM OPS 1.250.

3.255 - Fuel Policy

One must be established for flight planning and in-flight replanning to ensure that every flight carries enough fuel for the planned operation, with reserves to cover deviations from it. Planning of flights must only be based upon procedures and data in or derived from the Ops Manual or current helicopter-specific data, and the conditions under which the flight is to be conducted, including:

- Realistic fuel consumption data
- Anticipated masses
- Expected weather
- ATS procedures and restrictions

Pre-flight calculation of usable fuel must include:

- Taxy fuel
- Trip fuel
- Reserve fuel, consisting of:

- Contingency fuel

- Alternate fuel, if a destination alternate is required (you can use the departure heliport

- Final reserve fuel

- Additional fuel, if required by the operation (e.g. isolated heliports)

- Extra fuel if required by the commander

In-flight replanning procedures must include:

- Trip fuel for the remainder of the flight

- Reserve fuel, consisting of:

  - Contingency fuel

  - Alternate fuel, if a destination alternate is required (you can use the departure heliport)

  - Final reserve fuel

  - Additional fuel, if required by the operation (e.g. isolated heliports)

- Extra fuel if required by the commander

AMC OPS 3.255

Company fuel policy should be based on:

- *Taxy fuel*, which should be at least the amount expected to be used before takeoff, taking into account local conditions and APU consumption

- *Trip fuel*, which should include:

  - Fuel for takeoff and climb from heliport elevation to initial cruising level/altitude, for the expected routing

  - Fuel from top of climb to top of descent, including any step

  - Fuel from top of descent to where the approach procedure is initiated, for the expected arrival procedure

  - Fuel for approach and landing at the destination heliport.

- *Contingency fuel*, which should be:

- For IFR, or VFR in a hostile environment, 10% of planned trip fuel

- For VFR in non-hostile environments, 5% of the planned trip fuel

- *Alternate fuel*, which should be:

  - Fuel for a missed approach from MDA/DH at the destination heliport to missed approach altitude, for the complete missed approach procedure

  - Fuel from missed approach altitude to cruising level/altitude

  - Fuel from top of climb to top of descent

  - Fuel from top of descent to where the approach is initiated, taking into account expected arrival procedure

  - Fuel for an approach and landing at the destination alternate

  - For helidecks in hostile environments, 10% of the above

- *Final reserve fuel*, which should be:

  - For Day VFR navigating visually, 20 minutes at best range speed, or

  - For IFR or when VFR and navigating by other than visual means or at night, fuel for 30 minutes at holding speed at 1 500 ft (450 m) above the destination in standard conditions, calculated with the estimated mass on arrival above the alternate, or the destination, when no alternate is required

- *Extra fuel*, at commander's discretion

Isolated Heliport IFR

For an isolated heliport under IFR, or when VFR and navigating other than visually, where a destination alternate does not exist, the fuel at departure should include:

- Taxy fuel

- Trip fuel

- Contingency fuel as above

- Additional fuel for two hours at holding speed, including final reserve

- Extra fuel at commander's discretion

Enough fuel should be carried to ensure that, after a power unit fails at the most critical point, the helicopter can descend as necessary and proceed to a suitable heliport, hold there for 15 minutes at 1 500 ft (450 m) above heliport elevation in standard conditions, and make an approach and landing.

IEM OPS 3.255(c)(3)(i) - Contingency Fuel

At the planning stage, not all factors that could influence the fuel consumption can be foreseen. Contingency fuel is carried to compensate for items such as deviations from expected fuel consumption, forecast weather, planned routings and/or cruising levels/altitudes.

3.260 - Persons with Reduced Mobility

PRMs must not be allocated, nor occupy, seats where their presence could:

- Stop the crew from doing their job

- Obstruct access to emergency equipment

- Impede emergency evacuation

The commander must be notified when PRMs are to be carried on board.

IEM OPS 3.260

A PRM mean a person whose mobility is reduced due to physical incapacity (sensory or locomotory), intellectual deficiency, age, illness or other causes, who need special attention and adaptation of the service other passengers get. They should not be seated next to emergency exits.

Where their numbers form a significant proportion of the total number of passengers on board, there should not be more than the able-bodied people that can help with emergency evacuation.

3.265 - Inadmissible Passengers, Deportees or People in Custody

Procedures for their transportation must be esablished to ensure the safety of the helicopter and its occupants. The commander must be notified when the above-mentioned persons are to be carried on board.

3.270 – Stowage of Baggage and Cargo

Only such hand baggage and cargo may be carried into a helicopter and taken into the passenger cabin as can be adequately and securely stowed.

Baggage and cargo on board, which might cause injury or damage, or obstruct aisles and exits if displaced, must be stowed to prevent movement.

Appendix 1

Procedures that ensure that hand baggage and cargo are adequately and securely stowed must take account of:

- Items in cabins must be stowed only in locations capable of restraining them

- Mass limitations placarded on or next to stowages must not be exceeded

- Underseat stowages must not be used unless the seat has a restraint bar and the baggage may be adequately restrained by it

- Items must not be stowed in toilets or against bulkheads that are incapable of restraining articles against movement forwards, sideways or upwards and unless the bulkheads carry a placard specifying the greatest mass that may be placed there

- Baggage and cargo in lockers must not prevent latched doors being closed securely

- Baggage and cargo must not be placed where access to emergency equipment is impeded

- Checks must be made before takeoff, before landing, and whenever the *fasten seat belts* signs are illuminated (or it is otherwise so ordered) to ensure that baggage is stowed where it cannot impede evacuation or cause injury by falling or movement as may be appropriate to the phase of flight

AMC OPS 3.270

In establishing procedures for the carriage of cargo in the passenger cabin:

- The weight of the cargo must not exceed structural loading limit(s)

- The number and type of restraint devices and attachment points must be capable of restraining the cargo (see JAR 29.787)

- The cargo location should not hinder egress or impair the cabin crew's view

3.280 - Passenger Seating

Passengers must be seated where, if an emergency evacuation is required, they may best assist and not hinder evacuation.

IEM OPS 3.280

Procedures that ensure the above should allow for:

- Instructions on seating policy should be in the Ops Manual, relevant parts of which should be available to staff responsible for allocating passengers to seats and ensuring that emergency evacuation can be accomplished quickly and without difficulty (this includes check-in and crew)

- *Persons likely to assist evacuation.* Only those who appear reasonably fit and strong should be next to self–help (type III and IV) exits

- *Persons likely to impede evacuation.* Those who should be where they will not obstruct emergency equipment or exits, or otherwise stop the crew doing their jobs, include:

  - Persons who are physically or mentally handicapped to the extent that they would have difficulty in moving quickly if asked to do so

  - Persons whose sight or hearing is impaired to the extent that they might not readily become aware of instructions given to begin evacuation

  - Children and infants, whether or not accompanied by an adult

  - Persons in custody or being deported

  - Persons whose physical size would prevent them moving quickly

3.285 - Passenger Briefing

Passengers must be verbally briefed about safety matters, parts or all of which may be given by an audio-visual presentation. They must also be given safety briefing cards on which picture-type instructions indicate how to use emergency equipment and exits likely to be used.

Before Takeoff

Passengers must be briefed on the following:

- Smoking regulations

- Backs of seats upright and tray table stowed

- Location of emergency exits

- Location and use of floor proximity escape path markings

- Stowage of hand baggage

- Restrictions on portable electronic devices

- Location and contents of safety cards

Passengers must receive a demonstration of:

- The use of safety belts and/or harnesses, including how to fasten and unfasten them

- The location and use of oxygen equipment (passengers must also be briefed to extinguish all smoking materials when oxygen is being used)

- The location and use of life jackets, liferafts and survival suits

After Takeoff

Passengers must be reminded of smoking regulations and the use of safety belts and harnesses.

Before Landing

Passengers must be reminded of:

- Smoking regulations

- Use of safety belts and/or safety harnesses

- Backs of seats to be upright and tray table stowed

- Re-stowage of hand baggage

- Restrictions on portable electronic devices

After Landing

Passengers must be reminded of smoking regulations and the use of safety belts and/or safety harnesses. In an emergency during flight, they must be instructed in appropriate emergency action.

3.290 - Flight Preparation

An operational flight plan must be completed for each intended flight, which must not start unless the commander is satisfied that:

- The helicopter is airworthy

- The configuration is as per the CDL

- Instruments and equipment under Subparts K and L are available and working, except as in the MEL

- Parts of the Ops Manual required for the flight are available (see 3.120)

- Documents, additional information and forms required JAR OPS 3.125 and 3.135 are on board

- Current maps, charts and associated documents or equivalent data are available, including for diversions

- Ground facilities and services for the planned flight are available and adequate

- Provisions in the Ops Manual in respect of fuel, oil and oxygen requirements, minimum safe altitudes, heliport operating minima and availability of alternate heliports can be complied with*

- The load is properly distributed and safely secured

- The mass, at the start of takeoff, will allow the flight to be conducted in compliance with Subparts F to I*

- *Any operational limitations in addition to those covered can be complied with

3.295 - Selection of Heliports

The commander must select a takeoff alternate within one hours' flight time at normal cruise speed for IMC flights if it would not be possible to return to the departure point because of weather.

For an IFR flight, or when flying VFR and navigating non-visually, the commander must specify at least one alternate in the operational flight plan unless:

- The destination is a coastal heliport

- For a flight to any other land destination, the duration of the flight and prevailing weather are such that, at the ETA at the heliport of intended landing, an approach and landing may be made under VMC as prescribed, or

- The heliport of intended landing is isolated and no alternate is available, in which case a PNR must be determined

Two destination alternates must be selected when weather reports or forecasts for the destination, indicate that 1 hour either side of ETA, weather conditions will be below planning minima, or no weather information is available anyway.

Offshore alternates may be specified, subject to:

- Offshore alternates must be used only after a PNR. Otherwise, use an onshore alternate

- OEI capability is attainable

- Deck availability is guaranteed. Dimensions, configuration and obstacle clearance must be assessed for suitability as an alternate by each type to be used

- Weather minima must be established taking accuracy and reliability of meteorological information into account

- The MEL reflects essential requirements

- Offshore alternates must not be selected unless a procedure is in the Ops Manual

- Alternate(s) must be in the operational flight plan

AMC OPS 3.295(c)(1)

Alleviations from requirements to select alternate heliports for flights to coastal heliports under IFR apply only to helicopters from offshore, and should be based on individual safety assessments.

The following should be taken into account:

- Suitability of weather based on the landing forecast for the destination

- The fuel to meet IFR requirements of JAR OPS 3.255, less alternate fuel

- Where the destination coastal heliport is not directly on the coast it should be:

- Within a distance that, with the fuel above, the helicopter can, after crossing the coastline, return to the coast, descend safely and carry out a visual approach and landing with VFR fuel reserves intact, and

- Geographically sited so that the helicopter can, within the Rules of the Air, and within the landing forecast, proceed inbound from the coast at 500 ft AGL and carry out a visual approach and landing, or proceed inbound from the coast on an agreed route and carry out a visual approach and landing

- Procedures for coastal heliports should be based on a landing forecast no worse than:

  - *By Day*. A cloud base of DH/MDH + 400ft, and 4 km visibility (600 ft cloudbase if descending over the sea

  - *By Night*. A cloud base of 1 000ft and a visibility of 5km

- The descent to establish visual contact should take place over the sea or as part of the instrument approach

- Routings and procedures for coastal heliports nominated as such should be in the Ops Manual Part C

- The MEL should reflect the requirement for Airborne Radar and Radio Altimeter

- Operational limitations for coastal heliports should be acceptable to the Authority

IEM OPS 3.295(c)(1)

The procedures in AMC OPS 3.295(c)(1) above are weather critical, so a Landing Forecast conforming to the Regional Air Navigation Plan and ICAO Annex 3 has been specified. It consists of a concise statement of the mean or average weather expected at an aerodrome or heliport during the two-hour period immediately following the time of issue, containing surface wind, visibility, significant weather and cloud elements, and other significant information, such as barometric pressure and temperature, as agreed.

The above documents contain the details, with the operationally desirable accuracy of the forecast elements. In particular, the observed cloud height and visibility elements should remain within ±30% of the forecast values in 90% of cases.

The landing forecast most commonly takes the form of a routine or special selected meteorological report in the METAR code to which a TREND is added, using the codes NOSIG, i.e. no significant change expected, BECMG (becoming), or TEMPO (temporarily). The two-hour validity period starts at the time of the weather report.

AMC OPS 3.295[(e)]

Offshore Alternate Deck Environment

The landing environment of a helideck to be used as an Offshore Alternate should be pre-surveyed and the effect of wind direction and strength, and turbulence established, as well as physical characteristics. This information, which should be available to the Commander at the planning stage and in flight, should be published in an appropriate form in the Ops Manual Part C (including orientation of the helideck) so that its suitability can be assessed.

Performance

Use of Offshore Alternates is restricted to helicopters which can achieve OEI HIGE at an appropriate power rating at the alternate. Where the surface of the helideck, or prevailing conditions (especially wind), precludes OEI HIGE, OEI HOGE performance at an appropriate power rating should be used to compute landing mass, which should be calculated from graphs in Part B of the Ops Manual (due account should be taken of helicopter configuration, environmental conditions and systems with adverse effects on performance.) The planned landing mass, including crew, passengers, baggage, cargo plus 30 minutes Final Reserve fuel, should not exceed the OEI landing mass at the time of approach.

Weather

When use of an Offshore Alternate is planned, weather observations at the destination and alternate should be taken by an acceptable observer (although automatic stations may be used if acceptable).

The aerodrome forecast must indicate that, one hour either side of ETA, the weather conditions will be at or above the planning minima below:

	Day	Night
Cloud Base	600 ft	800 ft
Visibility	4 km	5 km

Where fog is forecast, or has been observed within the last two hours within 60 nm of the destination or alternate, offshore alternates should not be used.

Actions at PNR

Before passing the PNR (which should not be more than 30 minutes from the destination) the following should have been completed:

- Confirmation that navigation to the destination and offshore alternate can be assured

- Radio contact with the destination and offshore alternate (or master station) has been established

- The landing forecast at the destination and offshore alternate are confirmed to be at or above the required minima

- The requirements for OEI landing (see above) have been checked (in light of the latest reported weather) to ensure that they can be met

- To the extent possible, having regard to information on current and forecast use of the offshore alternate and on conditions prevailing, the availability of the offshore alternate should be guaranteed by the duty holder (the rig operator for fixed installations and the owner for mobiles) until the landing has been achieved (or until offshore shuttling has been completed).

Offshore Shuttling

Provided that the actions above have been done, offshore shuttling, using an offshore alternate, may be carried out.

IEM OPS 3.295(e) - Offshore Alternates

When operating offshore, spare payload capacity should be used to carry additional fuel if it would facilitate using an onshore alternate.

IEM OPS 3.295(e)(4) - Landing Forecast

The procedures in AMC OPS 3.295(e) are weather critical, so meteorological data (as per the Regional Air Navigation Plan and ICAO Annex 3) has been specified. As the following meteorological data is point-specific, caution should be exercised when associating it with nearby heliports (or helidecks).

METARs

Routine and special meteorological observations at offshore installations should be made at agreed periods and frequencies. They should comply with the meteorological section of the ICAO Regional Air Navigation Plan, and conform to ICAO Annex 3.

Routine and selected special reports are exchanged between meteorological offices in the METAR or SPECI code forms prescribed by the World Meteorological Organisation.

TAFS

The aerodrome forecast consists of a concise statement of the mean or average conditions expected during a specified period, which is normally between 9-24 hours, to include surface wind, visibility, weather and cloud, and expected changes. Additional elements may be included as agreed. Where forecasts relate to offshore, barometric pressure and temperature should be included to help with performance planning.

Aerodrome forecasts are most commonly exchanged in the TAF code form, and the detailed description is in the ICAO Regional Air Navigation Plan and ICAO Annex 3, with operationally desirable accuracy elements (see also Ops Manual). In particular, the observed cloud height should remain within ±30% of the forecast value in 70% of cases, and the observed visibility should remain within ±30% of the forecast value in 80% of cases.

Landing Forecasts (TRENDS)

The landing forecast consists of a concise statement of the mean or average conditions expected during the two hours immediately after issue. It contains surface wind, visibility, significant weather and cloud, and other significant information, such as barometric pressure and temperature, as agreed.

The detailed description is in the ICAO Regional Air Navigation Plan and ICAO Annex 3, together with desirable accuracy. In particular, the value of the observed cloud height and visibility should remain within ±30% of forecast values in 90% of the cases.

Landing forecasts most commonly take the form of routine or special meteorological reports in the METAR code, to which either the code words "NOSIG", i.e. no significant change expected; "BECMG" (becoming), or "TEMPO" (temporarily), followed by the expected change, are added. The two-hour validity starts at the time of the report.

3.297 - Planning Minima for IFR Flights
Takeoff Alternates
The appropriate weather reports or forecasts and aerodrome or landing forecasts, or any combination, must indicate that, for 1 hour either side of ETA, the weather will be at or above the minima under JAR OPS 3.225. The ceiling must be taken into account when only non-precision approaches are available. OEI limitations must be allowed for.

Destination and Destination Alternates
These may only be selected when appropriate weather reports or forecasts and aerodrome or landing forecasts, or any combination, indicate that, for 1 hour either side of ETA, the weather will be at or above the planning minima as follows:

- RVR/visibility under JAR OPS 3.225

- For a non-precision approach, the ceiling at or above MDH, and

- Planning minima for destination alternates:

Type of Approach	Planning Minima
Cat II and III	Cat I (Note 1)
Cat I	Plus 200ft/400m visibility
Non-Precision	Non-Precision (Note 2) plus 200ft/400 m visibility

Note 1: RVR

Note 2: The ceiling must be at or above the MDH

3.300 - Submission of ATS Flight Plan
Flights may not start unless an ATS flight plan has been submitted, or adequate information has been deposited, or transmitted as soon as possible after takeoff, to permit alerting services to be activated.

AMC OPS 3.300
For flights without an ATS flight plan, when unable to submit or to close, due to lack of ATS facilities or any other means of communication, operators should establish procedures, instructions and a list of authorised persons to be responsible for alerting SAR. To ensure that each flight can be located at all times, these instructions should:

- Provide the authorised person with at least the information needed in a VFR Flight plan, and the location, date and estimated time for re-establishing communications

- If an aircraft is overdue or missing, provide for notification to the appropriate ATS or SAR facility

- Provide that the information will be retained at a designated place until the completion of the flight

3.305 - Refuelling/Defuelling with Passengers Embarking, Onboard or Disembarking
No helicopter may be re/defuelled with Avgas or wide-cut type fuel (e.g. Jet-B or equivalent) or a mixture, when passengers are embarking, on board or disembarking. Otherwise, necessary precautions must be taken and the helicopter must be properly manned by qualified people ready to initiate and direct evacuation by the most expeditious means.

Appendix 1 to JAR OPS 3.305
The following precautions must be taken:

- Doors on the refuelling side must be closed

- Doors on the non-refuelling side must be open, weather permitting

- Fire fighting facilities must be positioned to be immediately available

- Enough personnel must be immediately available to move passengers clear

- Enough qualified personnel must be on board and prepared for an immediate emergency evacuation

- If fuel vapour is detected inside the helicopter, or any other hazard arises, fuelling must be stopped immediately

- The ground area beneath the exits for emergency evacuation and slide deployment areas must be kept clear

- Provision must be made for a safe and rapid evacuation

IEM OPS 3.305
When re/defuelling with passengers on board, ground servicing activities and work inside the helicopter, such as catering and cleaning, should be conducted so that they do not create a hazard, with aisles and emergency doors unobstructed.

3.307 - Re/Defuelling with Wide-cut Fuel
Procedures must be established.

IEM OPS 3.307
Wide-cut fuel (Jet B, JP 4, AVTAG) is an aviation turbine fuel falling between gasoline and kerosene with a higher volatility (vapour pressure), and lower flash and freezing points than JET A or A1.

Wherever possible, its use should be avoided, because mixtures with kerosene turbine fuels can result in the air/fuel mixture in the tank being in the combustible range at ambient temperatures. The extra precautions below are advisable to avoid arcing in the tank from electrostatic discharge, which can be minimised by static dissipation additive. When this additive is present in the proportions in the fuel specification, the normal precautions set out below are considered adequate.

Wide-cut fuel is involved when it is being supplied or when it is already present in fuel tanks. Its use should be recorded in the Tech Log, and the next two uplifts should be treated as though they also involved wide-cut fuel.

When using turbine fuels without static dissipators, but involving wide-cut fuels, a substantial reduction in the fuel flow rate is advisable, which:

- allows more time for static build-up in the fuelling equipment to dissipate before fuel enters the tank

- reduces charges building up from splashing

- until the fuel inlet point is immersed, reduces misting in the tank, and the extension of the flammable range

The flow rate reduction depends on the fuelling equipment and filtration system, so it is difficult to quote precise flow rates. Reduction in flow rate is advisable when pressure fuelling is employed.

3.310 - Crew Members at Stations
Flight Crew
During taxy, takeoff and landing, flight crew must be at their stations. During all other phases of flight, they must remain at their stations unless absence is necessary for their duties, or physiological needs, provided at least one suitably qualified pilot remains at the controls at all times.

Cabin Crew
On all decks occupied by passengers, cabin crew must be seated at their assigned stations during taxy, takeoff and landing, and whenever deemed necessary by the commander for safety.

IEM OPS 3.310(b) - Cabin crew seating positions
Cabin crew seats should be close to a floor level exit, with a good view of the area(s) of the passenger cabin for which the cabin crew member is responsible, and evenly distributed (this does not mean that, if there are more crew stations than cabin crew, their numbers should be increased).

3.320 - Seats, Safety Belts and Harnesses
Crew Members
During taxy, takeoff and landing, and whenever deemed necessary by the commander for safety, crew members must be properly secured by all safety belts and harnesses provided. During other phases of flight, flight crew members in the cockpit must keep safety belts fastened at their stations.

Passengers
Before takeoff and landing, and during taxying, and whenever deemed necessary for safety, the commander must ensure that each passenger on board occupies a seat or berth with his safety belt, or harness where provided, properly secured.

Multiple occupancy may only be allowed on specified seats and may not occur other than by one adult and one infant who is properly secured by a supplementary loop belt or other device.

3.325 - Securing of Passenger Cabin & Galley
Before taxying, takeoff and landing, exits and escape paths must be unobstructed. Before takeoff and landing, and whenever deemed necessary for safety, equipment and baggage must be secured.

3.330 - Accessibility of Emergency Equipment
Relevant emergency equipment must remain easily accessible for immediate use.

3.335 - Smoking on Board
No person on board is allowed to smoke:

- Whenever deemed necessary for safety

- While on the ground unless specifically permitted under the Ops Manual

- Outside designated smoking areas, in the aisles and in the toilets

- In cargo compartments and/or other areas where cargo is carried which is not stored in flame resistant containers or covered by flame resistant canvas

- In the cabin where oxygen is being supplied

3.340 - Meteorological Conditions
On an IFR flight, a commander must not start takeoff or continue beyond where a revised flight plan applies, unless information indicates that the expected weather at the destination and/or alternate are at or above the planning minima.

On a VFR flight, a commander must not start takeoff unless current weather reports or a combination of reports and forecasts indicate that the weather along the route (or that part to be flown under VFR) will, at the appropriate time, allow compliance with these rules.

On an IFR flight, a commander must not continue towards the planned destination unless the latest information indicates that, at the ETA, the weather at the destination, or at least one destination alternate are at or more than the minima above.

A flight to a helideck or elevated heliport must not be operated when the mean wind speed is reported as 60 knots or more.

3.345 - Ice and Other Contaminants
There must be procedures for when ground de/anti-icing and related inspections are necessary.

A commander must not start to take off unless the external surfaces are clear of deposits which might adversely affect performance and/or controllability, except as in the Flight Manual.

A commander must not start a flight under known or expected icing conditions unless the helicopter is certificated and equipped to cope with them.

3.350 - Fuel and Oil Supply
A commander must not commence a flight unless he is satisfied that the helicopter carries at least the planned amount of fuel and oil to complete the flight safely, taking into account the expected operating conditions.

3.355 - Takeoff Conditions
Before starting takeoff, commanders must be satisfied that the weather and condition of the FATO do not prevent a safe takeoff and departure.

3.360 - Application of Takeoff Minima
Before starting takeoff, a commander must be satisfied that the RVR/visibility and ceiling in the direction of takeoff is equal to or better than the applicable minima.

3.365 - Minimum Flight Altitudes
The Pilot Flying must not descend below specified minimum altitudes except when necessary for takeoff or landing, or descending under approved procedures.

3.370 - Simulated Abnormal Situations
Abnormal or emergency situations requiring abnormal or emergency procedures and simulation of IMC by artificial means must not be simulated on commercial air transport flights.

3.375 - In-flight Fuel Management
In-flight fuel checks and fuel management must be carried out.

The amount of usable fuel remaining in flight must be more than that needed to go to a heliport where a safe landing can be made, with final reserves.

The commander must declare an emergency when usable fuel on board is less than final reserve fuel.

Appendix 1 to JAR OPS 3.375

In-flight Fuel Checks
Fuel checks must be carried out in flight at regular intervals. The remaining fuel must be recorded and evaluated to:

- Compare actual consumption with planned consumption

- Check that the remaining fuel is enough to complete the flight

- Determine the expected fuel remaining on arrival at the destination

The relevant fuel data must be recorded.

In-flight Fuel Management
If, as a result of an in-flight fuel check, the expected fuel remaining on arrival at the destination is less than required alternate fuel plus final reserve fuel, the commander must divert or replan the flight as per JAR OPS 3.295(d)(1) unless he considers it safer to continue to the destination, if at an on-shore destination, when two suitable, separate touchdown and lift-off areas are available and the weather complies with JAR OPS 3.340(a)(2), the commander may permit alternate fuel to be used before landing.

If, as a result of an in-flight fuel check on a flight to an isolated destination heliport (see AMC OPS 3.255 para 3), the expected fuel remaining at the point of last possible diversion is less than the sum of fuel to divert, contingency fuel and final reserve fuel, a commander must divert, or proceed to the destination, provided that, at on-shore destinations, two suitable, separate touchdown and lift-off areas are available and the expected weather complies with JAR OPS 3.340(a)(2).

3.385 - Use of Supplemental Oxygen
Flight crew members engaged on duties essential to the safe operation of a helicopter in flight must use supplemental oxygen continuously whenever cabin altitude exceeds 10 000 ft for more than 30 minutes and whenever the cabin altitude exceeds 13 000 ft.

3.395 - Ground Proximity Detection
When undue proximity to the ground is detected by any flight crew member or by a GPWS, the commander must ensure that corrective action is initiated immediately to establish safe conditions.

3.400 - Approach and Landing Conditions
Before starting an approach to land, the commander must satisfy himself that, according to information available, the weather and the condition of the FATO should not prevent a safe approach, landing or missed approach, with regard to performance information in the Ops Manual.

IEM OPS 3.400
The in-flight determination of the FATO suitability should be based on the latest available report, preferably not more than 30 minutes before the expected landing time.

3.405 – Start and Continuation of Approach
The commander may commence an instrument approach regardless of reported RVR/Visibility, but the approach must not be continued beyond the outer marker, or equivalent, if the reported RVR/Visibility is less than the applicable minima.

Where RVR is not available, RVR values may be derived by converting the reported visibility under Appendix 1 to JAR OPS 3.430, sub-para (h).

If, after passing the outer marker (or equivalent), the reported RVR/visibility falls below the minima, the approach may continue to DA/H or MDA/H.

Where no outer marker or equivalent exists, the commander must make the decision to continue or abandon before descending below 1 000 ft above the heliport on the final approach segment.

The approach may be continued below DA/H or MDA/H and the landing completed, provided that the required visual reference is established at the DA/H or MDA/H and is maintained.

IEM OPS 3.405(a) - Equivalent Position
This can be established by DME distance, a suitably located NDB or VOR, SRE or PAR fix or any other suitable fix that independently establishes the position of the helicopter.

3.415 - Journey Log

The journey log must be completed.

3.420 - Occurrence Reporting

Flight Incidents

The operator or commander must submit a report to the Authority of any incident that has endangered or may have endangered safe operation of a flight, to be despatched within 72 hours of the event, unless exceptional circumstances prevent it.

Technical Defects and Exceedance of Technical Limitations

Technical defects and exceedances of limitations must recorded in the Tech Log.

Air Traffic Incidents

A commander must submit an air traffic incident report under ICAO PANS RAC whenever a helicopter in flight has been endangered by:

- A near collision with any flying device
- Faulty air traffic procedures or lack of compliance with procedures by ATS or the flight crew
- A failure of ATS facilities

Bird Hazards and Strikes

A commander must immediately inform the appropriate ground station whenever a potential bird hazard is observed, and submit a written bird strike report after landing whenever a helicopter for which he is responsible suffers a bird strike.

Emergencies with Dangerous Goods Onboard

If an in-flight emergency occurs and the situation permits, a commander must inform the appropriate ATS unit of any Dangerous Goods on board.

Unlawful Interference

Following an act of unlawful interference on board a helicopter, a commander must submit a report, as soon as practicable (if still alive ☺) to the local Authority and/or the Authority (if not, the hijackers must do it ☺).

Irregularities of Ground and Navigational Facilities and Hazardous Conditions

A commander must notify the appropriate ground station as soon as practicable when a potentially hazardous condition such as the following is encountered during flight:

- An irregularity in a ground or navigational facility
- A meteorological phenomenon
- A volcanic ash cloud
- A high radiation level

AMC OPS 3.420(e) - Dangerous Goods

To assist ground services in preparing for an emergency, it is essential that adequate and accurate information about any dangerous goods on board be given to ATC. Wherever possible, this should include the proper shipping name and/or the UN/ID number, the class/division and, for Class 1, the compatibility group, identified subsidiary risk(s), the quantity and the location on board.

3.425 - Accident Reporting

Operators must establish procedures to ensure that the nearest appropriate authority is notified by the quickest available means of any accident, involving the helicopter, resulting in serious injury (as per ICAO Annex 13) or death of any person or substantial damage to the helicopter or property.

A commander must submit a report to the Authority of any accident on board, resulting in serious injury to, or death of, any person on board while responsible for the flight.

3.430 – All Weather Operations - Heliport Operating Minima

Each heliport must have operating minima that are not lower than those in Appendix 1, or those of the State where the heliport is, except when specifically approved by that State.

Note: The above does not prohibit in-flight calculation of minima for a non-planned alternate if carried out under an accepted method.

Full account must be taken of:

- The type, performance and handling characteristics of the helicopter

- The composition of the flight crew, their competence and experience

- The dimensions and characteristics of FATOs and runways

- The adequacy and performance of visual and non-visual ground aids

- The equipment on the helicopter for navigation and/or control of the flight path during takeoff, approach, flare, hover, landing, roll-out and missed approach

- Obstacles in the approach, missed approach and climb-out areas for contingencies and necessary clearance

- The obstacle clearance altitude/height for the instrument procedures

- Means to determine and report weather

Appendix 1

Takeoff Minima

These must be expressed as visibility or RVR limits, taking into account relevant factors for heliports and helicopter characteristics. Where there is a specific need to see and avoid obstacles on departure and/or for a forced landing, other conditions (e.g. ceiling) must be specified.

The commander must not start takeoff unless the weather at the heliport of departure is equal to or better than minima for landing there, unless a suitable takeoff alternate is available.

When the reported visibility is below that required for takeoff and RVR is not reported, a takeoff may only be started if the commander can determine that RVR/Visibility along the takeoff FATO or runway is equal to or better than required minima.

With no visibility or RVR available, a takeoff may only be started if the commander can determine that the RVR/Visibility along the takeoff FATO or runway is equal to or better than required minima.

Visual Reference

Takeoff minima must be selected to ensure enough guidance to control the helicopter in the event of a discontinued takeoff in adverse circumstances and a continued takeoff after failure of the critical power unit.

At night, ground lighting must be available to illuminate the FATO/runway and obstacles unless otherwise agreed.

Required RVR/Visibility

For Performance Class 1, an RVR and visibility (RVR/VIS) must be established as takeoff minima under this table:

Onshore heliports with IFR departures	RVR/Visibility
No lighting and no markings (Day)	250m or the rejected takeoff distance, whichever is greater
No markings (Night)	800m
Runway edge/FATO lighting and centre line marking	200m
Runway edge/FATO lighting, centre line marking and RVR information	150m
Offshore Helideck	
Two pilot operations	250m (1)
Single pilot operations	500m (1)

Note 1: The takeoff flight path must be free of obstacles.

For Performance Class 2 onshore, the commander must operate to takeoff minima of 800 m RVR/VIS and remain clear of cloud during takeoff until Class 1 applies.

For Performance Class 2 offshore, the commander must operate to at least the minima for Class 1 and remain clear of cloud during the takeoff until Class 1 applies. (See note 1 to Table 1 above.)

The table below, for converting reported meteorological visibility to RVR, must not be used for calculating takeoff minima.

Non-Precision Approach

System Minima

These approaches must not be lower than the MDH values in the table below:

System Minima	
Facility	*Lowest MDH*
ILS (no glide path – LLZ)	250 ft
SRA (ending at ½ nm)	250 ft
SRA (ending at 1 nm)	300 ft
SRA (ending at 2 nm)	350 ft
VOR	300 ft
VOR/DME	250 ft
NDB	300 ft
VDF (QDM & QCH)	300 ft

Minimum Descent Height

The MDH for a non-precision approach must not be lower than either the OCH/OCL for the category of helicopter, or system minima.

Visual Reference

You may not continue an approach below MDA/MDH unless at least one of these visual references for the FATO/runway is distinctly visible and identifiable:

- Elements of approach light system

- The threshold, its markings or lights

- Visual glide slope indicator

- Touchdown zone, markings or lights

- FATO/Runway edge lights

- Other references as agreed

Required RVR

For non-precision approaches by Class 1 or 2 helicopters, these minima apply:

Onshore Non-Precision Approach Minima (5)(6)(7)				
MDH (ft)	*Facilities/RVR*			
	Full (1)	*Intermediate (2)*	*Basic (3)*	*Nil (4)*
250-299'	600 m	800 m	1 000 m	1 000 m
300-449'	800 m	1 000 m	1 000 m	1 000 m
450' +	1 000 m	1 000 m	1 000 m	1 000 m

Note 1: Full facilities are FATO/runway markings, 720 m or more of HI/MI approach lights, FATO/runway edge lights, threshold lights and FATO/runway end lights. Lights must be on.

Note 2: Intermediate facilities comprise FATO/runway markings, 420 - 719 m of HI/MI approach lights, FATO/runway edge lights, threshold lights and FATO/runway end lights. Lights must be on.

Note 3: Basic facilities are FATO/runway markings, <420 m HI/MI approach lights, any length of LI approach lights, FATO or runway edge lights, threshold lights and FATO/runway end lights. Lights must be on.

Note 4: Nil approach light facilities comprise FATO/runway markings, FATO/runway edge lights, threshold lights, FATO/runway end lights or no lights at all.

Note 5: The tables only apply to conventional approaches with a nominal descent slope of up to 4°. Greater slopes will usually require that visual guidance (e.g. PAPI) is also visible at MDH.

Note 6: The above figures are either reported RVR or meteorological visibility converted to RVR as in sub-paragraph (h) below.

Note 7: The MDH refers to the initial calculation. When selecting the associated RVR, there is no need to take account of a rounding up to the nearest ten feet, which may be done for operational purposes, e.g. conversion to MDA.

Where the missed approach point is within ½ nm of the landing threshold, the minima for full facilities may be used regardless of the length of approach lighting available, but FATO/runway edge lights, threshold lights, end lights and FATO/runway markings are still required.

Night Operations

Ground lighting must be available to illuminate the FATO/runway and obstacles unless otherwise agreed.

Single Pilot

The minimum RVR is 800 m or the Table 3 minima whichever is higher.

Precision Approach - Category I

A Cat I operation is a precision approach and landing using ILS, MLS or PAR with a DH of at least 200 ft and RVR at least 500 m.

Decision Height

The DH for a Cat I precision approach must be at least:

- The MDH in the Flight Manual

- The minimum height to which the approach aid can be used without the required visual reference

- The OCH/OCL for the helicopter

- 200 ft

Visual Reference

You may not continue an approach below MDA/MDH unless at least one of these visual references for the FATO/runway is distinctly visible and identifiable:

- Elements of approach light system

- The threshold, its markings or lights

- Visual glide slope indicator

- Touchdown zone, markings or lights

- FATO/Runway edge lights

Required RVR

For Cat I ops by Class 1 and 2 helicopters, these minima apply:

Onshore Precision Approach Minima Category I (5)(6)(7)				
DH (ft)	Facilities/RVR			
	Full (1)	Intermediate (2)	Basic (3)	Nil (4)
200	500 m	600 m	700 m	1 000 m
201-250	550 m	650 m	750 m	1 000 m
251-300	600 m	700 m	800 m	1 000 m
301 +	750 m	800 m	900 m	1 000 m

Note 1: Full facilities are FATO/runway markings, 720 m or more of HI/MI approach lights, FATO/runway edge lights, threshold lights and FATO/runway end lights. Lights must be on.

Note 2: Intermediate facilities comprise FATO/runway markings, 420-719 m of HI/MI approach lights, FATO/runway edge lights, threshold lights and FATO/runway end lights. Lights must be on.

Note 3: Basic facilities are FATO/runway markings, <420 m of HI/MI approach lights, any length of LI approach lights, FATO or runway edge lights, threshold lights and FATO/runway end lights. Lights must be on.

Note 4: Nil approach light facilities comprise FATO/runway markings, FATO/runway edge lights, threshold lights, FATO/runway end lights or no lights at all.

Note 5: The above figures are either the reported RVR or meteorological visibility converted to RVR under paragraph (h).

Note 6: The Table is applicable to conventional approaches with a glide slope angle up to and including 4°.

Note 7: The DH in the table refers to the initial calculation. When selecting the associated RVR, there is no need to take account of a rounding up to the nearest ten feet, which may be done for operational purposes, (e.g. conversion to DA).

Night Operations

Ground lighting must be available to illuminate the FATO/runway and obstacles unless otherwise agreed.

Single Pilot

Operators must calculate the minimum RVR for all approaches under JAR OPS 3.430 and this Appendix. Less than 800 m is not permitted except when using a suitable autopilot coupled to an ILS or MLS, in which case normal minima apply. The DH applied must not be less than 1.25 x the minimum use height for the autopilot.

Onshore Precision Approach - Category II

A Category II operation is a precision instrument approach and landing using ILS or MLS with DH between 100-200 ft and RVR at least 300 m.

Decision Height

This must not be lower than:

- The minimum in the Flight Manual

- The minimum height to which the approach aid can be used without the required visual reference

- The OCH/OCL for the helicopter

- That to which the crew is authorised

- 100 ft

Visual Reference

You may not continue an approach below the Cat II DH above unless visual reference with a segment of at least 3 consecutive lights (being the centre line of the approach lights), or touchdown zone lights, or FATO/runway centre line or edge lights, or a combination, is attained and can be maintained. This visual reference must include a lateral element of the ground pattern, i.e. an approach lighting crossbar or the landing threshold or a barette of the touchdown zone lighting.

Required RVR

For Cat II approaches by Class 1 helicopters the following minima apply:

Onshore Precision Approach Minima – Category II	
DH	Autocoupled to below DH (1) RVR
100 - 120 ft	300 m
121 - 140 ft	400 m
141 ft and above	450 m

Note 1: The reference to *autocoupled to below DH* means continued use of AFCS down to a height up to 80% of DH. Thus, airworthiness requirements may, through minimum engagement height for the AFCS, affect the DH to be applied.

Onshore Circling

Circling describes the visual phase of an instrument approach, to get into position for landing on a FATO/runway which is not suitably located for a straight in approach.

For circling, the MDH must be at least 250 ft, and the visibility at least 800 m.

Note: Visual manoeuvring (circling) with prescribed tracks is an accepted procedure within the meaning of this paragraph.

Visual Approach

RVR must be at least 800 m.

Conversion of Met Vis to RVR

A met vis to RVR conversion must not be used for calculating takeoff, Cat II or III minima or when a reported RVR is available.

Otherwise, use this table:

Lighting elements	RVR = met. vis multiplied by:	
	Day	Night
Hi approach and runway lighting	1.5	2.0
Any type of lighting	1.0	1.5
No lighting	1.0	Not applicable

ARA for Overwater Operations

Airborne Radar Approaches must be authorised, but they are only permitted to rigs or vessels under way when a multi-crew concept is used. They must not be undertaken unless the radar can provide course guidance to ensure obstacle clearance.

Before starting final approach, the commander must ensure that a clear path exists on the radar screen for the final and missed approach segments. If lateral clearance from any obstacle will be less than 1 nm, the commander must approach to a nearby target structure and thereafter proceed visually, or make the approach from another direction leading to a circling manoeuvre.

The cloud ceiling must be clear enough above the helideck to permit a safe landing.

Minimum Descent Height

Despite the minima below, MDH must be at least 50 ft above the elevation of the helideck.

When determined from a radio altimeter, the MDH for an ARA must be at least 200 ft by day and 300 ft by night. MDH for an approach leading to circling must be at least 300 ft by day and 500 ft by night.

Minimum Descent Altitude

An MDA may only be used if the radalt is unserviceable. MDA must be at least MDH +200 ft and based on a calibrated barometer at the destination or on the lowest forecast QNH for the region.

Decision Range

Decision Range must be at least 0.75 nm unless a lesser one has been demonstrated at an acceptable level of safety.

Visual Reference

Approaches may not continue beyond Decision Range or below MDH/MDA unless visual with the destination.

Single Pilot

The MDH/MDA for a single pilot ARA must be 100 ft higher than that calculated above. The Decision Range must be at least 1 nm.

AMC OPS 3.430(b)(4) - Effect of Temporarily Failed or Downgraded Ground Equipment

Aerodrome facilities are expected to be installed and maintained to the standards in ICAO Annexes 10 and 14. Any deficiencies are expected to be repaired without unnecessary delay.

These instructions are intended for pre- and in-flight use. It is not expected, however, that the commander would consult them after passing the outer marker or equivalent position - if failures of ground aids are announced at such a late stage, the approach could be continued at the commander's discretion. If, however, failures are announced before then, their effect should be considered as described in the tables below, and the approach may have to be abandoned to allow this to happen.

No DH

For aeroplanes (sic) authorised to conduct no DH operations with the lowest RVR limitations, the following applies in addition to the Tables below:

- At least one RVR value must be available at the aerodrome

- *no FATO/runway edge lights, or no centre lights* - Day only min RVR 200 m

- *No TDZ lights* - No restrictions

- *No standby power to FATO/runway lights* - Day only min RVR 200 m

Conditions for Tables

Multiple failures of FATO/runway lights other than indicated in Table 1B are not acceptable. Deficiencies of approach and FATO/runway lights are treated separately.

For Cat II or III operations, a combination of deficiencies in FATO/runway lights and RVR assessment equipment is not allowed.

Failures other than ILS affect RVR only and not DH

IEM to Appendix 1 - Aerodrome Operating Minima

The minima in this Appendix are based on the experience of commonly used approach aids, which is not meant to preclude other guidance systems, such as HUD and EVS, but the minima for them will need to be developed with need.

IEM to Appendix 1 - Onshore Heliport Departures

The cloud base and visibility should allow the helicopter to be clear of cloud at TDP, and for the PF to remain in sight of the surface until minimum speed for IMC flight in the Flight Manual.

IEM to Appendix 1 - Minimum RVR for Cat II

When establishing minimum RVR for Cat II Ops, operators should pay attention to the information from ECAC Doc 17 3rd Edition, Subpart A. It is retained as background information and, to some extent, for historical purposes, although there may be some conflict with current practices. Thus, it is not included here.

IEM to Appendix 1 - ARA for Overwater Operations

The ARA procedure may have up to five segments - arrival, initial, intermediate, final, and missed approach. In addition, the requirements of the circling manoeuvre to a visual landing should be considered. The individual segments can begin and end at designated fixes, but the segments of an ARA may often begin at specified points where no fixes are available.

The fixes or points are named to coincide with the associated segment. For example, the intermediate segment begins at the Intermediate Fix (IF) and ends at the Final Approach Fix (FAF). Where no fix is available or appropriate, the segments begin and end at specified points; e.g. Intermediate Point

(IP) and Final Approach Point (FAP). The order in which this IEM discusses the segments is the order in which the pilot would fly them in a complete procedure: that is, from the arrival through initial and intermediate to a final approach and, if necessary, the missed approach.

Only segments required by local conditions at the time of the approach need be included in a procedure. In constructing it, the final approach track, (which should be substantially into wind) should be identified first as it is the least flexible and most critical. When the origin and the orientation of the final approach have been determined, the others should be integrated to produce an orderly manoeuvring pattern which does not generate an unacceptably high workload for the flight crew.

Examples of ARA procedures, vertical profiles and missed approach procedures are in Figures 1 to 5 (not included here).

Obstacle Environment

Each segment is in an over-water area with a flat surface at sea level. However, due to the passage of large vessels which are not required to notify their presence, the exact obstacle environment cannot be determined. As the largest vessels and structures are known to reach elevations over 500 ft amsl, the uncontrolled offshore obstacle environment applying to the arrival, initial and intermediate approach segments can reasonably be assumed to be capable of reaching to at least 500 ft amsl. But, for final and missed approach segments, specific areas are involved within which no radar returns are permitted. In these areas, the height of wave crests and the possibility that small obstacles may be present which are not visible on radar, results in an uncontrolled surface environment which extends to 50 ft amsl.

Under normal circumstances, the relationship between the procedure and the obstacle environment is governed under the concept that vertical separation is very easy to apply during the arrival, initial and intermediate segments, while horizontal separation, which is much more difficult to guarantee in an uncontrolled environment, is applied only in the final and missed approach segments.

Arrival Segment

This starts at the last en-route navigation fix, where the aircraft leaves the helicopter route, and ends either at the IAF or, if no course reversals are required, it ends at the IF. Standard en-route obstacle clearance criteria should be applied to the arrival segment.

Initial Approach Segment

This is only required if a course reversal, race track, or arc procedure is necessary to join the intermediate approach track. The segment commences at the IAF and on completion of the manoeuvre ends at the intermediate point (IP). The MOC is 1 000 ft.

Intermediate Approach Segment

This starts at the IP, or in the case of "straight in" approaches, where there is no initial approach segment, at the IF. The segment ends at the FAP and should be at least 2 nm in length. The purpose of the intermediate segment is to align and prepare the helicopter for the final approach. During the intermediate segment, the helicopter should be lined up with the final approach track, the speed should be stabilised, the destination identified on the radar, and the final approach and missed approach areas identified and verified to be clear of radar returns. The MOC is 500 ft.

Final Approach Segment

This starts at the FAP and ends at the missed approach point (MAP). The final approach area, which should be identified on radar, is a corridor between the FAP and the radar return of the destination. The corridor should be at least 2 nm wide so that the projected track of the helicopter does not pass closer than 1 nm to the obstacles outside the area.

On passing the FAP, the helicopter will descend below the intermediate approach altitude, and follow a descent gradient which should not be steeper than 6·5%. At this stage vertical separation from the offshore obstacle environment will be lost, but, within the final approach area, MDH or MDA, will provide separation from the surface environment. Descent from 1 000 ft amsl to 200 ft amsl at a constant 6·5% gradient will take 2 nm. To follow the guideline that the procedure should not generate an unacceptably high workload for the flight crew, the required actions of levelling at MDH, changing heading at the Offset Initiation Point (OIP), and turning away at the MAP should not occur at the same time, so the FAP should not normally be less than 4 nm from the destination.

During final approach, compensation for drift should be applied and the heading which, if maintained, would take the helicopter directly to the destination, should be identified. It follows that, at an OIP at 1·5 nm, a heading change of 10° is likely to result in a track offset of 15° at 1 nm, and the extended centreline of the new track can be expected to have a mean position some 300-400 m to one side of the destination structure. The safety margin built in to the 0·75 nm Decision Range (DR) depends on the rate of closure with the destination. Although the airspeed should be 60-90 kt during the final approach, the ground speed, after due allowance for wind velocity, should be no greater than 70 kts.

Missed Approach Segment
The missed approach segment starts at the MAP and ends when the helicopter reaches minimum en-route altitude. The missed approach manoeuvre is a "turning missed approach" which must be at least 30° and not, normally, greater than 45°. A turn away of more than 45° does not reduce the collision risk factor any further, nor will it permit a closer decision range (DR), but may increase the risk of disorientation and, by inhibiting the rate of climb (especially in the case of a one engine inoperative (OEI) go-around), may keep the helicopter at an extremely low level for longer than is desirable.

The missed approach area should be identified and verified as a clear area on the radar screen during the intermediate approach segment. The base of the missed approach area is a sloping surface at 2·5% gradient starting from MDH at the MAP. The concept is that a helicopter executing a turning missed approach will be protected by the horizontal boundaries of the missed approach area until vertical separation of more than 130 ft is achieved between the base of the area, and the

offshore obstacle environment of 500 ft amsl which prevails outside the area.

A missed approach area, taking the form of a 45° sector orientated left or right of the final approach track, originating from a point 5 nm short of the destination, and terminating on an arc 3 nm beyond the destination, will normally satisfy the requirements of a 30° turning missed approach.

Required Visual Reference
The destination must be in view so that a safe landing may be carried out.

Radar Equipment
During the ARA procedure, colour mapping radar equipment with a 120° sector scan and 2·5 nm range scale selected, may result in dynamic errors of the following order:

- bearing/tracking error ± 4·5° with 95% accuracy

- mean ranging error - 250 m

- random ranging error ± 250 m with 95% accuracy

3.435 – Terminology
See *Terms & Definitions*.

3.440 - Low Visibility - General Rules
Category II or III operations may not be conducted unless:

- Helicopters are certificated, and equipped under JAR AWO or an equivalent

- A suitable system for recording approach and/or automatic landing success and failure is established and maintained to monitor overall safety

- Operations are approved

- The flight crew consists of at least 2 pilots

- DH is determined with a radio altimeter

Low visibility takeoffs may not be done in less than 150 m RVR, unless approved.

Appendix 1

This applies to the introduction and approval of low visibility operations. It contains details of operational demonstrations of Airborne systems, and is not included here.

3.445 - Heliports

Heliports may not be used for Cat II or III operations unless approved by the State in which the heliport is located.

Operators must verify that Low Visibility Procedures (LVP) have been established, and will be enforced, at those heliports where low visibility operations are to be conducted.

3.450 - Training & Qualifications

Before Low Visibility Takeoff, Category II and III operations, flight crew must complete the training and checking in Appendix 1, including flight simulator training to the limiting values of RVR and DH appropriate to the Cat II/III approval, and be qualified under Appendix 1.

The training and checking must be done under a detailed (approved) syllabus in the Ops Manual. It is in addition to that in Subpart N.

The flight crew qualification is specific to the operation and helicopter type.

3.455 - Procedures

Procedures and instructions for Low Visibility Takeoff and Cat II and III operations must be included in the Ops Manual and contain the duties of flight crew members during taxying, takeoff, approach, flare, the hover, landing, roll-out and missed approach as appropriate.

The commander must satisfy himself that:

- The status of the visual and non-visual facilities is enough before starting a Low Vis Takeoff or a Cat II or III approach

- Appropriate LVPs are in force according to information received from ATS, before starting a Low Visibility Takeoff or a Cat II or III approach

- The flight crew members are properly qualified before starting a Low Visibility Takeoff in an RVR of less than 150 m or a Category II or III approach

Appendix 1

Low Visibility Operations include:

- Manual takeoff (with or without electronic guidance systems)

- Autocoupled approach to below DH, with manual flare, hover, landing and roll-out

- Autocoupled approach followed by auto-flare, hover, autolanding and manual roll-out

- Autocoupled approach followed by auto-flare, hover, autolanding and auto-roll-out, when the applicable RVR is less than 400 m.

Note 1: A hybrid system may be used with any of these modes of operations.

Note 2: Other forms of guidance systems or displays may be certificated and approved.

The precise nature and scope of procedures and instructions depend upon the airborne equipment and the flight deck procedures. An operator must clearly define flight crew duties during takeoff, approach, flare, hover, roll-out and missed approach in the Ops Manual. Particular emphasis must be placed on responsibilities during transition from non-visual to visual conditions, and on procedures in deteriorating visibility or when failures occur. Special attention must be paid to the distribution of flight deck duties so as to ensure that the workload of the pilot making the decision to land or execute a missed approach enables him to devote himself to supervision and the decision making process.

The detailed procedures and instructions in the Ops Manual must be compatible with the limitations and procedures in the Flight Manual and cover the following items in particular:

- Checks for the satisfactory functioning of equipment, before departure and in flight

- Effect on minima from changes in ground installations and airborne equipment

- Procedures for takeoff, approach, flare, hover, landing, rollout and missed approach

- Procedures in the event of failures, warnings and other abnormal situations

- The minimum visual reference required

- The importance of seating and eye position

- Action when visual reference deteriorates

- Allocation of crew duties in the procedures above, to allow the Commander to devote himself to supervision and decision making

- The requirement for all height calls below 200 ft to be based on the radio altimeter and for one pilot to continue to monitor the instruments until landing is completed

- The requirement for the Localiser Sensitive Area to be protected

- The use of information relating to wind velocity, windshear, turbulence, runway contamination and multiple RVR

- Procedures for practice approaches and landing on runways at which the full Cat II or III heliport procedures are not in force

- Operating limitations resulting from airworthiness certification

- Information on the maximum deviation from the ILS glide path and/or localiser

3.460 - Minimum Equipment

Operators must include in the Ops Manual the minimum equipment to be serviceable at the start of a Low Visibility Takeoff or a Cat II or III approach under the Flight Manual or other approved document.

The commander must be satisfied that the status of the helicopter and relevant airborne systems is appropriate for the operation.

3.465 – VFR Operating Minima

VFR flights must be under the Visual Flight Rules and the table in Appendix 1 (below).

Subject to the sub-paragraphs below, helicopters must be operated in a flight visibility of at least 1500 m during daylight and 5 km by night (this may be reduced to 800 m for short periods during daylight, in sight of land, at speeds that will give adequate opportunity to observe other traffic and

obstacles in time to avoid a collision – at least the distance covered in 30 seconds – see ACJ). Low level overwater flights out of sight of land are only to be conducted under VFR when the cloud ceiling is greater than 600 ft by day and 1200 ft by night.

In Class G airspace, between helidecks where the overwater sector is less than 10 nm, VFR flights must be conducted under Appendix 2.

Special VFR flights must comply with any State or Zone minima in force.

Appendix 1 - Minimum Visibilities for VFR

Airspace	ABCDE	F	G
		Above 900 m (3 000 ft) AMSL or above 300 m (1000 ft) above terrain, whichever is the higher	At and below 900 m (3 000 ft) AMSL or 300 m (1 000 ft) above terrain, whichever is the higher
Dist from cloud	1 500 m horizontally 300 m (1 000 ft) vertically		Clear of cloud and in sight of the surface
Flight Vis	8 km at and above 3 050 m (10 000 ft) AMSL (Note 1) 5 km below 3 050 m (10 000 ft) AMSL (Note 2)		5 km (Note 2)

Note 1: When the height of the transition altitude is lower than 3 050 m (10 000 ft) AMSL, FL 100 should be used instead of 10 000 ft.

Note 2: Helicopters may operate in flight visibility down to 1500 m by day, ATS permitting, if the probability of encounters with other traffic is low, at 140 kts IAS or less. By agreement with ATS, helicopters may operate down to 800 m by day.

Appendix 2

Minima between helidecks in Class G airspace:

	Day		Night	
	Ht (1)	Vis	Ht (1)	Vis
Single Pilot	300 ft	3 km	500 ft	5 km
Two Pilots	300 ft	2 km (2)	500 ft	5 km (3)

Note 1: The cloud base must allow flight at the specified height below and clear of cloud

Note 2: Helicopters may operate down to 800 m with destination or intermediate structures continuously visible.

Note 3: Helicopters may operate down to 1500 m with destination or intermediate structures continuously visible.

ACJ OPS 3.465
When flight with a visibility of less than 5 km is permitted, the forward visibility should be at least the distance travelled in 30 seconds to allow adequate opportunity to see and avoid obstacles (see table below).

Visibility (m)	Advisory speed (kts)
800	50
1 500	100
2 000	120

3.470 – Performance General

Helicopters with more than 19 passenger seats, or operating to or from heliports in congested hostile environments, must operate under Subpart G (Performance Class 1). Helicopters with 9-19 passenger seats may operate under Subpart G or H (1 or 2). Helicopters with 9 or less passenger seats may operate under Subpart G, H or I (1, 2 or 3).

3.475 - General
The helicopter mass at the start of the takeoff or (if in-flight replanning) from where the revised operational flight plan applies, must not be greater than the mass at which the appropriate Subpart can be complied with, allowing for expected reductions in mass as the flight proceeds, and for fuel jettisoning as provided for in the requirement.

Performance data in the Flight Manual must be used to determine compliance, supplemented as necessary. When applying the factors, operational factors already incorporated in the Flight Manual may be allowed for to avoid double application.

When showing compliance, due account must be taken of helicopter configuration, environmental conditions and the operation of systems with an adverse effect on performance.

3.480 - Terminology
Refer to *Terms & Definitions*.

The terms *takeoff distance required, takeoff flight path, critical power unit inoperative en-route flight path* are defined in airworthiness requirements under which helicopters were certificated, or as specified by the Authority if it finds the data in the Flight Manual inadequate for showing compliance with performance limitations.

[IEM OPS 3.480(a)(1) and (a)(2) - Category A and B
Helicopters certificated under any of the following standards are considered to satisfy Category A. If they have the performance information in the Flight Manual, they are eligible for Performance Class 1 or 2:

- Certification as Cat A under JAR 27/29

- Certification as Cat A under FAR Part 29

- Certification as Group A under BCAR Section G or BCAR 29

In addition, certain helicopters certificated under FAR Part 27 complying with FAR Part 29 engine isolation requirements (as in FAA Advisory Circular AC 27-1) may be OK for Performance Class 1 or 2 if they comply with these additional requirements of JAR 29:

JAR 29.1027(a)	Independence of engine and rotor drive system lubrication
JAR 29.1187(e) JAR 29.1195(a) & (b) JAR 29.1197 JAR 29.1199 JAR 29.1201	Provision of a one-shot fire extinguishing system for each engine
JAR 29.1323(c)(1)	Ability of the airspeed indicator to consistently identify TDP

Note: The requirement to fit a fire extinguishing system may be waived if the manufacturer can demonstrate equivalent safety, based on service experience for the entire fleet showing that the actual incidence of fires in the engine fire zones has been negligible.

The performance rules of Subparts G, H and I were drafted with the performance requirements of JAR 29 Issue 1 and FAR Part 29 at Amendment 29-39. For helicopters certificated under earlier amendments, or under BCAR Section G or BCAR-29, performance data will have been scheduled in the Flight Manual, which may not be fully compatible. Before Class 1 or 2 operations are approved, scheduled performance data must be available which is compatible with G or H.

Any properly certificated and appropriately equipped helicopter is considered to satisfy Category B criteria, and are therefore eligible for Performance Class 3 operations.

[IEM OPS 3.480(a)(12) - Hostile Environment

Open sea areas considered to constitute a hostile environment should be designated by an Authority in the appropriate AIP or equivalent.

3.485 – Performance Class 1

Performance Class 1 helicopters must be certificated in Category A.

3.490 - Takeoff

The takeoff mass must not exceed the maximum in the Flight Manual's Category A performance section for the pressure altitude and ambient temperature at the heliport of departure.

For **Non-elevated Heliports,** the takeoff mass must be such that the rejected takeoff distance required does not exceed the rejected takeoff distance available, and the takeoff distance required does not exceed the takeoff distance available.

For **Elevated Heliports and Helidecks,** the takeoff mass must not exceed the maximum in the Flight Manual for the takeoff procedure, and the helicopter must be capable of:

- If a critical power unit failure is recognised at or before TDP, rejecting the takeoff and landing on the elevated heliport or helideck

- At or after TDP, continuing and clearing the heliport or helideck and all obstacles under the flight path by at least 35 ft vertically up to the end of the TODR. Obstacle clearance margins over 35 ft may be specified at a particular heliport.

Account must be taken of the following parameters at the heliport of departure:

- Pressure altitude

- Ambient temperature

- Takeoff procedure

- Up to 50% of reported headwind or at least 150% of reported tailwind (alternatives for specific sites may be approved)

The part of the takeoff up to and including TDP must be conducted in sight of the surface, so a rejected takeoff can be carried out.

IEM OPS 3.490(a)(1) & 3.510(a)(1)

The maximum mass in the Flight Manual's category A performance section must allow the helicopter to achieve rates of climb of 100 ft/min at 60 m (200 ft) and 150 ft/min at 300 m (1 000 ft) above the heliport, in the appropriate configuration, with the critical power unit inoperative and the remaining ones at an appropriate power rating.

IEM OPS 3.490(a)(3)(ii)

35 ft may be inadequate at particular elevated heliports subject to adverse airflow, turbulence, etc.

Obstacles beneath the level of the heliport but part of the same structure should be considered when approving the heliport (see Annex 14).

IEM OPS 3.490(b)(4) & 3.495(b)(4) - Headwind

When considering components in excess of 50% for takeoff and takeoff flight path, consider the proximity to the FATO, and accuracy of wind measuring equipment, appropriate procedures in a supplement to the Flight Manual and the establishment of a safety case.

3.495 - Takeoff Flight Path

Assuming that the critical power unit failure has been recognised at TDP, the takeoff flight path with the critical power unit inoperative must clear all obstacles vertically by at least 10.7 m (35 ft) in VFR and at least 35 ft plus 0.01 DR in IFR. An obstacle need not be considered if its lateral margin from the nearest point on the surface below the intended flight path exceeds 30 m or 1.5 times the overall length of the helicopter, whichever is greater, plus 0.15 DR for VFR, or 0.30 DR for IFR operations.

Obstacles may be disregarded if they are beyond:

- 7R by day (10R by night) if navigational accuracy can be achieved by suitable visual cues in the climb

- 300 m if navigational accuracy can be achieved by navaids

- 900 m in other cases

Where a change of direction of more than 15° is made, vertical obstacle clearance requirements must be increased by 5 m (15 ft) from where the turn is initiated (but not before reaching 30 m (100 ft) above the takeoff surface).

Account must be taken of the following at the heliport of departure:

- Mass of the helicopter at the start of takeoff

- Pressure altitude

- Ambient temperature

- Up to 50% of the reported headwind or at least 150% of the reported tailwind (alternatives for a specific site may be approved)

3.500 - En-route - Critical Power Unit Out

The en-route flight path with the critical power unit inoperative, appropriate to the expected weather, must comply with either of the next two paragraphs at all points along the route:

- When the flight will be out of sight of the surface, the mass of the helicopter must permit a rate of climb of at least 50 ft/minute with the critical power unit inoperative at at least 300 m (1 000 ft) or 600 m (2 000 ft) in mountainous areas above all obstacles within 18.5 km (10 nm)* either side of the intended track. When the flight will be in VMC and in sight of the surface, the same applies, except that only obstacles within 900 m either side of the route need be considered.

- The flight path must allow the helicopter to continue from cruising altitude to 300 m (1 000 ft) above the heliport where a landing can be made under JAR OPS 3.510. The flight path must clear vertically, by at least 300 m (1 000 ft) or 600 m (2 000 ft) in mountainous areas all obstacles within 18.5 km (10 nm)* either side of the intended track. The critical power unit is assumed to fail at the most critical point. When the flight will be in VMC and in sight of the surface, the same applies except that only obstacles within 900 m either side of the

route need be considered. Drift-down may be used.

*May be reduced to 9.3 km (5 nm) if required navigational accuracy can be achieved.

Account must be taken of the effects of winds.

Fuel jettisoning must be planned to take place only to an extent consistent with reaching the heliport with required reserves and using a safe procedure. It may not be planned below 1000 ft above terrain.

IEM OPS 3.500(a)(5) - Fuel Jettison

Where obstacles along the en-route flight path preclude compliance with JAR OPS 3.500(a)(1) at the planned mass at the critical point, fuel jettison at the most critical point may be planned, if AMC OPS 3.255 paragraph 3 is complied with.

3.510 - Landing

The landing mass at the estimated time of landing may not exceed the maximum in the Flight Manual for the pressure altitude and the temperature expected at the destination, or any alternate.

For **Non-elevated Heliports**, the landing mass must be such that, if a critical power unit failure is recognised during approach and landing, the helicopter must be able to:

- At or before LDP, perform a baulked landing, clearing all obstacles under the flight path

- At or after LDP, landing and stopping within the landing distance available

For Elevated Heliports and Helidecks, the landing mass must not exceed the maximum for the procedure, and the helicopter must be able to:

- At or before LDP, do a baulked landing, clearing the heliport or helideck and all obstacles under the flight path

- At or after LDP, land on the heliport or helideck

The following must be allowed for at estimated time of landing at destination or alternate:

- Pressure altitude

- Ambient air temperature

- Landing procedure

- Up to 50% of the expected headwind component

- Expected variations in mass during flight

That part from the LDP to touchdown must be conducted in sight of the surface.

IEM OPS 3.510(a)(3)(i)
The baulked landing at an elevated heliport may be done with drop down to accelerate to V_{TOSS}. As the drop down is carried out beyond the dimensions of the heliport, an obstacle clearance margin of at least 35 ft is considered more appropriate than the 15 ft required during certification of the surface level baulked landing profile.

3.515 – Performance Class 2

Performance Class 2 helicopters must be certificated in Category A. Operations other than those under JAR OPS 3.517 may not be conducted to or from elevated heliports or helidecks at night, or in a hostile environment.

3.517 - Applicability
Class 2 operations to or from helidecks or elevated heliports in non-hostile or non-congested hostile environments, may be conducted with an exposure time to a power unit failure during takeoff or landing until 31 December 2009, with approval.

Class 2 operations to or from elevated heliports in a non-congested hostile environment or helidecks, not approved as above, may continue until 31 March 2005, under approved procedures.

Appendix 1 - Exposure Time
Approval will be subject to:

- Powerplant system reliability assessment by the manufacturer to demonstrate eligibility

- Conditions to be implemented to obtain and maintain approval for the type

- Continuing surveillance

- Propulsion system monitoring

- Implementation of a Usage Monitoring System (see below)

The following must be implemented:

- A whole pile of stuff about the above in excruciating detail, not included here

AMC to Appendix 1
The data in Appendix 1 to JAR OPS 3.517(a), sub-paragraph (b)(1)(ii) should demonstrate the eligibility of the type by establishing that the probability of a power unit failure during the exposure time is not greater than 5×10^{-8} per takeoff or landing.

IEM to Appendix 1
Sub-paragraph (a)(2)(i) of Appendix 1 to JAR-OPS 3.517(a) introduces a powerplant system reliability assessment to demonstrate the eligibility of the helicopter for operations with an exposure time to a power unit failure during takeoff or landing. This requires establishing that the probability of power unit failure during the exposure time is not higher than 5×10^{-8} per takeoff or landing, on the basis of engine failure statistics and an evaluation (by analysis) of the exposure time for the recommended procedures.

The purpose of this IEM is to provide guidance on how to calculate the maximum permitted power unit failure rate for a given exposure time, or the maximum permitted exposure time for a given power unit failure rate, to achieve the appropriate probability of power unit failure during the exposure time.

However, the calculation and method are not included here as they are way too boring.

IEM OPS 3.517(a)
A continuous review of operations with an exposure time will be conducted until 1 April 2005. If the review indicates that satisfactory safety has been maintained, the applicability date of 31 December 2009 will be removed and the decision on whether to change the safety target from 5×10^{-8} to 1×10^{-8} taken.

IEM OPS 3.517(b) - Continued Ops to Helidecks
To take account of the considerable number of variables associated with the helideck environment, takeoffs and landings may require slightly different profiles. Factors such as mass and centre of gravity, wind velocity, turbulence, deck size, deck elevation and orientation, obstructions, power margins, platform gas turbine exhaust plumes etc., will all

have an influence. In particular, for the landing, additional considerations, such as a clear go-around flight path, visibility and cloud base etc., will affect the choice of profile. Profiles may be modified, taking account of the factors above and the characteristics of individual helicopter types.

Performance

To perform the following takeoff and landing profiles, adequate AEO hover performance at the helideck is required. To provide minimum performance, data (from the Flight Manual AEO OGE, with wind accountability) should be used to provide the maximum takeoff or landing mass. Where a helideck is affected by downdrafts or turbulence or hot gases, or where the profile is obstructed, or the approach or takeoff cannot be made into wind, it may be necessary to decrease this mass with a suitable calculation from the manufacturer. Helicopter mass should not exceed that required by JAR OPS 3.520(a)(1) or 3.535(a)(1).

Note 1: For types no longer supported by the manufacturer, data may be established by the operator, as acceptable.

Takeoff Profile

The takeoff should be done in a dynamic manner, ensuring that the helicopter continuously moves vertically from the hover to the Rotation Point (RP) and into forward flight. If the manoeuvre is too dynamic, there is an increased risk of losing spatial awareness (through loss of visual cues) in the event of a rejected takeoff, particularly at night.

If the transition to forward flight is too slow, the helicopter is exposed to an increased risk of contacting the deck edge if an engine fails at or just after the point of cyclic input (RP).

It has been found that the climb to RP is best made between 110% and 120% of the power required in the hover. This offers a rate of climb which assists with deck-edge clearance following power unit failure at RP, whilst minimising ballooning after a failure before RP. Individual types will require different values within this range.

Lateral Visual Cues

To obtain the maximum performance if an engine failure is recognised at or just after RP, the RP must be at its optimum value, consistent with maintaining necessary visual cues. If an engine failure is recognised just before RP, the helicopter, if at a low mass, may 'balloon' for a significant height before the reject action has any effect. Thus, it is important that the PF selects a lateral visual marker and maintains it until the RP is achieved, particularly on decks with few visual cues. In the event of a rejected takeoff, the lateral marker will be a vital visual cue in assisting with a successful landing.

Selection of Rotation Point

The optimum RP should ensure that the takeoff path continues up and away from the deck AEO, minimising the possibility of hitting the deck edge from the height loss from an engine failure at or just after RP.

The optimum RP may vary between types. Lowering the RP will result in a reduced deck edge clearance if an engine failure is recognised at or just after RP. Raising the RP involve a possible loss of visual cues, or a hard landing if an engine fails just before RP.

Pilot Reaction Time

This is an important factor affecting deck edge clearance if an engine fails before or at RP. Simulation has shown that a delay of one second can result in a loss of up to 15 ft in deck edge clearance.

Wind Speed

Relative wind is an important parameter in the achieved takeoff path after an engine failure; wherever practicable, takeoff should be made into wind. Simulation has shown that a 10 knot wind can give an extra 5 ft deck edge clearance compared to a zero wind condition.

Position Relative to Deck Edge

It is important to position the helicopter as close to the deck edge (including safety nets) as possible whilst maintaining visual cues, particularly a lateral marker.

The ideal position is normally achieved with rotor tips at the forward deck edge, which minimises the risk of striking the edge after recognition of an engine failure at or just after RP. Any takeoff heading which causes the helicopter to fly over obstructions below and beyond the deck edge should be avoided. The final takeoff heading and position will be a compromise between the takeoff path for least obstructions, relative wind, turbulence and lateral marker cue considerations.

Engine Failure at or just after RP

Once committed to the continued takeoff, it is important, if an engine fails, to rotate to the optimum attitude for the best chance of missing the deck edge. The optimum pitch rates and absolute pitch attitudes should be in the profile for the type.

Helidecks with Significant Movement

This technique should be used when helideck movement and other factors, e.g. insufficient visual cues, make a successful rejected takeoff unlikely. Weight should be reduced to permit improved OEI capability, as necessary.

The optimum takeoff moment is when the helideck is level and at its highest point, e.g. horizontal, on top of the swell. Enough collective should be applied positively for an immediate transition to climbing forward flight. Because of the lack of a hover, the takeoff profile should be planned and briefed before lift off.

Standard Landing Profile

Approach should be started into wind to a point outboard of the helideck. Rotor tip clearance from the helideck edge should be maintained until the aircraft approaches this position at the requisite height (type dependent) with approximately 10 kts of groundspeed and a minimal rate of descent. The aircraft is then flown on a flight path to pass over the deck edge and into a hover over the safe landing area.

Offset Landing Profile

If the normal landing profile is impracticable due to obstructions and prevailing wind, the offset procedure may be used. This involves flying to a hover position, approximately 90° offset from the landing point, at the

appropriate height and maintaining rotor tip clearance from the deck edge. The helicopter should then be flown slowly but positively sideways and down to position in a low hover over the landing point. Normally, CP will be the point when the helicopter begins to transition over the helideck edge.

Training

These techniques should be covered in the training required by Subpart N.

3.520 - Takeoff

Takeoff mass must not exceed that for a rate of climb of 150 ft/min at 300 m (1 000 ft) above the level of the heliport with the critical power unit inoperative and the remaining ones at an appropriate power rating.

Without an approval to operate with an **exposure time**, the takeoff mass must not exceed the maximum for the procedure, and the helicopter must be able, if the critical power unit failure is recognised at or before DPATO, to carry out a safe forced landing on the heliport or on the surface. After DPATO, the helicopter must be able to continue the flight. The part of takeoff where the failure may lead to a forced landing must only be over a surface that permits a safe forced landing.

For helidecks or elevated heliports in a non-hostile environment, **with an approval** to operate with an **exposure time**, the takeoff mass must not exceed the maximum for the procedure, and the helicopter must be able, if the critical power unit failure is recognised between the end of the exposure time and the DPATO, carrying out a safe forced landing on the heliport or on the surface. After DPATO, the helicopter must be able to continue the flight. The part of takeoff between the end of the exposure time and the DPATO must only be over a surface that permits a safe forced landing (if the failure occurs during the exposure time, a safe force landing may not be possible).

For helidecks or elevated heliports in a non-congested hostile environment, **with approval** for an **exposure time**, the takeoff mass must not exceed the maximum for the procedure, and must, if the critical power unit failure is recognised after the end of the exposure time, allow the helicopter to continue the flight. If the critical power unit failure occurs during the exposure time, safe forced landing may not be possible.

Account must be taken of the following at the heliport of departure:

- Pressure altitude

- Ambient temperature

- Takeoff procedure

- Up to 50% of the reported headwind, or at least 150% of the tailwind

The part of the takeoff before or at the DPATO must be conducted in sight of the surface.

IEM OPS 3.520
The DPATO should not be beyond where V$_Y$ is achieved AEO at takeoff power.

IEM OPS 3.520(a)(2) - Without Approval for Exposure Time
For takeoffs from elevated heliports or helidecks, the takeoff mass should allow, up to DPATO, a safe forced landing. This precludes operations where, if a power unit fails, there would be a risk of striking the deck edge.

IEM OPS 3.520 & 3.535 - Takeoff and Landing
This IEM describes three types of operation to or from helidecks and elevated heliports by Performance Class 2 helicopters. In two cases, exposure time is used, during which time the probability of a power unit failure is regarded as extremely remote - if it does happen, a safe force landing may not be possible.

- For a *Non-Hostile Environment* (without approval for exposure time), if an engine fails during the climb to RP, compliance with 3.520(a)(2) will enable a safe landing or a safe forced landing on the deck. If an engine fails between RP and DPATO, a safe forced landing on the surface, clearing the deck edge, is assured. At or after DPATO, the OEI flight path should clear all obstacles by the margins in JAR OPS 3.525. For **landing**, if an engine fails before DPBL, the pilot may elect to land or to execute a balked landing. After DPBL and before the committal point, compliance with 3.535(a)(2) will enable a safe force landing on the surface. After the committal

point, you will get a safe forced landing on the deck

- For a *Non-Hostile Environment* (with exposure time), if an engine failure occurs after the exposure time and before DPATO, compliance with 3.520(a)(3) will enable a safe force landing on the surface. At or after the DPATO, the OEI flight path should clear all obstacles by the margins in JAR-OPS 3.525. For **landing**, if an engine fails before DPBL, the pilot may elect to land or to execute a balked landing. If it happens before exposure time, compliance with 3.535(a)(3) will enable a safe force landing on the surface. After the exposure time, you will get a safe forced landing on the deck.

- For a *Non-Congested Hostile Environment* (with exposure time), if an engine fails after the exposure time, the helicopter can continue the flight. At or after DPATO, the OEI flight path should clear all obstacles by the margins in JAR-OPS 3.525. For **landing**, if an engine fails during the approach and landing phase up to the start of exposure time, compliance with JAR-OPS 3.535(a)(4) will enable the helicopter, after clearing all obstacles under the flight path, to continue the flight. After the exposure time, you will get a safe forced landing on the deck.

3.525 - Takeoff Flight Path
After the DPATO, the takeoff flight path with the critical power unit inoperative must clear all obstacles vertically by at least 10.7 m (35 ft) in VFR and 35 ft plus 0·01 DR in IFR. An obstacle need not be considered if its lateral margin exceeds 30 m or 1.5 times the overall length of the helicopter, whichever is greater, plus 0.15 DR for VFR or 0.30 DR for IFR.

Obstacles may be disregarded if they are situated beyond 7R by day if navigational accuracy can be achieved by suitable visual cues (10R by night), 300 m if navigational accuracy can be achieved by navigation aids, and 900 m in other cases.

Where a change of direction of more than 15° is made, vertical obstacle clearance requirements must be increased by 5 m (15 ft) from where the turn is initiated (not before 30 m (100 ft) above the takeoff surface).

Account must be taken of the following parameters at the departure heliport:

- Mass at the start of takeoff

- Pressure altitude

- Ambient temperature

- Up to 50% of the reported headwind when planning or at least 150% of tailwind

3.530 - En-route - Critical Power Unit Out

The en-route flight path with the critical power unit inoperative, appropriate to the expected weather, must comply with either paragraph below at all points along the route:

- When the flight will be out of sight of the surface, the mass of the helicopter must allow a rate of climb of at least 50 ft/minute with the critical power unit inoperative at at least 300 m (1 000 ft), or 600 m (2 000 ft) in mountainous areas, above all obstacles along the route within 18.5 km (10 nm)* either side of track. When the flight will be in VMC and in sight of the surface, the same applies, except that only obstacles within 900 m either side of the route need be considered.

- The flight path allows the flight to continue from cruising altitude to 300 m (1 000 ft) above the heliport where a landing can be made under JAR - OPS 3.535. The flight path must clear vertically, by at least 300 m (1 000 ft), or 600 m (2 000 ft) in mountainous areas, all obstacles along the route within 18.5 km (10 nm)* either side of the intended track (the critical power unit is assumed to fail at the most critical point). When the flight will be in VMC and in sight of the surface, the same applies, except that only obstacles within 900 m on either side of the route need be considered. Drift-down may be used.

*May be reduced to 9.3 km (5 nm) if the required navigational accuracy can be achieved.

Account must be taken of the effects of winds on the flight path.

Fuel jettisoning must be planned to take place only to an extent consistent with reaching the heliport with required reserves, using a safe procedure, and not planned below 1 000 ft above terrain.

IEM OPS 3.530(a)(5) - Fuel Jettison

The presence of obstacles along the en-route flight path may preclude compliance with JAR-OPS 3.530(a)(1) at the planned mass at the critical point along the route. In this case, fuel jettison at the most critical point may be planned, if AMC OPS 3.255 paragraph 3 is complied with.

3.535 - Landing

The landing mass at the estimated time of landing must not exceed the maximum for a rate of climb of 150 ft/min at 300 m (1000 ft) above the level of the heliport with the critical power unit inoperative and the remaining ones at an appropriate power.

Without an approval to operate with an exposure time, the landing mass must allow the helicopter, after clearing all obstacles under the flight path, to, if the failure is recognised before DPBL, continue the flight. At or after the DPBL, to carry out a safe forced landing on the heliport or surface. The part of the landing during which power unit failure may lead to a forced landing must be conducted only over a surface that allows a safe forced landing.

For helidecks or elevated heliports in a non hostile environment, **with an approval** for **exposure time**, the landing mass must allow (if the failure occurs before exposure time), the helicopter, after clearing all obstacles under the flight path, to, if the failure being recognised before DPBL, continue the flight. If the failure is recognised between DPBL and the start of exposure time, carrying out a safe forced landing on the heliport or surface. If the failure occurs during exposure time, a safe force landing may not be possible.

For helidecks or elevated heliports in a non-congested hostile environment, with an approval for an exposure time, the landing mass must allow, up to the beginning of the exposure time, the helicopter, after clearing all obstacles under the flight path, to continue the flight. If the critical power unit failure occurs during exposure time, a safe force landing may not be possible.

Account must be taken of the following parameters at the estimated time of landing at the destination heliport or alternate:

- Pressure altitude

- Ambient air temperature

- Landing procedure

- Up to 50% of the expected headwind

- Expected variations in mass during flight

That landing from DPBL to touchdown must be conducted in sight of the surface.

3.540 – Performance Class 3

Performance Class 3 helicopters may be certificated in Category A or B, but only used in non-hostile environments, except as under JAR OPS 3.005(e).

Operations may not be conducted with a ceiling of less than 600 ft above the local surface, or visibility less than 800 m, and always in sight of the surface.

Operations to or from elevated heliports in non-hostile environments may have an exposure time to a power unit failure during takeoff or landing until 31 December 2009, as approved.

Operations may not be conducted to or from helidecks or at night.

3.545 - Takeoff
Takeoff mass must not exceed the maximum for HIGE with all power units at takeoff power, or HOGE, in that order. Account must be taken of pressure altitude and ambient temperature the heliport of departure.

If a power unit fails, the helicopter must be able to perform a safe forced landing, except under the alleviation in sub-paragraph 3.540(a)(2) or 3.540(a)(4) above.

3.550 - En-route
The helicopter must be able, with all power units operating at maximum continuous power, to continue along its intended route or to a planned diversion without flying below the appropriate minimum flight altitude, and, if a power unit fails, perform a safe forced landing, except under the alleviation in sub-paragraph 3.540(a)(2) above.

3.555 - Landing
The landing mass at the estimated time of landing must not exceed the maximum for HIGE, with all power units at takeoff power, or HOGE, in that order.

Account must be taken of the pressure altitude and ambient temperature at the estimated time of landing at the destination or alternate.

If a power unit fails, the helicopter must be able to perform a safe forced landing, except under the alleviation in sub-paragraph 3.540(a)(2) or 3.540(a)(4) above.

3.605 – Mass & Balance

Loading, mass and C of G must comply with the more restictive of the Flight or Ops Manual.

The mass and C of G must be established by actual weighing before initial entry into service and thereafter every 4 years. The accumulated effects of modifications and repairs must be accounted for and properly documented, and helicopters must be reweighed if the effects are not accurately known.

Operators must determine the mass of all operating items and crew members in the dry operating mass by weighing or using standard masses. The influence of their position on the helicopter centre of gravity must be determined.

Operators must establish the mass of the traffic load, including any ballast, by actual weighing or determine the mass of the traffic load under standard masses as in JAR OPS 3.620.

The mass of the fuel must be determined with the actual density or, if not known, the density calculated under a method in the Ops Manual.

Appendix 1
Determination of DOM

Weighing
New helicopters are normally weighed at the factory and may be used without reweighing if the records have been adjusted for alterations or modifications. Helicopters transferred from one JAA operator with an approved mass control program to another need not be weighed before use unless more than 4 years have elapsed since the last weighing.

The individual mass and C of G position must be re-established periodically, with the maximum interval between two weighings being defined by the operator and meeting the requirements of JAR OPS 3.605(b). The mass and C of G must be re-established either by weighing or calculation whenever cumulative changes to the DOM exceed ± 0.5% of the maximum landing mass.

Weighing Procedure
Weighing must be done either by the manufacturer or an AMO. Normal precautions must be taken, consistent with good practices, such as:

- Checking for completeness of the helicopter and equipment

- Determining that fluids are properly accounted for

- Ensuring that the helicopter is clean

- Ensuring that weighing is done in an enclosed building

Equipment used for weighing must be properly calibrated, zeroed, and used under the manufacturer's instructions. Scales must be calibrated either by the manufacturer, a civil department of weights and measures or an appropriate organisation within 2 years or a period defined by the manufacturer, whichever is less.

Special Standard Masses
In addition to masses for passengers and checked baggage, operators may submit standard masses for other load items.

Helicopter Loading
Loading of helicopters must be done under the supervision of qualified people. Loading of freight must be consistent with the data used for calculation of the helicopter's mass and balance.

Operators must comply with additional structural limits, such as floor strength, maximum load per running metre, maximum mass per compartment, and/or the maximum seating limits.

Account must be taken of in-flight changes in loading (e.g. CAT hoist operations).

Centre of Gravity Limits

Operational C of G Envelope
Unless seat allocation is applied and the effects of the number of passengers per seat row, of cargo in individual compartments and of fuel in individual tanks is accounted for

accurately in the balance calculation, operational margins must be applied to the certificated C of G envelope. Possible deviations from the assumed load distribution must be considered. If free seating is applied, operators must introduce procedures to ensure corrective action by flight or cabin crew if extreme longitudinal seat selection occurs. C of G margins and associated procedures, including assumptions for passenger seating, must be acceptable.

In-flight Centre of Gravity
The above procedures must fully account for extreme variations in C of G travel from passenger/crew movement and fuel consumption or transfer.

IEM to Appendix 1 - Accuracy
The mass of the helicopter for establishing the DOM and C of G must be established accurately. Since a certain model of weighing equipment is used for widely different classes, one single criterion cannot be given, but weighing accuracy is considered satisfactory if the following criteria are met by the individual scales/cells:

- Below 2,000 kg - ± 1%

- Between 2,000-20,000 kg - ± 20 kg

- Above 20,000 kg - ± 0.1 %

IEM to Appendix 1 – C of G Limits
In the Limitations section of the Flight Manual, forward and aft C of G limits are specified, which ensure that the certification stability and control criteria are met through the whole flight. These limits must be observed by defining operational procedures or a C of G envelope which compensates for deviations and errors as listed below:

- Deviations of actual C of G from published values due, for example, to weighing errors, unaccounted modifications or equipment variations

- Deviations in fuel distribution in tanks

- Deviations in the distribution of baggage and cargo as compared with the assumed load distribution as well as inaccuracies in their actual mass

- Deviations in actual passenger seating from the distribution assumed when preparing documentation*

- Deviations of the actual C of G of cargo and passenger load within individual sections from the normally assumed mid position.

- Deviations of the C of G from application of the prescribed fuel usage procedure (unless already covered by the certified limits)

- Deviations from in-flight movement of cabin crew, pantry equipment and passengers

---

*Large errors may occur when free seating is allowed. Although even longitudinal passenger seating can be expected, there is a risk of extreme forward or aft seat selection causing very large and unacceptable C of G errors (assuming the balance calculation is done on an assumed even distribution). The largest errors may occur at a load factor of around 50% if all passengers are seated in either the forward or aft half of the cabin. Statistical analysis indicates that the risk of such extreme seating adversely affecting the C of G is greatest on small helicopters.

IEM OPS 3.605(e) - Fuel Density
If the actual fuel density is not known, the standard values in the Ops Manual may be used (or even the Flight Manual – *author*). They should be based on current measurements for the airports or areas concerned. Typical values are:

- Gasoline - 0.71
- JP 1 - 0.79
- JP 4 - 0.76
- Oil - 0.88

3.607 – Terminology
See *Terms & Definitions*.

3.610 - Loading, Mass and Balance
An operator must specify, in the Ops Manual, the principles and methods involved in the loading and mass and balance system that meet JAR OPS 3.605, to cover all types of intended operations.

3.615 - Mass Values for Crew
The following mass values must be used to determine DOM:

- Actual masses, including crew baggage
- Standard masses, including hand baggage, of 85 kg for crew members
- Others as acceptable

The DOM must be corrected to account for additional baggage, including position when establishing the C of G.

3.620 - Values for Passengers and Baggage
The mass of passengers and checked baggage must be computed with either the actual weighed mass or the standard mass values in the tables below, except where the passenger seats available are less than 6, when verbal statements may be used and added to a pre-determined constant to account for hand baggage and clothing. The procedures must be included in the Ops Manual.

When weighing (immediately before boarding at adjacent locations), passengers' personal belongings and hand baggage must be included. When using standard masses, use the tables below (which include infants under 2 carried by an adult on one passenger seat). Infants occupying separate seats are children for this purpose.

Where the total number of passenger seats is 20 or more, use the standard male and female masses in Table 1. As an alternative, where the total number of passenger seats is 30 or more, use the All Adult mass values.

Table 1

Pax Seats	20 +*		30 +*
	Male	*Female*	*All Adults*
All flights	82 kg	64 kg	78 kg
Children	35 kg	35 kg	35 kg
Hand Baggage	6 kg		
Survival Suit	3 kg		

Table 2

Pax Seats	10-19		
	Male	*Female*	*Child*
All flights	86 kg	68 kg	35 kg
Hand Baggage	6 kg		
Survival Suit	3 kg		

Table 3

Pax Seats	1-5	6-9
Male	98 kg	90 kg
Female	80 kg	72 kg
Children	35 kg	35 kg
Hand Baggage	6 kg	
Survival Suit	3 kg	

With 20 or more passenger seats available, the standard value for each piece of checked baggage is 13 kg. With 19 passenger seats or less, use the actual mass.

To use standard values other than those above, you must advise the Authority and gain approval in advance, with a detailed weighing survey plan, having applied the statistical method in Appendix 1 (revised values are only applicable to that operator, in circumstances consistent with those under which the survey was conducted). Where revised masses exceed those above, the higher values must be used.

On flights with a significant number of passengers who are expected to exceed standard masses, their actual masses must be determined by weighing or by adding an adequate mass increment. The same goes for checked baggage.

Commanders must be advised when a non-standard method has been used for determining load mass, which must be stated in the mass and balance documentation.

Appendix 1 - Procedure for Revised Mass Values

Passengers

The average mass of passengers and hand baggage must be determined by weighing, taking random samples, whose selection must be representative of passenger volume, considering the operation, the frequency of flights on various routes, in/outbound flights, applicable season and seat capacity.

The survey plan must cover the weighing of at least the greatest of:

- A number of passengers from a pilot sample, using normal statistical procedures and based on a relative confidence range of 1% for all adult and 2% for separate male and female average masses (see IEM OPS 3.620(h)) for the statistical procedure)

- For helicopters with 40 or more passenger seats, a total of 2000 passengers, or 50 x the passenger seating capacity if less

Passenger masses must include their belongings carried into the helicopter. When taking random samples, infants must be weighed with the accompanying adult.

Weighing of passengers must be done as close as possible to the helicopter, where a change in mass by disposing of or acquiring more personal belongings is unlikely to occur.

Weighing machines must have a capacity of at least 150 kg, with the display at minimum graduations of 500 g. Accuracy must be to within the greater of 0.5% or 200 g.

For each flight the mass of the passengers, the corresponding passenger category (i.e. male/female/children) and the flight number must be recorded.

The statistical procedure for determining revised standard baggage values based on average baggage masses of the minimum required sample size is basically the same as for passengers, with relative confidence range (accuracy) of 1%. At least 2000 pieces of checked baggage must be weighed.

To ensure that, in preference to actual masses, the use of revised standard values does not adversely affect operational safety, a statistical analysis (see IEM OPS 3.620(h)) must be carried out.

On helicopters with 20 or more passenger seats, these averages apply as revised standard male and female mass values. On smaller helicopters, all adult revised standard (average) values may be applied on helicopters with 30 or more passenger seats. Revised standard (average) checked baggage values apply to helicopters with 20 or more passenger seats.

Operators may submit a detailed survey plan and subsequently a deviation from the revised standard mass value, if determined by the procedure here. Such deviations must be reviewed at intervals not exceeding 5 years.

The male/female ratio must be 80/20. To use an alternative, data must be submitted showing that it is conservative and covers at least 84% of the actual male/female ratios on a sample of at least 100 representative flights.

The average values found are rounded to the nearest whole number in kg. Checked baggage mass values are rounded to the nearest 0.5 kg figure, as appropriate.

AMC to Appendix 1 - Passenger Weighing Surveys

Operators seeking approval to use different standard masses from those in JAR OPS 3.620, Tables 1 and 2, on similar routes or networks may pool their surveys, if prior approval has been given for a joint survey, which must meet the criteria of Appendix 1, and in addition to the joint results, results from individual operators in the joint survey are separately indicated to validate the joint survey.

IEM to Appendix 1

This IEM summarises elements of passenger weighing surveys and provides explanatory and interpretative information.

Operators should advise the Authority about the intent of the survey, explain the plan in general terms and obtain prior approval to proceed

A *representative survey plan* means a weighing plan in terms of weighing locations, and dates and flight numbers, giving a reasonable reflection of the operator's timetable and/or area of operation.

The minimum number of passengers to be weighed is the highest of:

- The number that follows from the general requirement that the sample should represent the total operation; this will often prove to be the overriding requirement

- The number that follows from the statistical requirement specifying the accuracy of the resulting mean values, which should be at least 2% for male and

female standard masses and 1% for all adult standard masses, where applicable. The required sample size can be estimated on the basis of a pilot sample (at least 100 passengers) or from a previous surveys. If analysis of the results of the survey indicates that the requirements on the accuracy of the mean values for male or female standard masses or all adult standard masses, as applicable, are not met, an additional number of representative passengers should be weighed in order to satisfy the statistical requirements.

To avoid unrealistically small samples, a minimum size of 2000 passengers (males + females) is also required, except for small helicopters where, in view of the burden of the large number of flights, a lesser number is considered acceptable.

At the beginning of the weighing program, it is important to note, and to account for, the data requirements of the weighing survey report (see below). As far as is practicable, the weighing program should be conducted in accordance with the specified survey plan.

Passengers and their belongings should be weighed as close as possible to the boarding point and the mass, as well as the associated passenger category (male/female/child), should be recorded.

The data should be analysed as per IEM OPS 3.620(h). To obtain an insight to variations per flight, per route etc. this analysis should be carried out in several stages, i.e. by flight, by route, by area, inbound/outbound, etc. Significant deviations from the weighing survey plan should be explained as well as their possible effect(s) on the results.

The results of the survey should be summarised. Conclusions and any proposed deviations from published standard mass values should be justified. The results are average masses for passengers, including hand baggage, which may lead to proposals to adjust the standard values in Tables 1, 2 and 3 above. These averages, rounded to the nearest whole number may, in principle, be applied as standard values for males and females on helicopters with 20 and more passenger seats. Because of variations in actual masses, the total passenger load also varies and statistical analysis indicates that the risk of a significant overload becomes unacceptable for helicopters with less than 20 seats. This is the reason for passenger mass increments on small helicopters.

The average masses of males and females differ by some 15 kg or more and, because of uncertainties in the male/female ratio, the variation of the total passenger load is greater if all adult standard masses are used than when using separate male and female standard masses. Statistical analysis indicates that all adult standard mass values should be limited to helicopters with 30 passenger seats or more.

As indicated in Appendix 1, standard values for all adults must be based on the averages for males and females found in the sample, taking into account a reference male/female ratio of 80/20 for all flights. A different ratio may be approved.

Weighing Survey Report
Reflecting the content of the paragraphs, this should be prepared in a standard format:

Introduction
Objective and brief description

Weighing Survey Plan
Discussion of the selected flight number, heliports, dates, etc. Determination of the minimum number of passengers to be weighed. Survey plan.

Analysis and Discussion of Results
Significant deviations from survey plan. Variations in means and standard deviations in the network. Discussion of the (summary of) results.

Summary of Results and Conclusions
Main results and conclusions. Proposed deviations from published standard values.

Attachment 1
Applicable summer and/or winter timetables or flight programs.

Attachment 2
Weighing results per flight (showing individual passenger masses and sex); means and standard deviations per flight, per route, per area and for the total network.

AMC OPS 3.620(a) - Verbal Statements
When asking passengers on helicopters with less than 6 passenger seats for their mass (weight), a specific constant should be added for clothing, which should be determined by the operator on the basis of relevant studies, but at least 4 kg.

People boarding passengers on this basis should assess the passenger's stated mass and clothing to check that they are reasonable. Such people should receive instruction.

IEM OPS 3.620(h) - Statistical Evaluation
For calculating the required sample size, it is necessary to make an estimate of the standard deviation on the basis of standard deviations calculated for similar populations or for preliminary surveys. The precision of a sample estimate is calculated for 95% reliability or 'significance', i.e. there is a 95% probability that the true value falls within the specified confidence interval around the estimated value. This standard deviation value is also used for calculating the standard passenger mass. The calculations are not included here.

IEM OPS 3.620(i) & (j) - Adjustment of Masses
When standard values are used, JAR OPS 3.620(i) and 3.620(j) require the operator to identify and adjust the passenger and checked baggage masses where significant numbers are suspected of exceeding standard values. This implies that the Operations Manual should contain appropriate directives to ensure that:

- Check-in, operations and cabin staff and loading personnel report or take appropriate action when a flight is identified as carrying such significant numbers (e.g. military or sports personnel)

- On small helicopters, where the risks of overload and/or C of G errors are the greatest, commanders pay special attention to the load and its distribution and make proper adjustments

3.625 - Mass and Balance Documentation
This must be established before each flight specifying the load and its distribution. It must enable the commander to determine that the mass and balance limits of the helicopter are not exceeded. The person preparing the documentation must be named on it. The person supervising the loading must confirm by signature that the load

and its distribution are as per the mass and balance documentation. This document must be acceptable to the commander, his acceptance being indicated by countersignature or equivalent.

Last Minute Change procedures must be specified.

Subject to approval, operators may use alternatives.

Appendix 1

Contents

- Registration and type
- Flight number and date
- Commander
- Person preparing the document
- DOM and C of G
- Mass of fuel at takeoff and trip fuel
- Mass of consumables other than fuel
- Components of the load including pax, baggage, freight and ballast
- Takeoff, Landing and Zero Fuel Mass
- Load distribution
- C of G positions
- Limiting mass and C of G values

Subject to approval, some may be omitted.

Last Minute Change

These must be brought to the attention of the commander, and entered on the documentation. The maximum allowed change must be specified in the Ops Manual. If this number is exceeded, new mass and balance documentation must be prepared.

Computerised Systems

The operator must verify the integrity of the output, establishing a system to check that amendments of input data are incorporated properly and that the system is operating correctly on a continuous basis by verifying output data at intervals up to 6 months.

On-board Systems

Approval is required to use an on-board system as a primary source for despatch.

Datalink

A copy of the final documentation as accepted by the commander must be available on the ground.

IEM to Appendix 1

The C of G position need not be mentioned if, for example, the distribution is in accordance with a pre-calculated balance table or if it can be shown that, for the planned operations, a correct balance can be ensured, whatever the real load is.

3.630 – Instruments & Equipment

Flight must not start unless the instruments and equipment required under this Subpart are approved and working, except as in the MEL.

Minimum performance standards are in the applicable JTSO (see JAR TSO), unless different ones are prescribed in operational or airworthiness codes. Instruments and equipment complying with other specifications on the date of JAR OPS implementation may remain in service, or be installed, unless additional requirements are prescribed in this Subpart. Items that have already been approved do not need to comply with a revised JTSO or specification, unless a retroactive requirement is prescribed.

The following do not need an equipment approval:

- Electric torches in JAR OPS 3.640(a)(4)
- An accurate time piece in JAR OPS 3.650(b) & 3.652(b)
- Chart holder referred to in JAR OPS 3.652(n)
- First aid kits in JAR OPS 3.745
- Megaphones in JAR OPS 3.810
- Survival and pyrotechnic signalling equipment in JAR OPS 3.835(a) and (c)
- Sea anchors and equipment for mooring, anchoring or manoeuvring amphibians on water in JAR OPS 3.840

Equipment to be used by one flight crew member at his station during flight must be readily operable from there. When a single item needs to be used by more than one flight crew member, it must be readily operable from any station it is needed. Indications must be seen readily, with the minimum practicable deviation from the position and line of vision normally assumed when looking forward along the flight path. Single instruments in multi-crew helicopters must be visible from each applicable flight crew station.

IEM OPS 3.630 - Approval & Installation

Approved means that compliance with the applicable JTSO design and performance specifications, or equivalent, in force at the time of application, has been demonstrated. Where a JTSO does not exist, applicable airworthiness standards apply unless otherwise prescribed in JAR-OPS 3 or JAR 26.

Installed means that the installation of Instruments and Equipment has been demonstrated to comply with the applicable airworthiness requirements of JAR 27/29, or the relevant code used for Type Certification, and any applicable requirement in JAR OPS 3.

Instruments and Equipment approved in accordance with other design requirements and performance specifications, before the applicability dates in JAR-OPS 3.001(b), are acceptable for use or installation on helicopters operated for commercial air transportation if any additional JAR OPS requirement is complied with.

When a new version of a JTSO (or other specification) is issued, Instruments and Equipment approved under earlier requirements may be used or installed on helicopters operated for commercial air transportation if such Instruments and Equipment are operational, unless removal from service or withdrawal is required by an amendment to JAR OPS 3 or JAR 26.

3.640 - Operating Lights

Helicopters require, for day VFR, an anti-collision light system. In addition, for IFR or by night:

- Lighting from the electrical system for adequate illumination for instruments and equipment essential to safe operation

- Lighting from the electrical system for illumination in all passenger compartments

- An electric torch for each required crew member, readily accessible when seated at their designated stations

- Navigation/position lights

- Two landing lights, of which at least one is adjustable in flight to illuminate the ground in front of and below, and on either side

- Lights to conform with the International regulations for preventing collisions at sea if the helicopter is amphibious

3.647 - Radio Communication and/or Navigation System

Whenever one is required, the helicopter must have a headset with boom microphone or equivalent and a transmit button on the flight controls for each pilot and/or crew member at their working station.

IEM OPS 3.647 – Equipment

A headset, as required by JAR-OPS 3.647, consists of a communication device which includes two earphones to receive and a microphone to transmit audio signals to the helicopter's communication system. To comply with the minimum performance requirements, the earphones and microphone should match with the communication system's characteristics and the flight deck environment. The headset should be adequately adjustable to fit the pilot's head. Headset boom microphones should be of the noise cancelling type.

3.650 - Day VFR– Flight and Navigational Instruments and Associated Equipment

Helicopters must have:

- A magnetic compass

- An accurate time-piece showing the time in hours, minutes, and seconds

- A sensitive pressure altimeter calibrated in feet with a sub-scale setting, calibrated in hectopascals/millibars, adjustable for any likely barometric pressure*

- An ASI in knots*

- A VSI*

- A slip indicator*

- A means of indicating in the flight crew compartment the OAT in degrees C**

*When two pilots are required, the second pilot's station must have these separate instruments. When duplicates are required, the requirement embraces separate displays and selectors for each pilot or other associated equipment where appropriate. In addition, helicopters over 3 175 kg MCTOM, or any over water, out of sight of land or when visibility is less than 1 500m, must have an attitude indicator and stabilised direction indicator.

All helicopters must have a means for indicating when power is not adequately supplied to the required flight instruments, and each airspeed indicating system must have a heated pitot tube or equivalent on helicopters over 3 175 kg MCTOM or with more than 9 passenger seats.

AMC OPS 3.650/3.652
Individual requirements of these paragraphs may be met by combinations of instruments or integrated flight systems, or a combination of parameters on electronic displays, if the information available to each pilot is at least that provided by the instruments and associated equipment in this Subpart.

The equipment requirements of these paragraphs may be met by alternative means when equivalent safety has been shown during type certification for the intended kind of operation.

Instrument	VFR		IFR or at Night	
	One Pilot	Two Pilots	One Pilot	Two Pilots
Magnetic Compass	1	1	1	1
Accurate Time Piece	1	1	1	1
OAT Indicator	1	1	1	1
Sensitive Altimeter	1	2	2	2
ASI	1	2	1	2
Heated Pitot	-	-	1	2
Pitot Heat Fail Indicator	-	-	1 (2)	2 (2)
VSI	1	2	1	2
Turn & Slip Indicator	1	2	1	2
Attitude Indicator	1/2 (1)	1/2 (1)	1	2
DGI	1 (1)	2 (1)	1	2
S'by Attitude Indicator	-	-	1	1

Note 1: An additional attitude indicator, for helicopters over 3 175 kg or when operating over water, out of sight of land or when visibility is less than 1 500 m.

Note 2: Required for helicopters over 3 175 kg with more than 9 passenger seats.

**AMC OPS 3.650(g) & 3.652(k)
A means to indicate OAT may be a temperature indicator with indications convertible to OAT.

3.652 - IFR or Night - Flight and Navigational Instruments and Associated Equipment
Helicopters must have:

- A magnetic compass

- An accurate time-piece showing the time in hours, minutes and seconds

- Two sensitive pressure altimeters calibrated in feet, with sub-scale settings in hectopascals/millibars, adjustable for any likely barometric pressure (for single pilot night VFR, one may be substituted by a radio altimeter)*

- An ASI with heated pitot tube or equivalent, including a warning indication of heater failure** (the failure warning does not apply to helicopters with 9 or less passenger seats or are below 3 175 kg, and with an individual C of A issued before 1 August 1999*

- A VSI*

- A slip indicator*

- An attitude indicator*

- A single, suitably illuminated, independent, standby attitude indicator (artificial horizon) capable of use from either pilot's station that provides reliable operation for at least 30 minutes, or the time to fly to a suitable alternate over hostile terrain or offshore, whichever is the greater, after total failure of the normal electrical generating system (automatically). It must be clearly evident to the flight crew when the standby attitude indicator is on its own or emergency power

- A stabilised direction indicator*

- A means of indicating in the flight crew compartment the OAT in degrees Celsius

- An alternate source of static pressure for the altimeter, ASI and VSI

Whenever two pilots are required the second pilot's station must have these separate instruments (only one altimeter is required, which may be one of the two required above). When duplicates are required, the requirement embraces separate displays and selectors for each pilot or other associated equipment where appropriate.

For IFR, there must be a chart holder in an easily readable position which can be illuminated at night.

All helicopters must have a means for indicating when power is not adequately supplied to the required flight instruments.

**AMC OPS 3.652(d) & (m)(2)

A combined warning indicator is acceptable if you can identify the failed heater in systems with two or more sensors.

3.655 – Extras for Single Pilot IFR

Helicopters must have an autopilot with, at least, altitude hold and heading mode, except those with 6 or less passengers seats first certified in a JAA State for single pilot IMC on or before 1 January 1979 and which are in service in a JAA State on 1 August 1999. Such helicopters may continue to be operated until 31 December 2004 as approved.

AMC OPS 3.655 - Without Autopilot

Operators approved for single pilot IFR in a helicopter without altitude hold and heading mode should establish procedures to provide equivalent safety, which should include appropriate training and checking, and increments to the operating minima in Appendix 1 to 3.430.

Any sector to be conducted in IMC should not be planned to exceed 45 minutes.

3.660 - Radio Altimeters

Required when operating over water:

- out of sight of land

- when visibility is less than 1 500 m

- at night

- at a distance from land corresponding to over 3 minutes at normal cruising speed

Radio altimeters must have an audio voice warning, or other approved means, operating below a preset height and with a visual warning capable of operating at a height selectable by the pilot.

3.670 - Airborne Weather Radar

Helicopters with more than 9 passengers seats under IFR or at night must have AWR when current weather reports indicate that thunderstorms or other potentially hazardous weather conditions, regarded as detectable with AWR, may reasonably be expected along the route.

3.675 – Icing Equipment

Helicopters must be certificated and equipped to operate in expected or actual icing conditions. At night, a means of illuminating or detecting the formation of ice is required that does not cause glare or reflection.

3.685 - Flight Crew Interphone

Helicopters requiring a flight crew of more than one must have a flight crew interphone system, including headsets and microphones (not handheld), for use by all members of the crew.

3.690 - Crew Interphone System

Helicopters carrying crew members other than flight crew must have a crew member interphone system, which must:

- Operate independently of the public address system, except for handsets, headsets, microphones, selector switches and signalling devices

- Provide two-way communication between the flight crew compartment and crew member stations

- Be readily accessible from each required stations in the flight crew compartment

In addition, for cabin crew members:

- Be readily accessible at required cabin crew stations close to each separate or pair of floor level emergency exits

- Have an alerting system with aural or visual signals for use by flight crew to alert the cabin crew and vice versa

- Have a means for the recipient of a call to determine whether it is a normal call or an emergency call

AMC OPS 3.690(b)(6)
The means of determining whether or not a call is a normal or an emergency one may be one or a combination of lights of different colours, codes (e.g. different rings), or others as acceptable.

3.695 - Public Address System
Helicopters with more than 9 passenger seats must have a public address system, which must:

- Operate independently of the interphone, except for handsets, headsets, microphones, selector switches and signalling devices

- Be readily accessible for immediate use from each required flight crew station

- Be readily accessible for use from at least one cabin crew station in the cabin, and each public address system microphone intended for cabin crew use must be next to a cabin crew member seat near each required floor level emergency exit in the passenger compartment

- Be capable of operation within 10 seconds by a cabin crew member at each station in from which it is accessible

- Be audible and intelligible at all passenger seats, toilets and cabin crew seats and work stations

- After a total failure of the normal electrical generating system, provide reliable operation for at least 10 minutes.

3.700 - Cockpit Voice Recorders - 1
Helicopters over 3 175 kg first issued with an individual C of A on or after 1 August 1999 must have a CVR which, against a time scale, records:

- Voice communications transmitted to or from the flight crew by radio

- The aural environment of the cockpit including, without interruption, audio signals from each microphone

- Voice communications of flight crew on the flight deck using the interphone system

- Voice or audio signals identifying navigation or approach aids

- Voice communications of flight crew using the public address system

The CVR must be able to keep information from at least the last hour of operation, but helicopters of 7 000 kg or less may use 30 minutes. It must start to record automatically before the helicopter moves under its own power and continue until the termination of the flight (when the helicopter can no longer do so). Depending on power, it must start to record as early as possible during the checks before engine start until the cockpit checks immediately after engine shutdown. The CVR must have a device to assist in locating it in water and may be combined with the FDR.

Helicopters may be despatched with the CVR not working if:

- It is not reasonably practical to repair or replace it before the start of the flight

- There are only 8 further consecutive flights with it unserviceable

- Not more than 72 hours have elapsed since it was found to be unserviceable

- The FDR is working, unless it is combined with the CVR

IEM OPS 3.700
The operational performance requirements for CVRs are in EUROCAE Document ED56A (*Minimum Operational Performance Requirements For Cockpit Voice Recorder Systems*) December 1993.

3.705 - Cockpit Voice Recorders-2
Helicopters first issued with an individual C of A up to and including 31 July 1999 over 7 000 kg or with more than 9 passenger seats must have a CVR which records pretty much the same stuff as above, under the same conditions, plus, for helicopters without an FDR, the parameters necessary to determine main rotor speed. Also, the CVR need

only keep at least the last 30 minutes' worth of information.

IEM OPS 3.705
Account should be taken of EUROCAE Documents ED56 or ED56A (*Minimum Operational Performance Requirements For Cockpit Voice Recorder Systems*) Feb 1988 and Dec 1993 respectively.

3.715 - Flight Data Recorders - 1
Helicopters first issued with a C of A or after 1 August 1999 over 3 175 kg must have a digital FDR (with a method of retrieving the data).

The FDR must be able to keep at least the last 8 hours' worth of information, against a timescale, including:

- Parameters necessary to determine altitude, airspeed, heading, acceleration, pitch and roll attitude, radio transmission keying, power on each engine, main rotor speed, use of rotor brakes, positions of primary flight controls, cockpit warnings, air temperature, use of AFCS and stability augmentation systems

- For helicopters over 7 000 kg, additional parameters necessary to determine main gearbox oil temperature and pressure, yaw rate, indicated sling load force (if an indicator is installed), radio altitude and landing gear position

- Any dedicated parameters relating to novel or unique characteristics

Data must be obtained from aircraft sources which enable accurate correlation with information displayed to the flight crew. The FDR must start to record automatically before the helicopter can move under its own power and stop automatically after it can no longer do so.

The FDR must have a device to assist in locating it in water, and it may be combined with the CVR.

Helicopters may be despatched with the FDR not working if:

- It is not reasonably practical to repair or replace it before the start of the flight

- There are only 8 further consecutive flights with it unserviceable

- Not more than 72 hours have elapsed since it was found to be unserviceable

- The CVR is working, unless it is combined with the FDR

AMC OPS 3.715(c)(3) – Parameters
The parameters to meet JAR OPS 3.715(c)(3) are in EUROCAE *Minimum Operational Performance Specification for Flight Data Recorder Systems*, Document ED 55 dated May 1990. The relevant sections are in tables not included here.

IEM OPS 3.715/3.720
The operational performance requirements for FDRs are in EUROCAE Document ED55 (*Minimum Operational Performance Specification For Flight Data Recorder Systems*) May 1990.

IEM OPS 3.715(h)/3.720(h) - Inoperative Recorders
An FDR is inoperative when any of the following conditions exist:

- Loss of the flight recording function is evident to the flight crew during the pre-flight check

- The need for maintenance has been identified by system monitors

- Analyses of recorded data or maintenance actions have shown that more than 5% of the total number of individual parameters (variable and discrete)are not being recorded properly (where improper recording affects 5% or less, timely corrective action should be taken in accordance with maintenance procedures

3.720 - Flight Data Recorders - 2
Note: This paragraph is intended to define FDR requirements for helicopters not covered by JAR OPS 3.715. Until an NPA, national regulations will apply, in which case the FDRs concerned should comply with the following.

The FDR must be able to keep at least the last 5 hours' worth of information.

Data must be obtained from aircraft sources for accurate correlation with information displayed to the flight crew.

Otherwise, the same as 3.715.

Appendix 1
A long, boring list of parameters to be recorded.

AMC OPS 3.720(c)(3) - Parameters
Compliance with JAR OPS 3.720(c)(3) may be shown by recording, so far as practicable, the relevant parameters in EUROCAE *Minimum Operational Performance Specification for Flight Data Recorder Systems*, ED 55 May 1990. The relevant sections are contained in tables not included here.

3.730 - Seats, Safety Belts, Harnesses and Child Restraints
Helicopters must have:

- A seat or berth for each person aged two or more

- For helicopters first issued with a C of A up to and including 31 July 1999, a safety belt, with or without a diagonal shoulder strap, or a safety harness for each passenger seat for each passenger aged two or more

- For helicopters first issued with a C of A on or after 1 August 1999, a safety belt, with a diagonal shoulder strap, or a safety harness for each passenger seat for each passenger aged 2 or more

- A restraint device for each passenger less than 2

- A safety harness for each flight crew seat which will automatically restrain the occupant's torso in rapid deceleration

- A safety harness for each cabin crew seat (this does not preclude use of passenger seats by extra cabin crew)

- Seats for cabin crew, where possible, near a floor level emergency exit. If the number of cabin crew exceeds the number of exits, the additional seats must be located such that the cabin crew member(s) may best be able to assist passengers in an emergency evacuation. Such seats must be forward or rearward facing within 15° of the longitudinal axis of the helicopter.

All safety harnesses and belts must have a single point release. A safety belt with a diagonal shoulder strap is permitted if it is not reasonably practicable to fit the latter.

3.731 - Fasten Seat Belt & No Smoking Signs
Helicopters in which all passenger seats are not visible from the commander's seat must have a means of indicating to all passengers and cabin crew when seat belts must be fastened and when smoking is not allowed.

3.745 - First-Aid Kits
Helicopters must have first-aid kits, readily accessible for use, which must be inspected and replenished periodically, under instructions on their labels, or as circumstances warrant.

AMC OPS 3.745
The following should be included in First Aid Kits:

- Bandages (unspecified)

- Burns dressings (unspecified)

- Wound dressings, large and small

- Safety pins and scissors

- Small adhesive dressings

- Antiseptic wound cleaner

- Adhesive wound closures

- Adhesive tape

- Disposable resuscitation aid

- Simple analgesic e.g. paracetamol

- Antiemetic e.g. cinnarizine

- Nasal decongestant

- First-Aid handbook

- Splints, suitable for upper and lower limbs

- Gastrointestinal Antacid +

- Anti-diarrhoeal medication (Loperamide)*

- Ground/Air visual code for survivors

- Disposable Gloves

- A list of contents in at least 2 languages (English and one other). This should include information on the effects and side effects of drugs carried.

Note: An eye irrigator, whilst not required to be in the first-aid kit should, where possible, be available for use on the ground.

*For helicopters with more than 9 passenger seats.

3.775 - Supplemental Oxygen - Non-pressurised Helicopters

Non-pressurised helicopters may not operate at pressure altitudes above 10 000 ft without supplemental oxygen equipment. The amount of supplemental oxygen required for a particular operation is determined on the basis of flight altitudes and flight duration, consistent with the Ops Manual and the routes to be flown.

A helicopter intended to be operated above 10 000 ft pressure altitude must have equipment capable of storing and dispensing the oxygen required.

Oxygen Supply

Flight Crew

Each member of the flight crew on duty in the cockpit must be supplied with supplemental oxygen under Appendix 1. If all occupants of cockpit seats are supplied from the flight crew source of oxygen supply then they must be considered as flight crew members on cockpit duty for the purpose of oxygen supply.

Cabin Crew, Additional Crew and Passengers

Cabin crew and passengers must have oxygen under Appendix 1. Extra cabin crew, and additional crew members, are passengers for this purpose.

Appendix 1

Supply for	Duration & Cabin PA
Occupants of flight deck seats on flight deck duty	Entire time at PAs over 10 000 ft
All cabin crew	Entire flight time cabin PA exceeds 13 000 ft, and between 10 000-13 000 ft after the first 30 minutes
100% Passengers*	Entire time PAs over 13 000 ft
10% of passengers*	Entire flight time at PAs between 10 000-13 000 ft after the first 30 minutes.

*Passengers means those actually carried and includes infants under 2.

3.790 - Hand Fire Extinguishers

Helicopters must have hand fire extinguishers for crew, passenger and cargo compartments and galleys as follows:

- The type and quantity of extinguishing agent must be suitable for the fires likely to occur where the extinguisher is intended to be used and, for personnel compartments, must minimise toxic gas concentration

- At least one hand extinguisher, with Halon 1211 (BCF), or equivalent, must be in the cockpit for the flight crew

- At least one hand fire extinguisher must be in, or readily accessible for use in, each galley not on the main passenger deck

- At least one readily accessible hand fire extinguisher must be available in each cargo compartment accessible to crew members during flight for fire fighting

- There must be at least the following number of hand fire extinguishers conveniently located for adequate availability in each passenger compartment:

Pax Seating	Minimum Hand Fire Extinguishers
7 to 30	1
31 to 60	2
61 to 200	3

AMC OPS 3.790

The number and location of hand fire extinguishers should provide adequate availability, allowing for the number and size of passenger compartments, the need to minimise toxic gas concentrations and the location of toilets, galleys etc. These considerations may result in the number being greater than the minima above.

There should be at least one extinguisher suitable for flammable fluid and electrical fires, on the flight deck. Additional extinguishers may be required for other compartments accessible to the crew in flight. Dry chemical extinguishers should not be used on the flight deck, or in any compartment not separated by a partition from it, because of the adverse effect on vision during discharge and, if non-conductive, interference with electrical contacts by the chemical residues.

Where only one hand extinguisher is required in passenger compartments, it should be near the cabin crew station, where provided.

Where two or more hand extinguishers are required in passenger compartments, and their location is not otherwise dictated by the above, one should be near each end of the cabin with the remainder throughout the cabin as evenly as is practicable.

Unless an extinguisher is clearly visible, its location should be indicated by a placard or sign, supplemented by appropriate symbols.

3.800 - Marking of Break-in Points

Designated areas of the fuselage suitable for break-in by rescue crews in emergency must be marked as shown (not here). The markings must be red or yellow, and, if necessary, outlined in white to contrast with the background. If the corner markings are more than 2 m apart, intermediate lines 9 cm x 3 cm must be inserted so that there is no more than 2 metres between adjacent marks.

3.810 - Megaphones

Helicopters with more than 19 passenger seats must have portable battery-powered megaphones readily available for use by crew members during an emergency evacuation.

AMC OPS 3.810

Where one megaphone is required, it should be readily accessible from a cabin crew assigned seat. Where two or more are required, they should be suitably distributed in the passenger cabin(s) and readily accessible to crew members assigned to direct emergency evacuations. This does not necessarily require megaphones to be positioned so they can be reached by a crew member when strapped in a cabin crew member's seat.

3.815 - Emergency Lighting

Helicopters with more than 19 passenger seats must have an emergency lighting system with an independent power supply to provide a source of general cabin illumination to facilitate evacuation, and illuminated emergency exit marking and locating signs.

3.820 - Automatic ELT

Helicopters must have automatic ELTs attached so that, in a crash, the probability of the ELT transmitting a detectable signal is maximised, and transmitting at any other time is minimised.

Performance Class 1 or 2 helicopters on flights over water in hostile environments (see JAR OPS 3.480(a)(12)(ii)(A)) at more than 10 minutes flying time at normal cruising speed from land, on offshore oil (and gas) flights must have Automatically Deployable ELTs.

ELTs must be able to transmit on the distress frequencies in ICAO Annex 10.

IEM OPS 3.820

Types of automatic ELT are as follows:

- *Automatic Fixed* (ELT (AF)). To be permanently attached before and after a crash and designed to aid SAR teams in locating a crash site

- *Automatic Portable* (ELT (AP)). To be rigidly attached before a crash, but readily removable after one, functioning as an ELT during the crash sequence. If the ELT does not employ an integral antenna, the aircraft-mounted antenna may be disconnected and an auxiliary (on the ELT case) attached. The ELT can be tethered to a survivor or a liferaft. This type is intended to aid SAR in locating the crash site or survivor(s)

- *Automatic Deployable* (ELT (AD)). To be rigidly attached before the crash and automatically ejected and deployed after the crash sensor has determined a crash has occurred. It should float in water and is intended to aid SAR teams in locating the crash site

To minimise the possibility of damage in crash impact, the Automatic ELT should be rigidly fixed to the helicopter structure as far aft as practicable, with antenna and connections arranged to maximise the probability of the signal being radiated after a crash.

3.825 - Lifejackets

Helicopters may not operate on water or on a flight over water:

- In Performance Class 3 beyond autorotational distance from land

- In Performance Class 1 or 2 at more than 10 minutes flying time at normal cruise speed from land

- In Performance Class 2 or 3 when taking off or landing over water

without lifejackets with survivor locator lights for each person on board, easily accessible, with safety belt or harness fastened, from the seat or berth of the person for whom use it is provided and an individual infant flotation device, with a survivor locator light, for each infant on board.

IEM OPS 3.825
Seat cushions are not flotation devices.

3.827 - Crew Survival Suits
Crews of Performance Class 1 or 2 helicopters on oil (or gas) flights over water more than 10 minutes flying time away from land at normal cruising speed, when the sea temperature will be less than 10°C during the flight, or when the estimated rescue time exceeds the calculated survival time, must wear a survival suit.

The same goes for Class 3 helicopters on flights over water beyond autorotational or safe forced landing distance from land when sea temperatures will be less than 10°C during the flight.

IEM OPS 3.827 - Calculating Survival Time
A person accidentally immersed in cold seas (typically offshore Northern Europe) will have a better chance of survival by wearing an effective survival suit as well as a lifejacket. This will slow down the rate at which body temperature falls and protect them from the greater risk of drowning from incapacitation due to hypothermia.

The complete system – suit, lifejacket and clothes worn under the suit – should be able to keep the wearer alive long enough to be recovered (in practice, the limit is about 3 hours). If a group of people in the water cannot be rescued within this time they are likely to have become so scattered and separated that location will be extremely difficult, especially in the rough water typical of Northern European seas. If it is expected that in water protection is required for longer than 3

hours, improvements should be sought in SAR procedures rather than immersion suits.

The *Clo value* is the unit defining the value of clothing insulation. A typical business suit and the usual undergarments have an in-air insulation value of 1 clo. Clo values are substantially reduced when clothing is compressed (as it is by hydrostatic compression under an immersion suit) or wet.

A *Ten-percentile thin man* is the tenth thinnest man in a sample of 100 representing the offshore population. Thinness is measured by mean skin fold thickness.

Survival Times
The aim must be to ensure that a man in the water can survive long enough to be rescued, i.e. survival time must be greater than likely rescue time. The factors affecting both times are shown in Figure 1. The figure emphasises that survival time is influenced by many factors, physical and human. Some of the factors are relevant to survival in cold water, some are relevant in water at any temperature.

(Rather meanigless chart here)

The relationship between water temperature, insulation of clothing and calm water survival is shown in Figure 2. The curves are appropriate for the 10-percentile thin man and assume that his survival time ends when core body temperature drops to 34°C, where he may not die from hypothermia, but be so incapacitated by cold to die from drowning. Fatter men with more body insulation can expect to survive longer than predicted by the curves. The curves show that the survival suit and clothing worn underneath must have an insulation value of about 0·5 clo if the wearer is likely to survive for more than 2 hours when immersed in water. If he is wearing summer clothes beneath a leak-free survival suit, the 0·33 clo line indicates that he will survive for less than 2 hours in water at 5° and for less than 3 hours in water at 10°.

(Another chart referring to thin individuals)

The effects of water leakage and hydrostatic compression on the insulation quality of clothing are well recognised. In a nominally dry system the insulation is provided by still air trapped within the clothing fibres and between the layers of suit and clothes. Many systems lose some insulative capacity either because the clothes under the 'waterproof' survival suit get wet or because of hydrostatic compression. As a result of water leakage and compression, survival times will be shortened: clothing of a greater dry and non-compressed clo value will maintain survival time.

It should not be forgotten that significant heat loss can occur from the head - a survival suit should have an insulated hood. Besides preventing heat loss, it will give the wearer some protection against accidental impact.

3.830 - Liferafts and Survival ELTs or Extended Overwater Flights

Helicopters on flights over water more than 10 minutes from land at normal cruising speed (Class 1 or 2), or 3 minutes (Class 3) must have:

- For those carrying less than 12 people, at least one liferaft with a capacity of at least the maximum people on board

- For those carrying more than 11 persons, at least two liferafts, enough together to accommodate all people capable of being carried on board. Should one of the largest capacity be lost, the overload capacity of the remaining ones must be enough to accommodate all people on the helicopter

- At least one survival ELT for each liferaft carried (but not more than 2 ELTs are required), capable of transmitting on the distress frequencies in ICAO Annex 10

- Emergency exit illumination

- Life saving equipment, including means of sustaining life appropriate to the flight

AMC OPS 3.830(a)(2)

Liferafts must be of an approved design and stowed to facilitate their ready use in an emergency. They must be conspicuous to standard airborne radar equipment. When carrying more than one liferaft on board, at least 50% must be jettisonable by the crew at their normal station, where necessary by remote control. Those not jettisonable by remote control or by the crew must allow handling by one person (40 kg as maximum).

Each liferaft must contain at least:

- One survivor locator light

- One visual signalling device

- One canopy (as a sail, sunshade or rain catcher)

- One radar reflector

- One 20 m retaining line to hold the liferaft near the helicopter but to release it if the helicopter becomes totally submerged

- One sea anchor

- One survival kit, for the route, containing at least:

  - One liferaft repair kit

  - One bailing bucket

  - One signalling mirror

  - One police whistle

  - One buoyant raft knife

  - One supplementary means of inflation

  - Seasickness tablets

  - One first-aid kit

  - One portable means of illumination

  - One half litre of pure water and one sea water desalting kit

  - One illustrated survival booklet in an appropriate language

Batteries used in ELTs should be replaced (or recharged) when the equipment has been in use for more than 1 cumulative hour, and when 50% of their useful life (or charge) has expired. The new expiration date must be legibly marked on the outside of the equipment. This does not apply to batteries (such as water-activated ones) that are essentially unaffected during storage intervals.

AMC OPS 3.830(a)(3) - Survival ELT

A survival ELT is meant to be removed from the helicopter and activated by survivors. It should be stowed to facilitate its ready removal and use in an emergency. An ELT(S) may be activated manually or automatically (e.g. by water activation), and be designed to be tethered to a liferaft or a survivor.

3.835 - Survival Equipment

Helicopters in areas where search and rescue would be especially difficult must have:

- Signalling equipment to make the pyrotechnical distress signals in Annex 2

- At least one survival ELT that can transmit on the distress frequencies in Annex 10

- Additional survival equipment for the route, taking account the people on board

IEM OPS 3.835

The expression *Areas in which search and rescue would be especially difficult* means:

- Areas so designated by the State responsible for managing search and rescue

- Areas that are largely uninhabited and where the State responsible for managing SAR has not published any information to confirm that search and rescue would not be especially difficult, and does not, as a matter of policy, designate areas as being especially difficult for search and rescue.

AMC OPS 3.835(c)

This additional survival equipment should be carried when required:

- 500 ml of water for each 4, or fraction of 4, persons on board

- One knife

- First Aid Equipment

- One set of Air/Ground codes

In addition, in polar conditions:

- A means for melting snow

- 1 snow shovel and 1 ice saw

- Sleeping bags for use by $1/_3$ of all people on board and space blankets for the remainder or space blankets for all passengers

- 1 Arctic/Polar suit for each crew member

Equipment already carried for other requirements need not be be duplicated.

3.837 - Helidecks in Hostile Sea Areas

For helicopters on oil (or gas) flights to or from helidecks in hostile sea areas more than 10 minutes at normal cruising speed from land:

- When the sea temperature will be less than 10°C during the flight, or when the estimated rescue time exceeds the calculated survival time, or the flight is planned at night, all persons on board must wear a survival suit

- All liferafts must be usable in the sea conditions in which the ditching, flotation and trim characteristics were evaluated to comply with the ditching requirements for certification

- The helicopter must have an emergency lighting system with an independent power supply to provide a source of general cabin illumination to facilitate evacuation

- All emergency exits and the means of opening must be conspicuously marked for the guidance of occupants using them in daylight or in the dark. Such markings must remain visible if the helicopter is capsized and the cabin is submerged

- All non-jettisonable doors designated as Ditching Emergency Exits must have a means of securing them open so they do not interfere with egress in all sea conditions up to the maximum to be evaluated for ditching and flotation

- All doors, windows or other openings in the passenger compartment suitable for the purpose of underwater escape must be operable in emergency

- Lifejackets must be worn at all times, unless an integrated survival suit is worn that meets the combined requirement of the survival suit and lifejacket

IEM OPS 3.837(a)(2) - Additional Requirements

Projections on the exterior surface, in a zone delineated by boundaries which are 1.22 m (4 ft) above and 0.61 m (2 ft) below the established static water line could cause damage to a deployed liferaft. Examples are aerials, overboard vents, unprotected split pin tails, guttering and any projection sharper than a three dimensional right angled corner.

While the boundaries above are intended as a guide, the total area to be considered should also take into account the likely behaviour of the liferaft after deployment in sea states up to the maximum in which the helicopter can remain upright.

Wherever a modification or alteration is made, the need to prevent it causing damage to a deployed liferaft should be taken into account in the design.

Particular care should also be taken during routine maintenance to ensure that additional hazards are not introduced by, for example, leaving inspection panels with sharp corners proud of surrounding fuselage surfaces, or allowing door sills to deteriorate to where sharp edges become a hazard.

The same considerations apply for emergency flotation equipment.

3.840 - Operating on Water - Miscellaneous

Helicopters certified for operating on water must not do so without:

- A sea anchor and other equipment necessary to facilitate mooring, anchoring or manoeuvring on water, appropriate to size, weight and handling characteristics

- Equipment for making the sound signals in the International Regulations for preventing collisions at sea

3.843 - Ditching

Performance Class 1 or 2 helicopters may not operate on flights over water in hostile environments at more than 10 minutes flying time at normal cruise speed from shore unless they are designed to land on water or are certificated under ditching provisions. In non-hostile environments, emergency flotation equipment is also required

Performance Class 2 helicopters taking off or landing over water must be designed for landing on water, be certificated under ditching provisions, or have emergency flotation equipment, except where, for minimising exposure, at a HEMS site in a congested environment.

Performance Class 3 helicopters on flights over water beyond safe forced landing distance from land must be designed for landing on water, be

certificated under ditching provisions or be fitted with emergency flotation equipment.

IEM OPS 3.843(c) - Class 2 Takeoff and Landing

Performance Class 2 helicopters taking off or landing over water are exposed to a critical power unit failure. They should therefore be designed to land on water, certificated under ditching provisions, or have appropriate floats fitted (for a non-hostile environment).

3.845 - Communication & Nav Eqpt

Flights must not start unless the communication and navigation equipment under this Subpart is:

- Approved and installed under applicable requirements, including the minimum performance standard and operational and airworthiness requirements

- Installed such that the failure of any single unit will not result in the failure of another

- Working for the kind of operation, except as provided in the MEL

- So arranged to be readily operable from any station

Minimum performance standards are those in the applicable JTSO, unless different ones are in the operational or airworthiness codes. Equipment complying with other design and performance specifications on the date of JAR OPS implementation may remain in service, or be installed, unless additional requirements are prescribed in this Subpart. Communication and navigation equipment which has already been approved does not need to comply with a revised JTSO or other specification, unless a retroactive requirement is prescribed.

IEM OPS 3.845 - Approval and Installation

Approved means that compliance with the applicable JTSO design and performance specifications, or equivalent, in force at the time of application, has been demonstrated. Where a JTSO does not exist, applicable airworthiness standards apply unless otherwise prescribed in JAR-OPS 3 or JAR 26.

Installed means that the installation of Instruments and Equipment has been demonstrated to comply with the applicable airworthiness requirements of JAR 27/29, or the relevant code used for Type

Certification, and any applicable requirement in JAR OPS 3.

Equipment approved under other requirements and specifications, before the applicability dates in JAR-OPS 3.001(b), are acceptable for use or installation on helicopters operated for commercial air transportation if any additional JAR OPS requirement is complied with.

When a new version of a JTSO (or other specification) is issued, Instruments and Equipment approved under earlier requirements may be used or installed on helicopters operated for commercial air transportation if such Instruments and Equipment are operational, unless removal from service or withdrawal is required by an amendment to JAR OPS 3 or JAR 26.

3.850 - Radio Equipment

Helicopters must have radios for the kind of operation. Where two independent (separate and complete) radio systems are required, each must have an independent antenna except that, where rigidly supported non-wire antennae or other installations of equivalent reliability are used, only one antenna is required. Equipment must also communicate on 121.5 MHz.

3.855 - Audio Selector Panel

Helicopters under IFR must have an audio selector panel accessible to each flight crew member.

3.860 - Radio for VFR, Visual Landmarks

Helicopters must have radio equipment (communication and SSR) necessary under normal operating conditions to:

- Communicate with appropriate ground stations and ATC from any point in controlled airspace within which flights are intended

- Receive meteorological information

- Reply to SSR interrogations as required for the route

3.865 - IFR, or VFR not visually navigated

Helicopters must have radio (communication and SSR) and navigation equipment suitable for the air traffic services in the area(s) of operation.

Radio Equipment
Must comprise of at least two independent radio communication systems normally necessary to communicate with an appropriate ground station from any point on the route, including diversions, and SSR equipment as required for the route.

Navigation Equipment
Must comprise at least:

- Two independent navaids for the route/area

- An approach aid suitable for destination and alternate heliports

- An Area Navigation System when required

- Two VORs where navigation is based only on VOR signals*

- Two ADFs where navigation is based only on NDB signals*

Alternatively, it may comply with RNP for the airspace concerned.

*A helicopter may operate without these, if it has alternative equipment which allows safe navigation as authorised.

The above requirements may be met by combinations of instruments or integrated flight systems, or a combination of parameters on electronic displays, if the information so available to each pilot is at least that provided by the instruments and equipment above.

Where not more than one item of equipment is unserviceable when about to begin a flight, the helicopter may nevertheless take off if:

- It is not reasonably practical to repair or replace that item before starting the flight

- The helicopter has not made more than one flight since the item was found to be unserviceable

- The commander is satisfied that, taking into account the latest information for the route/area and heliports (including planned diversions) and the likely weather, the flight can be made safely and under any relevant requirements of the appropriate ATC unit

3.875 - Maintenance

Helicopters must be maintained and released to service by JAR 145 organisations, except that preflight inspections need not necessarily be done by them.

This Subpart prescribes the requirements to comply with JAR OPS 3.180.

IEM OPS 3.875

Reference to *helicopters* includes *components*. De- and anti-icing activities do not need JAR 145 approval.

3.885 - Application for and Approval of the Maintenance System

Submit the documents in JAR OPS 3.185(b). Detailed requirements are in JAR OPS 3.180(a)(3) and 3.180(b), and JAR OPS 3.185.

IEM OPS 3.885(a)

The documents in JAR-OPS 3.185(b) are not expected to be submitted in a completed state with the initial application, since each will require approval in its own right and may be subject to amendment. Draft documents should be submitted at the earliest opportunity so that investigation of the application can begin. Grant or variation cannot be achieved until the Authority is in possession of completed documents.

The applicant should inform the Authority where base and scheduled line maintenance is to take place and give details of any contracted maintenance in addition to that in response to JAR-OPS 3.895(a) or (c).

At the time of application, operators should have arrangements for all base and scheduled line maintenance in place for an appropriate period of time, as acceptable. Operators should establish further arrangements in due course before the maintenance is due. Base maintenance contracts for high-life time checks may be based on one time contracts, when this is compatible with fleet size.

IEM OPS 3.885(b)

Approval of a maintenance system will be indicated by a statement with the following information:

- AOC number
- Name of the Operator

- Type(s) of helicopter and identification of the related maintenance programs
- Identification of the MME
- Any limitations imposed

Note: Approval may be limited to specified helicopters, to specific locations or by other means like operational limitations if considered necessary by the Authority in the interests of safe operation.

3.890 - Maintenance Responsibility

Airworthiness of helicopters and serviceability of operational and emergency equipment must be maintained by:

- Pre-flight inspections*
- Rectification of defects and damage affecting safe operation, according to the MEL and CDL
- Maintenance under the maintenance program and analysis of its effectiveness
- Accomplishment of operational directives, ADs and other continued airworthiness requirements. Until formal adoption of JAR 39, current national aviation regulations apply
- Modifications under approved standarda and, for non-mandatory ones, the establishment of an embodiment policy

The C of A must remain valid in respect of the requirements above, expiry dates and other conditions in the Certificate.

AMC OPS 3.890(a)

The operator is responsible for determining what maintenance is required, when it has to be one and by whom, and to what standard, to ensure continued airworthiness.

Thus, adequate knowledge of the design status (type specification, customer options, ADs, modifications, operational equipment) and required and performed maintenance is required. Status of design and maintenance should be adequately documented to support the quality system.

There should be adequate coordination between flight operations and maintenance to ensure that both receive all information on the condition of the aircraft for both their tasks.

The operator need not do the maintenance, which is to be done by a JAR 145 AMO, but carries the responsibility for the airworthy condition of aircraft operated, and should be satisfied before the intended flight that all required maintenance has been properly carried out.

When an operator is not JAR 145 approved, the operator should provide a clear work order to the maintenance contractor. The fact that an operator has contracted a JAR 145 AMO should not prevent him from checking the maintenance facilities.

*AMC OPS 3.890(a)(1)

This means all the actions necessary to ensure that the helicopter is fit for the intended flight, which should typically include but are not necessarily limited to:

- A walk-around inspection for condition including, in particular, obvious signs of wear, damage or leakage. In addition, the presence and condition of emergency equipment should be established

- Inspection of the Tech Log to ensure that the intended flight is not adversely affected by outstanding deferred defects and that no required maintenance in the maintenance statement is overdue or will become due during the flight

- That consumable fluids, gases, etc. uplifted before flight are of the correct specification, free from contamination, and correctly recorded

- That all doors are securely fastened

- Control surface and landing gear locks, pitot/static covers, restraint devices and engine/aperture blanks have been removed

- That external surfaces and engines are free from ice, snow, sand, dust, etc.

Tasks such as oil and hydraulic fluid uplift and inflation may be part of the preflight, as acceptable. The related instructions should address procedures to determine where the necessary uplift or inflation results from an abnormal consumption and possibly requires additional action by AMO.

There should be guidance to maintenance and flight personnel defining responsibilities for these actions and, where tasks are contracted to other organisations, how their accomplishment is subject to the quality system. It should be demonstrated that preflight inspection personnel have received appropriate training for the relevant tasks. The training standard for personnel performing preflights should be in the MME.

IEM OPS 3.890(a)(1)

The fact that preflights are an Operator's maintenance responsibility does not necessarily mean that people performing them report to the Nominated Postholder for Maintenance, but that the NPM is responsible for determining the content of the preflight inspection and setting qualification standards. Compliance with the qualification standard should be monitored by the Quality System.

AMC OPS 3.890(a)(2)

There should be a system to ensure that all defects affecting safe operation are rectified within the limits in the MEL or CDL and that no postponement of such a rectification can be permitted unless with the Operator's agreement under an approved procedure.

AMC OPS 3.890(a)(3)

There should be a system to ensure that all maintenance checks are done within the limits prescribed by the maintenance program and that, whenever a maintenance check cannot be done within the required time limit, its postponement is allowed with the Operator's agreement under an approved procedure.

AMC OPS 3.890(a)(4)

There should be a system to analyse the effectiveness of the maintenance program, with regard to spares, established defects, malfunctions and damage, and to amend the program (which will involve approval unless the operator has been approved to amend the program themselves).

IEM OPS 3.890(a)(5)

Any other continued airworthiness requirement made mandatory by the Authority includes Type Certification related requirements such as: Certification Maintenance Requirements (CMR's), Life Limited Parts, Airworthiness Limitations, yada, yada, yada.

AMC OPS 3.890(a)(6)

Operators should establish a policy (and work to it), to assess non-mandatory information related to airworthiness, such as Service Bulletins, Service Letters and other information the design organisation, the manufacturer or the related airworthiness authorities.

3.895 - Maintenance Management

Operators must be appropriately approved under JAR 145 to carry out the requirements in JAR OPS 3.890(a)(2), (3), (5) and (6), except when the Authority is satisfied that the maintenance can be contracted out.

Operators must employ acceptable people to ensure that maintenance is done on time to an approved standard (see JAR OPS 3.890). The senior person is the nominated postholder in JAR OPS 3.175(i)(2). The NMP is also responsible for corrective action from quality monitoring. The NPM should not be employed by a JAR 145 AMO under contract, unless specifically agreed.

When an operator is not JAR 145 approved, arrangements must be made with such an organisation to carry out the requirements in JAR OPS 3.890(a)(2), (3), (5) and (6). Except as otherwise specified below, the arrangement must take the form of a written maintenance contract. Base and scheduled line maintenance and engine maintenance contracts, with amendments, must be acceptable. Commercial elements of a maintenance contract are not needed, but operators may have contracts with organisations not JAR 145 approved/accepted, if:

- for helicopter or engine maintenance contracts, the contracted organisation is a JAR OPS Operator of the same type

- maintenance is ultimately performed by JAR 145 AMOs

- the contract details the functions in JAR OPS 3.890(a)(2), (3), (5) and (6) and defines the support of the quality functions of JAR OPS 3.900

- the contract, with amendments, is acceptable (commercial elements are not needed)

For occasional line maintenance, and component maintenance, including engines, the contract may take the form of individual work orders to the MO.

Suitable office accommodation must be provided at appropriate locations.

AMC OPS 3.895(a)

The requirement is meant to provide for the following three alternative options:

- An operator to be approved under JAR 145 for maintenance

- An operator to be approved under JAR 145 for some maintenance, which, as a minimum, could be limited line maintenance, or more, but still short of the above option

- An operator not approved for maintenance

The Authority will determine which is appropriate, applying the primary criteria of relevant experience if carrying out some or all maintenance on comparable helicopters. Thus, where an operator applies for *all maintenance*, the Authority needs to be satisfied the operator has enough experience on a comparable type. For example, adding a different large helicopter to an existing large helicopter fleet. If the experience is not satisfactory or too limited, the Authority may choose either to require more experienced management and/or release to service staff or may refuse to accept the new wide bodied aircraft if extra staff cannot be found.

Where an operator applies for *some maintenance*, or the Authority has been unable to accept an application for all maintenance, satisfactory experience is again the key, but related to the reduced maintenance. If the experience is not satisfactory or too limited, the Authority may choose to require more experienced staff or refuse the application if such staff cannot be found.

Not approved for maintenance accepts that the operator either does not have satisfactory experience or has only limited experience in someareas.

The Authority will require an operator to enter into a contract with an appropriately approved JAR-145 organisation except that, in some cases where it is possible to get enough satisfactorily experienced staff fot the minimal support for *some maintenance*.

Experience means staff with proven and demonstrated evidence that they were directly involved with at least line maintenance of similar aircraft types for at least 12 months.

There must be enough people meeting the requirement of 3.895(b) to manage maintenance responsibility, whichever option is used.

AMC OPS 3.895(b)

People employed should represent the maintenance management structure (for maintenance) and be responsible for all maintenance functions. Dependent on the size of the operation and the organisational setup, maintenance functions may be divided under individual managers or combined in nearly any number of ways, including combining the functions of accountable manager, the nominated postholder and the quality monitoring function, so long as the quality monitoring function remains independent of the functions to be monitored. In the smallest organisation this may lead to the quality monitoring function being performed by the accountable manager if suitably qualified. Consequently the smallest organisation consists of at least two people except that the Authority may agree to quality monitoring being sub-contracted to another operator's quality monitoring department or a suitably qualified independent person acceptable to the Authority.

The actual number of people to be employed and their necessary qualifications depends upon the tasks to be performed and the size and complexity of the operation (route network, line or charter, number of aircraft and the aircraft types, complexity of aircraft and their age), number and locations of maintenance facilities and the amount and complexity of maintenance contracting. Consequently, the number of people needed, and their qualifications, may differ greatly from one operator to another and a simple formula covering the whole range of possibilities is not feasible.

To enable the Authority to accept the number of people and their qualifications, an operator should make an analysis of the tasks to be performed, the way in which he intends to divide and/or combine these tasks, indicate how he intends to assign responsibilities and establish the number of man/hours and the qualifications to perform the tasks. With significant changes in the aspects relevant to the number and qualifications of persons needed, this analysis should be updated.

The Authority does not necessarily expect the credentials of each person of the Maintenance Management Group to be individually submitted, but the Manager of the Maintenance Management Group, and any manager reporting directly to him should be individually acceptable.

AMC OPS 3.895(c)

The Authority should only accept that the proposed person be employed by the JAR 145 Organisation when it is manifest that he/she is the only available competent person in a position to exercise this function, within a practical working distance from the Operator's offices.

IEM OPS 3.895(c)

This only applies to contracted maintenance and does not affect situations where the JAR 145 Organisation and Operator are the same.

AMC OPS 3.895([d])

Where an operator is not approved to JAR 145, or an operator's maintenance organisation is independent, a contract should be agreed that specifies, in detail, the work to be performed by the JAR 145 AMO.

The specification of work and assignment of responsibilities should be clear, unambiguous and detailed enough to ensure that misunderstanding does not arise between the parties (operator, maintenance organisation and the Authority) that could result in a situation where work with a bearing on airworthiness or serviceability is not or will not be properly performed.

Special attention should be paid to procedures and responsibilities to ensure that all maintenance work is performed, service bulletins are analysed and decisions taken on accomplishment, airworthiness directives are completed on time and that all work, including non-mandatory modifications is carried out to approved data and to the latest standards.

As to layout, the *IATA Standard Ground Handling Agreement* may be used as a basis, but this does not preclude the Authority from ensuring the content is acceptable, and especially that the contract allows the Operator to properly exercise maintenance responsibility. Parts of contracts with no bearing on technical or operational aspects of airworthiness are outside the scope of this paragraph.

AMC OPS 3.895(e)

In the case of a contract with a non-JAR 145 Organisation, the MME should include appropriate procedures to ensure that all this contracted maintenance is ultimately performed on time by JAR 145 approved/accepted organisations under acceptable data. In particular the Quality System procedures should place great emphasis on monitoring compliance with the above. The list of JAR 145 approved/accepted contractors, or a reference to this list, should be in the MME.

Such a maintenance arrangement does not absolve the Operator from overall Maintenance responsibility. Specifically, to accept the arrangement, the Authority should be satisfied that it allows the Operator to ensure full compliance with JAR-OPS 3.890 Maintenance Responsibility.

IEM OPS 3.895(e)

The purpose of JAR OPS 3.895(e) is to authorise a primary maintenance arrangement with an Organisation which is not a JAR 145 AMO, when it proves that such an arrangement is in the interest of the Operator by simplifying the management of its maintenance, and the Operator keeps appropriate control. Such an arrangement should not preclude the Operator from ensuring that all maintenance is performed by a JAR 145 AMO and complying with JAR-OPS 3.890 responsibility requirements. Typical examples follow:

Component Maintenance

The Operator may find it more appropriate to have a primary contractor, that would despatch the components to appropriately approved organisations, rather than himself sending different types of components to various approved/accepted maintenance organisations. The benefit for the operator is that the management of maintenance is simplified by having a single contact point for component maintenance. The Operator remains responsible for ensuring that all maintenance is performed by JAR 145 approved/accepted Organisations and in accordance with the approved standard.

Helicopter, Engine and Component

The operator may wish to have a maintenance contract with another non JAR 145 operator of the same type of helicopter. A typical case is that of a dry-leased helicopter between JAR

OPS Operators, where the parties, for consistency or continuity (especially for short term leases), find it appropriate to keep the helicopter under the current maintenance arrangement. Where this involves various JAR 145 AMOs, it might be more manageable for the lessee to have a single contract with the lessor. Such an arrangement should not be understood as a transfer of responsibility: the lessee, being the JAR-OPS approved Operator, remains responsible for maintenance, and employing the Maintenance Management Group.

In essence, JAR-OPS 3.895(e) does not alter the intent of JAR-OPS 3.895(a), (b) and (d) in that it also requires that the Operator has to establish a written maintenance contract and, whatever type of acceptable arrangement is made, the Operator must exercise the same level of control on contracted maintenance, particularly through the Maintenance Management Group and Quality System.

IEM - OPS 3.895(f) & (g)

The intent of this paragraph is that maintenance contracts are not necessary when the Operator's maintenance system specifies that the relevant maintenance activity may be ordered through one-time work orders. This includes, for obvious reasons, occasional line maintenance, and may also include component maintenance up to engines, so long as the maintenance is manageable through work orders, in term of volume and complexity. It should be noted that this paragraph implies that, even where base maintenance is ordered on a case-by-case basis, there must be a written contract.

AMC OPS 3.895([h])

Office accommodation means such that incumbents can carry out their tasks in a manner that contributes to good maintenance standards. For smaller operators, the Authority may agree to one office, subject to there being enough space and that each task can be done without undue disturbance. Offices should also include an adequate technical library and room for document consultation.

3.900 - Quality System

This must additionally include at least:

- Monitoring that the activities of JAR OPS 3.890 are done under accepted procedures

- Monitoring that contracted maintenance is carried out under the contract

- Monitoring compliance with this Subpart

For JAR 145 operators, the quality system may be combined with that required by JAR 145.

AMC OPS 3.900

There should be an acceptable plan to show when and how often the activities required by JAR OPS 3.890 will be monitored. In addition, reports should be produced at the completion of each investigation and include details of discrepancies.

The feedback part of the system should address who is required to rectify discrepancies and non-compliance in each case and the procedure if rectification is not done within appropriate timescales. The procedure should lead to the Accountable Manager in JAR-OPS 3.175(h).

To ensure effective compliance with JAR-OPS 3.900 the following have been shown to work well:

- Product sampling - part inspection of a representative sample of the fleet

- Defect sampling - monitoring of defect rectification performance

- Concession sampling - monitoring concessions to not carry out maintenance on time

- On time maintenance sampling - monitoring of when (hours/time/flight cycles etc.) helicopters and components are brought in for maintenance

- Sampling reports of unairworthy conditions and maintenance errors.

Note that JAR OPS 3.900 includes other self-explanatory monitoring elements.

IEM OPS 3.900

The primary purpose of the Quality System is to monitor compliance with the procedures in an MME to ensure compliance with Subpart M and thereby ensure the maintenance aspects of the operational safety of the helicopters. In particular, this part of the Quality System provides a monitor of the effectiveness of maintenance (see JAR OPS 3.890), and should include a feedback system to

ensure that corrective actions are identified and carried out in a timely manner.

3.905 – MME

One must be provided, with details of the organisation structure, including the nominated postholder responsible for the maintenance system and the people referred to in JAR OPS 3.895(b), and the procedures to satisfy the maintenance responsibility of JAR OPS 3.890 and the quality functions of JAR OPS 3.900, except that where the operator is a JAR 145 organisation, such details may be included in the JAR 145 exposition.

MMEs and amendments must be approved.

AMC OPS 3.905(a)

The purpose of the MME is to set forth the procedures, means and methods of the operator. Compliance with its contents will assure compliance with Subpart M, which, with an appropriate JAR 145 AMO Exposition, is a pre-requisite for obtaining acceptance.

Where an operator is a JAR 145 AMO the Exposition may form the basis of the operator's MME in a combined document as follows:

JAR-145 Exposition
- Part 1- Management
- Part 2 - Maintenance Procedures
- Part L2 - Additional Line Maintenance Procedures
- Part 3 - Quality System Procedures*
- Part 4 - Contracted JAA Operators
- Part 5 - Appendices (sample documents)

*Part 3 must also cover the functions in JAR OPS 3.900, Quality System.

Additional parts should cover:

- Part 0 - General Organisation
- Part 6 – JAR OPS Maintenance Procedures

Where an operator is not approved under JAR 145, but has a maintenance contract with a JAR-145 AMO, the MME should comprise:

- Part 0 - General Organisation

- Part 1 – JAR OPS Maintenance Procedures

- Part 2 - Quality System

- Part 3 - Contracted Maintenance

Personnel are expected to be familiar with relevant parts of the Exposition.

The operator will need to specify in the Exposition who should amend the document, particularly where there are several parts.

The person responsible for the management of the Quality System should be responsible for monitoring and amending the Exposition unless otherwise agreed, including associated procedures manuals, and the submission of proposed amendments. The Authority may agree a procedure, which will be stated in the amendment control section, defining the class of amendments which can be incorporated without the prior consent.

Electronic Data Processing (EDP) may be used, assuming compatibility and ease of use.

Part 0, *General Organisation* should include a corporate commitment, signed by the Accountable Manager, confirming that the MME and associated manuals define, compliance with Subpart M and will be complied with at all times. The following statement may be used without amendment (modifications should not alter the intent):

This exposition defines the Organisation and procedures upon which the Authority* Approval under JAR OPS 3 Subpart M is based.

These procedures are approved by the undersigned and must be complied with, as applicable, in order to ensure that all maintenance of …(quote Operator's name)… fleet of aircraft is carried out on time to an approved standard.

It is accepted that these procedures do not override the necessity of complying with any new or amended regulation published by the Authority* from time to time where these new or amended regulations are in conflict with these procedures.

It is understood that the Authority* will approve this Organisation whilst the Authority* is satisfied that

the procedures are being followed and the work standard maintained. It is understood that the Authority* reserves the right to suspend, vary or revoke the JAR-OPS Subpart M maintenance system approval of the Organisation, as applicable, if the Authority* has evidence that the procedures are not followed and the standards not upheld.

It is further understood that suspension or revocation of the approval of the maintenance system would invalidate the AOC.

Signed ……………

Dated ……………

Accountable Manager and…(position)……

For and on behalf of… (organisation)……"

* Where it states *Authority* please insert the actual name of the JAA-NAA, for example, RLD, RAI, LBA, DGAC, CAA, etc. etc.

Whenever the accountable manager is changed, the new one must sign the statement at the earliest opportunity as part of the acceptance by the JAA-NAA. Failure to do so action invalidates the JAR OPS M approval.

Appendices 1 and 2
Contain examples of Exposition layouts.

3.910 - Maintenance Program
The helicopter must be maintained under the operator's helicopter maintenance program, which must contain details, including frequency, of maintenance to be carried out. The program must require a reliability program when the Authority determines that one is needed.

Programs and amendments must be approved.

AMC OPS 3.910(a)
The program should be managed and presented by the operator to the Authority. Where implementation of the content is accomplished by a JAR 145 AMO, it follows that the AMO should have access to the relevant parts of the program when the organisation is not the author. *Implementation* means preparation and planning of maintenance tasks in accordance with the program.

The helicopter should only be maintained to one program at any time. Where an operator wishes to change from one to another, a transfer Check/Inspection may be needed, as agreed.

The program should contain a preface which will define the contents, the inspection standards, permitted variations to task frequencies and, where applicable, procedures to escalate established check/inspection intervals. Appendix 1 to this AMC provides detailed guidance on content.

Where an operator wishes to use a helicopter with the initial program based upon the MRBR process, associated programs for continuous surveillance of the reliability, or health monitoring of the helicopter should be considered as part of it.

Where a helicopter type has been subjected to the MRBR process, an operator should normally develop the initial program based on it.

Documentation supporting the development of programs for types subjected to the MRBR process should contain identification cross reference to the MRBR tasks so it is always possible to relate them to the current program. This does not prevent the program from being developed in the light of service experience to beyond MRBR recommendations, but will show their relationship.

Some programs, not developed from the MRB Process, utilise reliability programs, which should be considered as a part of the program. Reliability programs should be developed for maintenance programs based upon MSG logic or those that include condition monitored components or that do not contain overhaul time periods for all significant system components.

Reliability programs need not be developed for helicopters of 5 700 kg and below or that do contain overhaul time periods for all significant system components.

The purpose of a reliability program is to ensure that maintenance program tasks are effective and their periodicity is adequate. It follows that the actions resulting from the reliability program may be not only to escalate or delete maintenance task, but also to de-escalate or add maintenance tasks, as necessary.

A reliability program provides an appropriate means of monitoring the effectiveness of the maintenance program.

AMC OPS 3.910(b)

The documentation issued to approve the maintenance program may include details of who may issue certificates of release to service in a particular situation and define which tasks are base maintenance activity. Development of the program depends on sufficient satisfactory in-service experience which has been properly processed. In general, the task being considered for escalation beyond MRB limits should have been satisfactorily repeated at the existing frequency several times before being proposed for escalation. Appendix 1 to this AMC gives further guidance.

The Authority may approve a part of or an incomplete maintenance program at the start of operation of a new type or a new operator, subject to the limitation that the program is only valid for a period not exceeding any maintenance not yet approved. The following illustrate two possibilities:

- A new type may not have completed the acceptance process for structural inspection or corrosion control. The maintenance program cannot be approved as a complete program but may be approved for a limited period, say, 3 000 hours or 1 year

- A new operator may not have established suitable maintenance arrangements for the high-life time checks. The Authority may be unable to approve the complete program, preferring a limited period

If the Authority is no longer satisfied that a safe operation can be maintained, the approval of a program, or part, may be suspended or revoked. Events giving rise to such action include:

- An operator suspending the operation of that type for at least one year

- Periodic review of the maintenance program shows that the operator has failed to ensure that the program reflects the maintenance needs of the helicopter such that safe operation can be assured

Appendix 1
Contains an example program.

3.915 - Technical Log
Operators must use a tech log system containing the following for each helicopter:

- Information about each flight necessary to ensure continued flight safety

- The current certificate of release to service

- The current maintenance statement with the status of what scheduled and out-of-phase maintenance is next due, which may be kept elsewhere, as agreed

- All outstanding deferred defects that affect operation of the helicopter

- Guidance instructions on maintenance support arrangements

The tech log and amendments must be approved.

AMC OPS 3.915

The tech log is a system for recording defects and malfunctions discovered during operation and for recording details of maintenance done on the helicopter to which the tech log applies between scheduled visits to base maintenance. In addition, it is used for recording operating information relevant to flight safety and should contain maintenance data the crew need to know about.

The system may range from a single-section document to a complex system with many sections, but should always include the information in the example used here, which uses a 5-section system:

Section 1
Registered name and address of the operator, helicopter type and complete international registration marks.

Section 2
When the next scheduled maintenance is due, including, out-of-phase component changes due before the next check. In addition, this Section should contain the current Certificate of Release to Service, for the complete helicopter, issued normally at the end of the last check. The crew does not need these details if the next scheduled maintenance is controlled by other acceptable means.

Section 3
Information considered necessary for continued flight safety, including:

- The type and registration mark

- The date, place and times of takeoff and landing

- Running total of flying hours, so the hours to the next maintenance can be determined. The flight crew does not need these details if the next maintenance is controlled by other acceptable means

- Details of any defect affecting airworthiness or safe operation, including emergency systems, known to the commander. Provision should be made for the commander to date and sign such entries, including, where appropriate, the nil defect state for continuity. Provision should be made for a Certificate of Release to Service or, as agreed, the alternate abbreviated Certificate of Release to Service following rectification of a defect or any deferred defect or maintenance check. Such a certificate appearing on each page of this section should readily identify the defect(s) to which it relates or the particular check. The alternate abbreviated certificate of release to service consists of the following statement *JAR 145.50 release to service* instead of the full certification statement in AMC 145.50(b) para 1. When the JAA-NAA agrees to the use of the alternate abbreviated certificate of release to service, the introductory section of the technical log should include an example of the full certification statement from AMC 145.50(b) para 1 together with a note stating; *The alternate abbreviated certificate of release to service used in this technical log satisfies the intent of JAR 145.50(a) only. All other aspects of JAR 145.50(b) must be complied with.*

- The quantity of fuel and oil uplifted and the quantity of fuel in each tank, or combination, at the beginning and end of each flight; provision to show, in the same units, the amount of fuel planned to be uplifted and the amount actually uplifted; provision for the time when ground de-icing and/or anti-icing was started and the type of fluid applied, including mixture ratio fluid/water

- The preflight inspection signature

In addition to the above, it may be necessary to record (where the life of a helicopter or component is affected):

- The time in particular engine power ranges (Max Power is one example)

- The number of landings

- Flight cycles or flight pressure cycles

Note 1: Where Section 3 is 'part removable', such should contain the foregoing information where appropriate.

Note 2: Section 3 should be designed such that one copy of each page may remain on the helicopter and another retained on the ground until completion of the flight to which it relates.

Note 3: Section 3 layout should be divided to show clearly what is required to be completed after flight and in preparation for the next flight.

Section 4
Deferred defects that affect or may affect safe operation of the helicopter and should therefore be known to the commander. Each page should be pre-printed with the operator's name and page serial number and provide for recording:

- A cross reference for each deferred defect so the original can be identified in the particular Section 3 Sector Record Page

- The original date of occurrence of the defect deferred

- Brief details of the defect

- Details of the eventual rectification and its Certificate of Release to Service or a clear cross-reference back to the document that contains details of the eventual rectification

Section 5
Necessary maintenance support information that the commander needs to know, which

would include how to contact maintenance engineering if problems arise whilst operating the routes, etc.

The Technical Log System can be either a paper or computer system or a combination.

3.920 - Maintenance Records
The tech log must be kept for 24 months after the date of the last entry. The following records must be kept for:

- Detailed maintenance records - 24 months after the helicopter or component was released to service

- The total time and flight cycles of the helicopter and life-limited components - 12 months after the helicopter has been permanently withdrawn from service

- The time and flight cycles as appropriate, since last overhaul of the helicopter or component subjected to an overhaul life - Until the overhaul has been superseded by another of equivalent scope and detail

- The current inspection status such that compliance with the maintenance program can be established - Until the inspection has been superseded by another of equivalent work scope and detail

- The current status of ADs - 12 months after the helicopter has been permanently withdrawn from service

- Details of current modifications and repairs to the helicopter, engine(s), rotor and transmission components and components vital to flight safety - 12 months after the helicopter has been permanently withdrawn from service

When a helicopter is permanently transferred from one operator to another, the records must also be transferred and the time periods will continue to apply to the new operator.

AMC OPS 3.920
Operators should always receive a complete JAR 145 Certificate of Release to Service, so that records can be retained. The system to keep the maintenance records should be described in the MME or the relevant JAR 145 exposition.

When maintenance organisations retain copies of maintenance records on an operator's behalf, the operator remains responsible for their preservation and transfer to a new operator.

Acceptable form normally means on paper or in a computer database or a combination. Records in microfilm or optical disc form are also acceptable.

Paper systems should use robust material to withstand normal handling. Records should remain legible throughout the retention period.

Computer systems should have at least one backup system to be updated at least within 24 hours of any maintenance. Each terminal must contain safeguards against unauthorised personnel.

Microfilming or optical storage may be carried out at any time. The records should be as legible as the original and remain so for the retention period.

Information on times, dates, cycles etc. as required by JAR OPS 3.920 (*summary maintenance records*) are those that give an overall picture on the state of maintenance of the helicopter and life-limited components. The current status of life-limited components should indicate the component life limitation, total number of hours, accumulated cycles or calendar time and the number of hours/cycles/time remaining before the required retirement time is reached.

The current status of ADs should identify the applicable ones, including revision or amendment numbers. Where an AD is generally applicable to the helicopter or component type but not the particular item, this should be identified. The AD status includes the date when the AD was accomplished, and where the AD is controlled by flight hours or flight cycles, it should include the total flight hours or cycles, as appropriate. For repetitive ADs, only the last application should be recorded in the AD status. The status should also specify which part of a multi-part directive has been accomplished and the method, where a choice is available in the AD.

Details of current modification and repairs means data supporting compliance with airworthiness requirements. This can be in the form of a Supplemental Type Certificate, Service Bulletin, Structural Repair Manual or similar document. If the airworthiness data for modification and repair is produced by the JAR 145 organisation under existing national regulations, documentation

necessary to define the change and approval should be retained.

Substantiating data may include:

- Compliance program
- Master drawing or drawing list, production drawings, installation instructions
- Engineering reports (static strength, fatigue, damage tolerance, fault analysis, etc.)
- Ground and flight test program and results
- Mass and balance change data
- Maintenance and repair manual supplements
- Maintenance program changes and instructions for continuing airworthiness
- Flight manual supplement

Maintenance records should be stored in a safe way with regard to fire, flood, theft and alteration.

Computer backup discs, tapes etc., should be stored in a different location from the current working media, in a safe environment.

IEM OPS 3.920(b)(6)
Component vital to flight safety means one with Life Limited Parts or is subject to Airworthiness Limitations, or a major component, such as undercarriage and flight controls.

AMC OPS 3.920(c)
Where an operator terminates operation, all maintenance records should be passed on to the new operator or, if none, stored as required.

A permanent transfer does not generally include the dry lease-out when the duration of the lease is less than 6 months. However the Authority should be satisfied that all maintenance records necessary for the duration of the agreement are transferred to the lessee or made accessible to them.

3.930 - Continued Validity of AOC
Operators must comply with JAR OPS 3.175 and 3.180 to ensure continued validity of the AOC in respect of the maintenance system.

IEM OPS 3.930

This paragraph covers scheduled changes to the maintenance system. Whilst the requirements relating to AOCs, including their issue, variation and continued validity, are prescribed in Subpart C, this paragraph is in Subpart M to ensure that operators remain aware that there is a requirement elsewhere which may affect continued acceptance of the maintenance arrangement.

3.935 - Equivalent Safety Case

Operators must not introduce alternative procedures to those in this Subpart unless needed and an equivalent safety case has first been approved and supported by JAA Authorities.

IEM OPS 3.935

This paragraph is meant to provide the necessary flexibility to the Authority so it can accept alternate means of compliance with Subpart M, particularly with advances in technology. Once agreed by JAA, the alternative means will be proposed for inclusion in Subpart M following NPA consultation but, in the meantime, may be published as a Maintenance TGL.

3.940 - Composition of Flight Crew

The composition and number of flight crew members at designated stations must be as per, and at least the minima in, the Flight Manual.

The flight crew must include additional members as required, and must not be reduced below the numbers in the Ops Manual.

Flight crew members must hold an applicable and valid licence and be suitably qualified and competent to conduct their duties.

Procedures must be established to prevent the crewing together of inexperienced crew members.

One pilot must be designated as commander, who may delegate conduct of the flight to another suitably qualified pilot. Self-employed, freelance or part-time pilots must follow Subpart N.

Commanders must complete initial CRM training before starting unsupervised line flying.

Pilots

Commanders *and* co-pilots on IFR flights must hold valid instrument ratings, but you may fly in VMC at night, if appropriately qualified for the circumstances, airspace and flight conditions (including holding a pilot's licence). This must be entered in the Ops Manual and be acceptable.

For IFR operations using helicopters with more than 9 passenger seats, or helicopters with more than 19 passenger seats, the minimum flight crew is two qualified pilots, and the commander must hold a valid ATPL (H). Other helicopters may be operated by a single pilot under Appendix 1.

Appendix 1 - Single Pilot IFR or at Night

The Ops Manual must include a pilot conversion and recurrent training program which includes additional requirements for single pilot operation.

For training and recency, attention must be given to cockpit procedures, especially in respect of:

- Engine management and emergency handling
- Use of checklists
- ATC communication
- Cockpit procedures for departure and approach
- Autopilot management
- Simplified in-flight documentation

Recurrent checks must be done in the single-pilot role on type in a representative environment.

The pilot must meet Commander's minimum qualification requirements (JAR OPS 3.960).

For IFR, the pilot must have experience as follows:

- 25 hours total IFR experience in the relevant environment
- 25 hours on type, approved for single pilot IFR, of which 10 is as commander or commander under supervision, including 5 sectors of IFR line flying under supervision using single pilot procedures
- The minimum recent experience must be 5 IFR flights, including 3 instrument approaches, in the preceding 90 days on type in the single-pilot role. This may be replaced by an IFR instrument approach check on the helicopter type

Note: Additional equipment for alleviating pilot workload is in JAR OPS 3.655.

AMC OPS 3.940(a)(4) - Inexperienced Crew

After a Type Rating or command course, and associated line flying under supervision, a crew member is inexperienced until achieving 50 hours on type and/or in the role within 60 days, or 100 hours on type and/or in the role (no time limit). Fewer hours may be OK when a new operator is starting up, or a new type is introduced, or crew members have previously done a type conversion course with the same operator (re-conversion), subject to other conditions imposed.

IEM OPS 3.940(b)(1) - Composition

In some States, all flight at night are IFR, then provisions are made for flights at night to be under conditions similar to night VFR in other States. Where national legislation requires flight under IFR at night, in States who take advantage of this alleviation, operators should comply with guidance published by the Authority to ensure that pilots are appropriately qualified.

3.943 – Initial CRM Training

Unless previously done, flight crew members (either new employees or existing staff) must complete initial CRM training. New employees must do it inside the first year.

Commanders must complete initial CRM training before starting unsupervised line flying (3.940).

Initial CRM training must be conducted by suitably qualified people, under a detailed syllabus in the Ops Manual, and cover at least:

- Human error and reliability, error chain, error prevention and detection

- Company safety culture, SOPs, organisational factors

- Stress, its management, fatigue, vigilance

- Information acquisition and processing, situation awareness, workload management

- Decision making

- Communication and co-ordination inside and outside the cockpit

- Leadership and team behaviour, synergy

- Automation and philosophy of its use

- Specific type-related differences

- Case-based studies

- Additional areas which warrant extra attention, as identified by the accident prevention and flight safety program

3.945 - Conversion Training and Checking

Flight crew members must complete a Type Rating course which satisfies JAR FCL, and an operator's conversion course (which may be combined) before starting unsupervised line flying when changing to a helicopter for which a new type rating is required, or when changing operator.

Conversion training must be conducted by suitably qualified people under a detailed syllabus in the Ops Manual. The training required must be determined after note is taken of previous training (see training records in JAR OPS 3.985). Minimum standards of qualification and experience before conversion training must be in the Ops Manual

Each flight crew member must undergo the checks required by JAR OPS 3.965(b)* and the training and checks required by JAR OPS 3.965(d) before starting line flying under supervision. *For changing type, the check required by 3.965(b) may be combined with the type rating skill test. On completion of line flying under supervision, the check required by JAR OPS 3.965(c) must be done.

Once a conversion course has been started, a flight crew member must not undertake flying duties on another type until the course is completed or terminated, unless otherwise approved. CRM training must be incorporated.

AMC OPS 3.945 - Syllabus

The conversion course should be done in the following order:

- *Ground training* covering all systems and emergency procedures (with or without simulator or training device). Normally, classrooms, training aids, etc. are required, but private study may be OK for simple types if suitable materials are provided. Tests should be included

- *Emergency and safety equipment training* and checking (done *before* flying starts). Training should take place whenever practicable in conjunction with cabin crew doing similar training with emphasis on co-ordinated procedures and two-way communications. On completion of emergency and safety equipment training the flight crew member should undergo the check in JAR-OPS 3.965(c)

- *Flying training* (flight simulator and/or helicopter). Should be structured and done by suitably qualified TRIs and/or TREs. For multi-crew helicopters, emphasis should be placed on LOFT and CRM. Co-pilots should get the same as Captains. Training should include all elements of an IR if the flight crew member is likely to operate under IFR. Training should include proficiency training on a helicopter, including at least 3 takeoffs and landings, except where a zero-time STD is approved

- *Line flying under supervision.* Unless already covered above, before being assigned to line duty, flight crew should have successfully completed an OPC with a TRE. Flight crews should operate a minimum number of sectors and/or flying hours under the supervision of a nominated flight crew member. The minimum figures should be in the Ops Manual and should be selected after due note has been taken of the complexity of the helicopter and experience of the flight crew member. On completion of sectors and/or flying hours under supervision, a line check should be completed

For **new crew members**, or as applicable on conversion, aeromedical topics should be addressed, to include at least:

- First aid in general, and as appropriate to the type and crew complement

- Avoidance of food poisoning

- Possible dangers associated with contamination of skin or eyes by aviation fuel and other fluids and the immediate treatment

- Recognition and treatment of hypoxia and hyperventilation

- Survival training and guidance on hygiene appropriate to the routes

Training should also include:

- The importance of effective coordination between flight and cabin crew

- The use of smoke protection equipment and protective clothing where carried. In the case of the first type of helicopter so equipped, training should be associated with experience of movement in a cosmetic smoke filled environment

- Actual firefighting using equipment representative of that in the helicopter

- Operational procedures of security, rescue and emergency services

- Survival training appropriate to the area (e.g. polar, desert, jungle or sea), including survival equipment carried

- Ditching, where flotation equipment is carried, to include practice of the actual donning and inflation of a lifejacket, with a demonstration or film of the inflation of liferafts and/or sliderafts and equipment. This should, in initial training, be done in water, although previous certificated training with another operator or the use of similar equipment will be accepted in lieu of further wet drill training

- Location of emergency and safety equipment, correct use of appropriate drills, and procedures that could be required in different emergencies. Evacuation by a slide should be included when Ops Manual procedures require the early evacuation of flight crew to assist on the ground

- Passenger Handling. Other than general training on dealing with people, emphasis should be placed on advice on the recognition and management of passengers who appear or become intoxicated, under the influence of drugs or aggressive, motivation and crowd control, dangerous goods awareness, correct seat allocation with reference to mass and balance, with particular emphasis on disabled passengers and seating able-bodied passengers next to unsupervised exits

- Discipline and Responsibilities. Amongst other subjects, emphasis should be placed on discipline and an individual's responsibilities in relation to ongoing competence and fitness to operate as a crew member with special regard to flight time limitations

- Security procedures

- Passenger briefing/safety demonstrations. Training should be given in the preparation of passengers for normal and emergency situations

IEM OPS 3.945 - Line Flying under Supervision

This provides the opportunity to carry into practice the procedures and techniques from ground and flying training on a conversion course, under the supervision of a flight crew member specifically nominated and trained for the task. At the end of line flying under supervision the student crew member can perform a safe and efficient flight within the tasks of his station.

A variety of reasonable combinations may exist with respect to previous experience, complexity of the helicopter and the type of route/role/area.

IEM OPS 3.945(a)(8) – Conversion Course

A conversion course is deemed to have started when the flying or STD training has begun. The theoretical element may be undertaken ahead of the practical element.

Under certain circumstances, a conversion course may start and reach a stage where, for unforeseen reasons, it cannot be completed without delay, in which case the operator may apply to allow the pilot to revert to the original type.

Before the resumption of the conversion course the operator should establish how much of the conversion course needs to be re-covered before continuing with the remainder of the course.

3.950 - Differences & Familiarisation Training

Flight crew members must complete *differences training*, requiring additional knowledge *and training* on an appropriate training device, when operating a variant of a helicopter currently operated, or when

introducing a significant change of equipment and/or procedures on types or variants currently operated. They must also complete *familiarisation training*, requiring only the acquisition of additional knowledge, when operating another helicopter of the same type, or when introducing a significant change of equipment and/or procedures on types or variants currently operated.

3.955 - Upgrade to Commander

Pilots upgrading to commander must complete an appropriate command course. The Ops Manual must contain a minimum experience level for people from within the company and for direct entry commanders.

Appendix 1

Upgrade Training Course

The command course must be specified in the Ops Manual and include at least:

- Flight sim training (including LOFT) and/or flying training including a proficiency check as commander

- Operator command responsibilities

- Line training in command under supervision. At least 10 hours including at least 10 sectors is required for pilots already qualified on type

- Completion of a commander's line check and route/role/area competency qualification

- For initial upgrade to commander the course must also include CRM

Combined Upgrading and Conversion Course

The Command Course must also include a Conversion Course under JAR OPS 3.945 and additional sectors for a pilot transitioning on to a new type.

IEM to Appendix 1 - CRM training

The idea behind this training is to enhance communication and management skills, with emphasis on the non-technical aspects of flight crew performance.

CRM training should contain these elements:

- The Basic Module

- Situational awareness

- Assertiveness/guidelines for effective speaking up

- Effective communication within the crew

- Enhancing crew co-operation

- Identifying and managing stress

- The Specific Module, aimed at management skills

    - Information management including the effective utilisation of all available resources such as other crew members, aircraft systems, supporting facilities and information from outside

    - Leadership

    - Delegation

    - Judgement and decision making

    - Effective communication skills as desired for commanders

This training should include classroom training and practical exercises, including group discussions and accident reviews to analyse communication problems and instances or examples of a lack of information or crew management.

3.960 - Commander - Minimum Qualifications

An ATPL(H), but a CPL(H) wll do if:

- Under **IFR**, the commander has at least 700 hours total time on helicopters which includes 300 as PIC (see JAR FCL) and 100 under IFR. The 300 hours as PIC may be substituted by co-pilot hours on a 2 for 1 basis if they were gained within an established two pilot crew concept system described in the Ops Manual.

- Under **VMC at night**, a commander, without a valid instrument rating, has 300 hours total time on helicopters which includes 100 as PIC and 10 at night as PF.

3.965 - Recurrent Training and Checking

Flight crew members must undergo recurrent training and checking relevant to the type or variant which they are certificated to operate.

A recurrent training and checking program must be in the Ops Manual, as approved.

Recurrent **training** must be done by suitably qualified people, but helicopter/simulator training must be done by a TRI/SFI, if they satisfy the operator's experience and knowledge requirements to instruct on the items in Appendix 1 to JAR OPS 3.965(a)(i)(A) and (B).

Recurrent **checking** must be done by:

- *OPCs* - by a TRE or, if the check is done in an STD, a TRE or SFE (flight crews must undergo OPCs as part of a normal crew)

- *Line Checks* - by commanders nominated by the operator, as acceptable

Operator Proficiency Check

Flight crews must do OPCs to demonstrate competence in normal, abnormal and emergency procedures. The check must be done without external visual reference when it is likely that the crew member will be operating under IFR.

The period of validity is 6 months, plus the remainder of the month of issue. If issued within the final 3 months of a previous check, the validity extends from the expiry date of the previous check. Before a flight crew member, without a valid IR, may operate VMC at night he must undergo a proficiency check at night. Thereafter, each second check must be done at night.

Line Check

Flight crews must do line checks to demonstrate competence in normal line operations as in the Ops Manual. The period of validity is 12 months, plus the remainder of the month of issue. If issued within the final 3 months of a previous line check, the validity extends until 12 months from the expiry date of the previous check.

Emergency and Safety Equipment

Flight crews must undergo training and checking on the location and use of emergency and safety equipment carried. The period of validity is 12 calendar months in addition to the remainder of the month of issue. If issued within the final 3 calendar months of validity of a previous emergency and safety check, the validity extends until 12 calendar months from the expiry date of the previous check.

Crew Resource Management

Must be done as part of recurrent training.

Ground and Refresher Training

Must be done at least every 12 months. If done within 3 months of the expiry of the 12-month period, the next training must be done within 12 months of the original expiry date.

Helicopter/Flight Simulator Training

Must be done at least every 12 months. If the training is done within 3 months of the expiry of the 12-month period, the next training must be done within 12 months of the original expiry date.

Appendix 1

Recurrent Training

Must consist of:

- *Ground and Refresher Training* (including systems), operational procedures and requirements (including ground de-/anti-icing and incapacitation), and accident/incident and occurrence review. Knowledge must be verified by questionnaire or other method

- *Helicopter/Flight Simulator Training*, to cover all major failures of systems and associated procedures over a 3-year period. When engine problems are simulated, if no STD is available, emergencies may be covered in the helicopter using a safe airborne simulation, with due consideration given to the effect of subsequent failures. The exercise must be preceded by a comprehensive briefing. This may be combined with the OPC.

- *Emergency and Safety Equipment Training*, which may be combined with emergency and safety equipment checking, in a helicopter or a suitable training device. **Every year**, the program must include:

  - Actual donning of a lifejacket

- Actual donning of PBE

- Actual handling of fire extinguishers

- Instruction on location and use of emergency & safety equipment carried

- Instruction on the location and use of all types of exits

- Security procedures

Every three years, the training must include:

- Actual operation of all exits

- Actual fire-fighting with ship's equipment on an actual or simulated fire, except Halon, for which alternatives may be used

- The effects of smoke in enclosed areas and actual use of relevant equipment in a simulated smoke-filled environment

- Demonstration of liferafts, or, demonstration *and* use of liferafts where fitted for extended overwater operations

- First aid

- *Crew Resource Management*

Recurrent Checking

Must comprise:

- *Operator Proficiency Checks*, to include the following abnormal/emergency procedures:

  - Engine & fuselage fire

  - Emergency operation of undercarriage

  - Fuel dumping

  - Engine failure and relight

  - Hydraulic failure

  - Electrical failure

- Engine failure during takeoff before and after DP

- Engine failure during landing before and after DP

- Flight and engine control system malfunctions

- Recovery from unusual attitudes

- Landing with one or more engine(s) inoperative

- IMC autorotation techniques

- Autorotation to a designated area

- Pilot incapacitation

- Directional control failures and malfunctions

For IFR, also include:

- Precision instrument approach to minima with simulated failure of one engine

- Go-around on instruments from minima with simulated failure of one engine

- Non-precision approach to minima

- Landing with a simulated failure of one or more engines

- Approach with FCS/flight director system malfunctions, flight instrument and navigation equipment failures

- *Emergency and Safety Equipment Checks.* Items are those for which training has been carried out above.

- *Line checks.* These must establish the ability to do a complete line operation, including pre- and post-flight stuff and use of equipment, as per the Ops Manual. Crews must be assessed on CRM Skills. PFs and PMs must be checked in both functions. Checks must be done in a helicopter by acceptable nominated by the operator.

- *Single Pilot.* The checks above must be performed in the single pilot role on a particular type in a representative environment.

IEM to Appendix 1

Training and checking provides an opportunity to practice abnormal or emergency procedures which rarely arise in normal operations and is a part of a structured program of recurrent training. It should be done in an STD whenever possible.

Where there is a Flight Manual limitation on emergency power ratings, procedures to permit realistic engine-failure training and demonstration of competence, without using ratings, must be developed with the manufacturer and included in the flight manual (these procedures must also be approved by the Authority). Where the emergency drills require action by the Pilot Monitoring, the check should additionally cover knowledge of these drills.

Because of the unacceptable risk when simulating emergencies such as rotor failure, icing problems, certain types of engine(s) (e.g. during continued take-off or go-around, total hydraulic failure etc.), or because of environmental considerations associated with some emergencies (e.g. fuel dumping) these should preferably be done in an STD. If none is available, these may be covered in the helicopter with safe airborne simulation, bearing in mind the effect of subsequent failures, and discussion on the ground.

The OPC may include the annual IR test, in which case a combined check report may be used, details of which should be in the Operations Manual.

AMC to Appendix 1 - Water Survival Training

Where liferafts are fitted for extended overwater operations (Sea Pilot transfer, offshore operation, regular, or scheduled, coast to coast overwater operations, or others as designated), a comprehensive wet drill to cover ditching procedures should be practised. This drill is to include practice of the actual donning and inflation of a lifejacket, together with a demonstration or film of the inflation of life-rafts. Crews should board the same (or similar) liferafts from the water whilst wearing a lifejacket. Training should include the use of all survival equipment carried on liferafts and any additional survival equipment separately on board the aircraft.

Consideration should be given to further specialist training such as underwater escape training.

Note: Wet practice drill is always to be given in initial training unless similar training has been received from another operator and is acceptable to the Authority.

AMC OPS 3.965
The line check is performed in the helicopter. All other training and checking should be done in the helicopter or an appropriate STD or, in the case of emergency and safety equipment training, a suitable alternative training device. The type of equipment used for training and checking should be representative of the instrumentation, equipment and layout of the type operated.

Line Checks
Operators have a statutory obligation to check that pilots are competent. The line check is a particularly important factor in the development, maintenance and refinement of high operating standards, and can provide a valuable indication of the usefulness of training policy and methods. The requirement is for a test of the ability to perform satisfactorily a complete line operation from start to finish, including pre- and post-flight procedures and use of equipment, and for an involvement of an overall assessment of the ability to perform the duties as in the Ops Manual. The route should give adequate representation of a pilot's normal operations. The check is not meant to determine competence on any particular route.

CRM Skills
The commander, in particular, should also demonstrate ability to manage the operation and take appropriate command decisions. Pilots should be checked in PF and PM roles. When assessing CRM skills, the examiner should normally occupy an observer's seat.

Proficiency Training and Checking
When a flight simulator is used, the opportunity should be taken, where possible, to use LOFT.

Emergency and Safety Equipment Training
This should take place with cabin crew doing similar training with emphasis on coordinated procedures and two-way communication between the flight deck and cabin.

IEM OPS 3.965
Line checks, route competency and recency requirements are intended to ensure the crew member's ability to operate efficiently under normal conditions, whereas checks and emergency and safety equipment training are primarily intended to prepare the crew member for abnormal/emergency procedures.

AMC OPS 3.965(e) - Crew Co-ordination & CRM
The successful resolution of emergencies requires effective co-ordination between flight and cabin crew, who should receive combined training, since most of it covers common ground.

There should be an effective liaison between flight and cabin crew training departments; to promote consistency of drills and procedures, provision should be made for instructors to observe and comment on each others' training.

CRM training is the effective utilisation of *all* available resources i.e. crew members, aircraft systems and supporting facilities to achieve safe and efficient operations.

Emphasis should be placed on the importance of effective co-ordination and two-way communication between flight and cabin crew in various emergency situations. Initial and recurrent CRM training should include joint practice in evacuations so that all who are involved are aware of the duties other crew members must perform. When such practice is not possible, combined flight and cabin crew training should include joint discussion of emergency scenarios.

3.968 - Operating in Either Pilot's Seat
Pilots who may be assigned to operate in either pilot's seat must complete appropriate training and checking, with the program in the Ops Manual.

Appendix 1
Commanders who may also be co-pilots, or commanders required to train or examine, must complete additional training and checking as per the Ops Manual, concurrent with OPCs. This training must include at least an engine failure during takeoff, an OEI approach and go-around, and an OEI landing (*simulated* engine failures!).

Commander's checks must be valid and current.

Pilots relieving the commander *must have demonstrated*, concurrent with the OPC, practice of drills and procedures which would not, normally, be the relieving pilot's responsibility. Where the differences between left and right seats are not significant (for example because of the autopilot), practice may be done in either seat.

A pilot other than the commander in the commander's seat *must demonstrate* practice of drills and procedures, concurrent with the OPC, which would otherwise be the commander's responsibility as PM. Where the differences between seats are not significant (for example because of the autopilot), practice may be done in either seat.

3.970 - Recent Experience
Pilots may not operate helicopters unless they have carried out at least three takeoffs, circuits and landings as PF in a helicopter or simulator of the same type, in the preceding 90 days (may be extended up to 120 days by line flying under supervision of a nominated commander).

For night VMC, a pilot without an IR must do at least three takeoffs, circuits and landings at night in the preceding 90 days (may be done in an STD).

A pilot with an IR satisfies the night recency requirement with at least 3 instrument approaches in the preceding 90 days (may be done in an STD).

3.975 - Route/Role/Area Competence
Before being assigned as commander, pilots must obtain adequate knowledge of the routes and of heliports (including alternates), facilities and procedures to be used.

The validity of the route/role/area competence qualification is 12 months, plus the remainder of the month of qualification or latest operation on the route, in the role or area.

The qualification is revalidated by *operating on the route* (i.e. no specific check), in the role or area within the validity period above. If revalidated within the final 3 months of previous qualifications, the validity extends from the date of revalidation until 12 months from the previous expiry date.

AMC OPS 3.975
Route/role/area competence training should include knowledge of:

- Terrain and MSAs

- Seasonal weather

- Meteorological, communication and air traffic facilities, services and procedures

- Search and rescue procedures

- Navigational facilities for the route

- Obstructions, physical layout, lighting, approach aids and arrival, departure, holding and instrument approach procedures and operating minima

For the less complex route/role/area and/or heliport, familiarisation by self-briefing with route documentation, or by means of programmed instruction may be used. For more complex routes and/or heliports, in-flight familiarisation as a commander, co-pilot or observer under supervision, or familiarisation in an approved flight simulator using an appropriate database must be used as well.

Route competence may be revalidated by operating on the route within the previous period of validity instead of the procedure above.

3.980 - More than One Type or Variant
Flight crews may not operate more than one type or a variant unless they are competent, and appropriate procedures are in the Ops Manual.

AMC OPS 3.980
Operators of more than one helicopter variant or type should provide (in the Ops Manual), flight crew minimum experience levels, and the process where flight crew qualified on one type or variant will be trained and qualified on another, plus any additional recency requirements required.

If a flight crew member operates more than one type or variant the following should be satisfied:

- Recency requirements (see JAR OPS 3.970) should be met and confirmed before starting commercial air transport operations, as must the minimum number of flights on each type within a 3-month period specified in the Operations Manual

- JAR-OPS 3.965 requirements with regard to recurrent training

- JAR-OPS 3.965 requirements for proficiency checks may be satisfied by a 6-monthly check on any one type or variant, but a proficiency check on each type or variant should be done every 12 months

- For helicopters **over 5 700 kg**, or with **more than 19 passenger seats**, the flight crew member should not fly more than two types, having achieved at least 3 months and 150 hours experience before the conversion course. 28 days and/or 50 hours flying should then be achieved exclusively on the new type or variant, a flight crew member should not be rostered to fly more than one type or significantly different variant of a type during a single duty period (this para covers the next two)

- For all other helicopters, a flight crew member should not operate more than three types or significantly different variant

- For a combination of helicopter and aeroplane, a flight crew member may fly one helicopter type or variant and one aeroplane type, irrespective of MCTOM or passenger seating configuration

3.985 – Training Records

Operators must maintain records of all training, checking and qualification in JAR OPS 3.945, 3.955, 3.965, 3.968 and 3.975 by a flight crew member, make the records of all conversion courses and recurrent training and checking available, on request, to the crew member.

IEM OPS 3.985

A summary of training should be maintained to show trainee completion of each stage.

3.988 – Crew Other than Flight Crew

All crew members, other than flight crew, assigned to duties in the helicopter, must comply with this Subpart, except for cabin crew who will comply *only* with Appendix 1.

Appendix 1 - Cabin Crew

Cabin crew must comply with JAR OPS 1 Subpart O, except for:

- The term *crew members* does not mean crew members in the sense of JAR OPS 3 Subpart O

- For *aeroplane* read *helicopter*

- The term *airport(s)* includes *heliport(s)*

- Reference to other subparts of JAR OPS 1 means the appropriate one of JAR OPS 3

Alleviation

The following rules do not apply to helicopter cabin crew:

- paragraph (d); evacuation slide training

- paragraph (e)(2)(ii); severe air turbulence

- paragraph (e)(2)(iii) sudden decompression

- paragraph (h)(1); slides

- paragraph (h)(2); slide rafts

- paragraph (h)(4); dropout oxygen

3.995 - Minimum Requirements

Crew members must be at least 18 years old, and have passed an initial medical examination or assessment to be found medically (and remain) fit to discharge the duties in the Ops Manual. Crew members must be competent to perform duties under the Ops Manual.

ACJ OPS 3.995(a)(2)

Medical examination or assessments should be done by, or under the supervision of, an acceptable medical practitioner. A medical record should be for each crew member.

The following medical requirements apply:

- Good health

- Free from physical or mental illness which leads to incapacitation or inability to work

- Normal cardiorespiratory function

- Normal central nervous system

- Adequate sight 6/9 with or without glasses

- Adequate hearing

- Normal function of ear, nose and throat

3.1005 - Initial Training

Crew members must successfully complete initial training, as accepted, and the checking in JAR OPS 3.1025 before undertaking conversion training.

ACJ OPS 3.1005

All elements of initial training must be done by suitably qualified people.

Fire and Smoke Training
Must include:

- Emphasis on the responsibility of crew to deal promptly with emergencies involving fire and smoke and, in particular, the importance of identifying the actual source of the fire

- Classification of fires and appropriate extinguishing agents and procedures for particular situations, techniques of application of extinguishing agents, consequences of misapplication, and use in a confined space

- General procedures of ground-based emergency services at heliports

Water Survival Training
When extended overwater operations are to be conducted, this must include the actual donning and use of personal flotation equipment in water by each crew member. Before first operating on a helicopter fitted with liferafts or other similar, training must be given on the use of it, as well as actual practice in water.

Survival Training
Must be appropriate to the area (e.g. polar, desert, jungle, sea or mountain).

Medical Aspects and First Aid
Must include instruction on first aid and the use of first-aid kits, and the physiological effects of flying and with particular emphasis on hypoxia.

Passenger Handling
Must include:

- Regulations covering safe stowage of cabin baggage and the risk of it becoming a hazard to occupants or otherwise obstructing or damaging emergency equipment or exits

- Duties in the event of turbulence, including securing the cabin

- Precautions when live animals are carried in the cabin

- Dangerous Goods training as per Subpart R

- Security, including Subpart S

Communication
During training, emphasis must be placed on the importance of effective communication between crew members and flight crew including technique, common language and terminology.

Discipline and Responsibilities
Must include at least:

- The importance of crew members working under the Ops Manual

- Continuing competence and fitness to operate as a crew member with special regard to flight and duty time limitations and rest requirements

- Awareness of aviation regulations relating to crews and role of Authority

- General knowledge of relevant aviation terminology, theory of flight, passenger distribution, meteorology and areas of operation

- Preflight briefing of crew members and provision of necessary safety information for specific duties

- The importance of ensuring that relevant documents and manuals are kept up-to-date with amendments

- The importance of identifying when crew members have the authority and responsibility to initiate an evacuation and other emergency procedures

- The importance of safety duties and responsibilities and the need to respond promptly and effectively to emergency situations

Crew Resource Management

Appropriate JAR-OPS 3 requirements must be included in the training of crew members.

3.1010 - Conversion and Differences Training

Appropriate training, as per the Ops Manual, must be done before undertaking duties as follows:

- *Conversion Training*. A conversion course must be done before being first assigned as a crew member, or to another type

- *Differences Training*. Must be completed before operating on a variant of a type currently operated, or with different safety equipment, safety equipment location, equipment relevant to duties, or normal and emergency procedures on currently operated helicopter types or variants

Operators must determine the content of training, taking account of previous training, which must be done in a structured and realistic manner.

Conversion training, and, if necessary, differences training, must include the use of all relevant equipment (including safety equipment) and emergency procedures for the type or variant and involve training and practice on either a training device or the actual helicopter.

ACJ OPS 3.1010

Conversion and differences training must be done by suitably qualified people, and given on the location, removal and use of all safety and survival (and additional) equipment carried, as well as all normal and emergency procedures for the type, variant and configuration.

Fire and Smoke Training

Crews must be given realistic and practical training in the use of all fire fighting equipment, including protective clothing representative of that carried in the helicopter. This training should include:

- Extinguishing a fire characteristic of a helicopter interior fire except that, for Halon extinguishers, an alternative agent may be used

- Donning and use of PBE by each crew member in enclosed, simulated smoke-filled environments, or

- Crews must fulfil the recurrent training requirements of ACJ OPS 3.1015 3.3.

Doors and Exits

Each crew member operates and actually opens all normal and emergency exits for passenger evacuation in a helicopter or representative training device, and all other exits are demonstrated.

Evacuations, etc.

Emergency evacuation training includes the recognition of planned or unplanned evacuations on land or water. This must include recognition of when exits are unusable or when evacuation equipment is unserviceable, and each crew member must be trained to deal with an in-flight fire, with particular emphasis on identifying the actual source, and other in-flight emergencies.

Pilot Incapacitation

Where the flight crew is more than one, crew members must be trained to assist if a pilot becomes incapacitated. This training should include a demonstration of:

- The pilot's seat mechanism

- Fastening and unfastening the pilot's seat harness

- Use of the pilot's oxygen equipment, when applicable

- Use of pilots' checklists

Safety Equipment

Crew members must be given realistic training on, and demonstration of, the location and use of safety equipment, including:

- Life-rafts, including equipment attached to, and/or carried in them

- Lifejackets, infant lifejackets and flotation cots

- Fire extinguishers

- Fire axe or crow-bar

- Emergency lights including torches

- Communications equipment, including megaphones

- Survival packs, including their contents

- Pyrotechnics (actual or representative devices)

- First-aid kits, their contents and emergency medical equipmen

- Other safety equipment or systems where applicable

Passenger Briefing/Safety Demonstrations

An operator should ensure that training is given in the preparation of passengers for normal and emergency situations in accordance with JAR - OPS 3.285.

All appropriate JAR OPS 3 requirements must be included in the training of crew members.

3.1012 - Familiarisation Flights

After completion of conversion training, each crew member must undertake familiarisation flights before operating as a crew member.

3.1015 - Recurrent Training

Crew members must undergo recurrent training, covering the actions assigned in normal and emergency procedures and drills relevant to the type(s) and/or variant(s) of helicopter.

The program accepted by the Authority must include theoretical and practical instruction, together with individual practice.

The validity of recurrent training and associated checking is 12 months, plus the remainder of the month of issue. If issued within the final 3 months of a previous check, the validity extends until 12 months from the previous expiry date.

ACJ OPS 3.1015

Recurrent training must be done by suitably qualified people. **Every year**, the program of practical training must include:

- Emergency procedures, with incapacitation

- Evacuation procedures

- Touch-drills by each crew member for opening normal and emergency exits for passenger evacuation

- Location and handling of emergency equipment, and donning by each crew member of lifejackets, and PBE

- First aid and contents of first-aid kit(s)

- Stowage of articles in the cabin

- Dangerous goods as in Subpart R

- Security procedures

- Incident and accident review

- Crew Resource Management

Every 3 years, recurrent training must also include:

- Operation and actual opening of normal and emergency exits for evacuation in a helicopter or representative training device

- Demonstration of all other exits

- Being given realistic and practical training in the use of fire-fighting equipment, including protective clothing, representative of that carried in the helicopter, to include extinguishing a fire characteristic of a helicopter interior fire except that, for Halon extinguishers, an alternative agent may be used, and the donning and use of PBE by each crew member in an enclosed, simulated smoke-filled environment, plus use of pyrotechnics, and demonstration of the use of the life-raft, where fitted.

Appropriate JAR OPS 3 requirements must be included in the training of crew members.

3.1020 - Refresher Training

Crew members who have been absent from flying duties for more than 6 months must do refresher training as per the Ops Manual.

When a crew member has not been absent from flying duties, but has not, in the preceding 6 months, undertaken duties on a type of helicopter as a crew member, before undertaking such duties on that type, the crew member must either completes refresher training on the type, or operates two re-familiarisation sectors.

ACJ OPS 3.1020

Refresher training must be done by suitably qualified persons and, for each crew member, must include at least:

- Emergency procedures, with incapacitation
- Evacuation procedures
- Operation and actual opening of normal and emergency exits for passenger evacuation in a helicopter or representative training device
- Demonstration of other exits
- Location and handling of emergency equipment, donning of lifejackets, and PBE

3.1025 - Checking

During or following completion of the training required by JAR OPS 3.1005, 3.1010 and 3.1015, crew members must undergo a check covering the training received to verify proficiency in carrying out normal and emergency safety duties. These checks must be performed by acceptable people. Crew members must undergo Initial Training, Conversion and Differences Training and Recurrent Ttraining

ACJ OPS 3.1025

Elements of training requiring individual practical participation should be combined with practical checks, which should be accomplished by the method appropriate to the training, including:

- Practical demonstration
- Computer based assessment
- In-flight checks
- Oral or written tests

3.1030 - More than One Type or Variant

Crew members may not operate on more than three helicopter types except that, with approval, they may operate on four, if safety equipment and emergency procedures for at least two are similar.

Variants of a type are considered to be different if they are not similar in emergency exit operation, location and type of safety equipment and emergency procedures.

3.1035 - Training Records

Operators must maintain records of all training and checking required by JAR OPS 3.1005, 3.1010, 3.1015, 3.1020 and 3.1025, and make them available, on request, to the crew member.

3.1040 - Manuals, Logs & Records

Most of this is pretty much the same as 1.1040 (just change the numbers, substitute *helicopter* for *aeroplane* and apply the appropriate procedures).

3.1150 – Dangerous Goods

As for JAR OPS 1.1150.

3.1235 - Security

As for JAR OPS 1 (1.1235).

Index

By The Same Author

Operational Flying

A book that has little to do with flying, but everything to do with being a pilot, covering the practical and admin sides of working with aeroplanes and helicopters. If you're a corporate pilot, with no Public Transport experience to fall back on, but faced with operating an aircraft without any help, this should be the manual you don't have the incentive to write for yourself, and it will be especially useful to Operations Staff, who often have to put themselves in a pilot's shoes, such as when inspecting Pleasure Flying sites. It is an updated version of *The Professional Pilot's Manual*, published by Airlife. Here's what they said about it then....

> *"Phil Croucher has approached the complex and intricate subject of becoming a professional pilot in a readable colloquial style."* Christopher Orlebar, *MRAeS, Aerospace magazine.*

> *"...should have appeared 20 years ago. It would have saved many prospective pilots lots of anguish and budding Air Taxi Operators lots of money...there is much useful technical information, making the book suitable reference material for most pilots, from airline to PPL instructor, including helicopter pilots...easy reading, even when it comes to Weighty matters such as air and company law... in a style that actually makes it worth reading... performance made easy..."* Mike Richards, *Flyer magazine.*

Here's what they say about it now.....

> *"...an intriguingly cynical attitude towards the official documentation which he tries, in this chunky book, to turn into something the average pilot has a chance of understanding. He makes a pretty good job of this task too.* James Allen, *Pilot Magazine.*

Aside from passing on tricks of the trade, it's a commentary on Operations Manuals, since they never seem to be written in English. It covers the Joint Airworthiness Requirements, as well as containing information on setting up your own company, Legal Stuff, writing your own Ops Manual, and more!

The Helicopter Pilot's Handbook

The problem with helicoptering is that there are no flying clubs, at least of the sort that exist for fixed wing, so pilots get very little chance to swap stories, unless they meet in a muddy field somewhere, waiting for their passengers. As a result, the same mistakes are being made and the same lessons learnt separately instead of being shared.

This book is an attempt to correct the above problems by gathering together as much information as possible for helicopter pilots, old and new, professional and otherwise, containing all the helicopter-specific information from *Operational Flying*, plus additional chapters about two popular helicopters, the Bell 206 and AS 350.

JAR Professional Pilot Studies

Just as important as the exams is the interview, and this is the book for both. It covers the exams for the ATPL for aeroplanes *and* helicopters, not forgetting OPC and recurrent training subjects.

The BIOS Companion

A book that deals with all those secret settings in your computer's BIOS, plus tons of data for troubleshooters.

I already had about HALF of the information, and to get THAT much, I had to get several books and web pages. GOOD JOB!!

I had more time to go thru the book and think that you should change the word "HALF" to "FOURTH".

I commend you on the great job you did. That's a hell of a lot of work for any major company to do, let alone an individual.

Again, Thank you

Craig Stubbs

Thank! I really appreciated this. I read it and was able to adjust my BIOS settings so that my machine runs about twice as fast. Pretty impressive.

Thanks again.

--Tony

"I thought the BIOS Companion was quite good. Just chock full of the kind of info I had been looking for. First book I've gotten that was worth the more than price I paid."

Tony